ROUGH
GUIDES

CW00351817

Man Utd

2003–04 SEASON
A Fan's Handbook

by **Jim White** and **Andy Mitten**

with extra stats from Michael Crick

Rough Guide Credits

Editor: Mark Ellingham   **Design and layout**: Henry Iles
Photos: EMPICS; Iain McCartney (archive).

Acknowledgments

Rough Guides and the authors thank Peter Draper at United for saying yes to
this book, and Carlton Books for again granting us a sublicense.

Jim and Andy thank: Cat; Andy Walsh; Michael Crick – the Cantona of
stats; and Mark for the idea, the enthusiasm, and the quality editing.

Jim thanks Bols, as always; Andy thanks: all the family,
the UWS heads, Sid RIP, and the lovely Helen.

Publishing Information

This 3rd edition published August 2003 by
Rough Guides Ltd, 80 The Strand, London WC2R 0RL

Distributed by the Penguin Group

Penguin Books, 80 The Strand, London WC2R 0RL
Penguin Putnam, Inc., 375 Hudson Street, New York 10014, USA

Typeset in Minion and Helvetica to an original design by Henry Iles.
Printed in Spain by Graphy Cems. 464pp.

Contents

Reds in review

Introduction

Any United fan living in exile will have grown weary of the mantra that prevailed south of Manchester at the end of last term: it wasn't United who won the title, it was Arsenal who lost it. Arsène Wenger, of course, led the whinging, but ABUs across the country were all at it, complaining that United, despite the evidence of the Premiership table, were not worthy champions. Sure, Arsenal's late season cockups did much to tilt the title United's way. Yet the season was in many ways a mirror of what had happened a year earlier, when United began dropping points, and Arsenal put together their championship run. United's campaign was equally remarkable: unbeaten from Boxing Day as they bagged 51 of 57 available points. That can hardly be defined as a gift, however much the Arsenal manager might be in denial. And the facts are these: United won the title two games before the end of Arsenal's season, by five clear points. Ferguson had timed his run to perfection, easing across the line with enough time and energy to wave cheerily to the crowd, even as early as the Reds' visit to Highbury for the championship 'clincher' in mid-April.

   That said, if a clairvoyant had predicted at virtually any point in the season that the Premiership would be decided when Arsenal still had two games to play, even the most die-hard United fan would have assumed that meant the title was already Highbury bound. When United drew at Bolton on Saturday 22 February and the same afternoon Arsenal trounced Manchester City at Maine Road, racing to a four goal lead before the half hour and thus re-establishing a five point lead at the top of the Premiership, there cannot have been a Red in the country who thought that their team would finish anything better than second. As late as mid-March it seemed a foregone conclusion. Arsenal, as they had shown coming to Old Trafford and winning in the fifth round of the FA Cup, were a very good side, built on a roster of fabulously-gifted attacking players, and they looked well set for successive championships. But, as Alex Ferguson knows better than anyone, the league is not won in February, or March. John Toshack got it about right in his days as a Liverpool forward and part-time poet. 'Easter time is very vital,' he once rhymed horrendously, 'that's when we decide the title.'

The championship is never over until it is over, in other words, and in cruising past Arsenal on the home bend of the last lap, Ferguson achieved what – as he himself claimed – was undoubtedly his most satisfying championship win at Old Trafford since the first back in 1993. He knew how good Arsenal were. He knew how tough it was to beat them. And he will have enjoyed putting one over on Arsène Wenger, a man who he has never warmed to on a personal level. But most of all, he will have enjoyed the manner of United's win.

At Christmas, when his team lost at Middlesbrough, United had looked anything but champions. Laurent Blanc was clearly past his sell-by date in defence, the midfield was patchy and hamstrung with injury, the attack misfiring. But that was the last league defeat. And gradually, Ferguson pulled the disparate, apparently defeated individual parts into a slick machine once more. He was hugely assisted by Ruud van Nistelrooy embarking on the most acquisitive striker's scoring streak seen in a United shirt since Denis Law forty years before. He was privileged to have in Paul Scholes and Ryan Giggs two home-grown talents finding the form of their lives. He was, it could be argued, lucky that his youthful defence suddenly coalesced, with John O'Shea in particular excelling. Yet you make your own luck in football, and the way Ferguson paced his team's season was the work of a master craftsman.

And it ought to be recorded before the 'Arsenal blew it' theory becomes established history, that the very way United moved into form contributed to the undermining of their rivals. Just as Newcastle had crumbled back in 1996, the fact that they could feel United breath on their collars contributed to Arsenal's downfall.

Although too canny to falter on screen as Kevin Keegan had, Arsène Wenger's body language was there for all to see as United closed remorselessly on his boys. Edgy, nervy, drawn – what a contrast he made to made to Ferguson's calm authority. And the United man's constant reminder of Wenger's over-confident prediction at the start of the season – that his side would retain the title without even losing a game – was a masterstroke of psychological warfare, succeeding as it did in negating the air of invincibility the Frenchman had sought to create at Highbury.

So that was the season, then, a title made all the richer by the excellence of the team beaten into second place. It is a story re-told from a fans' perspective in these pages, through match reports, player assessments and our guide to rival teams. And, of course, we also cover the rest of United's season – a season in which the League, for a time, looked set to be the least memorable component. There was the unexpected run to the final of the previously-mocked Worthington Cup and the all-too predictable outcome in Cardiff against United's recent nemesis, Liverpool. And once more, the Champions League provided huge drama, with second round group opponents Juventus spurring the best Red display of this and many a season.

True the 4-0 home win over Liverpool was fun, yes the 6-2 away at Newcastle majestic, but that night in Turin, United played as only they can. The Quarter Final defeat to Real Madrid was almost as thrilling, too, for pure football. Real beat United with a display that most of us there, or watching on TV, will, in a perverse way, be glad to have witnessed. The Spaniards (with their French, Portuguese and Brazilian team mates) went about the game the way it should be approached, and at times played it better than it has been attempted before. But then, United are in many ways their ideal opponents, a team that allows them room to demonstrate their gifts. When Madrid encountered the more pragmatic Italians of Juventus in the next round, they could not cope.

It is from that Juventus performance that Fergie and his team will draw for the future. With two years left on his contract, the manager has set his sights on the Champions League. He needs, he says, a little bit more imagination in his squad, he needs one or two players to give that extra sparkle. As this guide was being edited, the news didn't look encouraging. The loss of Beckham, followed by assitant manager Carlos Queiroz, to Madrid seemed like a step back in terms of European domination, and spark – and such feelings were compounded by the failure to capture United's key summer target, Ronaldinho, by reports that both Kewell and Viera had said no to United, and by the on-off sale of Juan Sebastian Veron.

That said, as we go to press, and as the manager ticks off the names on his summer shopping list, the squad surely has more strength and depth than previously. Sir Alex may not have secured Ronaldinho as his first Brazilian Red but his compatriot Kleberson may yet prove the buy of the summer: a player whose holding and carrying work was vital to Brazil's World Cup victory. Alongside Paul Scholes and Roy Keane – or his Cameroon alter-ego, the newly-signed Eric Djemba Djemba – and with Giggs and the young French winger David Bellion on the flanks – United's midfield will be formidable. And then there is a major intrigue in goal, with American keeper Tim Howard looking to compete in the starting line-up with Fabien Barthez.

With these players on board, Ferguson and his squad should relish the chance to prove wrong all the tabloid critics who implied that United need Beckham to be a major European force. Certainly, these writers are happy to pledge their faith in a manager who ended our desperate 26-year hunt for the League title, then delivered it eight times out of eleven in the following seasons, along with the Champions League in 1999.

Jim White and Andy Mitten, July 2003.

Season Review

Game by game: how United's
2001-02 campaign unfolded

Pre-season talk

SUMMER 2002, and a disappointing World Cup for United players. Argentina's Juan Veron, Uruguay's Diego Forlan, South Africa's Quinton Fortune and France's Mikael Silvestre and Fabien Barthez were all on the first plane home after their teams imploded in the group phase. Diego had at least shown the world that he could score, contrary to last season's evidence, with a spectacular volley against Senegal. But it was disaster for France and Argentina. Somewhat against expectation, the English boys proceeded the furthest, to the quarter final, until Ronaldinho decided to lob Seaman, and the country's expectation was blown apart. Still, they were in it long enough for David Beckham to enhance his reputation as the hottest commercial property on planet football, for Paul Scholes to do his bit and Nicky Butt to turn a few heads, including Pele's, who nominated him the player of the first phase.

But the biggest impact of any United player in Japorea was that of Rio Ferdinand: the gawky West Ham Bambi of old had been replaced by an authoritative centre back, a towering presence at the back with assured distribution. And he wasn't even a United player at the time, even if he had apparently taken a bunch of Cheshire estate agent's particulars to Japan as holiday reading. Reds everywhere looked forward with glee to what he might bring to the party when he finally signed on the dotted line for a record £30m. Alex Ferguson, doubtless, was just as pleased that several of his senior squad missed out on the World Cup altogether, saving limbs and ambition for the more important task ahead. Ruud van Nistelrooy's Holland, Ole Gunnar Solskjaer's Norway and Ryan Giggs's Wales had all pooped the party. And the poor Neville brothers had both

He picked this one up from the Brazilians – Rio shows off his skills at Bournemouth

been left behind, one with a snapped metatarsal, the other with injured pride. As for Roy Keane, well, he had kept journalists' note-books filled for the entire summer after his exasperated walkout from the Ireland squad before a ball had been kicked. He didn't rate Mick McCarthy it seemed; but then it is hard for anyone to live up to the man he answers to in his day job.

All six players would be anxious to prove themselves on the world stage that United offered in the season ahead, where the challenges looked as demanding as they had been for years. Domestically, Arsenal, the double winners, were according to their many admir-ers the best club side Britain had seen since Liverpool's demise. Their manager reckoned they would cruise through the season unbeaten now that the power had irrevocably shifted down south. Liverpool too fancied their chances, particularly after Gérard Houllier had spent big bringing in some exotic talents to pad out the squad that had won a treble of sorts in 2001. And as for Europe, this was the season for the Reds to go one better than last year and reach the final of the Champions League. After all it was to be held at Old Trafford. Perhaps destiny awaited ...

20–30 July 2002	Pre-Season Friendlies

With most United players needing a break after their World Cup travels, and Roy Keane tired for reasons of his own after his sortie in the Far East, the club sensibly didn't arrange any exhausting long-distance pre-season tours. The World Cup players returned later to pre-season training after Sir Alex let them have nearly a month off, which meant that few of them featured in the first pre-season friendly against Irish league side Shelbourne on July 20 2002. United have a link-up with the North Dublin club, but it was news of Roy Keane's return to Ireland that made the headlines. Some pre-dicted that the United captain would be subjected to abuse from supporters of the national team who might accuse him of treachery after his early departure from Ireland's World Cup training camp. The reality was very different, the media again underestimating the affection in which Keane is held by United fans – and that's who packed Tolka Park to its 10,500 capacity. Keane's every touch was applauded to the echo, T-shirts were sold with 'Two Famous Cork Leaders Shot in the Back' (the other being Michael Collins) and his team mates looked on with bemusement at the hero-worship of their captain. United easily beat the Shels 5-0, with a hat-trick from Van Nistelrooy and further goals from Forlan and a soon to be on his bike Dwight Yorke. The players, under new assistant manager Carlos Queiroz, reflected on a job well done on their private day-return jet back to Manchester.

The Keano faithful show their support at Shelbourne

A week later, United played two friendlies in one day…at the same time. Such is the number of big names in the squad, the club felt comfortable fulfilling two testimonial requests – at Chesterfield and Bournemouth, with the first teamers spread evenly amongst the two teams. Seven thousand turned out at the Spireites' (named after Chesterfield's famous crooked church spire) arthritic Saltergate ground to witness another 5-0 victory, this time in the

Derbyshire sun. As well as scoring, Blanc, Van Nistelrooy, Forlan, Keane and Kieran Richardson illustrated the mixture of youth and experience on display in the game, held as manager John Duncan's testimonial.

Two hundred miles to the south, slightly more attention was cast on another United XI given that it was Rio Ferdinand's first appearance in the red shirt since his £30 million transfer from Leeds. With Bournemouth £600,000 in debt and unable to afford a fourth stand at their nearly redeveloped Dean Court ground, observers were not slow to compare the contrasting financial fortunes of the two teams. Desperation is nothing new to the south coast side, though; they once changed their name to AFC Bournemouth in the hope that they would somehow prosper from heading the alphabetical table of the 92 league teams. Historians were not fooled. Events were much closer on the field than the state of the club's finances off it, with United running out 3-2 winners after goals from Veron, Ben Muirhead and Michael Stewart in a testimonial for the ex-Man City manager Mel

Ben Muirhead – United's new goalscorer?

Machin, an old friend of Sir Alex's and a supportive manager for the fledgeling Rio. Sixty million Chinese viewers were claimed to be watching MUTV's feed of the game, and together with 8,104 inside the ground, they witnessed Ferdinand's 17-minute substitute cameo. He would have been oblivious to the fact that around the same time, Leeds fans were holding up a banner that read: 'Rio's scum and he knows he is!' at one of their friendly games. Hell hath no fury like Yorkshire's scorn.

Oslo's Valerenga were United's next opponents on July 30th in a game played at Norway's national stadium, the Ullevaal. Norwegian hero Solskjaer was captain for the night in front of a capacity 27,200 crowd, half of them enthusiastic Scandinavian United fans – United's Scandinavian branch boasts 23,000 members, 17,000 of them from Norway. When Berg, Johnsen and Nevland played for the Reds, that number was nearer 30,000 and the people at the sup-porters' club were trying to educate the more fickle members that there is more to supporting United than Norwegian nationals. Their main man Solskjaer did his bit, converting a first half penalty, and a late Keane goal gave United a 2-1 win in the toughest pre-season game so far.

| 2–4 August 2002 | Amsterdam Tournament |

Ajax Amsterdam beat United 2-1 in the first game of the annual Amsterdam Tournament on August 2nd. Over 48,000, including a couple of thousand travelling Reds, watched in the stunning ArenA. Fuelled by a day on the beer and other Amsterdam lad-friendly attractions, the travelling fans were loud and proud. Scholes scored United's only goal against the hosts in the first game back for United's England World Cup performers.

Two days later, in the second Amsterdam game, United beat a sloppy Parma side 3-0 in their most convincing pre-season per-formance to date. Giggs, Veron and Solskjaer got the goals, the Argentine in outstanding form. Ajax won the tournament, beating Barcelona in the game which followed United's victory.

United in Holland: back to the serious business after the World Cup

August 6–10 2002	Pre-Season Friendlies

On August 6, after a brief return to Manchester, United headed to Denmark's chilled-out second city Aarhus for a game against the city's second team, FC Aarhus. The Danish side started with ringers made up from players with roots in Aarhus, including players from their rival team AGF. FC Aarhus's usual semi-pro players, who play to crowds of 500, came on in the second half. Imagine City playing Milan and requesting some United players and you get the picture. A turnout of 21,000, the vast majority of them United fans, saw Van Nistelrooy score twice, and Giggs, Solskjaer and Forlan bag the rest of the customary five. United weren't always convincing against the unusual selection they faced, not that the fans cared.

The final pre-season game was the first to be played at Old Trafford, against Seba Veron's old club, the Argentine giants Boca Juniors. A largely and appropriately youthful crowd of 56,724 attended the game to raise money for United favoured charity, UNICEF, whose ambassador, Roger Moore, led the teams onto the

He's got Becks's number – Moore, 007

pitch in a 'Moore 007' shirt. What ensued, though, was far from fraternal, as a tempestuous clash saw the Boca player Tevez sent off and Rio Ferdinand limping off after 23 minutes with a badly twisted ankle. It overshadowed a 2-0 United victory and two fantastic finishes from Van Nistelrooy, who, without a World Cup to drain his energies, is looking in awesome shape.

Ferdinand's twist apart, United's pre-season preparations had gone well, with the Dutchman, Veron and Beckham the best performers. And with the coffers of two struggling clubs, a couple of long-standing old pros and a charity plumped up, it seemed a more generous way to sharpen limbs for the battle ahead than the usual money-making pre-season effort. Though with the seasonal scrap about to commence, the intent was that this would be the last time for a while that United extended any charitable thoughts.

The Season – August

Wednesday 14 August 2002   Champions League qualifier 1st leg

Zalaegerszeg 1   Manchester United 0
Koplarovics 90.

Kick-off: 8.45pm. Népstadion. **Att**: 28,000 (550 Reds) **Ref**: W Stark

United: (4-4-2) Barthez | Brown (P Neville 5), O'Shea, Blanc, Silvestre | Keane, Beckham, Veron, Giggs | Solskjaer (Forlan 80), Van Nistelrooy. Booked: Van Nistelrooy, Beckham.

Zalaegerszeg: (5-3-2) Ilic | Babati, Csóka, Urban, Budisa, Szamosi | Farago, Ljubojevic, Vincze, | Egressy (Molnár 65), Kenesei (Koplarovics 83). Booked: Ilic.

The first competitive game of the season and a rare sighting of United playing a qualifier for the Champions League. The only other time it happened, against Lodz in 1998, United won the competition. But they'll be lucky to do the same again if they continue to play as they did tonight.

Hungary may have provided some great teams and players in the 1950s, but that was then. And few had ever heard of Zalaegerszeg, a team from an industrial town of 60,000 in the southwest of the country, who had recently been crowned champions for the first time. Old Trafford scouts watched their surprise win over NZ Zagreb in the second round qualifier, but didn't count on the Hungarians shifting to a defensive 5-3-2 formation at home.

Such was the demand for tickets, the game was shifted to the national Népstadion in Budapest (officially known as the Ferenc Puskas stadium after the Hungarian hero, whose twinkling toes bedazzled England in the 1950s). The capacity was well down from the 100,000 that it accommodated as a Socialist super-bowl, and, like the stadium, the pitch was in poor condition. That said, nothing should excuse United's dire display. Despite having seven shots on target to the Hungarians' one, the Reds failed to score and it was with a crushing sense of inevitability that Zalaegerszeg netted in the closing minutes after a cross-field ball floated over Phil Neville's head for Koplarovics to slot past stand-in Carroll.

No mistaking the message as the Magyars go one-up

'They fought like tigers,' said Sir Alex after the game, aware of the significance of the result to Hungarian football and surely confident of victory at Old Trafford. Some United fans were less complimentary to their own players at Budapest airport the following day.

United performance: 3/10. Man of the match: Solskjaer – he tried, he hit the post, but even he couldn't score.

Saturday 17 August 2002	Premiership

Manchester United 1   West Bromwich Albion 0
Solskjaer 79.

Kick-off: 3pm. Old Trafford. Att: 67,645 Ref: S Bennett

United: (4-4-1-1) Carroll | P Neville (Scholes 71), O'Shea, Blanc, Silvestre (Forlan 76) | Keane, Beckham, Veron (Solskjaer 59), Butt | Giggs | Van Nistelrooy. Booked: Keane.

West Brom: (3-5-2) Hoult | Gilchrist, Moore, Sigurdsson | Clement, Johnson, McInnes, Gregan (Taylor 83), Balis | Dichio (Dobie 61), Roberts (Marshall 70). Sent off: McInnes

The first home game of the season is a favourite. It's about seeing the people you see only at the match for the first time in months.

They may not be close friends, but mates all the same, bonded by United memories. It's handshakes all round and it makes you appreciate the community that exists amongst fans. I'm sure it was the same for West Brom followers; only they had the extra bonus of it being their first game in England's top league since 1986. Baggies fans were loud and proud. There is no better way to start life in the Premiership than with a trip to Old Trafford and they savoured the moment, posing for photos by the Busby statue and taking their seats when the rest of the ground was still empty.

Game underway, United set about the task of expected victory. The atmosphere was loud in the visitors' section – they even had the cheek to sing 'it's just like being in church' – but it soured considerably with their *Dambusters* tune, complete with arms outstretched. Unsurprisingly, United fans took it to be an offensive slur on the Munich air crash. Unintentionally, West Brom fans had shown their naivety, for no offence was intended – they always sing this song and it's nothing to do with Munich. This misunderstanding led to a one-sided enmity.

On the field, United created chances they didn't convert. Many were surprised to see just Van Nistelrooy up front with Keane given

Ton up: Ole starts the season as he means to go on

an advanced midfield role behind, and with the score still goalless after an hour, Solskjaer was introduced. West Brom were soon down to ten men but their defensive resolve wasn't broken. 4-5-1 soon became 2-5-3 when full backs Silvestre and Phil Neville were sacrificed for Scholes and Forlan as United chased that elusive goal.

Eleven minutes from time, Solskjaer (who else?) got that goal, his 100th in a United shirt. Sir Alex was quick to praise him, purring: 'Ole always assesses what is happening round the field and to score 100 goals is a fantastic achievement considering he has spent so much time on the bench.'

United performance: 7/10. Man of the match: Keane – under pressure off the field, pressuring defenders on it. Premiership position: Several teams on three points, just as many on none.

Friday 23 August 2002	Premiership

Chelsea 2
Gallas 3, Zenden 45.

Manchester United 2
Beckham 26, Giggs 65.

Kick-off: 8pm. Stamford Bridge. Att: 41,541 (3,000 Reds) Ref: G Poll

United: (4-4-1-1) Carroll | P Neville (Scholes 71), O'Shea, Blanc, Silvestre | Keane, Beckham, Butt, Giggs (Veron 85) | Scholes | Van Nistelrooy. Booked: Beckham, P Neville.

Chelsea: (4-4-2) Cudicini | Melchiot, Gallas, Desailly, Babayaro | De Lucas, Lampard, Petit (Gronkjaer 75), Zenden | Zola (Gudjohnsen 81), Hasselbaink (Cole 81). Booked: De Lucas, Hasselbaink, Desailly.

At £40 a ticket in the away end, this outing had the unholy distinction of being the most expensive league game in United's history. Greedy though they are, the truth is that Chelsea could charge twice that amount for the visit of United and still sell out, such is the number of monied London business types and wealthy tourists prepared to spend big when the Reds are in town.

The game, moved to a Friday night by police because of the Notting Hill Carnival, was preceded by a minute's silence for the two Soham schoolgirls, Jessica Chapman and Holly Wells, who had been abducted and murdered wearing United 'Beckham' shirts.

With just one loss in the previous ten visits, United's record at Stamford Bridge was a good one, although they didn't get off to the best start when Chelsea took the lead through Gallas in the third minute. United were pallid in the first half, a rare highlight being

Beckham's delightful equalising chip over Cudicini in the 26th minute, but they still went in 2-1 down at the break after an unmarked Zenden scored from the edge of the area.

If Sir Alex's half-time team talk mirrored the fans' own chat during the break – in which concern at the unconvincing nature of United so far this season was rapidly developing into alarm – then it showed in a marked second half improvement. United came out with more verve, more passion, and created the better chances. Giggs's equaliser came when he knocked in a Silvestre cross (one of many from the full back) for his 100th United goal. United failed to convert further

Another ton up: this time it's Giggs

chances, but visiting fans who filed out into the prosperous west London streets after the game left encouraged.

United performance: First half 5/10. Second half 9/10. **Man of the match:** Silvestre – he set both goals up with some first-rate crosses. **Premiership position:** 1. Arsenal 7pts (pl 3); 2. Tottenham 7pts (pl 3); 3. Leeds 6pts (pl 2)…7. United 4pts (pl 2).

⚽ **TON UP** On the opening day of the league season, Ole Gunnar Solskjaer scores his 100th goal for United in a 1-0 win over West Bromwich Albion. Six days later Ryan Giggs joins him in the United centurions' club by scoring in the 2-2 draw at Chelsea.

Wednesday 27 August 2002   Champions League qualifier 2nd leg

Manchester United 5   Zalaegerszeg 0

Van Nistelrooy 6, 76 (pen), Beckham 15, Scholes 21, Solskjaer 84.

Kick-off: 7.45pm. Old Trafford. **Att:** 66,814 (1,500 Zeta) **Ref:** C Batista

United: (4-4-2) Carroll | P Neville, Ferdinand (O'Shea 62), Blanc, Silvestre | Keane, Beckham (Forlan 72), Veron, Giggs | Scholes (Solskjaer 50) | Van Nistelrooy.

Zalaegerszeg: (5-3-2) Ilic | Babati (Turi 75), Csóka, Urban, Budisa, Szamosi | Molnár, Ljubojevic (Farago 59), Vincze (Balog 64) | Egressy, Kenesei (Koplarovics 83). Booked: Molnár. Sent off: Ilic.

Did you know that there are only 72 words in the *Oxford English Dictionary* that begin with the letter 'Z'? Zola is in there, Zidane should be, and after their victory over United two weeks ago in Budapest, a few ABUs would no doubt advocate the inclusion of Zalaegerszeg, or Zeta as they are known to their fans.

No problems – Ruud gets the rout underway

The Hungarians had conceded three goals in each of their four league games. Surely United could breach the defensive shroud that had somehow survived in Budapest? With Rio Ferdinand making his competitive debut and newspapers speculating how much money United would lose if they didn't progress to the group stage (Peter Kenyon confidently said that the club hadn't considered the option of not qualifying), United needed a good start. They got it.

Three up inside 21 minutes, fans relaxed and watched some quick passing football that left the Hungarians outclassed. Van Nistelrooy struck the first, a low shot under the keeper; Beckham the second with a free kick that we have all come to call his 'trademark' over a flimsy wall, and Scholes the third after a brilliant move involving Keane and Beckham. Ferdinand was relaxed and was applauded when he made way for O'Shea.

When keeper Ilic, formerly of Charlton, was sent off, Van Nistelrooy stepped up to take the ensuing penalty, despite many chanting for Forlan to have the opportunity of a first goal. But Keane handed the ball to the Dutchman, who converted his second, and Solskjaer made it five with seven minutes to play. 'Are you City in disguise?' asked the Red hordes, to the appreciation, no doubt, of Kevin Keegan who was sitting in the directors' box.

United performance: 8/10. Man of the match: Beckham – always involved and always eager.

⚽ OFF TO THE SUN United's qualification to the first group stage of the Champions League proper saw them grouped with Olympiakos, Maccabi Haifa and Bayer Leverkusen.

Saturday 30 August 2002	Premiership

Sunderland 1
Flo 70

Manchester United 1
Giggs 7

Kick-off: 3pm. Stadium of Light. Att: 47,586 (1,800 Reds) Ref: U Rennie

United: (4-4-2) Carroll | P Neville (Forlan 89), Blanc, Ferdinand, Silvestre (O'Shea 25) | Beckham, Keane, Veron, Giggs | Solskjaer, Van Nistelrooy. Booked: Beckham, P Neville. Sent off: Keane

Sunderland: (4-4-2) Sorensen | Wright, Bjorkland, Babb, Gray | Piper (Thirwell 89), McAteer, Reyna, Butler | Flo (Quinn 79), Phillips. Booked: McAteer.

Roy Keane. Those two words currently dominate the sports headlines. Whether United's captain should have committed to his brutally honest (and therefore controversial and highly profitable) autobiography whilst still playing is debatable. Whether he deserved to be sent off today, for elbowing the Scouse urchin Jason McAteer, is not. In the last minute of this 1-1 game, the two Irish midfielders got caught up in an off the ball incident. They have rarely got on, and McAteer's little mime suggesting Keane might like to write about a foul in his next book wasn't clever, but the United captain couldn't have expected to get away with clipping his opponent round the ear like a teacher admonishing a ten-year-old. Ferguson, of course, defended his captain, letting off a torrent at Niall Quinn, as he came trotting up to share wise words with his departing one-time Irish colleague.

United had started so brightly, too, taking the lead through Giggs and threatening to add to that total with every advance. Peter Reid's struggling side, bolstered by lanky new addition Tore Andre Flo, improved in the second period as a series of personal duels developed all over the pitch. Ferdinand contained Flo, Gray had the better of Beckham, Keane and McAteer snapped at each other and nobody could get near Veron. Sunderland meanwhile got an equaliser, when Flo stabbed in a loose ball past Carroll, but events in the 90th minute overshadowed the disappointing result.

Some United fans who previously considered Roy to be beyond reproach will continue to back him, principally because he's built up so much credit as Manchester United's best player in the last decade, but cracks are in danger of appearing in the relationship. They say a change is as good as a break. United fans don't want Roy

Keane faces up to his literary critics

to change, they'll accept the package if it means more of the same on the field from one of the very best on the planet, but a timely break for a hip operation might be the best thing for all parties, to allow the current storm to pass over.

United performance: First half 7/10; second half 5/10. **Man of the match:** Blanc – composed and even managed to lead one attack. **Premiership position:** 1. Arsenal 7pts (pl 3); 2. Tottenham 7pts (pl 3); 3. Leeds 6pts (pl 2)…7. United 9pts (pl 6).

OLD OFFENDERS Roy Keane's dismissal at Sunderland is the tenth of his United career – a new club record. The next worse offenders are Eric Cantona and Nicky Butt on five each.

September

Manchester United 1   Middlesbrough 0
Van Nistelrooy 28 (pen).

Kick-off: 8pm. **Old Trafford. Att:** 67,508 **Ref:** M Riley

United: (4-4-1-1) Barthez | P Neville, Ferdinand, Blanc, Silvestre | Beckham, Butt, Veron, Giggs | Scholes | Van Nistelrooy (Solskjaer 71). Booked: Veron.

Middlesbrough: (5-3-2) Schwarzer | Quedrue (Whelan 73), Cooper, Southgate, Ehiogu, Stockdale | Greening, Boateng, Geremi | Job, Maccarone (Marinelli 62). Booked: Southgate, Ehiogu.

The subject of Roy Keane continued to dominate talk amongst United fans. How long would he be banned for 'bringing the game in disrepute'? How serious would the operation be on his hip? And perhaps most important for fans always angling from the point of self-interest, how would United survive without him?

Unconvincing so far this season, victory was imperative against Steve McClaren's side who had nailed United's Championship hopes with a single goal victory at Old Trafford six months ago. Beckham (who had become a father again after Victoria gave birth to Romeo three days before the game) was given the captain's armband, but he failed to motivate his colleagues to the level of performance expected. A flat crowd failed, too, in stirring the players out of their directionless slumber. Still, United won the game, when Van Nistelrooy converted a penalty, awarded controversially when the Dutchman made the most of a slight tug by Ehiogu. For all his many, many qualities, Van Nistelrooy does have a questionable habit of going down like City in the '90s, and not always when there has been contact.

It takes more than three men to stop Paul Scholes

The bright side was that these three points taken from a stubborn Boro lifted United up to fourth in the league. 'We made it hard for ourselves,' said Sir Alex, 'with all that possession we had, all the control, we should have killed our opponents off.' Thankfully for United, Middlesbrough, with rated new Italian signing Maccarone up front, never looked close to scoring a goal of their own.

United performance: 6/10. **Man of the match:** Ferdinand – whilst he did nothing wrong, he'll have busier games. **Premiership position:** 1. Arsenal 11pts (pl 4); 2. Tottenham 10pts (pl 4); 3. Leeds 9pts (pl 5); 4. United 8pts (pl 4).

Wednesday 11 September 2002   **Premiership**

Manchester United 0   **Bolton 1**
Nolan 76.

Kick-off: 8pm. Old Trafford. Att: 67,623 Ref: G Barber

United: (4-4-2) Barthez | P Neville, Ferdinand, Blanc, Silvestre | Beckham, Butt, Veron (Forlan 77)
Giggs | Solskjaer, Van Nistelrooy. Booked: P Neville.

Bolton Wanderers: (4-5-1) Jaaskelainen | Charlton, Whitlow, Bergsson, Barness | Gardner, Nolan,
Frandsen (Holdsworth 87), Djorkaeff (Warhurst 73), Pedersen (Campo 90) | Ricketts. Booked: Nolan.

My selective short-term memory recalls only the lighter moments
from this game. Like when, at half time, the PA announcer request-
ed that 'Ray Von' contact his nearest steward. Von is a character from
Boltonian Peter Kay's brilliant *Phoenix Nights* show and the away
fans loved the announcement almost as much as they cheered
Nolan's goal, the only one of the game. But, before we get drawn on
another embarrassing home defeat by our pie-eating neighbours,
it's worth telling the story of the Bolton right back Barness, who, the
morning after this game, went to purchase a copy of *The Sun* in a
newsagents' not too far from Old Trafford. He did so using a vouch-
er offering a 10p discount. Bolton chairman Phil Gartside is always
saying that money's tight at Planet Reebok, but this tight?

Bogey men: Bolton make a habit of winning at Old Trafford

As for the game, Bolton did exactly what they did a season earlier at Old Trafford when they were also victorious. They battled and fought for every ball as if their lives depended on it and a watching Roy Keane wouldn't have questioned their hunger. Liverpudlian Nolan, Bolton's only home-grown player, scored the winner 14 minutes from time after Beckham failed to control a loose ball in his area. Bet his scouse mates loved him for that.

Veron should be called Veron-and-off. Sublime one move, sloppy the next, he needs to add a thread of consistency to his game. Up front, United have scored just five goals in as many league games – and only one of them from a forward in open play. It's the worst record since 1992-93 when Sir Alex recruited Cantona to make the difference. Now, the implementation of the transfer window means that any new signings will have to wait until January.

United performance: 5/10. **Man of the match:** Bergsson – born in 1965 and the oldest player in the Premiership, he controlled Bolton's defence magnificently. **Premiership position:** 1. Arsenal 11pts (pl 5); 2. Tottenham 10pts (pl 5); 3. Leeds 9pts (pl 5)…7th. United 8pts (pl 5).

Saturday 14 September 2002	Premiership

Leeds United 1   Manchester United 0
Kewell 67.

Kick-off: 12pm. Elland Road. **Att:** 67,623 (4,200 Reds) **Ref:** J Winter

United: (4-4-2) Barthez | O'Shea, Ferdinand, Blanc, Silvestre | Beckham, Butt (Chadwick 63), P Neville, Giggs | Solskjaer, Van Nistelrooy (Forlan 71). Booked: Solskjaer.

Leeds United: (4-4-2) Robinson | Mills, Woodgate, Matteo (Radebe 45) Harte | Smith, Bowyer, Dacourt, Barmby (Bakke 45) | Viduka (McPhail 73), Kewell. Booked: Smith, Harte.

Rio Ferdinand's return to Elland Road provided a chance for the natives to air their grievances, just as they did in the past when Jordan, McQueen and King Cantona returned to their jilted ex at the Elland Road hovel. Aside from a few 'Judas' banners that looked as if they'd been painted by an inebriated dog, the hostile reception was not as bad as the papers had led us to believe, but since when have tabloid journalists had their fingers on the pulse of fan culture? It was left to the United fans to stir things, with a chorus of 'Leeds are our feeder club'. But once Kewell had scored the game's only goal, heading unmarked from a Harte cross, it was advantage to the

He's up for it: Rio treads in the footsteps of Eric

home fans, who untiringly belted out: 'Rio, Rio, what's the score?'

One result will hardly make Ferdinand think twice about whether he made the right decision. However, the defeat, Leeds' first victory over the Reds in five years, means that United have endured their worst ever league start in a Premiership season, having dropped ten points from the opening six matches. It's true that the injury list is substantial (United finished the game without the services of Keane, Butt, Veron and Scholes in midfield), but it's also true that Arsenal have a six-point advantage after as many games. Ruud needs to find his scoring touch and United need to rediscover their cutting edge if another league championship is not to be kissed goodbye before the clocks go back.

'You have to dig in at times like this. It's not easy but it is where the character comes into it and we have character OK,' opined Sir Alex after the match. In Ferguson we trust.

United performance: 6/10. **Man of the match**: Kewell – one of his on days. He has plenty of off ones. **Premiership position**: 1. Arsenal 14pts (pl 6); 2. Leeds 12pts (pl 6); 3. Chelsea 12pts (pl 6)…9th. United 8pts (pl 6).

Manchester United 5   Maccabi Haifa 2

Giggs 9, Solskjaer 35, Veron 46, Van Nistelrooy 54,   Katan 6, Cohen 85.
Forlan 89 (pen).

Kick-off: 7.45pm. Old Trafford. **Att:** 63,439 (4,600 Haifa) **Ref:** P Allearts

United: (4-4-2) Barthez (Ricardo 66) | O'Shea, Blanc, Ferdinand, Silvestre | P Neville, Beckham,
Veron, Giggs (Forlan 55) | Van Nistelrooy (Pugh 76), Solskjaer.

Maccabi Haifa: (4-5-1) Awate | Harazi (Cohen 74), Benado, Ejiafor, Keise | Rosso, Badir, Zandberg
(Israilevich 65), Almoshnino (Zano 55), Pralija | Katan. **Booked:** Rosso.

Following two successive league defeats, United were under pressure
to win convincingly against the Israeli champions Maccabi Haifa to
show that all is still well at Old Trafford. The game commenced
United's eighth Champions League campaign, a record matched,
but not bettered, by any other team.

Sir Alex had complimented the wrong Israeli team before the game,
much like an opposition manager confusing United with Liverpool,
but he was well intentioned when he spoke of advances in the standard of Israeli football. Haifa proved as much in becoming the first
Israeli team to qualify for UEFA's gravy train, and backed by 4,600
fans – the largest ever visiting contingent at Old Trafford in the
Champions League – they seemed intent on enjoying the experience.
The fans, a mass of green who pointed, clapped, jumped and
swayed to their own Hebrew rhythm, seemed content just to see
their team at Old Trafford. But suddenly they found themselves celebrating, almost disbelievingly, when Katan gave them an early lead.
Giggs, who has incurred recent criticism from disgruntled fans,
equalised a minute later, heading in a Phil Neville cross, and he continued to cause problems. Had it not been for the heroics of keeper
Awate, United would have taken a 2-1 lead well before Solskjaer
made it two on 35 minutes. Veron, another player with critics,
struck United's third a minute after half-time as the self-belief and
confidence began to rise. 'Are you watching Liverpool?' sang the
Red fans, in gloating reference to Liverpool's 2-0 defeat by Valencia
the night before. The chant rang a bit hollow, given that the Spanish
champions are a far superior side to Maccabi Haifa. But it was sung
with gusto anyway.

It's a goal! No, really! Forlan's first

When **Van Nistelrooy** made it 4-1, substitutes **Ricardo** and **Danny Pugh** were introduced for their competitive debuts. But the loudest cheer came with **Forlan**'s introduction. The Uruguayan has endured fourteen goalless hours in a red shirt, yet the support has never wavered. With 35 minutes to score, Forlan looked as if he was in for more frustration until United were awarded an 89th minute penalty. 'Diego, Diego' roared the crowd, and captain Beckham bowed to the pressure and later attested: 'I think I would have been hated by 67,000 if I would have denied Diego the penalty.' Forlan scored. I'll write that again. **Forlan scored**. It might have been a penalty, but it was still a goal. It was a moment and a night to enjoy, but tougher tests lie ahead.

United performance: 8/10. **Man of the match:** Veron – fine range of passing. **Group F position:** (pl 1) 1. United 3pts; 2. Olympiakos 3pts; 3. Maccabi Haifa 0pts; 4. Bayer Leverkusen 0pts.

⚽ **WHO'S GOING IN GOAL, THEN**? Ricardo Lopez (signed on August 30th) makes his debut against Maccabi Haifa, as a substitute for Fabien Barthez, and becomes United's tenth first team goalkeeper in three and a half years, the greatest turnover in keepers in United history. The ten hail from ten different countries. United currently have three international goalkeepers on the books: Barthez (France), Carroll (Northern Ireland) and Ricardo (Spain).

⚽ **DI-E-GO, WHOA-OH!** Forlan finally scores for United, from the penalty-spot. It is his 27th appearance for the club since his signing in January 2002 (though most of those games were as a late substitute).

---

21 September 2002	Premiership

Manchester United 1   Tottenham Hotspur 0
Van Nistelrooy 63 (pen).

Kick-off: 3pm. Old Trafford. **Att:** 67,611 Ref: R Styles

United: (4-4-2) Barthez | P Neville, Ferdinand, O'Shea, Silvestre | Beckham, Butt, Veron, Giggs (Pugh 85) | Solskjaer (Forlan 76), Van Nistelrooy. Booked: Van Nistelrooy.

Tottenham Hotspur: (4-4-2) Keller | Thatcher, Doherty, Richards, Davies | Etherington, Bunjevcevic, Redknapp, Iversen, | Sheringham, Keane. Booked: Richards.

Tottenham arrived at Old Trafford in the unusual position of being above United in the league. Early tables can be misleading though, and with Spurs' quite dreadful record in M16 of just one win in the last 24 matches, United were clear favourites for victory, especially after Glenn Hoddle revealed that thirteen of his players were on the injury table. It must be as big as his ego then.

With Giggs on form, United created plenty of chances and for a while it looked like a rout was on the cards. But the forward pairing of Van Nistelrooy and Solskjaer seemed oddly nervous – that, and Spurs keeper Keller was in outstanding form – and the goal glut never took off. At the other end, Barthez made two top-class saves from Bunjevic and Richards. The game's only goal came from a penalty – converted of course by Van Nistelrooy – after Doherty had tussled with Solskjaer in the 63rd minute. Minutes earlier, Ruud had reason to claim for a penalty himself when the clumsy Doherty brought him down.

United's three home wins this season have all been by a single goal – two of them have been from the spot – and whilst we've not been exactly lucky, neither with injuries nor refereeing decisions, the side who laboured over a depleted Tottenham were devoid of the creative spark of previous models. Exceptional players do not become mediocre overnight and the relative loss of form may be temporary,

Plenty of chances, but just the one goal for Ruud

but while the English Premiership has yet to pass its quarter mark, Arsenal look a far superior side.

United performance: 6/10. **Man of the match:** Giggs – full of invention and sparkle. **Premiership position:** 1. Arsenal 17pts (pl 7); 2. Liverpool 15pts (pl 7); 3. Tottenham 13pts (pl 7)…7th. United 11pts (pl 7).

Tuesday 24 Sept 2002   **Champions League, 1st Group Stage**

Bayer Leverkusen 1   Manchester United 2
Berbatov 51.   Van Nistelrooy 31, 44.

Kick-off: 8.45pm. **Bay Arena. Att:** 22,500 (1,500 Reds) **Ref:** J Wegereef

United: (4-4-1-1) Barthez | O'Shea (G Neville h-t), Blanc, Ferdinand, Silvestre | P Neville, Butt, Veron (Solskjaer 87), Beckham | Giggs | Van Nistelrooy (Forlan h-t)
Booked: Butt, Ferdinand.

Bayer Leverkusen (3-3-3-1) Juric | Zivkovic, Ramelow, Lucio | Balitsch (Franca 81), Babic, Ojigwe (Simak 64) | Schneider, Basturk, Brdaric | Neuville (Berbatov 21)
Booked: Balitsch.

Leverkusen went into this match a dismal fourth from bottom in the Budesliga, and having been hammered 6-2 by Olympiakos in the previous week's Champions League game. So they were hardly the force which knocked United out of Europe five months previously. With star players Ballack and Ze Roberto enticed south to Bayern Munich, the team who used just fourteen players in last season's 19-game European run had started to show signs of fatigue.

Nevertheless, Leverkusen opened well and looked the likelier team to score until **Van Nistelrooy** netted his first goal of the season from open play when he chested down a high ball from Veron (playing his 50th United game), before threading the ball through the legs of Juric. It was his 14th goal in as many European games for United. Ruud then added a calming second goal, thirteen minutes later, when he finished an excellent move that had started when Phil Neville won the ball in midfield and involved neat passes between Giggs and Butt.

Revenge on Leverkusen: Ruud accepts the acclaim

Van Nistelrooy and O'Shea were lost to injury at half-time, and with United losing their threat, Berbatov pulled a goal back after a pass from Basturk. Klaus Toppmoller, the Leverkusen coach who looks like a cross between David Gower, Ronald McDonald and Tony Wilson, urged his side on for an equaliser, and the plastic Leverkusen fans who had sung 'You'll Never Walk Alone' thought they had a goal when a glancing header from Berbatov beat Barthez but not the post with three minutes left.

Victory made United the first English team to win at the Bay Arena and it was United's first win in Germany since 1965. Not a classic, but an excellent result.

United performance: 8/10. Man of the match: Van Nistelrooy – two first half goals and no signs of a lack of confidence suggested by some. Group position: (pl 2) 1. United 6pts; 2. Olympiakos 3pts; 3. Maccabi Haifa 3pts; 4. Bayer Leverkusen 0pts.

28 September 2002   Premiership

Charlton Athletic 1   Manchester United 3
Jensen 43   Scholes 54, Giggs 83, Van Nistelrooy 63.

Kick-off: 3pm. The Valley. Att: 26,630 (2,400 Reds) Ref: D Gallagher
United: (4-4-2) Barthez | P Neville, Ferdinand, Blanc, O'Shea | Giggs, Butt (G Neville 77), Scholes, Beckham | Solskjaer, Forlan (Van Nistelrooy 55). Booked: Forlan, Beckham, P Neville.
Charlton: (4-4-2) Kiely | Young (Johansson 85), Rufus, Fortune, Powell | Robinson, Mustoe (Kishishev 88), Jensen, Konchesky | Euell, Bartlett. Booked: Mustoe, Robinson.

When **Paul Scholes** scored United's equaliser nine minutes into the second half of this match, it was the Reds' first league goal from open play in eight hours and 17 minutes. George Best rarely went that long without having sex. There has been no shortage of critics of United's form so far this season, and for whatever reason, Sir Alex no longer sees it necessary to give post-match press conferences. But to his credit, the manager never loses faith in his players, even if he changes personnel when things don't go to plan. That's football.

Despite his two goals in Leverkusen, Van Nistelrooy's troublesome hamstring meant he started on the bench with Forlan in the uncustomary right-wing position and Beckham just inside. The system would have engendered fierce criticism had United not won, and after an unconvincing first half, the knives were being sharpened in the press box. Charlton's early confidence, however, belied that of a team who had lost all their home games so far this season, a team who have taken just four points off United in the previous eleven meetings. They went ahead two minutes before half time when Jensen found himself in space and had time to blast an unstoppable shot past Barthez into the top corner. But they seemed almost as surprised to find themselves in pole position.

Whatever Ferguson said at half-time, it worked. Giggs, always United's most dangerous performer, set Scholes up for the first after a penetrating run. Van Nistelrooy's introduction gave United a more familiar and menacing feel, but it wasn't until seven minutes before the end that the visitors took the lead, Giggs the scorer after dodging past Kiely. And it was Giggs who supplied the cross that led to third, a simple header for Van Nistelrooy, in the final minute. Arsenal's awesome 4-1 win at Leeds took the weekend newspaper plaudits, but United are not quite to be written off yet.

United performance: 8/10. **Man of the match**: Giggs – yet again, he was irresistible. **Premiership position**: 1. Arsenal 20pts (pl8); 2. Liverpool 18pts (pl 8); 3. Middlesbrough 14pts (pl 8); 4. United 14pts (pl 8).

Giggs tears them apart, again

October

Manchester United 4   Olympiakos 0
Giggs 19, 66, Veron 26, Solskjaer 77.

Kick-off: 7.45pm. Old Trafford. **Att:** 66,902 (3,000 Olympiakos) **Ref:** G Veissiere.

United: (4-4-2) Barthez | G Neville, Blanc (O'Shea 69), Ferdinand, Silvestre | Giggs (Fortune 63), Veron, Butt, Beckham | Scholes (Forlan 77), Solskjaer. Booked: G Neville, Veron, Ferdinand.

Olympiakos: (4-5-1) Eleftheropoulos | Anatolakis, Antzas, Venetidis, Amanatidis (Patsatzoglou 73) | Giannakopoulos (Dracena 45), Zetterberg, Karembeu, Djordjevic, Ze Elias | Ofori Quaye (Alexandris 59). Booked: Karembeu, Anatolakis. Sent off: Ze Elias.

Not for the first time for a European game at Old Trafford, United took to the field in an all blue strip. The referee had decided the Olympiakos black outfit would clash with the dark side panels on the red home shirt: a decision that seemed decidedly pedantic. Still, the omens were good for United; they had won on the previous four occasions at home when they've not played in red.

Olympiakos are formidable in Greece but away from home they have a reputation for crumbling against stronger teams, despite the backing of their forever shouty fans. They've not won once in nineteen Champions League away games and they've yet to score a goal in England. So, few were surprised when they fell 2-0 behind in the first half hour. Solskjaer crossed neatly to Giggs for the first, and then Beckham picked Veron out with an exquisite pass that elicited an equally sublime finish as the Argentinian chipped over Eleftheropoulos. Veron was the game's outstanding player in the first half, his range and quality of passes mesmerising. He also managed to escape serious injury when the Brazilian Ze Elias made an atrocious attempt at a tackle, which, if it had connected, would have chopped him off at the knee. Ze Elias was sent off with little debate.

After the break, Giggs inadvertently made it three when his cross clipped defender Anatolakis on 66 minutes. Then with 13 minutes left, Scholes set up Solskjaer and United's fourth.

Veron – a cut above the rest

All of which means, defying the Premiership lack of form, it's three convincing wins out of three for United in the Champions League group stage.

United performance: 8/10. **Man of the match:** Veron – a cut above everyone else on the pitch, as he was last season against the same side. **Group position:** (pl 3) 1. United 9pts; 2. Maccabi Haifa 3pts; 3. Olympiakos 3pts; 4. Bayer Leverkusen 3pts.

Manchester United 3   Everton 0

Scholes 86, 90. Van Nistelrooy 89 (pen).

Kick-off: 8pm. Old Trafford. **Att:** 67,629 **Ref:** M Riley

United: (4-4-1-1) Barthez | G Neville, O'Shea, Blanc, Silvestre | Beckham, Butt (Forlan 85), Veron (Solskjaer 63), Giggs | Scholes | Van Nistelrooy (P Neville 89).

Everton: (4-4-2) Wright | Hibbert, Weir, Yobo, Unsworth | Carsley, Li Tie, Gravesen, Pembridge | Campbell, Radzinski (Rooney 74).

Booked: Graveson, Unsworth. Sent off: Weir.

With no win since 1992, Everton have an appalling recent record at Old Trafford. But under new googly-eyed boss David Moyes – who played alongside Beckham when he made his league debut at Preston – they are much improved and fancied themselves for a point at least. In an absorbing first half played out in front of Old

Trafford's best atmosphere of the season so far, United continually pressed forward, while Everton defended well, hoping for a counter-attacking opportunity.

The story was much the same in the second half until a sixteen-year-old Croxteth-built tank by the name of Rooney entered the field with 16 minutes to play – and charged his way towards goal to threaten the game's first goal. In the Everton fanzine *When Skies Are Grey* they list players that they have spotted in the previous

The late, late show: Scholes concludes operations

month. Usually they are seen in the typical footballer hang-outs of restaurants, mobile phone shops and fancy trouser emporia. Rooney was spotted on his mountain bike, by the shops, with his mates.

Just as Everton's tight and disciplined approach looked as if it might be rewarded, Scholes seized on a poor clearance and clipped the ball past Wright four minutes from time. Relief. When Weir was sent off for pulling back Solskjaer minutes later, Van Nistelrooy struck his third penalty of the season. Yet another goal, easily the best, came in injury time when Scholes smashed a scorching 25 shot past the ex-Ipswich and Arsenal keeper.

The scoreline was harsh on Everton, but luck hasn't always run United's way recently. With the victory, United doubled the amount of goals they have scored so far in the league at Old Trafford.

United performance: 7/10. **Man of the match:** Scholes – late, great, double. **Premiership position:** 1. Arsenal 23pts (pl 9); 2. Liverpool 21pts (pl 9); 3. Middlesbrough 17pts (pl 9); 4. United 17pts (pl 9).

Saturday 19 October 2002	Premiership

Fulham 1
Marlet 15.

Manchester United 1
Solskjaer 62.

Kick-off: 3pm. Loftus Road. **Att:** 18,103 (2,800 Reds) **Ref:** M Dean

United: (4-4-1-1) Barthez | G Neville, O'Shea, Blanc, Silvestre (Forlan 81) | Beckham, Veron, P Neville (Fortune 59), Giggs | Scholes | Solskjaer. Booked: Beckham, Blanc, Barthez.

Fulham: (4-4-2) Van der Sar | Ouaddou, Knight, Goma, Brevett | Finnan, Davis, Malbranque, Legwinski | Marlet, Sava (Hayles 78).

With black market tickets going for £150 outside Fulham's temporary base at Loftus Road, and Giggs making his 500th appearance in a United shirt, United's travelling support were disappointed with a limp first-half performance that saw the jet-heeled Marlet put Fulham ahead after out-sprinting Silvestre to sidefoot in.

United reshuffled their formation at half-time to deal with Fulham's midfield dominance and emerged a greater threat. A long ball from Gary Neville didn't look as though it would trouble the Fulham defence but Ouaddou and Knight's hesitation meant Solskjaer nipped the ball away before hitting a meanly angled volley past Van der Sar. What followed ten minutes later will go down as one of the

It's a penalty – Giggs isn't happy but Barthez plans a spot of boot-cleaning

season's most bizarre acts. Featuring a cast of four Frenchmen, it started when Fulham were awarded a penalty after Blanc, knowing that he
was beaten for pace, pushed his compatriot Marlet inside the box. As
Malbranque stood waiting to take the spot kick, Barthez (as he had
done last season against Leicester) began walking around behind his
goal, feigning the need to clean his boots. He was booked for time-
wasting, which created a further delay. Then at last, the usually decisive penalty taker hit a mediocre shot, which Fabien saved, to be
rewarded with a famous kiss on the bald bonce by Blanc. United were
unlucky not to be awarded a penalty themselves in added time for
handball, but in truth the draw was a fair, and disappointing, result.

At least no further ground was lost to Arsenal, who were beaten by
Rooney FC – or so the media, in a froth of excitement at the Scouse
wunderkind, had us believe.

United performance: 6/10. Man of the match: Sean Davis – the England under-21 player dominated
in midfield. Premiership position: 1. Liverpool 24pts (pl 10); 2. Arsenal 23pts (pl 10); 3. United 18pts
(pl 10).

Wednesday 23 October 2002   **Champions League, 1st Group Stage**

Olympiakos 2
Choutos 70, Djordjevic 76.

Manchester United 3
Blanc 21, Veron 59, Scholes 84.

Kick-off: 9.45pm. Apollon Rizoupolis. **Att:** 15,000 (300 Reds) **Ref:** P Collina

United: (4-5-1) Barthez | G Neville, Blanc, O'Shea, Silvestre | Giggs (Fortune 63), Veron (Richardson 87), P Neville, Scholes, Beckham (Chadwick 63) | Forlan. Booked: G Neville.

Olympiakos: (4-4-2) Eleftheropoulos | Anatolakis, Antzas, Venetidis, Patsatzoglou | Giannakopoulos (Mavrogenidis 88), Zetterberg (Ofori Quaye 71), Karembeu, Djordjevic | Giovani (Choutos h-t), Dracena. Booked: Anatolakis, Venetidis.

This was United's fourth trip to Athens in eighteen months if you include the journey on September 12 2001 for a game cancelled after the Twin Towers bombing. Three hundred determined souls still purchased tickets, a snip at £52 each, for a game in a stadium more suited to the English third division than to the Champions League paraphernalia with which it was decorated. Olympiakos are currently playing home games at the ground of second division Apollon whilst they wait to build their own stadium. Meantime, the 76,000-seater Olympic stadium, where United played both Panathinaikos and Olympiakos last

Veron – irresistible again in Europe

year, is being refurbished to stage the event it is named after in 2004. It is hard to find anyone in Athens who believes it will be ready in time.

Apollon's ground holds just 15,000, but it sounded a lot more. Like the Turks, Greek fans are impressively noisy and they put us Reds to shame with their firebrand fervour. No kind of support can turn a team into the best in Europe, though, and United outclassed a mediocre Olympiakos for the first hour, cruising into a 2-0 lead with goals from **Blanc** and a thumping cracker from **Veron** after a surging run. The travelling fans, who included the United under-20s team, relaxed and savoured the atmosphere, until a suspect early substitution saw Beckham and Giggs replaced by Fortune and Chadwick, both of whom were lacking match practice. Olympiakos could hardly believe their luck and scored twice, before a **Scholes** goal put United back in front just before time.

The Olympiakos fans were friendly with the visiting supporters before the game but edgy during it, and the police escorted the United followers back to a chartered metro which took them into the city centre after the game. Nobody much minded the herding as after this the Reds, or should that be Blues, were through to the second phase after our 100th win in European competition.

United performance: 8/10. **Man of the match:** Scholes – a bundle of problems for the Greeks and scored when it mattered. **Group position:** (pl 4) 1. United 9pts; 2. Bayer Leverkusen 6pts; 3. Maccabi Haifa 3pts; 4. Olympiakos 3pts.

⚽ **GOAL-DEN OLDIES** Laurent Blanc's goal at Olympiakos makes him United's second oldest scorer since the war, at 36 years and 338 days. (The oldest was Bryan Robson.)

Blanc's up, the marking's shocking

Saturday 26 October 2002   Premiership

Manchester United 1   Aston Villa 1
Forlan 77.   Mellberg 35.

Kick-off: 3pm. **Old Trafford. Att:** 67,619 **Ref:** G Poll

United: (4-4-2) Barthez | G Neville, Ferdinand, Blanc, Silvestre | Beckham, P Neville (Fortune 59), Veron, Forlan | Solskjaer, Scholes. **Booked:** Beckham.

Aston Villa: (4-4-2) Enckelman | Delaney, Mellberg, Staunton, Samuel | Leonhardsen, (Hitzlsperger 84), Kinsella, Taylor, Barry | Dublin (Crouch 65), Moore (Angel 65).

Sandwiched in between away games in Athens and nearby Nicosia, Sir Alex asked the Premiership authorities if this match could be postponed in the hope of his players spending the intervening week catching the last of the Mediterranean autumnal sun. The league refused, and the United squad returned to a city that had registered over thirty recent earthquakes. Yes – that was Manchester.

When Aston Villa scored their first away goal of the season ten minutes before half-time, Manchester continued to be the stage of the surreal. With news of Arsenal losing at home to Blackburn (thanks, Dwight), United had the chance to close the gap at the top and yet the team were, in the words of the manager, 'shoddy and lacked urgency.'

789 minutes: the wait is over

With thirteen minutes to play, defeat looked on the cards. That, however, was reckoning without Diego. Silvestre had time to pick out **Forlan** with a cross and the Uruguayan, who had already come characteristically close to scoring four times, finally seized his chance and judged his header perfectly for his first Premiership goal in 789 minutes. Seven hundred and eighty-nine minutes. Manchester's bizarre week was complete and the relief was tangible, not just for the United fans who had stuck by Forlan against his countless critics, but by the man himself who whipped off his top to expose a chest that had last seen the light of day trying to impress the *chicas* on the beach in Punta del Este.

The goal gave brief respite, but it didn't mask another inadequate United performance nor prevent talk of the team simply not being as good as they were. After all, a home win against the likes of Aston Villa used to be taken for granted.

United performance: 6/10. **Man of the match**: Barry – attacked, defended and kept Beckham quiet.
Premiership position: 1. Liverpool 27pts (pl 11); 2.Arsenal 23pts (pl 11); 3. Chelsea 19pts (pl 11); 4. United 19pts (pl 11).

Tuesday 29 October 2002	Champions League, 1st Group Stage

Maccabi Haifa 3   Manchester United 0
Katan 40, Zutauttas 56, Ayegbeni 77 pen.

Kick-off: 8.45pm. **Att**: 22,000 (1,500 travelling Reds) **Ref**: A Lopez Nieto
United: (4-4-2) Ricardo | G Neville, O'Shea, Ferdinand, Silvestre | Richardson (Nardiello 62), P Neville, Scholes, Fortune | Solskjaer, Forlan (Timm 79). Booked: Ricardo, O'Shea, Silvestre.
Maccabi Haifa: (4-4-2) Awate | Harazi, Benado, Zano, Keise | Rosso, Zutauttas (Zandberg 81), Badir, Pralija | Katan, Ayegbeni (Almoshnino 85).

With UEFA insisting that the Israeli champions play all their games away from home because of the political situation in Israel and the Palestinian Territories, Haifa reluctantly switched their games to Nicosia, a forty-minute flight away. Ironically, Nicosia is the last divided capital city in the world and Greek and Turkish soldiers swap stares either side of a UN administered buffer zone, untouched except for nearly thirty years of dust. Along with other United fans, we saw some Turks on the other side of the fence. One waved and shouted. 'Why are you here?' 'For a football game.' 'Which Turkish team do you know?' he hollered. 'Galatasaray, Fenerbahce, Besiktas.' 'Galatasaray is my team,' he said, smiling, and pointing to himself. Mad.

The game was a shocker, an easy victory for Haifa. United rested a few key players, sure, and they didn't need the points. But the team that started featured nine full international players who should have put up a more convincing performance. The Maccabi fans appeared to be having the time of their life, singing non-stop for ninety minutes. The 1,500 travelling United fans, whose ranks were swollen to 14,000 by day-tripping Cypriots enjoying seeing United players in the flesh, couldn't come close in comparison.

Two hours after the game and the departures board at Larnaka airport was full with early morning return flights to two destinations: Haifa and Tel Aviv. The concourses were flushed with Maccabi's green and their cheery, drum-beating followers. Applause went up when their manager Itzhak Shun appeared on a TV screen and fans huddled closer to hear his post-match comments. A minute later, there was an ovation. 'What did he say?' I asked a nearby fan. 'He said that for two hours, Israel could forget its problems.' He paused. 'He is right. That game was the happiest moment of my life, we have shocked European football.'

I could have begged to differ, but thought better of it. Let them have their moment in the sun, even if it was at United's expense.

United performance: 4/10. **Man of the match:** Katan – scored a lucky goal, but troubled the experienced United defence. **Group position:** (pl 5) 1. United 12pts; 2. Bayer Leverkusen 9pts; 3. Maccabi Haifa 6pts; 4. Olympiakos 3pts.

⚽ **MADS' ELEVEN** Mads Timm plays for eleven minutes as a substitute in the 3-0 defeat at Maccabi Haifa, which currently gives him the second shortest United career on record (after Nick Culkin's 7.5 seconds at Arsenal in 1999).

Mads about the boy

FERGIE'S NAGS

As those who have ever been in a car driven by him will attest, Alex Ferguson enjoys a touch of pace, and as a manager he has always admired sprinters: Giggs, Kancheslskis, Ferdinand – gallopers, all of them. It will have come as some small consolation, then, that after a barren season on the football pitch he won the 2002 Racehorse Owner of the Year award with a horse so quick it was the stuff of legend. In its first season of racing, **Rock of Gibraltar** beat Mill Reef's long-standing record of five consecutive class one victories, by notching up seven, including the 2000 Guineas. It would have made that eight, but for an appalling start in the **Breeder's Cup Mile** in Kentucky. Unsure of the American way, the Rock ambled out of the starting gate to find itself way behind, and blocked in; it then produced a burst of acceleration few had ever witnessed before, to ease through the field into second place.

After that race, the Rock was retired and sent off to sire as many foals as is equinely possible. Not a bad life for a two-year-old. If you wonder why Fergie didn't keep the horse running, in the hope of picking up every classic in the record book, the answer is simple: £30m. Which is the Rock's value as a stud. Yes, a full Rio. Now it had proven its pedigree, particularly in America, there was no point risking its pristine physique in training and racing. Better to keep it perky for sex at £70,000 a shot.

With the Rock otherwise engaged, the horse Ferguson will have an interest in for the 2003 flat season is **Gatwick**, trained by former blue Mick Channon. As with the Rock – which he co-owned with Susan, wife of John Magnier, the man behind Coolmore stables, and a recent investor in Manchester United plc – Gatwick is not entirely Fergie's own. He is in a consortium with several long-standing racing friends, including Henry Ponsonby, who ran the Manchester United Racing Club, the institution which first introduced Ferguson to horse ownership back in 1997.

Rock of Gibraltar   Andrei Kanchelskis

November

Manchester United 2   Southampton 1
P Neville 15, Forlan 85.   Fernandes 18.

Kick-off: 3pm. Old Trafford. **Att:** 67,691 **Ref:** U Rennie

United: (4-4-2) Barthez | G Neville, Ferdinand, Blanc, Silvestre (Solskjaer 68) | Beckham, P Neville (Forlan 79), Veron, Giggs | Scholes, Van Nistelrooy (O'Shea 87).

Southampton: (4-4-2) Niemi | Dodd, Lundekvam, M Svensson, Bridge, | Fernandes, A Svensson, Marsden (Delgado 88), Oakley | Beattie, Ormerod (Delap 74) **Booking:** Dodd.

In the climate of disappointment and inconsistency that has been the season so far, one stable factor has been the unflinching support

Shirts against skins: Diego models the new kit

for Diego Forlan from United fans. Maybe it's because they see how hard he works in games, maybe they can see a certain comedy value in a goalscorer who, er, doesn't score. Whatever, Diego enjoyed his finest hour in (and out of) a red shirt today just as United appeared to be about to draw their third league game on the trot.

There was no chance of repeating the 6-1 victory of last season, as a tenacious Southampton side played their part in an absorbing end to end encounter, save for a couple of minutes' break when a loon United fan stole onto the pitch and broke the north west record for evading stewards on a slippery playing surface during a match whilst fully clothed. Phil Neville's fine early strike had been cancelled out just three minutes later when the tricky Gaul Fernandes slotted past Barthez.

Then, five minutes from time, cue Forlan, on as a sub for the free-scoring Neville junior. He instantly made himself busy around the Saints' goal and the headlines were assured when he hit a stunning shot from 30 yards in front of the Stretford End. It was more than a winner, and for a minute, you wondered whether Diego was going to run out of the stadium, never to be seen again as he did a celebration world tour to mark the occasion, red shirt swinging above his head like a lasso. Fantastic. As was the aftermath, when Forlan couldn't get the shirt back on, and set off chasing James Beattie, still waving the shirt.

United performance: 7/10. **Man of the match:** Ferdinand – his confidence seems unaffected after an injury-pockmarked start to his Old Trafford career. **Premiership position:** 1. Liverpool 30pts (pl 12); 2.Arsenal 23pts (pl 11); 3. United 22pts (pl 22).

Tuesday 5 November 2002	Worthington Cup 3rd Round

Manchester United 2   Leicester City 0
Beckham 80 (pen), Richardson 90.

Kick-off: 8pm. Old Trafford. **Att:** 47,848 **Ref:** C Foy

United: (4-4-2) Carroll | G Neville, Ferdinand, May, O'Shea | Beckham, P Neville (Scholes 59), Forlan, Fortune (Veron 65) | Solskjaer, Nardiello (Richardson 74). Booked: Beckham, P Neville.

Leicester City: (4-4-2) Walker | Sinclair, Heath, Elliott (Summerbee 51), Rogers (Stevenson 81) | Impey, Izzet, Davidson, Stewart | Dickov (Benjamin 56), Scowcroft. Booked: Heath, Impey, Sinclair.

The Cup formerly known as Worthless does have its uses. Reduced priced tickets allow youngsters who wouldn't otherwise get a chance to see United the opportunity to appreciate their heroes, while on the field many a youngster, from Beckham to O'Shea, has been blooded in the competition. That 47,848 chose to attend a night game against unappealing opposition indicates the strength of United's support. And perhaps the number of tickets sold persuaded Sir Alex to have more of a crack than usual at the competition. It was certainly no youth team that took the pitch.

Kieran Richardson: no fear in front of goal, but he'll have to drop the Spitfire celebration

The Foxes, in administration off the field but rejuvenated on it and riding high in the Nationwide, were not daunted and matched United in every area in the first period. Despite Forlan looking lively and pumped with confidence after his recent goalscoring deeds, the score remained goalless at the hour mark, when Sir Alex pulled out the heavyweights, and introduced Veron and Scholes. Still, it wasn't until ten minutes before the end that the net was breached by a Beckham penalty after Impey had pushed Solskjaer. The captain of England and (for tonight at least) United then set up United's second goal in the final minute, crossing for the tricky Kieran Richardson to head in on his home debut.

United performance: 7/10. **Man of the match:** Beckham – kidnap threats off the field, rousing on it.

Saturday 9 November 2002	Premiership

Manchester City 3   Manchester United 1
Anelka 5, Goater 26, 50.   Solskjaer 8.

Kick-off: 12.15pm. Maine Road. **Att:** 34,649 (3,100 Reds) **Ref:** P Durkin
United: (4-4-2) Barthez | G Neville (O'Shea 62), Ferdinand, Blanc, Silvestre | Giggs, Veron (Forlan 62), Scholes, P Neville | Solskjaer, Van Nistelrooy. Booked: Solskjaer, P Neville.
City: (3-5-2) Schmeichel | Dunne, Wiekens, Mettomo | Jensen, Berkovic (Wright-Phillips 78), Foe, Tiatto (Horlock 87), Jihai | Anelka, Goater. Booked: Weikens.

The Derby day highlight for some Reds inside Maine Road's mishmash of stands came when a flag was unfurled in City's Kippax Street side which read: 'Manchester Is Red.' How we chortled watching so many clueless Blues pass the banner above their heads. The fun was meant to serve as a fitting prelude to United's final visit to Maine Road but, instead, it presaged a terrible afternoon. Even now, well after the debacle, I'm still fuming and, like every Red in the stadium, I feel cheated at the inadequate and passionless performance by the players of Manchester United. United fans have not had to deal with a Derby defeat since 1989, and this was as painful as the 5-1 of '89. It was that bad.

City were a goal up after five minutes, Anelka the scorer after he hustled Ferdinand off a poor ball from Phil Neville. Solskjaer equalised three minutes later with a routine finish, and for a while

United looked the better team. Then, in the 26th minute, Shaun Goater robbed Gary Neville of possession and scored City's second. The Goat. It was a terrible piece of defending, and one which ensured Neville was cheered ironically by Blues for the rest of the game. Anelka could, and should, have made it 3-1 when he was put one on one with Barthez but it was Goater who eventually scored City's third, five minutes after half-time. United were briefly stirred, but appeared devoid of both the quality and inspiration to turn the game – and it's naïve to blame the deficiencies solely on injuries. Giggs came close, and O'Shea missed a sitter that will surely re-appear on a TV 'What Happened Next?' sequence, but City were worthy victors.

Queiroz and Ferguson: not happy, not happy at all

This defeat wasn't a freak one. It had been coming. What concerns many Reds is how quickly United have slipped from a team that won the Premiership at a canter in 2001 to a side that have looked utterly unconvincing all of this season and through much of the last one. Many fear for the outcome when United play a top-class side.

There are only so many excuses that Sir Alex and the United players can offer before the fans' patience wears thin. We keep hearing talk of 'hunger', 'desire' and determination' but where is the evidence? Something is clearly wrong, and the derby result confirmed the fact to United fans who are becoming bored and frustrated at the current situation. Strong words, but the truth. No less.

United performance: 4/10. **Man of the match:** Berkovic – pocket-sized battler allowed to perform like Platini. **Premiership position:** 1. Liverpool 30pts (pl 13); 2. Arsenal 29pts (pl 13); 3. Chelsea 23pts (pl 13)…5th. United 22pts (pl 13).

Wednesday 13 Nov 2002	Champions League, 1st Group Stage

Manchester United 2   Bayer Leverkusen 0
Veron 42, Van Nistelrooy 69.

Kick-off: 7.45pm. Old Trafford. **Att:** 66,185 **Ref:** V Hrinak

United: (4-4-1-1) Ricardo | O'Shea, Blanc (G Neville 77), Ferdinand, Silvestre | Fortune, Veron, Beckham (Solskjaer 77), Giggs (Chadwick 81) | Scholes | Van Nistelrooy.

Booked: Ricardo.

Bayer Leverkusen: (4-1-3-2) Butt | Sebescen, Zivkovic, Ramelow, Kleine | Balitsch (Preuss 81) | Bierofka (Dogan 78), Babic, Simak | Berbatov, Brdaric.

After the appalling result at Maine Road, United needed to convince doubtful fans of their quality. Qualification to the second Champions League group stage had been assured, but that wasn't the point. The game at Maine Road had brought matters to a head and many fans were questioning the validity and purpose of the Manchester United's first team players after the poor start to the season. For his part, Sir Alex issued a rare stinging criticism of his squad immediately after the derby, stating publicly that he wasn't afraid to rebuild his side and that each of his players has until the end of the season to save their skin. Citing one of the players under the most criticism, Veron, as an example, Ferguson said: 'His European form has always been great but there is always the question: Is he a European or Premiership player? The one thing he has is quality, it's an important year for him, just as it is for the rest of us. We are all going to get judged.'

But this was Europe, and Veron was at his beguiling best – albeit that this was an exercise in irrelevance, with both teams already through, and Leverkusen leaving six regular starters in Germany. Veron had a point to prove, though, and whilst too many of his passes still went astray, he was the game's most influential per-

Ruud again, as the Reds make amends

former, scoring one before half-time and starting a move that allowed **Van Nistelrooy** to tap in United's second. Throughout, Leverkusen looked an imitation of the side that knocked United out of the European Cup six months earlier, which, with hindsight, made the failure to reach Glasgow 2002 even more frustrating.

All of which validates UEFA's decision to change the format of the Champions League next season to a single group phase, followed by a two-leg knock-out tournament for the last sixteen.

United performance: 7/10. **Man of the match**: Veron – an artist, consistently United's top performer in Europe. **Final Group position**: (pl 6) 1. United 15pts; 2. Leverkusen 9pts; 3. Maccabi Haifa 7pts; 4. Olympiakos 4pts.

⚽ **RETURN TO TURIN** United are drawn with Juventus in the second group stage of the European Cup, the sixth time we have been drawn against the Turin team, making them our most frequent continental opponents.

West Ham 1
Defoe 86.

Manchester United 1
Van Nistelrooy 37.

Kick-off: 4pm. **Att:** 35,049 (2,900 Reds) **Ref:** M Halsey

United: (4-4-2) Barthez | Blanc, Brown, Silvestre, O'Shea | Scholes, Fortune, Giggs, Veron | Solskjaer, Van Nistelrooy. Booked: Fortune.

West Ham: (4-4-2) James | Dailly, Pearce, Schemmel, Winterburn | Carrick, Sinclair, Cole, Cisse | Defoe, Di Canio. Booked: Cisse, Di Canio.

United went into this game boasting an enviable record against a Hammers side who hadn't recorded a single home league win so far.

Cheer up lads, we've just scored

But then United's away form – with just one victory at Charlton – was hardly formidable, either. And feelings of disgruntlement were shared. Home fans protested against their board before the game. According to them, money has been lavished on a colossal new main stand but not on the team. The board have retorted publicly with the claim that their wage bill is the seventh highest in the

Premiership. United, of course, remain the top payers, although with an acute injury problem, many of the big earners are not even playing at the moment and with that in mind, the return of Wes Brown after a three-month absence was most welcome.

After a Defoe 'goal' was disallowed for being offside in the 20th minute, United took the lead seven minutes before half-time after Fortune picked up a poor Sinclair clearance and nudged it wide to Solskjaer. The Gunnar crossed for Van Nistelrooy, who had actually been offside when the move started, to finish at the near post. With the day approaching that marked a decade since the arrival of Eric, the away fans roared 'Twelve Cantonas'. Either that or they were feeling prematurely festive. West Ham searched for an equaliser, which, as Sir Alex later admitted, they deserved. Defoe came close when he hit the bar with a lob twenty minutes from time and just as an away win was looking the most likely result an offside Defoe, who had been a nuisance all afternoon, equalised with four minutes left after being put clear by the impish Di Canio.

The spark is still missing and with Arsenal now nine points ahead, any title prospects look remote.

United performance: 8/10. **Man of the match:** Defoe – it must be easier to juggle snakes than mark him. **Premiership position:** 1. Arsenal 35pts (pl 16); 2. Liverpool 31pts (pl 16); 3. Chelsea 30pts (pl 16); 4. United 29pts (pl 16).

Saturday 23 November 2002	Premiership

Manchester United 5   Newcastle United 3

Scholes 25, Van Nistelrooy 38, 45, 52, Solskjaer 54.   Bernard 35, Shearer 51, Bellamy 74.

Kick-off: 12.15pm. Old Trafford. **Att:** 67,619 **Ref:** S Dunn

United: (4-4-2) Barthez | O'Shea, Blanc (Roche 69), Brown, Silvestre | Solskjaer, Fortune, Scholes, Giggs | Van Nistelrooy (Richardson 63), Forlan (Veron 79).

Booked: Solskjaer, Van Nistelrooy.

Newcastle: (4-4-2) Given | Griffin, Dabizas, O'Brien, Hughes | Speed, Bernard (Solano 71), Jenas, Dyer | Bellamy, Shearer.

Booked: Dabizas, Speed.

One of many criticisms of United of late is that they've stopped entertaining, that the once indomitable goal machine now stutters and stalls. Reds were nervous before this game, Magpies confident.

Alan Shearer? No problem for the ever-confident John O'Shea

Or as Mark Jensen, editor of their fanzine *The Mag*, put it: 'For the first time in a long time I fancy us to beat you at Old Trafford.'

United's players reckoned otherwise. Coming out onto a new pitch that cut up easily, we were the best team from the start, and the goals looked sure to come. The first arrived on 25 minutes as Solksjaer, after brilliantly controlling a poor ball and beating two defenders, set up Scholes. Ten minutes later Bernard equalised when a cross left Barthez flat-footed and bewildered, but the lead was restored inside three minutes when Silvestre centred for Van Nistelrooy to head in his first Premiership goal from open play all season. Ruud then made it 3-1 just before the break when he tapped in a finish after Forlan had dragged a shot across goal.

Alan Shearer, a man who is still consistently booed at Old Trafford for having the audacity to turn United down twice, struck a net-busting free kick that Lev Yashin on steroids would have struggled to get near: 3-2 after 51 minutes. A minute later, United were 4-2 up when **Van Nistelrooy** secured his hat-trick, again converting an assist from Forlan. **Solskjaer** made it 5-2 after 54 minutes when he found himself clean through on goal. He didn't waste his chance. Bellamy got a consolation header to make it 5-3 and prompt the Geordies to sing: 'We're gonna win 6-5.'

There may have been some suspect defending from both teams, but the game was a fine attacking showcase and the feel-good factor increased by news that both Arsenal and Liverpool had lost. Considering the absence of Beckham, Butt and Ferdinand, the relief was best summed up by Van Nistelrooy: 'It has been hard to say what has been missing but this result gives us confidence with the big games coming up.' Let's hope the action is equal to his words.

United performance: 9/10. **Man of the Match:** Van Nistelrooy – tireless contribution…and three goals. **Premiership position:** 1. Arsenal 32pts (pl 15); 2. Liverpool 31pts (pl 15); 3. Everton 29pts (pl 15)… 5th. United 26pts (pl 15).

<hr>

Tuesday 26 November 2002   Champions League, 2nd Group Stage

FC Basle 1   Manchester United 3
Gimenez 1.   Van Nistelrooy 62, 63. Solskjaer 68.

Kick-off: 8.45pm. St. Jacob-Park. **Att:** 29,501 (1,400 Reds) **Ref:** V Ivanov

United: (4-5-1) Barthez | P Neville, Brown (May 90), O'Shea, Silvestre | Fortune, Veron, Solskjaer (Chadwick 90), Giggs, Scholes | Van Nistelrooy (Forlan 73).
Booked: Fortune, Scholes, Veron, Van Nistelrooy.
Basle: (4-3-1-2) Zuberbuhler | Haas, M Yakin, Zwyssig, Atouba | Ergic (Barberis 85), Cantaluppi, Chipperfield (Tum 72) | H Yakin | Gimenez, Rossi.
Booked: Zwyssig.

Such is Beckham's appeal on the continent that Miss Switzerland invested in a seat for this game (and seats were being touted at £300 plus). Then it was announced that Beckham, like many of his injury laden colleagues, wasn't going to play, so Miss Switzerland did the

Basle fans in full voice, Miss Switzerland not pictured

unnatural thing and saved on dragging her pampered limbs to the impressive St Jacob-Park.

She missed out. Pundits had warned about Basle's penchant for grabbing an early goal, which had set the template for their impressive European form so far this season. United paid little attention to such talk, and Basle scored early. Very early. After 31 seconds, in fact, making it the fastest goal in Champions League history, and by the first Swiss side to reach the Champions League, let alone the second group stage. Basle's further threats to deliver a knock-out blow were averted by some fine goalkeeping by **Barthez** – encouraging after his patchy form this season. Still, Basle displayed the confidence of a team that had disposed of Celtic and Liverpool in earlier rounds.

Half-time saw the teams switch role as well as ends, United becoming dominant, Basle subservient. United were irresistible as they hit three goals in just seven minutes. **Van Nistelrooy** scored the first two – his second appeared implausible as he turned the right-back Haas on the by-line before hitting a shot through a crowded area. It somehow went in off the far post from the tightest angle. **Solskjaer** got the third after he ran onto a long pass and found himself one on one with the keeper with time to choose his spot. He doesn't miss those types of opportunities and even Miss Switzerland would have enjoyed the abandon with which the United players celebrated.

United performance: 8.5/10. **Man of the match:** Van Nistelrooy – five goals in four days. **Group position:** (pl 1) 1. United 3pts; 2. Deportivo 1pt; 3. Juventus 1pt; 4. Basle 0pt.

STAMP COLLECTING United's trip to Basle in the European Cup makes Switzerland the 30th country we have visited in UEFA tournaments. The most significant countries United have yet to visit in European competition are Romania and Norway (where there is huge Red support).

December

Sunday 1 December 2002   **Premiership**

Liverpool 1
Hyppia 82.

Manchester United 2
Forlan 64, 67.

Kick-off: 12.15pm. Anfield. **Att:** 44,250 (3,000 Reds) **Ref:** A Wiley

United: (4-4-2) Barthez | G Neville, Brown, Silvestre, O'Shea | Solskjaer, Scholes, Fortune (P Neville 82), Giggs | Forlan (Stewart 90), Van Nistelroy (May 90). Booked: Van Nistelrooy, Brown, Silvestre, Forlan.

Liverpool: (4-4-2) Dudek | Carragher, Traore (Riise 79), Henchoz, Hyppia, | Smicer (Diouf 70), Gerrard, Hamann, Murphy | Barros (Heskey 59), Owen. Booked: Murphy, Smicer.

Last year 12,000 held up coloured cards on the Kop to make a giant 'G.H' collage. They're calling for him to be sacked now. For this game, the same fans continued educating the rest of the ground with a collage that spelled out: 'This Is Anfield.' What can await us next season?

He comes from Uruguay ... a legend is born

A giant '13' – to remind Scousers of the number of years since they won the league?

For the first 45 minutes, Sir Alex's injury-sapped team were put under pressure by a side which has become accustomed to beating United. Anfield nasalled away its roars, and diverted itself with its booing for Gary Neville, when the man they love to hate had possession. United never looked entirely comfortable.

All that changed in the second half, which will go down as one of the most memorable of the season among Red supporters. The United defence, with Silvestre at centre half, was unconquerable, and upfront a new cult hero was born, as Forlan scored two goals in three minutes, the first a gentle tap-in after the fumbling Dudek allowed Carragher's soft header to roll unchallenged through his legs. When Hyppia, a player usually thought of as Liverpool's bedrock, failed to intercept a pass three minutes later, Diego was on hand to thump the ball past the hopeless Pole.

Hyppia made partial amends with a low strike eight minutes from time but an equaliser would have been unjust and there was only one song emanating from Anfield at the end of the day. And that came from the United fans singing: 'Who put the ball in the Scousers net? Jerzy, Jerzy Dudek.' Ace.

United performance: 8/10. **Man of the match**: Gary Neville edges Fortune for the honour – both had their best performance of the season. **Premiership position**: 1. Arsenal 35pts (pl 16); 2. Liverpool 31pts (pl 16); 3. Chelsea 30pts (pl 16); 4. United 29pts (pl 16).

Burnley 0   Manchester United 2
Forlan 35, Solskjaer 65.

Kick-off: 8pm (delayed due to crowd congestion). Turf Moor. **Att:** 22,034 (4,000 Reds) **Ref:** N Barry
United: (4-4-2) Carroll | P Neville, Brown, May, Silvestre | Pugh, Chadwick, Stewart (Scholes 48), O'Shea | Van Nistelrooy (Solskjaer 46), Forlan (Giggs 76). Booked: Brown.
Burnley: (4-4-2) Beresford | West, Davis, Gnohere (A Moore 73), Branch | Weller, Cook (Grant 57), Briscoe (Papadopoulos 67), Little | Blake, Taylor.

Once again, the merits of the Worthington Cup were emphasized at Burnley. As against Leicester in the previous round, this wasn't a United side of fresh-faced youngsters without a razor in their Vuitton washbags. But a number of fringe team players – look, there's David May – enjoyed a rare start, and a 4,000 away ticket allocation at an impressively redeveloped ground resulted in a belting local cup-tie played in a febrile atmosphere.

Burnley's 88,000 population makes the town the smallest to have hosted top-flight football on a consistent basis, and whilst the days of the Clarets playing at the highest level are long gone, their recent revival under Stan Ternant has seen them establish themselves as a

It's that man again

first division side once again. In doing so, they have lifted spirits in a depressed and challenged town.

Over at the United end, the atmosphere was rocking, and a chant went up of 'You're just a small town in Blackburn'. It was intended to rile the locals, who despise their neighbours to the west, and it did. The evening also gave vent to a hearty rendition of a tune that might well become a classic – 'Diego, he came from Uruguay, he made the Scousers cry' – celebrating Forlan's Anfield brace.

It was indeed the man who now can't stop scoring, who made the difference for United at Turf Moor. The first half was evenly matched, fast paced and goalless until United's man of the moment slid in his sixth of the season from a John O'Shea pass on 35 minutes. United were easily stronger in the second period and Danny Pugh had three good chances to score. Maybe on another day. Half-time substitute Solskjaer, who had set Pugh up for two of the openings, made it 2-0 on 65 minutes after Luke Chadwick had beaten two defenders and crossed the ball back.

United looked likely to score again, but the partisans in the away end didn't end up celebrating another goal, but instead the incredulous news that a Burnley player, Glen Little, had been awarded the man of the match award: 'Fergie, sign him on', sang the irony-heavy Reds. Who said we couldn't enjoy the Worthington Cup?

United performance: 7/10. **Man of the match:** Diego Forlan – flush with confidence and involved in everything.

Saturday 7 December 2002   **Premiership**

Manchester United 2   Arsenal 0
Veron 22, Scholes 73.

Kick-off: 12.15pm. Old Trafford. **Att:** 67,650 **Ref:** D Gallagher
United: (4-5-1) Barthez | G Neville, Brown, Silvestre, O'Shea | Solskjaer, P Neville, Scholes, Veron, Giggs | Van Nistelrooy. Booked: P Neville.
Arsenal: (4-4-2) Shaaban (Taylor 42) | Luzhny, Keown, Cygan, Cole | Ljungberg, Vieira, Silva, Pires (Toure 77) | Wiltord (Bergkamp 67), Henry. Booked: Luzhny.

Some of the praise for Arsenal so far this season has been justified, some of it almost sickeningly obsequious. Arsenal were worthy

Phil's finest hour: he tackled everyone, even his brother

champions last season and they are league leaders on merit so far this, but for a team that has never come close to winning the European Cup to be labelled 'England's greatest' is a tag too far. Manager Wenger, quoted eight weeks ago, said that he thought his team were capable of remaining unbeaten this season. Only arrogance, no matter how self-assured, can lead a man to make such a comment in the full knowledge that it could come back and slap you in the face. After all, Beckham had said the same thing last season, suggesting it might be a nice parting gift to Uncle Alex. And look what that got us.

With three league defeats already since that quote, Arsenal must be beginning to regret their manager's hype. And the fourth came today, after Phil Neville delivered a command performance to quell the presence of the colossus Vieira, combining a series of crunching tackles with faultless distribution in midfield. For the first time in 55 Premiership games, Monsieur Wenger's side failed to score. Not only that, they were outmanoeuvred by the tactical acumen of Sir

Alex and his coaches in a 2-0 defeat. Ex-Highbury captain Tony Adams was purring about United after the game, especially the defence. He described John O'Shea as 'a fantastic player' and praised Gary Neville, Silvestre and Brown. United fielded eleven stars, though, with the two goalscorers Veron and Scholes shining radiantly too. 'We got a warning,' confessed a stunned Wenger post match. He got a lesson in spirit and hunger too.

United are back, and who would have thought that four weeks ago, after the derby?

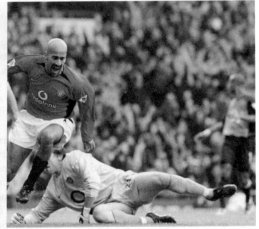

A season unbeaten? Veron begs to differ

United performance: 9/10. **Man of the match**: Phil Neville – morphed into Keane and Butt to become the main man against Vieira and Gilberto. Hugely effective. **Premiership position**: 1. Arsenal 35pts (pl 17); 2. Chelsea 33pts (pl 17); 3. United 32pts (pl 17).

⚽ **BRING ON CURZON ASHTON** United are drawn against First Division Portsmouth in the FA Cup third round, which means it is now fifty years since we met non-league opposition in the FA Cup (the last was Walthamstow Avenue in 1953). Alex Ferguson never has much luck in the FA Cup third round draw. In sixteen third round pairings in his time at Old Trafford, United have met opponents from the top flight ten times, and on another three occasions we met teams who, like Portsmouth, were top of the division immediately below.

Manchester United 2   Deportivo La Coruña 0
Van Nistelrooy 7, 55.

Kick-off: 7.45pm. Old Trafford. Att: 67,014 Ref: T Hague

United: (4-4-1-1) Barthez | G Neville, Brown, Silvestre, O'Shea (Forlan 81) | Solskjaer, P Neville (Beckham 81), Veron, Giggs | Scholes | Van Nistelrooy (Richardson 89).
Booked: Veron, Solskjaer.

Deportivo: (4-3-1-2) Juanmi | Scaloni, Cesar, Romero, Capdevila | Victor (Luque 75), Segio, Mauro Silva, Amavisca (Tristan h-t) | Valeron (Acuna 65) | Makaay.
Booked: Capdevila.

Manchester United and Deportivo La Coruña were happy to exist without ever troubling each other throughout their entire histories up until 2001. Now, the pair can't stop meeting. Tonight's game was the fifth between the clubs in fifteen months, which reflects well on the achievement of the Galician club – from a city of 250,000 – in establishing themselves as Champions League regulars.

If anything, though, expectations of the club are now too high and leading goalscorer Roy Makaay was keen to inject a sense of reality: 'We're very ambitious but people have to understand that we are not as big a club as Manchester. In the last ten years Deportivo have grown bit by bit, but we don't have the history or the money that Manchester has. Manchester can spend a lot of money on the best players when they need to – it's not like that here. Manchester has injuries which they can cover for. We have injuries which we can't.'

The night belonged to Makaay's Dutch team mate Van Nistelrooy as he equalled then overtook Andy Cole's 18 Champions League goals for the club. Van Nistelrooy has now scored 53 goals in 66 Red starts. His first came when he outjumped two defenders to head in Scholes's enchanting cross after seven minutes. The second came just as Depor were becoming more adventurous. A Scholes shot was saved by Depor's reserve keeper (the first choice Molina is recovering from cancer) but he could only parry it toward Solskjaer who turned it into the path of Van Nistelrooy.

Despite the freezing Manchester night which obliged most of United's foreign players to wear gloves, the Reds' had mounted a slick, controlled display in searching for that second, killer, goal.

After they had gained it, they relaxed, and when Beckham, sporting a new hairstyle, was introduced with nine minutes to play, the fans kicked off an impromptu chant of 'One Rod Stewart'.

United performance: 8/10.
Man of the match: Veron – the renaissance continues.
Group position: (pl 2) 1. United 6pts; 2. Juventus 4pts; 3. Deportivo 1pt; 4. Basle 1pt.

Riverdance – Ole and Ruud try out a few steps

⚽ **RUUD RECORD** Ruud van Nistelrooy's two strikes against Deportivo La Coruña bring his tally to 20 goals for United in the European Cup, overtaking Andy Cole's club record of 19.

Saturday 14 December 2002   **Premiership**

Manchester United 3   West Ham 0
Solskjaer 15, Veron 17, Schemmel (og) 61.

Kick-off: 12.15pm. Old Trafford. **Att:** 67,555 **Ref:** R Styles

United: (4-4-2) Barthez | G Neville, Brown, Silvestre, O'Shea (Blanc 76) | P Neville, Scholes (Forlan 74), Giggs, Veron | Solskjaer, Van Nistelrooy. Booked: Fortune.
West Ham: (4-4-2) James | Repka, Dailly, Pearce, Schemmel | Carrick, Sinclair, Minto (Breen 88), Lomas (Moncur 84) | Defoe, Cole. Booked: Cisse, Di Canio.

Just a month after playing West Ham away, United's fortunes have changed completely. Today was the seventh straight win and Arsenal's lead has been chipped away to nothing but a game in hand. 'It has been a proud period, which has produced some thrilling football to close the gap on the leaders,' beamed Sir Alex.

The game was effectively won in the first quarter, the first goal

David who? Veron shows he can bend it, too

symbolising the confidence in United's play. Phil Neville knocked the ball to Van Nistelrooy from his own half, who in turn fed the older Neville. Gary crossed for Solskjaer who headed in. A minute later, in the area of the pitch known by TV commentators as prime Beckham free-kick territory, United were awarded a free kick after Ruud Van Nistelrooy's ankles became the target of the aggressive attention of the ever belligerent Repka. With a fully fit Beckham on the bench, Veron took responsibility, nonchalantly sizing up his options as the Hammers wall assembled. From a distance of 31 yards, Veron then bent a delightful free kick over the wall and inside the far post. A match-winning moment that he was to top with a man of the match performance.

So limp were West Ham that Barthez waited until the 82nd minute to make his first save. By that time, United had added a third after another Gary Neville cross had been turned in past James, this time inadvertently by Schemmel.

United's attack dominated the headlines, but the defence deserves equal praise for keeping a fourth consecutive clean sheet. O'Shea was once again as excellent as he is versatile – he has played at right back, left back, centre half and, against Burnley in the Worthington Cup, in central midfield so far this season. A jack of all trades and a master of the lot.

United performance: 8/10. **Man of the match:** Veron – continues to confound those who question his relevance at United with a panoply of passes. **Premiership position:** 1. Arsenal 35pts (pl 17); 2. United 35pts (pl 18); 3. Chelsea 34pts (pl 18).

Tuesday 17 December 2002	Worthington Cup Quarter Final

Manchester United 1   Chelsea 0
Forlan 80.

Kick-off: 8pm. Old Trafford. **Att:** 57,985 **Ref:** S Bennett

United: (4-5-1) Barthez | G Neville, Brown, Silvestre, O'Shea | Beckham, Veron, P Neville, Scholes, Giggs | Forlan. Booked: P Neville.

Chelsea: (4-3-1-2) Cudicini | Gallas, Le Saux, Melchiot, Terry | Lampard, Morris, Stanic | De Lucas (Zenden 66), | Zola, Hasselbaink (Gudjohnsen 78). Booked: Terry, Stanic.

No English team betters Chelsea's recent record at Old Trafford. With just three defeats in their last 19 games in M16 and an eleven-match unbeaten run before this game, both managers fielded full strength sides to illustrate their seriousness about the Worthington Cup, now that the final is just two rounds away.

The game was dominated by good defending, making it one for the football connoisseur rather than the fans who'd taken advantage of tickets being on sale on match day in the hope of seeing goals. Brown and Silvestre have developed a fine understanding in central defence in recent games that must leave Sir Alex pondering how he will find room for the world's most expensive centre half. The clearest chance came in the 69th minute when Zola was through with only Barthez to beat. The number one repeated the type of top class save he'd made at the start of the game from Hasselbaink.

With Forlan and Beckham – the latter back after five weeks out with a rib injury – peripheral figures, United's great threat came from Scholes as he attempted to crack Chelsea's defensive code. Then, ten minutes before time, Beckham at last found his touch and threaded a pass through to Forlan who finished confidently through Cudicini's legs. A low Zenden shot a minute later required

Silvestre enjoying himself at centre back

yet another top save from Barthez, but United won this tightest of games to their eighth win on the bounce.

'See you on the motorway,' sang the observant Chelsea fans who had struggled to shift their tickets. We won't be seeing them at Cardiff, that's for sure.

United performance: 7/10. **Man of the match:** Silvestre – another excellent performance at centre half. On the day he signed a new contract at the club too.

Sunday 22 December 2002   Premiership

Blackburn Rovers 1   Manchester United 0
Flitcroft 40.

Kick-off: 2pm. Ewood Park. **Att:** 30,475 (7,000 Reds) **Ref:** D Elleray

United: (4-4-2) Barthez | G Neville, Brown, Silvestre, O'Shea | Solskjaer, P Neville (Blanc 84), Scholes, Giggs (Beckham 69) | Van Nistelrooy, Forlan (Keane 59). Booked: G Neville.

Blackburn: (4-4-2) Friedel | Neill, Taylor, Short, Johansson | Flitcroft, Tugay, Dunn, (Gillespie 55), Duff | Cole, Yorke.

In a game played in the miserable half-light of a Lancashire winter day, United hoped to add to their eight-match run of consecutive victories against a team without a win against the Reds in eight years. It should have been straightforward, with United not only on a good run, but spurred by the presence of Roy Keane on the bench after a 26-game absence through injury and ill discipline. And so it promised, as United showed their superiority in the first period, passing the ball around with the confidence of a team in form. Backed by a highly vocal following of 7,000 who completely out-sang the home supporters, Sir Alex's men almost toyed with their opponents. Chances and openings were created with a series of quick attacking movements, but poor finishing meant that the score remained goalless.

At the other end, Barthez was seldom troubled and even a spec-tacular-looking save from Dunn seven minutes before half-time looked more dramatic than it actually was. Two minutes later though, the Frenchman had little chance when Flitcroft half volleyed a poor clearance through a crowded box. Coming against the run of play, it was not only the first goal United had conceded in over eight hours, but also prompted the wonderful 'Flitcroft finally scores at home!' headline in *The Sun*. The ex-Blue had recently been caught playing away. And not just with his team.

Blackburn were more assertive in the second period, taking the game to United with Cole and Yorke troubling the Red defenders. Luckily, the two ex-Reds showed a profligacy in front of goal similar to Van Nistelrooy. In one of several good goal-scoring opportunities, Van Nistelrooy was pressed into a one-on-one with goalkeeper Friedel. The American, the best in the Premiership this season according to many, did well to smother the Dutchman's line of vision, but Ruud will be disappointed that he didn't do better.

When Keane was introduced into the mist with 29 minutes to play, the boos that rang out in the home end were easily eclipsed by the cheers of the Red partisans in the Darwen End. 'Keano, there's only one Keano,' came the cry that complimented a large banner which read: 'And on the Eighth Day God Created Keane.' Neither Keane, nor fellow substitute Beckham, could break Blackburn's initiative, though, and if anything, their introduction confused the formation. Long before time, you sensed that a goal just wasn't going to happen.

United performance: 6/10. **Men of the match:** Yorke and Cole – constant running, even though ultimately ineffective in front of goal. **Premiership position:** 1. Arsenal 39pts (pl 19); 2. Chelsea 37pts (pl 19); 3. United 35pts (pl 19).

Grim faces – it's time for Keano

Middlesbrough 3   Manchester United 1
Boksic 44, Nemeth 48, Job 85.   Giggs 60.

Kick-off: 4pm. Old Trafford. **Att:** 34,673 (1,800 United) **Ref:** G Barber

United: (4-4-1-1) Barthez | G Neville (Beckham 72), Brown, Blanc, O'Shea (Ferdinand 83) | Solskjaer, Keane, Veron, Giggs | Scholes | Van Nistelrooy (Solskjaer 71). Booked: Scholes, Brown.

Middlesbrough: (4-3-1-2) Schwarzer | Parnaby, Southgate, Ehiogu, Quedrue | Greening, Wilson, Geremi | Job | Boksic (Wilkshire 64), Nemeth (Maccarone 83).

After the run of nine straight wins, the slip-up at Blackburn could be excused. Teams lose games. But when a second game is lost in succession and Arsenal move seven points clear it is serious.

It seems unfair to cast a slur against someone with a career as distinguished as Laurent Blanc, but all three of the younger Boro forwards gave him problems and each of this unlikely triumvirate scored. Boksic is no youth team player, but the goal United conceded to him a minute before half-time would have looked shoddy even at that level. A pass from Veron was cut out, and left-back Quedrue advanced right up the field to the edge of the area where he slipped a pass for Boksic who flicked the ball over Barthez. Steve McClaren's side further lifted their fans three minutes after the break when Nemeth was allowed to drift past Blanc and beat O'Shea before cracking a shot past Barthez into the top corner. Bad news.

United had to take risks to get back into the game and Giggs's goal on the hour gave hope in the Teeside murk after he turned in a ball from Solskjaer, whose new role as a right winger had kept Beckham on the bench. Beckham's introduction in the 72nd minute increased United's attacking momentum, but with so many men pushed forward, there was always going to be risk against a side so efficient at home. And so it proved, when Geremi, on a season-long loan from Real Madrid, crossed for Maccarone who headed the ball down for Job to finish. We'll spare you the puns.

McClaren obviously was delighted with his third victory over United in the teams' five meetings since he left Old Trafford.

United performance: 6/10. **Men of the match**: Southgate and Ehiogu – showed how central defenders should play. **Premiership position**: 1. Arsenal 42pts (pl 20); 2. Chelsea 38pts (pl 20); 3. United 35pts (pl 20).

Manchester United 2   Birmingham 0
Forlan 37, Beckham 73.

Kick-off: 3pm. Old Trafford. **Att:** 67,640 **Ref:** M Dean

United: (4-4-2) Barthez | O'Shea, Brown, Ferdinand, Silvestre | Beckham, Veron, Keane, Scholes | Forlan, Solskjaer. Booked: Brown.

Birmingham City: (4-5-1) Vaesen | Kenna, Cunningham, Johnson, Sadler | Lazaridis, Cisse, Savage, Devlin, Kirovski | Morrison. Booked: Cisse, Kirovski.

United's ninth game of the month saw them pitted against a side with strong Red connections. As well as being a club stalwart with 410 games and probably as many scars, Steve Bruce didn't let the glut of emerging talent at Old Trafford escape his attention, and now that he's finally settled on a club to manage, he's called on their services. Two of Birmingham's midfielders, the American Kirovski and the Welshman who looks like an extra in *Neighbours*, Savage, were both youngsters training at the Cliff in the mid-1990s. United were disappointed to lose Kirovski to Dortmund after a work visa

Veron – right on top of his game

wrangle, just as referees still are when they hear that they are to officiate a game involving Savage.

Birmingham fans have been satisfied with their return to the Premiership but a recent poor run, and seven injured defenders, has seen them slide down the table. They could have hoped for more than to meet a United side who contrived one of their best performances of the season after two successive defeats. Blanc, Giggs and Neville G were relegated to the subs' bench and despite Van Nistelrooy being out with a poisoned toe (don't think about it), United created so many chances that the only surprise was that only two resulted in goals. The first came when a deep Silvestre cross was headed on by Beckham for Forlan (who else?) to finish. Veron, frequently at the centre of United's attacks with his sublime array of passing, set up the second, but only after Birmingham had twice required Barthez to make important saves. The Argentine put Beckham through and the England captain chipped keeper Vassen from 25 yards.

United performance: 9/10. Man of the match: Veron – the trick meister was incredible throughout.
Premiership position: 1. Arsenal 42pts (pl 20); 2. Chelsea 38pts (pl 20); 3. United 35pts (pl 20).

January

Manchester United 2 Sunderland 1
Beckham 81, Scholes 90.   Veron o.g 4.

Kick-off: 2pm. Old Trafford. Att: 67,609 Ref: G Poll
United: (4-4-2) Barthez (Carroll 29) | O'Shea (Giggs 63), Brown, Ferdinand, Silvestre | Beckham, Veron (G Neville 90), Keane, Scholes | Forlan, Solskjaer. Booked: Ferdinand, Solskjaer.
Sunderland: (4-1-4-1) Macho | Wright, Craddock, Babb, McCartney | Thirlwell | Flo (Proctor 72), McCann (Williams 14), Kilbane, Stewart (Oster 84) | Phillips. Booked: Wright.

I took the better half today after we were offered a couple of tickets together. It's not that she has no interest in football, it's just that she can't understand why thousands pay to 'get cold'. She also struggled to understand why all the players weren't running all the time 'like they do on the telly', but was cheered by our proximity to the pitch and, therefore, Beckham.

The icon actually covered so much ground today that everyone was close to him and his new barnet at some point. Most of his chasing on Old Trafford's heaviest pitch of the season was done in vain after Veron headed a bizarre own goal in the fifth minute following a breakdown in communication between the Argentinean and the cockney Ferdinand (Veron, it is rumoured, speaks the better English).

Non-stop: Beckham is there when it matters

United's efforts to get back in the game thereafter were all encompassing: 32 attempts were made on Sunderland's goal compared with three on United's, but such was the form of cat Macho that the struggling Mackems held out until nine minutes from time. It was Ferdinand who finally unlocked things, knocking one of his goal kicks into the path of Beckham, who went through one-on-one to score. The comeback was on, but it wasn't until the PA announcer Alan Keegan was informing the crowd that there would be three minutes' stoppage time that Silvestre stretched to hook a misguided

Forlan header into the box. In a crowd of desperate defenders, Scholes managed to head the ball past the devastated Macho.

Two late goals – how very unlike United to start the New Year as they've finished so many games in previous years. And yes, the drama was enough to make both of us go home with a smile.

United performance: 7/10. Man of the match: Beckham – the energy, the quality of passing, the goal. Premiership position: 1. Arsenal 46pts (pl 22); 2. United 41pts (pl 22); 3. Chelsea 38pts (pl 22).

Saturday 4 January 2003   **FA Cup 3rd Round**

Manchester United 4   Portsmouth 1
Van Nistelrooy 5, 81 (pens), Beckham 17, Scholes 90. Stone 39.

Kick-off: 12.30pm. Old Trafford. Att: 67,222 (9,000 Pompey) Ref: M Riley

United: (4-4-2) Carroll | G Neville, Blanc, Ferdinand, Silvestre (Brown 82) | Beckham, Keane, P Neville, Richardson (Scholes 60) | Van Nistelrooy, Giggs.

Portsmouth: (3-5-1-1) Hislop | Tavlaridis, Foxe, Primus | Taylor, Quashie, Harper, Diabate, Stone | Merson | Todorov. Booked: Diabate, Tavlaridis.

Unperturbed by the fact that eighteen lower league sides have tried and failed to knock United out of the FA Cup since Bournemouth last achieved the honour in 1984, 9,000 Pompey fans travelled north to take their part in the biggest crowd their team have played in front of since the 1939 FA Cup final.

They sang their chimes and hoped that a side who had performed so impressively in the First Division would be capable of a shock. Unfortunately, a United team with seven changes and Van Nistelrooy back attacked from the first minute and were a goal up after five when Ruud converted a penalty. A brilliant Beckham free kick from 25 yards flew past Hislop's huge frame to make it two after seventeen minutes. An embarassment looked on the cards, but Harry Redknapp's side were surprisingly allowed back into the game when Stone scored with their first attack on 39 minutes.

United's second-half laziness meant a game that should have been finished off before the interval was kept alive. Quashie ought to have equalised when he was one-on-one with Carroll after 62 minutes but order was restored when Van Nistelrooy scored his second penalty on 81 minutes to secure the victory. The visitors were

He's bent it again, and even Keane's impressed

aggrieved when Todorov looked to have made it 3-2 a couple of minutes later, only to be ruled offside. 'Who's the scummer in the black,' they sang. A scummer is Pompey speak for a resident of Southampton.

Scholes finally made the score comfortable with another of his injury-time goals, lifting a Ferdinand through ball over Hislop. A tough lesson for Portsmouth, who were shown the levels they'll have to reach next season if they come up. And talking of a different level, Fergie invited his old mates Redknapp and assistant Jim Smith back for a glass of wine afterwards. The bottle of claret he produced cost over £600: 'more than my entire entertaining budget for a season,' Redknapp said. Welcome to the top table.

United performance: 8 /10. **Man of the match:** Beckham – exquisite, he's found his best form of the season.

THIRD ROUND? NO PROBLEM United's 4-1 defeat of Portsmouth preserves Alex Ferguson's unbeaten record in the third round of the FA Cup.

Tuesday 7 January 2003　　　**Worthington Cup Semi-Final (1st leg)**

Manchester United 1　　**Blackburn Rovers 1**
Scholes 58　　　　　　　　　　　　Thompson 61.

Kick-off: 8pm. Old Trafford. Att: 62,740 Ref: U Rennie

United: (4-4-1-1) Barthez | G Neville, Ferdinand, Brown, Silvestre | Beckham, Veron, P Neville (Forlan 82), Giggs (Solskjaer 74) | Scholes | Van Nistelrooy. Booked: P Neville.

Blackburn: (4-4-2) Friedel | McEveley, Taylor, Todd, Neill | Dunn (Gillespie 19), Tugay, Flitcroft, Thompson (Jansen 66) | Cole, Yorke. Booked: Neill, McEveley.

The night of the Blackburn away defeat last month, the younger brother hit the town. He ended up back at Dwight Yorke's house for a party which was held, according to whom you believe, to celebrate either a) the birth of his baby boy, or b) Blackburn's victory over United. He described the scenes of high living *chez* Yorke, and noted the frankly stunning array of females in attendance. He later talked to Blackburn's scouse midfielder David Thompson, whom he described as a 'decent lad'. With the benefit of hindsight, we mused over the idea that had he laced Thompson's drinks with a substance that would have laid him low for a few days, it could have caused

Chilled Worthington's – Ruud toasts Scholes

him to lose his place in the team and not be in a position to score an equaliser against United a couple of weeks later.

In truth, a draw was the least Blackburn deserved on a freezing night played in front of a poor atmosphere. If the United fans were hoarse, they had reason to be – this was the team's eighth home game in a month. But there was still audible displeasure when Giggs left the field, with many fans not satisfied with his recent form.

Scholes put United ahead with his tenth of the season after a Beckham cross but three minutes later Thompson scored the first goal United have conceded in the Worthington Cup this season. And it could have been worse, as a penalty might well have been awarded just before time when the 17-year-old McEveley went down in the box.

United performance: 6/10. **Man of the match:** Tugay – composed, no matter how much pressure he was under.

Saturday 11 January 2003	Premiership

West Bromwich Albion 1 Manchester United 3
Koumas 6.   Van Nistelrooy 8, Scholes 22, Solskjaer 79.

Kick-off: 3pm. **The** Hawthorns. **Att:** 27,129 (3,000 Reds) **Ref:** N Barry

United: (4-4-2) Barthez | G Neville, Ferdinand, Brown, Silvestre | Beckham, Keane (O'Shea 80), Scholes, P Neville, | Solskjaer (Forlan 68), Van Nistelrooy. Booked: Scholes.

West Brom: (3-5-2) Hoult | Gilchrist, Moore, Sigurdsson (Dobie 75) | Clement, Johnson, Wallwork, Koumas, Chambers (Balis 86) | Dichio, Roberts.

The last time United played at the Hawthorns they registered a 5-1 win, their ninth straight victory at the start of the '85-86 season. United were favourites for the title then, but fell away badly and finished fourth. Much has changed since. The Hawthorns has three new stands, the Baggies no longer sport the no-smoking logo on their shirt and United aren't quite the chancers in the league they were. Expectations have risen with success to the point that not winning the Championship is now deemed failure.

With Giggs dropped after a spell of ineffectiveness and papers milking and exaggerating the criticism that he's been getting off Reds, the United fans were loud in their chants of support for the

Walking on air – another man of the match award for Becks

absent winger (we're a perverse bunch). In fact, we were loud all afternoon, so loud that the West Brom fans gave the travelling Reds credit for being the noisiest to visit all season.

After the brief shock of going behind to a speculative low shot past Barthez after six minutes, parity was restored 22 seconds later when Van Nistelrooy turned in a brilliant Beckham cross. The immense gulf in class between the two sides was evident thereafter and United took the lead in the 23rd minute when Scholes volleyed in a Keane cross from the near post. West Brom let none of their fans down with their battling endeavour, but any chance of a result was put beyond them in the 55th minute when Solskjaer struck the ball into the roof of the net after Gary Neville had centred.

United performance: 7.5/10. Man of the match: Beckham – superb, on top of his game at the moment. Premiership position: Several teams on three points, just as many on none. Premiership position: 1. Arsenal 46pts (pl 22); 2. United 44pts (pl 23); 3. Chelsea 41pts (pl 23).

Manchester United 2   Chelsea 1
Scholes 39, Forlan 90.   Gudjohnsen 30.

Kick-off: 12.30pm. Old Trafford. **Att:** 67,606 **Ref:** P Durkin

United: (4-4-1-1) Barthez | G Neville, Ferdinand, Brown, Silvestre (Veron 86) | Keane, Beckham, P Neville (Giggs 45), Solskjaer | Scholes | Van Nistelrooy (Forlan 71).

Chelsea: (4-4-2) Cudicini | Melchiot, Gallas, Desailly, Babayaro | Le Saux, Lampard, Petit, Gronkjaer (De Lucas 56) | Gudjohnsen (Zenden 84), Hasselbaink (Zola 16).

United left it late to record a seventh consecutive home win: 93rd minute late. Before the game, Chelsea lay in third, three points behind the Reds. But despite talk of being Championship contenders, they've never quite managed to compete with United and Arsenal in the Premiership years. Their quality cannot be denied, though, and throughout large tracts of today's game, Ranieri's foreign legion looked the better side, and they deserved their lead after Gudjohnsen flicked in

Keane's away ... and Forlan's waiting to do the rest

a clever ball from Petit, the best player on the field in the first half. Given Chelsea's excellent record at Old Trafford, the omens were hardly encouraging but United benefited from a rare error by their defence six minutes before the break. An appalling clearance by the normally judicious Cudicini went as far as Beckham and the United no. 7 crossed perfectly for Scholes to head in his fifth goal in as many games.

United improved in the second half with Scholes and Solskjaer causing the most problems, but it wasn't until the last ten minutes that they really asserted pressure for a crucial winner. In a dramatic end, Keane won the ball from United fans' favourite Le Saux and two of the United substitutes contrived to do the rest. A quick-minded Veron hit a pass to Forlan and the Uruguayan hit a left foot finish firmly into the roof of the goal. It wasn't the first time he took his shirt off to celebrate a goal, but it was easily the most satisfying sight seen at Old Trafford all day. Stirring stuff.

United performance: 7/10. **Man of the match:** Scholes – the catalyst for so many United attacks.
Premiership position: 1. Arsenal 49pts (pl 23); 2. United 47pts (pl 24); 3. Newcastle 42pts (pl 23).

Wednesday 22 January 2003 Worthington Cup Semi-Final (2nd leg)

Blackburn Rovers 1   Manchester United 3
Cole 12.   Scholes 30, 42, Van Nistelrooy 77 (pen)

Kick-off: 8pm. Ewood Park. **Att:** 29,048 (7,000 United) **Ref:** J Winter
United: (4-4-2) Barthez | G Neville, Ferdinand, Brown, Silvestre | Beckham, Keane, Veron, Scholes (Butt 79) | Giggs, Van Nistelrooy (Forlan 84).
Blackburn: (4-4-2) Friedel | McEveley, Taylor, Todd, Neill | Duff (Gillespie 34), Tugay, Flitcroft, Thompson | Cole, Yorke. Booked: Friedel, Thompson.

Backed by a another beery and boisterous following, United came from behind – to a 12th minute chipped goal by Cole – to offer one of their most assured displays of the season. A brace in 12 minutes from Scholes swung the tie into United's favour, the first on the half hour after he initially failed to control a Beckham cross before instinctively chasing the ball and firing into the net. Three minutes before the interval, Gary Neville surged forward down the right after Keane had broken up an attack. Neville centred perfectly for Scholes to sidefoot past Friedel. A Van Nistelrooy penalty on 77 minutes made it 3-1, after the Dutchman had carried a Beckham pass from his own half before being brought down by Friedel.

The post-match quotes became a meeting of the Scholes appreciation society with Rovers' manager Souness saying: 'Paul Scholes caused us lots of problems. They're a super team and I've got no complaints. There's no disgrace going out to a very good team.' Sir Alex Ferguson added: 'Our away form has been questionable and we need more performances like that tonight if we going to go for the league. Paul Scholes has settled into the position he's good at, he's maturing and having a fantastic season.'

And judging by the manner in which the players celebrated reaching their first cup final since '99, the Worthington seems anything but worthless.

United performance: 8.5/10. **Man of the match:** Scholes – and not just for scoring in his sixth successive game.

SEMI-FINALS? NO PROBLEM United's victory over Blackburn in the League Cup semi-final means that Alex Ferguson has won all nine of United's domestic semi-finals in his time at Old Trafford.

Paul Scholes – everyone's talking about him

Sunday 26 January 2003   **FA Cup 4th Round**

Manchester United 6   West Ham 0

Giggs 8, 29, Van Nistelrooy 49, 58, P Neville 50,
Solskjaer 69.

Kick-off: 1pm. Old Trafford. **Att:** 67,181 (9,000 Hammers) **Ref:** S Bennett

United: (4-4-1-1) Barthez | Blanc, Ferdinand, O'Shea, P Neville | Beckham, Veron, Keane, Giggs |
Scholes | Van Nistelrooy. Booked: Veron.

West Ham: (4-4-2) James | Minto, Pearce, Breen (Dailly 79), Lomas | Carrick, Sinclair (Johnson 79),
Fowler, Cisse (Garcia 79) | Cole, Defoe. Booked: Minto.

David James wonders if the nightmare will ever end

The incessant Manchester rain made for a heavy and patchy pitch
but it didn't stop United recording their biggest FA Cup win in three
decades. United were ruthless and exploited the weak defence and
low morale of struggling West Ham from the start. **Giggs** rebuffed
some of the recent criticism with two goals in the first 29 minutes,
the first after a Scholes shot was blocked on the line allowing the
Welshman to drive the ball in. He then started and finished the
move that led to his second, combining well with Veron.

The gaping chasm between the teams was always evident in the first half, when United's exhilarating play seemed the exhibition stuff of a practice game rather than the fourth round of the most famous domestic competition in the world. Every pass was met with roars of approval. Quiet it wasn't, especially with the odious Bowyer being booed whenever he touched the ball. Three more goals in nine minutes at the start of the second half gave the game a realistic scoreline, for at one stage the unhappy Hammers didn't have a shot on goal for 35 minutes. United's sixth came with 21 minutes still left on the clock, and had they kept their foot on the pedal you felt double figures were actually on the cards.

West Ham fans will have long given up hopes of a repeat of the 2001 victory, so they cheered their spirits with a good ol' cockney knees-up and a version of the 'hokey cokey'. They knew that life was much tougher in the Blitz. There was further amusement at the end of the game when David James seemed far from distraught at conceding six as he laughed and joked with Phil Neville when the two teams left the field. Ronny and Reggie wouldn't have approved.

United performance: 9.5/10. Man of the match: Van Nistelrooy – led from the front as ever.

February

Saturday 1 February 2003	Premiership

Southampton 0   Manchester United 2
Van Nistelrooy 15, Giggs 22.

Kick-off: 3pm. St. Mary's. Att: 32,085 (3,000 Reds) Ref: P Dowd

United: (4-4-2) Barthez (Carroll 38) | O'Shea, G Neville, Ferdinand, Silvestre | Beckham (Scholes 69), Keane, Veron, Giggs | Solskjaer, Van Nistelrooy (Forlan 88).

Southampton: (4-4-2) Niemi (Jones 87) | Telfer, Lundekvam, M Svensson, Benali | Fernandes, A Svensson, Marsden, Oakley | Beattie, Tessem (Davies 69). Bookings: A Svensson, Benali.

Southampton are twice the club they were two years ago. Literally. Gates have doubled since they moved to St Mary's and, under

Gordon Strachan, fans have had to get used to missing out of the excitement of a relegation battle – the prospect of European travel being far more likely than Nationwide football these days. With a top scorer James Beattie who has 17 goals in the past 19 games, beating the Saints in their new home was a challenge. Why, it was difficult enough at Old Trafford where United left it late.

Still, an in-form United conspired to give Sir Alex a rare treat for his 900th game in charge. Not only did United control an exciting if slightly dishevelled game and get the three points to stay in touch with Arsenal, but a clean sheet was recorded for the first time away from home all season. Given that Southampton started with three dangerous attacks in the first ten minutes, this feat looked particularly unlikely, but the home side failed to do what United did twice in the first 22 minutes – score.

United's first two attacks brought a goal apiece. The first, after fifteen minutes, came when a cross-field pass from Silvestre found

Ruud points the way – it was never this easy at The Dell

Beckham on the right. The no. 7 lofted the ball into the path of Gary Neville on the overlap. He had time to measure a low cross and Van Nistelrooy half volleyed past Niemi. A classic move. A similar build-up seven minutes later allowed Solskjaer to cross for Veron, the Argentine cleverly stepped over the ball allowing Giggs to shoot. His first shot was saved but rebounded into his path and he made sure with the follow-up. And that was that.

Further incident came with both goalkeepers being stretchered off at different stages, Southampton missing out on what looked like a clear penalty and United controlling the game. It wasn't always pretty, but it was highly effective.

United performance: 8.5/10. Man of the match: Solskjaer – didn't score, but kept the Saints' defence busy. Premiership position: 1. Arsenal 56pts (pl 26); 2. United 50pts (pl 25); 3. Newcastle 48pts (pl 25).

Tuesday 4 February 2003	Premiership

Birmingham 0   Manchester United 1

Van Nistelrooy 56.

Kick-off: 7.45pm. St. Andrews. Att: 29,475 (3,000) Ref: S Dunn

United: (4-4-2) Carroll | G Neville, Brown, Ferdinand, Silvestre | Beckham, Veron, Keane, Scholes | Giggs, Van Nistelrooy (Solskjaer 82). Booked: Keane.

Birmingham City: (4-4-2) Vaesen | Kenna (Devlin 84), Cunningham, Upson, Clapham | Clemence, D Johnson, Dugarry, Savage | Morrison (Kirovski 78), John (Lazaridis 63). Booked: Clemence.

Without a win in nearly two months, Birmingham had found themselves drawn towards the fringes of a relegation battle. But whilst recent form showed that the Brummies had won just three of their eleven home games so far, no side under Steve Bruce was going to be an uncomplicated opposition.

In windswept and freezing conditions, Birmingham appeared content to contain United in a slack first half. Satisfied with not being a goal down, the Blues attempted to be more adventurous in the second half, but their inferior ability meant that Carroll wasn't forced to make a single save. United needed a goal, though, and it came on 56 minutes when Van Nistelrooy received the ball with his back to goal. After effectively creating a chance out of nothing, he shot on the turn past Vaesen. With Keane at his best since his return

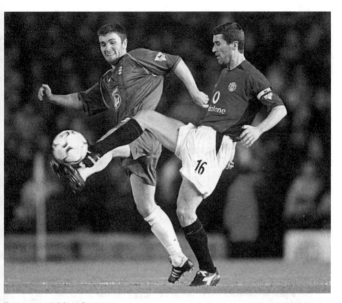

Keane – a captain's performance

from injury, United controlled possession thereon.

As Solskjaer warmed up to replace the goalscorer, Birmingham fans hollered: 'Who the f****** hell are you?' – surely a bit rich coming from someone who had Jeff Kenna in their side.

This wasn't vintage United, but it didn't need to be. Any side with aspirations of winning the league needs to show many facets, and whilst a highlights video of this game would be a non-starter, the battling type of performance which United demonstrated tonight is as important as any.

A sixth consecutive league win, another clean sheet and the gap at the top is down to three points.

United performance: 6.5/10. **Man of the match**: Keane – as selfless and successful as we've seen recently. **Premiership position**: 1. Arsenal 56pts (pl 26); 2. United 53pts (pl 26); 3. Newcastle 48pts (pl 25).

Sunday 9 February 2003 Premiership

Manchester United 1   Manchester City 1
Van Nistelrooy 18. Goater 86.

Kick-off: 12.30pm. Old Trafford. **Att:** 67,646 **Ref:** P Dowd

United: (4-3-1-2) Carroll | G Neville, Ferdinand, Brown, Silvestre | Beckham, Keane, Veron (Butt 76) | Scholes | Giggs (Solskjaer 89), Van Nistelrooy (Forlan 88). Booking: G Neville.

City: (3-5-2) Nash | Distin, Howey, Sommel | Jensen, Horlock (Wright-Phillips 67), Berkovic (Bernarbia 86), Foe, Sun Jihai | Fowler (Goater 86), Anelka. Bookings: Foe.

For all the hype and talk of revenge after the humiliation of 11/9, this Manchester derby was an anticlimax – just like the previous one at Old Trafford. It began, though, in an amusing farce, with a loud-speaker appeal for City keeper Nicky Weaver to report to the changing rooms after Schmeichel injured himself in the warm-up. Weaver could not be tempted away from the pie concession and missed his chance to be a City reserve. And they said he was going to be England keeper, too.

United were more fired up for the return derby – but the goals didn't come

United were so dominant in the first half that payback seemed inevitable. Ahead after eighteen minutes, the opener came when a move started by Keane set Giggs free to cross for Van Nistlerooy, who had loped away from marker Distin and steered the ball past Nash. Keane was the game's key figure as United peppered the City goal, but no further goals were forthcoming.

The second half contrasted sharply with the first. City had a greater urgency and purpose – well, ten of them did for Robbie Fowler appeared embarrassingly unfit. As soon as the Scouse urchin was substituted (and how he remained on the field for 86 minutes is a mystery), City equalised through Shaun Goater's head. The Goat had been on the field only nine seconds and the Blues fans in the self-proclaimed 'Mancunian Section' – a sea of pale complexions, moustaches, triple chins and *Kickers*-wearing social zeroes – relished their highlight of the season. No doubt Keegan loved it.

United performance: First half: 8.5/10. Second half: 5/10. **Man of the match**: Keane in the first, Berkovic in the second. **Premiership position**: 1. Arsenal 57pts (pl 27); 2. United 54pts (pl 27); 3. Newcastle 49pts (pl 26).

Saturday 15 February 2003	FA Cup 5th Round

Manchester United 0   Arsenal 2
Edu 34, Wiltord 52.

Kick-off: 12.15pm. Old Trafford. **Att**: 67,209 (9,000 Gooners) **Ref**: J Winter

United: (4-4-2) Barthez | G Neville, Brown, Ferdinand, Silvestre | Beckham, Scholes, Keane, Giggs (Forlan 71) | Solskjaer, Van Nistelrooy. Booked: Scholes, Van Nistelrooy, Keane.

Arsenal (4-4-2) Seaman | Lauren, Keown, Campbell, Cole | Pires (Van Bronkhorst 84), Edu, Vieira, Parlour | Wiltord (Toure 90), Jeffers (Henry 73). Booked: Vieira.

A new *United We Stand* hit the streets today. The cover featured Ryan Giggs with the caption: 'I told you I didn't fire blanks'. The line had a double meaning. Firstly, Giggs's form has improved in recent weeks and he's resembled a genuinely effective winger and not the imitation of one that some have accused him of. Secondly, he was about to become a dad. But how were we to know that Giggsy was just about to fire the biggest blank of his career, an opportunity to tap into an open goal which he somehow shot over? Never mind feeling sorry for the United players after Arsenal won 2-0 and

Giggs fires his blank

knocked United out of the cup, what about the *UWS* sellers whose attempts to shift copies were met with abuse?

In truth, the most saddening aspect about today was the realisation that Arsenal are currently the best team in the country, a point proved as they recorded a convincing victory against their biggest rivals away from home. And not only that: they did it without Bergkamp and, for most of the game, their most outrageous talent, Thierry Henry. On a day when five million or so Britons were advocating peace by marching against the war in Iraq, the players ignored the public mood and embarked on a series of personal battles, nasty challenges and petty squabbles. Arsenal, as the result suggests, often came out on top.

The result could have been so different if Giggs had converted his first-half chance. But he didn't, and Arsenal dominated once they had taken a scruffy lead through Edu on 34 minutes. Their second goal, scored after 52 minutes, was of a far higher order after Edu cleverly set Wiltord up and the Frenchman beat his compatriot in the United goal from 18 yards. The day belonged to Arsenal, although their confidence seemed a little too self-assured when their fans sang 'We'll be back again in May' (for the European Cup final). We'll see about that.

United performance: 6/10. **Man of the match**: Vieira – on today's evidence, the best midfielder in Britain.

⚽ **GOING FOR THE QUADRUPLE** United's defeat to Arsenal in the FA Cup fifth round dashes (unreal) hopes of an unprecedented quadruple of trophies. Nonetheless it is the latest date in a season United have still been in contention for all four top trophies.

Wednesday 19 February 2003 Champions League, 2nd Group Stage

Manchester United 2   Juventus 1
Brown 3, Van Nistelrooy 85.   Nedved 90.

Kick-off: 7.45pm. Old Trafford. **Att:** 66,703 **Ref:** K M Nielson.

United: (4-4-2) Barthez | G Neville, Brown, Ferdinand, Silvestre (O'Shea 52) | Beckham, Keane, Butt, Giggs (Forlan 90) | Scholes (Solskjaer 80), Van Nistelrooy. Booked: Keane, Scholes.

Juventus (4-5-1) Chimenti | Zenoni, Montero, Ferrara, Pessotto | Nedved, Tacchinardi, Davids, Camoranesi, Zalayeta | Trezeguet (Olivera 65). Booked: Davids, Tacchinardi.

Three minutes on the clock, and it's Wes Brown

The pre-match headlines were dominated by an incident that occurred five days previously and involved a football boot, a manager who wasn't noted for his accuracy as a player and David Beckham's forehead. Only the news that this game may have been postponed diverted attention from the media obsession with all things Beckham. The Juventus squad was so ravaged by flu that they were forced to field a near reserve side after UEFA turned down their request for a postponement.

Fergie's Fury

I've done things I'm not proud of, but the temper is exaggerated. It's good to let the pressure out of your system. I don't believe in this English thing of not complaining.

Alex Ferguson, *Managing My Life*.

Any player who has served under the Manchester United manager, will have a line about him losing his temper. The few that have entered the public arena have become the stuff of football folklore, but none with such immediate dramatic impact as the incident of Beckham and the boot. Sir Alex, it was reported, had not been happy with the icon's performance against Arsenal in the cup, and had picked him out for special attention, climaxing in kicking a boot in his direction. A boot that caught the football model just above his eyebrow. And the Beckham reaction? Why, to go shopping in central Manchester, of course, with the eyebrow stitched, and an Alice band neatly keeping the hair out of the way for the cameras.

The press seized on the boot as if it was a weapon of mass destruction, and even Madame Tussaud's got in on the act, popping a plaster on their wax dummy. And the incident became a focus of national debate. Was it deliberate, we needed to know, and had Ferguson apologised? The first question is easy enough. Ferguson was a feisty professional footballer, renowned more for the sharpness of his elbows than the caress of his boot on ball, and he would, frankly, have struggled to direct a football boot towards the face of his most photogenic player. As to an apology, it seems that was immediately forthcoming. But it was almost certainly another step on the road that led towards Beckham's summer transfer to Real Madrid.

Ironically, the England captain had spoken of Ferguson mellowing with age at the start of the season. Beckham could only compare him with the man he knew when he joined the club as a boy in the late-80s, but older players could testify to Ferguson's infamous temper well before that. Back as a fledgeling manager, whatever he may say now about the use of anger as a judicious motivational tool, Fergie's eruptions were very much a blunt instrument. When playing for Aberdeen, for instance, Gordon Strachan chose to ignore Ferguson's instructions during a game. Worse still, he told him to 'shut his face' from the relative safety of the pitch. Ferguson was visibly outraged and weighed up his options. He could have encroached into the playing area and dealt with Strachan there and then. Or, he could wait until half-time and deal with the issue then. He chose the latter, and Strachan takes up the story:

'As soon as we reached the dressing room I could see him making a beeline for me. There was trouble in store. What happened next could have looked like comedy to a bystander but laughter was totally out of order in my position. As he swung one hand away to the left, he swept a row of tea cups in the direction of Willie Miller and Alex McLeish.' Ferguson recalled how he then kicked the tea urn which stood in the middle of the room. 'I just booted the whole thing up in the air, and of course the tea and everything was all over the place, cups everywhere. And wee Strachan – the tea's dripping down the wall behind him – sat there and didn't say a word.'

Perhaps the most amusing explosion of Fergie fury also occurred during his time at Pittodrie. No matter that it was a reserve game at Forfar Athletic, Ferguson entered the dressing room in an apoplectic mood and kicked out at the laundry basket. Hard. A pair of underpants flew through the air and landed on a player's head like a hat. So frightened was the player that he sat there rigid. Ferguson didn't notice until he had finished raging, when he looked up at the player and said, 'and you can take those f***ing pants off your head. What the hell do you think you're playing at?'

As the Beckham incident proved, he can still rant. And United followers are largely grateful that he still can. After the derby defeat at Maine Road this season, when he threatened the team that he would open the dressing room to furious Reds still raging in the stands, so that the players could give a direct explanation for their pitiful showing, how many fans would seriously have preferred him to pat them on the head and say better luck next time?

When an unmarked Wes Brown headed United in front after three minutes – his first ever goal for the club – it seemed that the Reds were going to punish the weakened old lady of Turin. And yet despite missing captain Conte, Buffon, Del Piero, Thuram, Tudor and Iuliano, the Juve midfield contained enough talent for them to enjoy great tracts of possession and pin United back in a mediocre game. April '99 it wasn't, especially for Keane who struggled to keep pace with Davids.

It wasn't until the 85th minute, when Beckham provided his second goal assist of the night, that the crowd truly relaxed. Van Nistelrooy controlled a diagonal pass from the no. 7 to chip the ball over Chimenti for his 21st European goal for United.

A last-minute goal from the sublime Nedved gave the scoreline a sense of perspective, even though it was a freak effort as the Czech winger had intended to cross. Nine points from three games. Only disaster will prevent United reaching the quarter finals.

United performance: 7/10. **Man of the match**: Brown – did a good job on Zalayeta and the tired Trezeguet. **Group position**: (pl 3) 1. United 9pts; 2. Juventus 4pts; 3. Basle 3pts; 4. Deportivo 0pts.

BROWN 1 O'SHEA 0 Wes Brown's goal for United against Juventus was his first for the club – on his 111th appearance. Of current outfield players John O'Shea has now played most often for United without scoring.

Saturday 22nd February 2003   **Premiership**

Bolton Wanderers 1   Manchester United 1
N'Gotty 61.   Solskjaer 90.

Kick-off: 12pm. The Reebok Stadium. **Att**: 27,409 (3,000 Reds) **Ref**: A D'Urso

United: (4-4-2) Barthez | G Neville, Ferdinand, O'Shea, Brown (P Neville 74) | Beckham, Keane, Veron (Butt 80), Giggs (Forlan 58) | Solskjaer, Van Nistelrooy. Booked: Keane.

Bolton Wanderers: (4-3-3) Jaaskelainen | Charlton, Laville, Bergsson, N'Gotty | Okocha, Campo, Gardner | Mendy (Barness 82), Djorkaeff (Nolan 85), Pedersen (Salva 58). Booked: Campo.

And you thought the derby was bad in November. Today, United were at their sloppy, lazy and overwrought worst against Sam Allardyce's highly motivated Bolton side and the unbeaten run which stretches back to Boxing Day scarcely deserves to be intact. If the defence had a passable game, the midfield and forwards didn't. Veron seemed incapable of passing to a red shirt, Giggs was as effective as a rubber carving knife, Keane and Beckham weary, Van Nistelrooy and Solskjaer quiescent.

Bolton, meanwhile, were happy to benefit from United's sluggishness and the only surprise was that they took over an hour to take the lead – although they came close on numerous first-half occasions. The goal came when N'Gotty headed an inswinging free kick towards the United goal. Barthez, not sure whether to come out or not, was stranded as the ball sailed over him and went in off the post. United were

Trickmasters: Okocha and Veron face up

stirred from the slumber and Keane missed a high-quality opportunity two minutes later when the ball fell to him after Forlan had an inviting one-on-one with Jaaskelainen.

Then, with the whistle about to blow, Bolton lost a lead in the final minute for the fifth time this season. Keane fed Beckham who crossed for Solskjaer …and the Gunnar lashed the ball in by the near post. Whether it masked a dire performance or maintained the momentum remains to be seen, but one thing's for sure – returning to Manchester and listening to Arsenal destroy Man City on the radio, the title seems an unrealistic prospect with just ten games left.

United performance: 5/10. **Man of the match**: Okocha – terrific trickery throughout. **Premiership position**: 1. Arsenal 60pts (pl 28); 2. United 55pts (pl 28); 3. Newcastle 52pts (pl 27).

Wednesday 25 February 2003 Champions League, 2nd Group Stage

Juventus 0

Manchester United 3
Giggs 15, 41, Van Nistelrooy 60.

Kick-off: 8.45pm. Delle Alpi. **Att:** 59,111 (3,800 Reds) **Ref:** M Merk.

United: (4-4-2) Barthez | G Neville, Keane, Ferdinand, O'Shea (Pugh 60) | Beckham, Butt, P Neville, Veron | Solskjaer, Forlan ((Giggs 8) Van Nistelrooy 48).

Juventus: (4-5-1) Buffon | Thuram, Montero, Ferrara, Zambrotta (Pessotto 66) | Conte (Tudor 45), Nedved, Davids, Camoranesi, Di Vaio (Salas 45) | Trezeguet.

Last night was special. United provided one of those pure buzzes that they serve up once or twice a year – and when most of us fans least expect it. But football astonishes as often as it enthrals, and United did both in Turin.

After the game, I dropped into an Internet cafe outside Milan's imposing Central Station. With a freshly-minted copy of *La Gazzetta dello Sport*, I ordered a coffee and struck up a conversation with the owner. 'You don't look like a hooligan,' he said, assuming that all English football fans fitted the stereotype. 'We're not all hooligans, mate,' I replied. He supported Juve's great rivals Milan, but he enthused as much about Giggs as their defeat, purring: 'Giggs

Giggs – the Italians love him

was like Maradona against Juve'. High praise…either that or he was angling for a tip.

La Gazzeta is renowned for strict player ratings. Roy Keane received an '8' for his world-beating performance in Turin nearly four years ago. Today, the number '8' sits by the side of the word **Giggs**, who scored two of United's goals. Ryan's confidence has seemed shot in recent months, so I hope he gets to hear how highly the Italians, who know their football, rated him. **Veron** and **Keane** were the next highest rated United players with '7'. It might not sound it, but such recognition is rare. Maradona once got a nine. Or so they say.

Was the sublime Veron of last night really the same person who was so gauche at Bolton? It appears so. Is Keane's future at the back? He was faultless so who knows? Those United fans who filled three sections over as many tiers in the Delle Alpi's giant febrile cavity couldn't quite believe what they saw. To get a draw in Turin is a feat. To outclass Juventus in their own home, in front of their first full house in the Champions League, was the stuff of fantasy.

United performance: 9.5/10. **Man of the match:** Veron – a dazzling assortment of passing. **Group position:** (pl 4) 1. United 12pts; 2. Juventus 4pts; 3. Deportivo 4pts; 4. Basle 3pts.

Take your partners: United waltz through

March

Manchester United 0   Liverpool 2

Gerrard 39, Owen 86.

Kick-off: 2.00pm. Millennium Stadium. **Att:** 74,500 (31,000 Reds) **Ref:** P Durkin

United: (4-4-2) Barthez | G Neville, Brown, Ferdinand, Silvestre | Giggs, Veron, Keane, Beckham | Scholes | Van Nistelrooy.

Liverpool: (4-4-2) Dudek | Carragher, Traore (Riise 79), Henchoz, Hyppia, | Smicer (Diouf 70), Gerrard, Hamann, Murphy | Barros (Heskey 59), Owen. Booked: Murphy, Smicer.

This game was so predictable of both United and Liverpool this season that we should all have put big money on the result. United have been spellbinding in one game, awful the next. Incredible against Juventus five days previously, we should have known that they would perform as their alter egos in Cardiff, no matter their pre-match fancied status.

Keano can't believe it

As for Liverpool, the majority of their fans haven't been enamoured by Houllier's interpretation of Association Football this season. Boring, monotonous and turgid were but three descriptions fulminated before Sunday's game – by Liverpool fans. In conversation, two Scousers said the same thing: that Liverpool will attempt to nick a goal before defending their lead with little imagination or entertainment value. They hadn't put money on the game either.

The Worthington Cup has been long derided by United fans, but 31,000 endured an awkward journey to Wales, and touts asked £250 for tickets. The scene was set – a rare sunny day in Cardiff, the finest venue in the United Kingdom and a match between the biggest two clubs in the British Isles. Suddenly, the worthless moniker was forgotten as United and Liverpool fans partied well away from each other on separate sides of the Millennium Stadium.

Then the game. The decision to close the roof was questionable, for it created a darkened, almost surreal environment against the Cardiff sun, and as the match lumbered on, my attention was attracted to the numerous Liverpool flags. Scousers reserve affection for their banners; indeed some appear to have more pride in them than their own appearance. 'Don't bomb Iraq, nuke Manchester,' suggested one; 'Owen is a weapon of Manc destruction' read another. More puzzling to the international TV audience was 'Hillman is a Scouser' – a reference to the murderer in Manchester's *Coronation Street*.

United performance: 6/10. **Man of the match**: Gerrard – 'You can keep Veron, you can keep Keane, we've got a superstar who wears 17'…according to another flag.

WORTHLESS LOSERS United's defeat to Liverpool in the League Cup final means they are the first club to lose the final four times (after previous defeats in 1983, 1991 and 1994).

Wednesday 5 March 2003	Premiership

Manchester United 2   Leeds United 1
Radebe 20 o.g, Silvestre 79.   Viduka 64.

Kick-off: 8pm. **Old Trafford. Att**: 67,135 **Ref**: G Poll

United: (4-4-1-1) Barthez | O'Shea, Ferdinand, Keane, Silvestre | Beckham, Butt, Veron (P Neville 56), Fortune (Giggs 64) | Scholes | Van Nistelrooy (G Neville 89). Booked: Scholes.

Leeds United: (4-4-1-1) Robinson | Mills, Radebe, Lucic, Harte | Smith, Johnson, Okon, Bravo (McPhail 85) | Barmby (Milner 85) | Viduka. Booked: Smith.

With Arsenal eight points clear and the mood amongst Reds downbeat after the Worthington Cup final defeat, victory against Leeds was imperative. Following the lumbering performance in Cardiff, Sir Alex implemented changes, with Gary Neville and Ryan Giggs relegated to the bench, the latter just eight days after he had earned

What Leeds need is a quality centre back ...

the headline 'Fantastico' in *La Gazzetta dello Sport* for his triumphs in Turin.

United started brightly, as they have often done this season, and a 20th minute own-goal from Radebe rewarded the early supremacy against a Leeds side missing six regulars and unrecognisable from the version that last visited Old Trafford. The goal came after Beckham crossed for Butt before Radebe turned the ball into his own net through a crowded penalty area. Despite chances, a second goal wasn't forthcoming, while Leeds themselves offered little in the first period aside from a wicked Alan Smith shot acrobatically saved by Barthez. 'Liverpool,' chanted their fans, obviously in dire need of a team, any team, to cheer on.

Venables' side, however, looked more self-assured after the interval, and when Viduka headed an equaliser after 64 minutes it was difficult to feel sorry for England's premier 'United' – for just as against City a month earlier, Sir Alex's players were letting inferior opposition nudge back into the game. Still, with eleven minutes remaining and the vast majority inside Old Trafford overwrought at the prospect of more dropped points, Silvestre ran onto a lofted Beckham free kick to head his first goal of the season: 2-1.

With Keane, Veron, Silvestre and Fortune all picking up knocks, Sir Alex rightly pointed out that victory had come at a cost, but no matter how maladroit and halting the performance, the one thing that really mattered was eventually achieved. Victory.

United performance: 7/10. **Man of the match**: Rio Ferdinand – seemed determined to impress against his old club. **Premiership position**: 1. Arsenal 63pts (pl 29); 2. United 58pts (pl 29); 3. Newcastle 55pts (pl 29).

Wednesday 12 March 2003	Champions League 2nd Group Phase

Manchester United 1　　FC Basle 1
G Neville 53.　　　　　　　　　　Gimenez 1.

Kick-off: 7.45pm. Old Trafford **Att**: 66,870 **Ref**: C Larsen

United: (4-4-2) Carroll | G Neville, Blanc (Scholes 73), Ferdinand, O'Shea | Fletcher (Beckham 73), P Neville, Butt, Richardson (Giggs 45) | Solskjaer, Forlan. Booked: P Neville.

Basle: (4-3-1-2) Zuberbuhler | Haas, M Yakin, Zwyssig, Atouba | Barberis, Cantaluppi, Chipperfield | H Yakin | Giminez (Tum 77), Rossi (Huggel 63). Booked: Cantaluppi.

With qualification to the quarter-finals assured, Sir Alex used this effectively meaningless game to give younger players valuable first team and European experience. That these opportunities arise most frequently in the continent's premier competition and not the League Cup is somewhat ironic. And make of it what you will that Laurent Blanc, playing his first game since January, was playing professional football before United's callowist youngsters, Darren Fletcher and Kieron Richardson, were even born. Fletcher's talent has never been doubted by coaches at Carrington since he signed for the club at fifteen – and that following a personal visit from Sir Alex to the family home in Scotland and a return meet *chez* Fergie – but his subsequent progress has been stifled by injury. Tonight, he was a rare shard of light in a dark, disjointed Red performance, exhibiting a passing ability that belied his inexperience.

Basle's reward for their early possession came in the 14th minute when Ferdinand misjudged a cross and Giminez was left unmarked with time to control the ball and smash it past Carroll. The noisy

Collector's item: a goal from Neville G

visiting fans couldn't believe it and even had the front to strike up 'Sing When You're Winning' in English.

United's patchy performance barely improved but **Gary Neville** equalised with a deflected left foot shot that kept up his average of a goal for every three years he's been at the club. Sir Alex pulled some of the more established talent off the bench in search of a winner on a strange night against the Champions League's surprise team. Then again, what did we expect against a club whose female owner joined the players in the bath to celebrate winning the league last season?

United performance: 5.5/10. **Man of the match**: Fletcher – the 19-year-old deserved every plaudit.
Group position: (pl 5) 1. United 13pts; 2. Juventus 7pts; 3. Deportivo 4pts; 4. Basle 4pts.

Saturday 15 March 2003   Premiership

Aston Villa 0   Manchester United 1
                                    Beckham 12.

Kick-off: 12pm. Villa Park. **Att**: 42,602 (3,000 Reds). **Ref**: M Dean

United: (4-4-2) Barthez | G Neville, Ferdinand, Silvestre, O'Shea | Beckham, Butt, Scholes, Giggs | Solskjaer, Van Nistelrooy. Booked: Scholes.

Aston Villa: (4-4-2) Postma | Wright, Mellberg, Johnsen, Samuel | Hendrie, Hitzlsperger, Hadji, Barry | Dublin (Cooke 79), Vassel. Booked: Wright, Hadji.

Aston Villa haven't beaten United in the league since August '95 – the game which prompted Alan Hansen to make his assertion that you don't win trophies with kids. Double that with the fact that Villa have lost four on the trot and you can see why the bookmakers made them 4/1 to win at home. Villa are like Everton pre-Moyes – a team that contributes so little to the Premiership that you question their existence. However, following the disgraceful Birmingham derby two weeks previous, Graham Taylor's side desperately needed to rediscover some pride.

David Beckam, already looking good in white

With a section of the M6 closed due to an accident and another lunchtime kick-off catching many off guard, the majority of United fans were only just in the ground to see Beckham tap in a Giggs cross from four yards: 1-0. And that was about the fun of it.

Villa weren't as woeful as their form suggests, though they seemed clueless in front of goal. Dublin, Vassel, Hitzlsperger, Hendrie and Hadji all came close to equalising – the latter four times – but Barthez was on form, as was the United defence. They needed to be, for the personnel in front weren't.

United improved in the second half, but this was not the team at their swaggering best. Still, the cliché that three points matter more than anything was true today and if the performance was unconvincing, then the news that Arsenal had lost at Blackburn made Reds forget it. Just two points now separate United and Arsenal. Maybe it's game on, after all.

United performance: 6/10. **Man of the match:** Barry – as at Old Trafford earlier in the season, he never stopped running and crosses like Beckham. **Premiership position:** 1. Arsenal 63pts (pl 30); 2. United 61pts (pl 30); 3. Newcastle 58pts (pl 30).

Tuesday 18 March 2003	Champions League 2nd group phase

Deportivo La Coruña 2   Manchester United 0
Victor 32, Lynch og 47.

Kick-off: 8.45pm. **Estadio Riazor. Att:** 20,000 (500 Reds) **Ref:** V Hrinak

United: (3-5-2) Ricardo | Roche (Stewart 45), Blanc, O'Shea | Pugh, P Neville, Lynch, Butt, Fletcher | Giggs (Richardson 72), Forlan (Webber 72). Booked: P Neville.

Deportivo: (4-4-1-1) Dani Mallo | Manuel Pablo, Cesar, Andrade (Djorovic 64), Capdevila | Victor (Hector 77), Acuna, Duscher, Fran (Scaloni 52) | Valeron | Luque. Booked: Acuna

As pointless games go, this was up with the best of them. United had already qualified for the quarter finals. Deportivo hadn't – and couldn't. Neither author made the journey to La Coruña (a wonderful place, but not for the third time in eighteen months) and instead watched an ITV commentary team almost penitential that the game was afforded a spot on prime-time television.

Whilst Depo rested some star players, Giggs and Butt were the only recognised first teamers for United – indeed, between them the duo had played more games in the competition than all their team mates put together. However, those who criticised United for a lightweight eleven should understand that the management had earned the right to give players like **Pugh**, **Lynch** and **Roche** experience on the back of winning the group early. The

Danny Pugh: in at the deep end

team, by far United's most inexperienced fielded for a big cup game, boasted an average age of 24 only thanks to the presence of Blanc.

Sir Alex won't have been disappointed as he cast a paternal eyes over his young charges. True, Depor were the dominant side but cliche that it sounds, sprit and endeavour were to be found in spades amongst the young Reds. It seems a shame, then, that the two goals could have been avoided. **Blanc**, who these days turns slower than the Prestige oil tanker that continues to pollute Galician shores, was beaten for pace – no, really – which allowed Luque to score after 32 minutes. Then, two minutes into the second half, **Lynch** found himself in the wrong place and headed into his own goal.

One thing's for certain, though, the United that will return to Spain in three weeks' time for the glorious/ominous prospect of a quarter-final tie against the Madrid Globetrotters will be a very different side.

United performance: 7/10. **Man of the match**: Darren Fletcher – showed the quality first touch that will give him a realistic chance of making it at Old Trafford. **Group position**: (pl 6) 1. United 13pts; 2. Juventus 10pts; 3. Deportivo 7pts; 4. Basle 4pts.

⚽ **OWN GOAL DEBUT** It's every defender's nightmare – and it happened for Mark Lynch, who scored an own goal on his debut in the 2-0 defeat at Deportivo La Coruña.

Manchester United 3   Fulham 0
Van Nistelrooy 45, 68, 90.

Kick-off: 12.30pm. **Old Trafford. Att:** 67,706 **Ref:** S Bennett

United: (4-4-1-1) Barthez | G Neville, O'Shea, Ferdinand, Brown | Beckham, Butt, Scholes, Giggs | Solskjaer, Van Nistelrooy. Booked: Ferdinand, G Neville.

Fulham: (4-4-2) Taylor | Ouaddou, Knight, Harley, Melville | Boa Morte, Djetou, Malbranque, Legwinski | Marlet, Saha.

Another 12.30pm kick-off, but rather than curse the fact, 5,000 United fans held up cards showing the number '3' - in the hope of getting more 3pm kick-offs. At least Sky TV, who were broadcasting the game, acknowledged the effort when it would have been convenient not to. Mind you, in the press box, several Sunday newspapermen mocked the protest by flourishing signs reading 12.30: they love the longer time to meet deadlines afforded by an early start.

Whilst United have closed on Arsenal and remain unbeaten in the league since Christmas, there have been no high scoring league victories as in years of yore. And it looked like it was going to be a goal-less first half against a Fulham side not lacking flair players – most notably Malbranque – until Djetou pulled Solskjaer's arm in the box and a penalty was awarded. Van Nistelrooy inevitably converted it – his first Premiership goal in six weeks.

The Dutchman got a second, a glorious solo effort worthy of being goal of the season on 68 minutes. Picking the ball up inside his own half with his back to goal, he outran the Fulham midfield and feinted past Melville before rolling the ball past keeper Taylor before he'd barely had chance to reduce the angle. After the game, Jean Tigana, Fulham's manager, complained that Van Nistelrooy had levered himself off on the run by pushing an elbow into Malbranque's face, but no-one else saw it like that: they were stunned by the excellence.

Van Nistelrooy's hat-trick was confirmed in the last minute when he hit a back post volley from a Giggs cross. The win put United top of the league for the first time this season and although Arsenal still have a game in hand, Old Trafford sang 'United – top of the league', loud and proud in the Manchester sunshine. Who said all early kick-offs were miserable?

Three-up for Ruud before lunchtime – and United are top of the league

United performance: 7.5/10. **Man of the match**: Van Nistelrooy – a hat-trick and his best United goal so far. **Premiership position**: 1. United 64pts (pl 31); 2. Arsenal 63pts (pl 30); 3. Newcastle 61pts (pl 31).

⚽ **TEN UP FOR ENGLAND REDS** On March 29, David Beckham scores his tenth goal for England in a 2-0 Euro Championship qualifying win over Liechtenstein. He is the fifth player to score ten goals for England while at United, following in the footsteps of Tommy Taylor, Bobby Charlton, Bryan Robson and Paul Scholes.

Remember 3pm?

United fans were so frustrated by the lack of games played at the traditional time of 3pm on a Saturday that they organised a protest that received widespread coverage before the Fulham game.

The parties responsible for the proliferation of kick-offs at 12.15pm, 12.30pm or whatever other time is deemed feasible – United played Chelsea on a Friday night at the start of last season – are Sky television, the police and both competing clubs. All try and shift the blame to each other when criticised, although it's Sky who hold the real power, not to mention the contract that allows them to propose that games are shifted. The police prefer earlier games because it means less time for fans in the pubs, a point rarely raised in the past when trouble was more commonplace.

For their part, Sky move the times of the games because matches are not allowed to be televised between 3pm and 5pm on a Saturday for fear that it will affect attendances at other matches. With each competing club receiving £597,000 per televised game, United have been shy in expressing the concerns of their fans, Sir Alex Ferguson and several players not endeared towards early kick-offs. At other clubs, Leeds and Charlton for example, they have been critical of Sky for not televising them enough.

The majority of United fans appreciate the importance of television revenue and don't object to some games being shifted, but not the majority as happened last season. The atmosphere isn't at its best for early games, fans often have to set off when people are still clubbing and many quite enjoyed the tradition of hearing the other half-time and full-time scores whilst at the game. Expect this one to rumble on, especially in view of the proposed TV deals on offer from the Premiership for 2004–05, which will comprise 38 'first pick' games to be played on Sundays at 4pm, 38 'second pick' games played on Sunday at 2pm or Monday at 8pm, and a further 62 'third pick' games to be played on Saturday at 1pm and 5pm.

April

Manchester United 4   Liverpool 0
Van Nistelrooy 5, 65 (pens), Giggs 78, Solskjaer 90.

Kick-off: 12.30pm. **Old Trafford. Att**: 67,639 **Ref**: M Riley

United: (4-4-1-1) Barthez | Silvestre (O'Shea 68), Ferdinand, Brown, G Neville | Giggs, Keane, P Neville (Beckham 65), Solskjaer | Scholes | Van Nistelrooy. Booked: Silvestre.

Liverpool: (4-4-2) Dudek | Carragher, Traore, Hypia, Riise | Gerrard, Diouf (Smicer 71), Hamann, Murphy (Cheyrou 79)| Heskey, Baros (Biscan 7). Booked: Diouf, Murphy, Gerrard. Sent off: Hypia.

The song sheet went like this:

'Di-e-go whoa-oah, Di-e-go whoa-oah, he came from Uruguay,
   he made the Scousers cry.'

'Sit Down Pinocchio.' (to Phil Thompson)

'You're not famous anymore.'

'Big nose, what's the score?' (to Phil Thompson)

'If you all hate Scousers clap your hands.'

'Get those nostrils off the pitch.' (to Phil Thompson)

'Sign on, sign on, with hope in your heart, 'cos you'll never get a job, you'll
   never get a job.'

'Twelve long years.'

'He's only a poor little Scouser, his face is all tattered and torn, he made me feel
   sick, so I hit him with a brick, and now he don't sing any more.'

'If you want to go to heaven when you die, you must keep the Red flag flying
   high, you must wear a red bonnet, with f**k the Scousers on it…if you
   want to go to heaven when you die.'

'Build a bonfire, put the Scousers on the top. Put Man City in the middle and
   burn the f***ing lot.'

'Gary Neville is a Red, he hates Scousers.'

'Get to work you lazy t***s.'

'Part-time supporters.'

'In your Liverpool slums, you look in the dustbin for something to eat, you find
   a dead rat and you think it's a treat, in your Liverpool slums.'

Gary Neville – he cares about these games with the Scousers

The vitriol can be strong, the language mordant, but the United-Liverpool game remains the most eagerly awaited in English football. And today? 4-0: the biggest win over Liverpool for fifty years, Giggs's first league goal at Old Trafford in two years, and with Arsenal only drawing at Villa, United drew level at the top with the same number of games played. That's six league points off Liverpool this season…and about time too.

United performance: 7.5/10. **Man of the match**: Scholes – great close control and vision.
Premiership position: 1. Arsenal 67pts (pl 32); 2.United 67pts (pl 32) 3. Newcastle 61pts (pl 31).

Real Madrid 3   Manchester United 1

Figo 12, Raul 28, 49.   Van Nistelrooy 52.

Kick-off: 8.45pm. Estadio Santiago Bernabeu. **Att:** 75,000 (4,500 Reds) **Ref:** A Frisk

United: (4-4-1-1) Barthez | G Neville (Solskjaer 86), Ferdinand, Brown Silvestre (O'Shea 58) | Giggs, Keane, Butt, Beckham | Scholes | Van Nistelrooy. Booked: Neville, Scholes, Van Nistelrooy, Keane.

Real Madrid: (4-4-2) Casillas | Salgado, Helguera, Hierro, Roberto Carlos | Figo, Makelele, Flavio Conceicao, Zidane | Raul, Ronaldo (Guti 83).

Over four thousand United fans descended on the Spanish capital for a game billed by the local media as 'the biggest in the world'. Serious problems were narrowly averted outside the Bernabeu after dangerous crushes, mainly as a result of nervous police. And inside, in one of the world's great footballing citadels, a towering mass of 75,000 blue seats, the hosts produced a first half performance that justified the hyperbole that accompanies their every move. So slick, so inspired were the reigning European and World Club Champions that United seems outclassed by their beguiling brilliance. 'It was if they were from another planet,' commented Gary Neville. So that's why the Spanish press have taken to calling them *galacticos*.

Beckham – second best on the Bernabeu turf

Ruud takes on Real singlehanded

Luckily, United fared better in the second period – that's after Raul had given our alien cousins a 3-0 lead, a perfect 20 yard shot after being set up by Figo. Added to earlier goals by Figo – a 12th minute cross cum shot that looped over Barthez, and a 28th minute goal by Raul after he turned past Ferdinand and fired hard and low, Madrid seemed peerless.

United, though, are better than their performance suggested, and that frustrated fans. Despite the speculation, Beckham didn't look like a player who could get on the Madrid bench, Giggs was peripheral and Scholes drifted. But Van Nistelrooy's contribution cannot be doubted. He never stopped chasing and challenging, and was rewarded with a goal when Casillas could only parry a shot into his path on 52 minutes for him to head in.

Three-one is how it stayed, the fickle Castillians chirping 'olé' with every touch, the United fans learning to accept their technical inferiority. It could be possible to turn the game round at Old Trafford in two weeks' time…in the same way that it is possible that Leeds United will be held up as an example of a well-run company by the Department of Trade and Industry.

United performance: 7.5/10. **Man of the match**: Zidane – the best footballer on this planet, and probably in the solar system.

Newcastle United 2
Jenas 21, Ameobi 89.

Manchester United 6
Solskjaer 32, Scholes 34, 38, 52, Giggs 44,
Van Nistelrooy 58(pen)

Kick-off: 12.30pm. St. James's Park. **Att:** 52,164 (3,000 Reds) **Ref:** S Dunn

United: (4-4-1-1) Barthez | O'Shea (G Neville 49), Silvestre, Ferdinand, Brown (Blanc 65) | Scholes, Butt, Keane, Solskjaer | Giggs (Forlan 45) | Van Nistelrooy.

Newcastle: (4-4-2) Given | Hughes, Bramble, Woodgate, Bernard | Solano (Ameobi 66), Jenas, Dyer, Robert (Viana 15, Lua Lua 66) | Bellamy, Shearer.

Booked: Shearer.

A night out in Newcastle – or Newcastle-Gateshead as the tourist literature now calls it – is not for the timid. Large groups of sparsely attired young females roam the streets from pub to pub, the shrill of their voices filling the Georgian splendour of Grey Street, the tawdriness of the Bigg Market. It's the brassy being brash, even when the weather's brass. And there was an air of alcopop-fuelled confidence the night before this game. Pubs advertised 'United v Man Utd' on florescent boards, and pundits in the *Evening Chronicle* were unanimous in their predictions of the big game: Newcastle would win. No doubt.

When the gifted Jenas hit a belting shot which swerved past Barthez after twenty minutes, a bright day became a brilliant one for all but 3,000 inside St James's Park. However, United – that's the one with a trophy cabinet – were level twelve minutes later when a clever Giggs cross let Solskjaer beat the offside trap to score. Substitute Gary Neville was barely able to stay off the pitch. So he didn't. He managed to restrain himself when a second went in two minutes later. Giggs was again the provider, Scholes the finisher – 2-1.

Incredibly, United scored again, a third in six minutes. Giggs – who else? – played a ball to Brown who knocked it back for Scholes. The ginger prince struck a wicked effort past Given. 'Shearer, what's the score?' sang the travelling Reds, their anger at Alan's early transgression towards half the United team now subsided. A minute before the break, O'Shea beat Hughes with a drag back and hit a shot that smashed off the cross bar. Giggs netted the rebound. 4-1 at half-time, and cue chants of 'Shearer for Sunderland'.

He's on my team. The captain makes his choice

The rout continued after the break. **Scholes** sealed his hat-trick on 51 minutes when he hit a Gary Neville cross in between the post and the hapless Given, and a sixth goal followed seven minutes later after a penalty was awarded when Bramble brought down Forlan. **Van Nistelrooy** doesn't miss. To their credit, the Newcastle fans who had seen their team concede just ten goals at home in sixteen previous games this season got behind their lads whilst the United fans rubbed it in with a chant of: 'Who put the ball in the Geordies net, half of Man United.' Amoebi's late goal was a goal-difference annoyance. But it had been an absorbing, outstanding show.

United performance: 10/10. **Man of the match**: Scholes – a beautiful hat-trick from some quite exquisite attacking play. **Premiership position**: 1. United 70pts (pl 33); 2. Arsenal 67pts (pl 32); 3. Newcastle 61pts (pl 33).

Wednesday 16 April 2003   Premiership

Arsenal 2
Henry 51, 62.

Manchester United 2
Van Nistelrooy 24, Giggs 63.

Kick-off: 7.45pm. Highbury. **Att**: 38,164 (2,900 Reds) **Ref**: M Halsey

United: (4-4-1-1) Barthez | Brown, Ferdinand, Silvestre, O'Shea (G Neville 45) | Solskjaer, Butt, Keane, Scholes |Giggs | Van Nistelrooy. Booked: Keane, Butt.

Arsenal: (4-4-2) Taylor | Lauren, Keown, Campbell, Cole | Ljungberg, Gilberto, Vieira, Pires (Kanu 80) | Bergkamp (Wiltord 75), Henry. Sent off: Campbell.

The biggest Premiership game of the season so far on the hottest day of the year so far. Black market tickets fetched £300 and hundreds of loyal Reds stood outside the Clock End hoping for a spare. Inside, United's recent form fuelled considerable optimism amongst fans, a sanguinity vindicated by the first half performance. The Reds, attired in the fetching all blue third strip, governed from the start and took the lead when **Van Nistelrooy** exchanged passes with Giggs before embarrassing Campbell and loping past Keown to lift the ball over Taylor on

A classic from Ruud ... worth all of £300 admission

24 minutes. O'Shea caused problems on the left side and Keane controlled midfield. Even to neutrals, we were ruthlessly in control.

Arsenal emerged for the second half, however, a distinctly resurgent team and they drew level fortuitously when a Cole shot deflected off Henry and past Barthez on 51 minutes. A greater injustice eleven minutes later allowed them to take the lead, when a linesman failed to signal that Henry was offside by 2.8 nautical miles. But their advantage was unmerited and United, enraged, surged forward, restoring parity just a minute later when Giggs equalised with a header from a deep cross from Scholes. Wenger's shot daggers, and the game bubbled on with pride and belligerence, exemplified when Sol Campbell was sent off with seven minutes to play after flinging an elbow at Solskjaer, but ultimately to a stalemate.

When Sir Alex uncharacteristically strode onto the pitch after the final whistle and clenched his fists whilst saluting the travelling fans, Arsene Wenger was back in the dressing room, his face drawn and wan with nerves.

Fergie delighted: he can almost feel that trophy

The body language said it all: United may not have won, but the Reds are on a roll towards the Championship. Such talk would have been unheard of only six weeks ago, when the Arse were preening themselves about the inevitability of a double Double.

United performance: 8.5/10.
Man of the Match: Keane – who said he was past it?
Premiership position: 1. United 71pts (pl 34); 2.Arsenal 68pts (pl 33); 3. Newcastle 61pts (pl 33).

Saturday 19 April 2003   Premiership

Manchester United 3   Blackburn Rovers 1
Van Nistelrooy 20, Scholes 42, 61.   Berg 24.

Kick-off: 3pm. Old Trafford. **Att**: 67,626 **Ref**: A D'Urso

United: (4-4-1-1) Barthez (Ricardo 45) | P Neville, Ferdinand, Silvestre, Brown | Butt (Keane 54), Beckham, Scholes, Fortune | Giggs (Solskjaer 83) | Van Nistelrooy.

Blackburn: (4-4-2) Friedel | Neill, Berg (Taylor 63), Short, Gresko | Flitcroft, Tugay, Dunn, Duff (Suker 65) | Cole, Yorke.

Statistics can belie facts. Whilst you can't argue that Manchester City haven't won a major domestic trophy for 27 years or Newcastle for 48, the statistics which make Mark Viduka the Premiership's best striker must be viewed with suspicion. Today, one stat gave an accurate portrayal of this game: United had twelve shots on target, Blackburn two.

Come on Henning, you're never going to catch him

United's form of late has been as impressive as at any time under Sir Alex and the confidence continued to flow against a potentially troublesome opposition that contained three United old boys – that's after Blackburn had two chances to take the lead in the first ten minutes. After that, Scholes (bizarrely the only Red to be named in the PFA Premiership eleven) began to create and Giggs caused the Blackburn defence more problems than Duff was doing at the other end. Which was something.

Scholes, Giggs, Fortune and Beckham were all involved in the move that led to Van Nistelrooy heading United's first on twenty minutes. Then Blackburn equalised, Berg heading across an empty net from a Dunn cross. Phil Neville, on for the injured O'Shea, did one of his nifty step overs and crossed for Scholes to smash the ball past Friedel just before half-time: 2-1.

An injured Barthez was replaced at the interval by Ricardo, the Spaniard keen to make a name for himself with a rare first team opportunity. He did this within sixty seconds of entering to field by showing the nimbleness of a blindfolded elephant and fouling Cole. Luckily, humiliation was avoided with a fine save from the resulting penalty. United eventually made it 3-1 when Giggs beat three Blackburn defenders to create space for Van Nistelrooy to cross for Scholes to pot his second. No wonder the crowd began to cheer the team's every move.

United performance: 8.5/10. Man of the match: Giggs – the better he plays, the less likely a transfer seems. Quick and confident. Premiership position: 1. United 74pts (pl 35); 2. Arsenal 71pts (pl 34); 3.Newcastle 61pts (pl 34).

GIGGS: THE CHASE IS ON Ryan Giggs plays his 540th game for United in the 3-1 home win over Blackburn Rovers, and so reaches third place in the all-time club appearance table, behind Bill Foulkes (688) and Bobby Charlton (759). During the season Giggs has overtaken four players – Joe Spence (510 games), Denis Irwin (528), Tony Dunne (535) and Alex Stepney (539).

TON UP FOR SCHOLES Paul Scholes scores twice against Blackburn to become the third player this season (after Solskjaer and Giggs), and the seventeenth in United history, to reach 100 goals for the club.

PENALTIES? NO PROBLEM Ricardo saves a penalty in the second minute of his league debut, preserving United's extraordinary record that no visiting team has scored a league penalty at Old Trafford since Norwich City in December 1993.

Wednesday 23 April 2003   Champions League Qtr-Final 2nd Leg

Manchester United 4   Real Madrid 3
Van Nistelrooy 43, Helguera og 52, Beckham 71, 84.   Ronaldo 12, 50, 59.

Kick-off: 7.45pm. Old Trafford. **Att:** 66,708 **Ref:** P Collina.

United: (4-4-1-1) Barthez | Brown, Ferdinand, Silvestre, O'Shea | Solskjaer, Keane, Butt, Veron (Beckham 63) | Giggs | Van Nistelrooy. Booked: Veron.

Real Madrid: (4-2-3-1) Casillas | Salgado, Helguera, Hierro, Roberto Carlos | Makelele, McManaman (Portillo 69) | Figo (Pavon 86), Zidane, Guti | Ronaldo (Solari 69).

United's home form in Europe is largely formidable. Largely: their home form when it matters most in Europe is not. A failure at Old Trafford to beat Dortmund in '97, Monaco in '98, Real Madrid in '00, Bayern Munich in '01 and Leverkusen in '02 contributed largely to eventual elimination. And after the 3-1 defeat in Madrid, United not only had to win tonight – they had to win by at least two clear goals. It looked some order, especially when Beckham was announced as substitute. However, United fans were less surprised than the media, given Beckham's recent form, and his limp showing against Roberto Carlos in the first leg. As Sir Alex made clear, Solskjaer deserved to start ahead of England's captain after his performances on the right in recent weeks.

He came, he conquered

Old Trafford was a cauldron of noise, as it needed to be, for United to have any chance of a much mooted early goal. The Reds opened brightly and a goal was scored in the 12th minute, but it went to Ronaldo who struck a shot past Barthez, the keeper having deserted the near post. It was a knock-out blow, but United heads went down only for a minute. The crowd roared on the Reds, as Solskjaer twice went close and Giggs shot wide before eventually crossing for Van Nistelrooy to make it 1-1 in the 43rd minute.

Madrid regained the lead again in the 50th minute, Ronaldo guiding a Roberto Carlos cross in. United now needed five, which seemed implausible, and for a while, again, the crowd and the match went numb, and a kind of training ground automatism took hold. Then the ageing Helguera turned a Veron shot past Casillas, and the crowd roared again. Game on. Solskjaer shot and Veron volleyed, but it was again Real who scored next, Ronaldo netting his hat-trick

And he was almost as good: Ruud gets one back

with an unstoppable 25-yard shot. The Brazilian was substituted, to a standing ovation from all parts of the ground, that was heartfelt and spontaneous. He later commented at how humbled he had felt.

Whilst one world-renowned player moved towards the bench, another had come off it to take centre stage: Beckham. His two goals in thirteen minutes, including a perfect free kick, couldn't save the tie, but for a few minutes, again, Real seemed thrown, and a United miracle not beyond chance. It didn't happen, but Beckham had exorcised much of his hurt, and restored his reputation.

The crowd – Manchester and Madrid followers alike – left the ground drained and buzzing, witness to what has to be one of the great games of football seen in this young century. The result was a 4-3 win to the Reds, and a 5-4 aggregate victory to Real. Both had played like winners.

United performance: 8.5/10. **Man of the match:** Ronaldo – a cool hat-trick at the very highest level.

ALL IN VAIN Despite being favourites to win a 10th European Cup, Real Madrid were eliminated by Juventus – the team United had humbled earlier in the competition - at the semi-final stage. And then, of course, Juve lost out in an all-Italian no score bore final, on penalties, to Milan. None of which games will be remembered like the United-Real shoot-out.

YOUTH VICTORY On April 25, United win the FA Youth Cup for a record ninth time, with a 3-1 aggregate victory over Middlesbrough. Next in line are Arsenal who have won the trophy six times. United have also appeared in a record twelve finals.

Tottenham Hotspur 0 Manchester United 2

Scholes 69, Van Nistelrooy 90

Kick-off: 4.05pm. White Hart Lane. **Att:** 36,073 (3,000 Reds) **Ref:** J Winter

United: (4-4-1-1) Carroll | Brown (Brown 54), Ferdinand, Silvestre, O'Shea | Beckham, Keane, Scholes, Solskjaer (Fortune 71) | Giggs | Van Nistelrooy.

Tottenham Hotspur: (4-4-2) Keller | Carr, King, Taricco, Richards (Gardner 30) | Davies, Poyet, Toda (Iversen 78), Etherington (Bunjevcevic 78) | Sheringham, Keane.

United had an unexpected lift the day before this game when Bolton's two-goal comeback against Arsenal ensured that for the first time this season the title destiny was in Red control. The task was simple: three wins in the final league games and the title went back to Old Trafford. Tottenham fans felt compromised. They would rather see anyone but Arsenal win the league, but they were hardly going to support United. (Well, to be honest, a few in the crowd did indeed seem to know their priorities.)

United responded to their destiny with a composed, positive first half. The score only remained goalless thanks to the shot saving exploits of Keller, the American enjoying a

Keller – he did this all afternoon

contrast in fortunes compared to United's Barthez, dropped for this one after his failure to stop any of the shots Ronaldo fired his way on Wednesday. And so it continued, right until 21 minutes to the whistle, with tension rising amongst the travelling fans, when Scholes deftly headed a Beckham cross wide to Giggs. The Welsh-Mancunian spun the ball back in for Scholes to head his 20th goal of the season.

Even though Tottenham continued with the threat of a bunch of sparrows, nerves weren't settled until injury time, when Van Nistelrooy became the first player since Denis Law in '63/64 to score 40 goals in a season when he controlled a beautiful ball from Fortune to stab past the magnificent Keller. He also kept up a record of scoring every time he's played against Spurs.

The United end erupted with chants of: 'We want our trophy back' and 'We're gonna win the league' sung against the back drop of a flag that read: 'We've got Wesley Brown, We've got John O'Shea. Manchester is dreamin', of silverware in May.'

The dream just could be about to happen…

United performance: 8/10. **Man of the match:** Keane – although it could have easily been Keller.
Premiership position: 1. United 77pts (pl 36); 2. Arsenal 72pts (pl 35); 3. Newcastle 65pts (pl 36).

RUUD FACTS Ruud Van Nistelrooy scores his fortieth goal of the season in United's 2-0 win at Spurs, only the second player in United history to score 40 goals in a season.

Saturday 3 May 2003	Premiership

Manchester United 4   Charlton Athletic 1
Beckham 11, Van Nistelrooy 31, 37,53.   Jensen 12.

Kick-off: 12.30pm. Old Trafford. **Att:** 67,721 **Ref:** M Halsey

United: (4-4-2) Carroll | Brown, Silvestre, Ferdinand, O'Shea | Giggs (Butt 77), Scholes (Veron 69), Keane, Beckham | Solskjaer (Forlan 77), Van Nistelrooy.

Charlton: (5-3-2) Kiely | Young, Kishishev (Sankofa 73), Konchesky, Fortune, Powell | Parker, Jensen, Lisbie (Johansson 84) | Euell (Bart Williams 78), Bartlett. Booked: Fortune.

The mood was happy inside Old Trafford. 'Just like a team that's gonna win the football league, we shall not be moved,' roared the Stretford. And the North, East and even the South stand.

Then the game. When Beckham struck a left foot shot from the edge of the box that took a deflection on its way into Kiely's goal

Beckham opens the scoring – and it's looking good for the Premiership

after 11 minutes, it was expected to be the first of many against the faded Addicts. It was, but only after a doubtful Keane back pass forced Carroll to make a poor clearance… straight to Jensen. The Charlton playmaker took his time to shoot into an open goal. It was all a bit nervy until **Van Nistelrooy** hooked a Silvestre header in with his right foot for United's second on 31 minutes, and then made it three six minutes later with a beautiful chip over Kiely in a move started by Silvestre. Eight minutes after the break, the Dutchman completed his third hat-trick of the season and his 79th goal in his 100th United game since joining from PSV – he controlled a Beckham cross and hit it with power from ten yards.

As his players thanked the supporters, **Sir Alex** took the microphone and announced that any celebrations would have to wait until Goodison Park on the final day of the season. So there was no traditional lap of honour with the kids: no premature assumptions here. Unlike at Highbury. That didn't stop Mancunian pubs from rocking to the strain of the John O'Shea song that night.

And the following day, **Leeds**' surprise victory at Arsenal confirmed United's eighth title in eleven brilliant years.

United performance: 8/10. **Man of the match**: Keane - smart. **Premiership position**: 1. United 80pts (pl 37); 2. Arsenal 72pts (pl 35); 3. Newcastle 66pts (pl 37).

⚽ **THROUGH THE TURNSTILES** United's final game at Old Trafford against Charlton on May 3 is the 33rd competitive home game of the season, a new club record exceeding the 31 home fixtures of 1998-99. The attendance of 67,721 is the highest for a competitive game at Old Trafford since 1939, and the second highest-ever for a league game at the ground. (Though the highest post-war crowd officially remains the 67,957 for Ryan Giggs's testimonial against Celtic in 2001). United also set a new average crowd of 67,630 for the season, beating the previous English league record of 67,586, set by United the year before. The seasonal aggregate is 1,284,969, another record.

⚽ **RUUD'S HATFULL** May 3 2002 Van Nistelrooy is the first United player since Denis Law in 1968-69 to score three hat-tricks in the same season, and the first since Law in 1963-64 to score three League hat-tricks.

⚽ **CHAMPIONS AGAIN!** On May 4, United are declared champions as Arsenal lose 3-2 at home to Leeds. It's the club's **eighth league title** in eleven years, matching Liverpool's eight titles between 1976 and 1986. United have now won the League **fifteen times**, three behind Liverpool's eighteen, but three ahead of Arsenal on twelve. **Ryan Giggs** equals Phil Neal and Alan Hansen's all-time record of eight Championship medals. Giggs has now won thirteen major medals, another club record.

It is **Alex Ferguson**'s eighth English league title, a new managerial record (next best is Bob Paisley of Liverpool with six). Ferguson has now won twenty-four major trophies in England and Scotland, only two short of Jock Stein's twenty-six, the post-war British record. Sir Alex has also won fifteen major honours at Old Trafford, which is more than all other United managers combined (Ernest Mangnall (3), Sir Matt Busby (8), Tommy Docherty (1) and Ron Atkinson (2)). Sir Alex, asked earlier in the season what he felt was his greatest achievement, had replied: 'Knocking Liverpool off their f***ing perch.' Quite so.

'We've won nothing yet.' The boss puts celebrations on hold ...

Sunday 11 May 2003   Premiership

Everton 1   Manchester United 2
Campbell 8.   Beckham 43, Van Nistelrooy 79 (pen).

Kick-off: 3pm. Goodison Park. **Att:** 40,168 (5,000 Reds) **Ref:** M Riley

United: (4-4-1-1) Carroll | Brown (G Neville 40), O'Shea (Blanc 45), Ferdinand, Silvestre | Beckham, Keane, Scholes, Giggs | Solskjaer (Fortune 78), Van Nistelrooy. Booked: Ferdinand, Blanc, G Neville.

Everton: (4-4-2) Wright | Yobo, Stubbs, Unsworth, Watson | Carsley, Gravesen (Chadwick 75), Hibbert, Naysmith (Pistone 83) | Campbell (Ferguson 40), Rooney.

Booked: Graveson, Hibbert, Rooney, Stubbs, Ferguson.

Weeks before the final game of the season at Goodison, press and fans alike anticipated the nervy prospect of United going to Merseyside needing victory against a much-improved Everton. But United had been crowned champions a week previously. Relaxed in that knowledge, 3,000 Reds (plus a few thousand more in the home sections) made the short trip west in celebratory mood.

Even Keano's smiling – but then who wouldn't after Beckham's free kick

Together for the last time: Fergie's fledgelings

The atmosphere within Goodison's archaic stands was charged given that Everton required three points to qualify for the UEFA Cup, but as the game swung against them and the reality dawned that they would be cruelly dropping out of the top six for the first time since November, it became as changeable as the weather. United's usual medley of anti-Scouse songs and a flag bearing the message 'The only time the Premiership will be won on Merseyside' hardly endeared the Reds to the home fans, but Evertonians were still honourable enough to applaud Wes Brown as he was carried around the pitch on a stretcher.

They had seen their team go ahead with an eighth minute Campbell header, but despite Rooney having three sound scoring chances, it was United who dominated with some strutting play and twice as many efforts on goal. A wondrous Beckham free kick, his first from a dead ball in the league this season, levelled the score two minutes before half-time. Everton's vexed frustration was complete

2002 — 2003

We've got our trophy back

in the 78th minute when ref Mike Riley issued his sixth and seventh yellow card after Stubbs fouled Van Nistelrooy for a penalty. Ruud of course converted, a goal that lifted his total to 44 for the season and confirmed him as the golden boot winner with 25 league goals.

The United fans applauded the disappointed Everton players after the final whistle prior to the real celebrations when the champions were presented with the Premiership trophy. The players' reactions illustrated their unbridled joy as they joined in the terrace anthems 'We've got our trophy back' and 'Champions'. They continued for half an hour but just when they seemed finished and were applauded for one last time, Van Nistelrooy ran back across the field and, ignoring the orders of a policeman, whipped his shirt off and threw it into the United end. Happy days.

United performance: 8.5/10. **Man of the match**: Giggs – one of many champions on top of their game. **Premiership final positions**: 1. United (Champions) 83pts (pl 38); 2. Arsenal 78pts (pl 38); 3. Newcastle 69pts (pl 38).

W25, D8, L5 In winning the final game at Everton, United finish the season with twenty-five wins and eight draws, one of the club's best ever title campaigns. Statistically it is exceeded in points per game (adjusting for differ-ent points systems) only by the 1999-2000 and 1993-94 championships. It is United's 63rd competitive game of the season, matching the club record totals of 1993-94 and 1998-99.

RUUD'S GOALS Ruud van Nistelrooy's hat trick makes it 130 goals for United this season, a club total exceeded only by the 143 goals of 1956-57. The strikes also mean that Ruud has scored in **ten successive United games** in all competitions, beating the club record he established only the season before. The run began with his hat-trick at Old Trafford against Fulham on March 22 and involved fifteen goals (five of them penalties). Van Nistelrooy has also scored in both games he has played for Holland in that time – a run of twelve first-class matches in which he has never failed to score. In addition Van Nistelrooy equals his own club record (shared with Billy Whelan in 1956) of scoring in eight consecutive league matches.

Van Nistelrooy's **44 goals for the season** are second in United history only to Denis Law's 46 in 1963-64. The Dutchman's 80 goals in 101 games over two seasons are a rate of 79.2%, by far the best in United history. The next highest rates are Charlie Sagar (1905-07) on 72.7%, and Tommy Taylor (1953-58) with 68.6%.

Ruud also ends the season with the Golden Boot as the **Premier League's top scorer** with 25 goals, one ahead of Thierry Henry. Astonishingly, this is only the second time in history that a United player has been outright leading scorer in the top division – the other occasion was Dennis Viollet with 32 league goals in 1959-60. George Best in 1967-68, and Dwight Yorke in 1998-99, both shared the feat with other players.

ON THE SPOT Ruud van Nistelrooy's first Everton goal is his nineteenth successful penalty for United in just two seasons, exceeding the post-war club record of eighteen spot-kicks, held jointly by Albert Quixall and Eric Cantona. Van Nistelrooy has failed with only one penalty he has taken for United (against Olympiakos in the European Cup in 2001). Cantona failed twice and Quixall four times. United have now scored fourteen penalties this season (Van Nistelrooy 12, Forlan 1, Beckham 1), a new post-war club record, exceeding the twelve of 1990-91.

Barclaycard Premiership 2202-03 — Final Table

		HOME					AWAY						
	Pl	W	D	L	F	A	W	D	L	F	A	GD	Pts
1. Manchester United	38	16	2	1	42	12	9	6	4	32	22	40	83
2. Arsenal	38	15	2	2	47	20	8	7	4	38	22	43	78
3. Newcastle United	38	15	2	2	36	17	6	4	9	27	31	15	69
4 Chelsea	38	12	5	2	41	15	7	5	7	27	23	30	67
5. Liverpool	38	9	8	2	30	16	9	2	8	31	25	20	64
6. Blackburn Rovers	38	9	7	3	24	15	7	5	7	28	28	9	60
7. Everton	38	11	5	3	28	19	6	3	10	20	30	-1	59
8. Southampton	38	9	8	2	25	16	4	5	10	18	30	-3	52
9. Manchester City	38	9	2	8	28	26	6	4	9	19	28	-7	51
10. Tottenham Hotspur	38	9	4	6	30	29	5	4	10	21	33	-11	50
11. Middlesbrough	38	10	7	2	36	21	3	3	13	12	23	4	49
12. Charlton Athletic	38	8	3	8	26	30	6	4	9	19	26	-11	49
13. Birmingham City	38	8	5	6	25	23	5	4	10	16	26	-8	48
14. Fulham	38	11	3	5	26	18	2	6	11	15	32	-9	48
15. Leeds United	38	7	3	9	25	26	7	2	10	33	31	1	47
16. Aston Villa	38	11	2	6	25	14	1	7	11	17	33	-5	45
17. Bolton Wanderers	38	7	8	4	27	24	3	6	10	14	27	-10	44
18. West Ham United	38	5	7	7	21	24	5	5	9	21	35	-17	42
19. West Brom Albion	38	3	5	11	17	34	3	3	13	12	31	-36	26
20. Sunderland	38	3	2	14	11	31	1	5	13	10	34	-44	19

Month by Month 2002–03

	Pld	W	D	L	F	A	Pts	Rank
August	3	1	2	0	4	3	5	8
September	5	3	0	2	5	3	9	4
October	3	1	2	0	5	2	5	9
November	4	2	1	1	9	8	7	8
December	6	4	0	2	10	5	12	2
January	3	3	0	0	7	3	9	3
February	4	2	2	0	5	2	8	2
March	3	3	0	0	6	1	9	3
April	5	4	1	0	17	5	13	1
May	2	2	0	0	6	2	6	2

United's Scorers 2002–03 [01–02] ● League ● Cup ● Europe

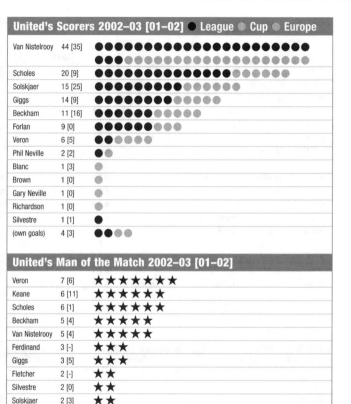

Van Nistelrooy	44 [35]
Scholes	20 [9]
Solskjaer	15 [25]
Giggs	14 [9]
Beckham	11 [16]
Forlan	9 [0]
Veron	6 [5]
Phil Neville	2 [2]
Blanc	1 [3]
Brown	1 [0]
Gary Neville	1 [0]
Richardson	1 [0]
Silvestre	1 [1]
(own goals)	4 [3]

United's Man of the Match 2002–03 [01–02]

Player	Rating
Veron	7 [6]
Keane	6 [11]
Scholes	6 [1]
Beckham	5 [4]
Van Nistelrooy	5 [4]
Ferdinand	3 [-]
Giggs	3 [5]
Fletcher	2 [-]
Silvestre	2 [0]
Solskjaer	2 [3]
Blanc	1 [0]
Brown	1 [1]
Forlan	1 [1]
Gary Neville	1 [1]
Phil Neville	1 [0]
Butt	0 [3]
Carroll	0 [1]
Andy Cole	0 [2]

From ratings in the *Rough Guide* (all competitive fixtures).

Team by Team: 2002–03 [2001–02]

HOME		TEAM	AWAY		POINTS	
02–03	[01–02]		[01–02]	02–03	02–03	[01–02]
W 2-0	[L 0-1]	Arsenal	[L 1-3]	D 2-2	4	[0]
W 5-3	[W 3-1]	Newcastle United	[L 3-4]	W 6-2	6	[3]
W 2-1	[L 0-3]	Chelsea	[W 3-0]	D 2-2	4	[3]
W 4-0	[L 0-1]	Liverpool	[L 1-3]	W 2-1	6	[0]
W 3-1	[W 2-1]	Blackburn Rovers	[D 2-2]	L 0-1	3	[4]
W 3-0	[W 4-1]	Everton	[W 2-0]	W 2-1	6	[6]
W 2-1	[W 6-1]	Southampton	[W 3-1]	W 2-0	6	[6]
D 1-1	–	Manchester City	–	L 1-3	1	[–]
W 1-0	[W 4-0]	Tottenham Hotspur	[W 5-3]	W 2-0	6	[6]
W 1-0	[L 0-1]	Middlesbrough	[W 1-0]	L 1-3	3	[3]
W 4-1	[D 0-0]	Charlton Athletic	[W 2-0]	W 3-1	6	[4]
W 2-0	–	Birmingham City	–	W 1-0	6	[–]
W 3-0	[W 3-2]	Fulham	[W 3-2]	D 1-1	4	[6]
W 2-1	[D 1-1]	Leeds United	[W 4-3]	L 0-1	3	[4]
D 1-1	[W 1-0]	Aston Villa	[D 1-1]	W 1-0	4	[4]
L 0-1	[L 1-2]	Bolton Wanderers	[W 4-0]	D 1-1	1	[3]
W 3-0	[L 0-1]	West Ham United	[W 5-3]	D 1-1	4	[3]
W 1-0	–	West Bromwich Albion	–	W 3-1	6	[–]
W 2-1	[W 4-1]	Sunderland	[W 3-1]	D 1-1	4	[6]
					83	[77]

League Record 2002–03

	Pld	W	D	L	F	A	GD	Pts	Rank
Home Record	19	16	2	1	42	12	30	50	1
Away Record	19	9	6	4	32	22	10	33	1
Overall Record	38	25	8	5	74	34	40	83	1

League Record 2001–02

	Pld	W	D	L	F	A	GD	Pts	Rank
Home Record	19	11	2	6	40	17	23	35	6
Away Record	19	13	3	3	47	28	19	42	2
Overall Record	38	24	5	9	87	45	42	77	3

The Cast

United's first team squad for the new season

No-one is an automatic choice. *That's what Sir Alex made clear when he put his whole cast on notice after that shocking display against City last term. And he was as good as his word. It seems unlikely that anyone in the squad, with the exception of Ruud van Nistelrooy, and probably Roy Keane and Paul Scholes, could have considered themselves definitely in the first eleven for the remainder of the season. Sir Alex ended up giving run-outs to no less than xx players – although, admittedly, he did use a cup competition (the Champions League, this time, rather than the Worthington, once United had qualified in their group phases) to blood most of the youngsters. And then came the summer, with transfer frenzy bubbling from the moment United got their hands on the Premiership trophy, much of it focussed on the mercurial Ronaldinho – the Reds' first ever Brazilian signing. At time of writing, it looks like Alex has got his man, along with midfield enforcer Eric Djemba Djemba (United's first Cameroon signing), French wonder-winger David Bellion, and, if a work permit can be sorted out, American keeper Tim Howard.*

Towards the end of our main coverage, we also review a few of the players on the periphery: bright new hopes like Jimmy Davis or Mads Timm, who might just get the call from the Boss this term. And there are entries, too, for the back-room staff, from Sir Alex to Trevor Lea (the man who orders the pre-match breakfast pasta).

Players who left United at the end of last season (Laurent Blanc, David May, Lee Roche – oh, and the bloke with the haircut) are covered in the following chapter – Once Were Reds – along with details of their appearances and ratings for the season.

Keepers

Fabien Barthez

Born: Lavelanet, France, 28.6.71.
Height: 5'11". **Weight:** 11st 13lbs.
Previous clubs: Toulouse, Marseille, AS Monaco (£7m, 2.6.00).
Debut: 13.8.00 v Chelsea (Wembley CS) 0-2.
Appearances: 139. **Goals:** 0.

At the end of the season, as the United players drenched the Goodison turf in champagne (not a commodity the grass will have seen much of this past twenty years), it is hard to imagine a bunch of footballers happier with their lot. Job satisfaction was written all over their bubbly-soaked faces. Except for one figure, a hair-free, Donald Pleasance look-alike, who skulked sheepishly at the back, looking decidedly embarrassed to be there. Fabien Barthez, a man usually delighted to join in goal celebrations by running thirty yards and leaping on top of the huddle, this time bore the expression of a participant in *I'm A Celebrity Get Me Out Of Here*, who suddenly finds that the jungle does not come complete with room service. He looked horribly out of place, as if he wanted to be anywhere other than there. And maybe soon he will be.

Alex Ferguson has a record of being ruthless with keepers – Jim Leighton, Mark Bosnich, Massimo Taibi – and the latest to join the line of those ostracised and banished was poor Barthez. After the defeat against Real Madrid in the Champions League quarter final when two of Ronaldo's goals were of the sort that, say, Peter Schmeichel in his prime might have got at least a finger to, Barthez did not appear again in his half-sleeved United shirt.

Cruel as it may be to cut a keeper like that (after all Rio Ferdinand was left flat-footed by the hot streak that was the Brazilian that Old Trafford night), it was a judgement that long seemed pending. Ferguson had been growing increasingly suspicious of the heavy smoker from the rugby-playing south of France. Not because of his

A crucial season ahead for the flying Frenchman

attitude, which has been beyond reproach (don't judge by appearances: he may have been photographed stepping out with some of the globe's top crumpet, but this is no dilettante playboy). More it is that his powers seem to be on the wane. Maybe the six years at the top experienced by the French national side has taken its toll on his body; maybe the reflexes are slowing with age; maybe his confidence has received an irrevocable knock after being caught out trying his tricks once too often last season, or maybe his face doesn't fit at Carrington where he's far from the most popular member of staff and frequently accused of being aloof.

Whatever, the blinding shot-stopping has increasingly been accompanied by less distinguished positioning and lame kicking. Ferguson looks and studies and then acts. And the fans knew something was up, too: Fab's signature chant sung to the tune of *Dirty Old Town* became heard with decreasing frequency during the season. 'He needed a rest,' the manager said. 'It seems I'm no longer up to it,' Barthez reckoned. Unlike for those Real goals, he can't be faulted for his self-assessment.

Last season Appearances: 46. Goals: 0. Rating: 5.5/10.

Roy Carroll

Born: Portadown, Northern Ireland, 30.9.77.
Height: 6'2". **Weight:** 13st 2lbs.
Previous clubs: Hull, Wigan (£2.5million, 1.7.01).
Debut: 26.9.01 v Aston Villa (away PL) drew 1-1 (own goal Alpay).
Appearances: 23 (3). **Goals:** 0.

Sixteen appearances in a season for a reserve keeper tells you all you need to know about the sitting tenant. As Barthez wobbled in both confidence and fitness, this was Roy Carroll's chance to make his bid for the top job, and the save he pulled out at the last to ensure his team finished the Championship with a win at Everton implies he is keen to take every opportunity to show his worth. Yet his future at Old Trafford seems far from assured, and hard to read, after a distinctly odd season.

United have lost just twice with Carroll in goal

With Barthez out injured at the start, Carroll played the season's first five games, then promptly discovered that the signing of Ricardo meant that when Barthez returned, he wasn't even on the bench. As votes of confidence go, few chairmen could have delivered a more pointed one to their manager. But Carroll fought back, and by the new year when Barthez's hamstrings were playing up, it was he not the Spaniard who was deemed the natural understudy. And when Barthez was dispensed with, he was handed the gloves. Whether that was a temporary measure, whether he will be allowed to progress beyond that is unlikely. United were linked over the summer with virtually every goal keeper who has drawn breath (except David Seaman) before settling on Tim Howard as a possible long-term first choice.

Still, the fact remains Carroll is a good, solid shot-stopper, a big physical presence in the box, and distinctly brave – as illustrated by his attempt to blame Roy Keane for his own Barthez-style howler at home to Charlton. Not to mention a lucky omen: in 26 appearances for the club he has been on the losing side only twice. As keepers' strike rates go that is almost the equivalent of Ruud van Nistelrooy's scoring touch.

Last season Appearances: 14 (2). Goals: 0. Rating: 6/10.

Tim Howard

Born: North Brunswick, New Jersey, USA 6.3.79.
Height: 6'2". Weight: 14st 3lbs.
Previous clubs: North Jersey Imperials, MetroStars (£1.8m – *predicted* July 03).
Debut: n/a.
Appearances: n/a. Goals: n/a.

America has a history of producing quality goalkeepers. There are almost as many Yanks playing between the sticks in the Premiership as there are Englishmen, and Brad Friedel was reckoned the best in the league last season. No surprise there, perhaps, as most American kids are immersed in games involving ball-handling skills from almost as soon as they can walk. And Howard is, apparently, a blinding basketball player, capable of a slam dunk worthy of Michael Jordan.

Physically, this US youth and Under-21 international is a huge presence, strong, agile and such a good shot-stopper he has been voted the Major Soccer League's goalkeeper of the year on three occasions. But much of the attention he will receive now he is at United will doubtless centre on his mental condition. He has a mild form of Tourette's

The new keeper? T-Ho on US international duty

Syndrome, the congenital brain problem which involves involuntary nervous spasms. Fortunately for Howard, he does not suffer from the extreme verbal Tourette's – whose sufferers cannot stroll down a supermarket aisle without bawling out obscenities. Rather, Howard is prone to muscular twitches and tics. Bravely, he has not tried to hide his condition, but has used his prominence in American professional sport to campaign for greater awareness and tolerance of Tourette's sufferers. He was awarded the New York Humanitarian award in 2002 for his work encouraging kids with the condition to engage in sport, and he doesn't stop there: he's also a keen amateur hip hop DJ who calls himself T-Ho.

Howard's arrival in Britain – work permits permitting – has been hugely welcomed by Tourette's sufferers, for whom his signing is the single best piece of publicity in years. However, football crowds are not known for their sensitivity, and the new keeper can anticipate serious stick the moment he steps out for United. How he copes with that will probably define his Old Trafford career.

Last season Appearances: n/a.

Ricardo

Born: Madrid, Spain, 31.12.71.
Height: 6'0". **Weight:** 13st 12lbs.
Previous Clubs: Avila, Club Atlético de Madrid, Real Valladolid (£1.5million, 30.8.02).
Debut: 29.10.02 v Maccabi Haifa (away CL) lost 0-3.
Appearances: 3 (2). **Goals:** 0.

Before the Champions League quarter final against Real Madrid, Ricardo was all over Spanish television giving his guided tour to Manchester. It included, inevitably, hints on how to buy a pint of warm bitter in a local pub. Which, if he has learned anything in his time at Old Trafford, Ricardo will appreciate was something of poetic licence: most of the drinking population of Manchester these days stick to cold Guinness or chilled beers.

Ricardo Lopez Felipe is one of Ferguson's odder purchases. Why a keeper on the wrong side of 30 was suddenly required back in

Ricardo with Forlan. Sound on primary school advice, but will he even make the bench this year?

September has never been fully explained: was there really such a paucity of youth team goalies that an emergency third choice couldn't be summoned up from the stiffs in the event of disaster higher up the food chain? Or was it that the manager thought he was getting more and that it was the number one jersey he was looking to fill? Whatever, no-one can fault the player's ambition in leaping at the chance to come to United. He hoped the move from unfashionable Valladolid – the worst supported team in Spain's La Liga – might leapfrog him up the Spanish international pecking order. Sitting on the bench if he was lucky, though, can hardly have helped his cause, and when he was finally summoned for the game against Blackburn – following yet another injury to Barthez – he was so eager to get involved, he brought down David Dunn in his first bit of action, then immediately saved the resultant penalty. Where next is a bigger challenge, since it was Roy Carroll not him who was promoted following Fabien's implosion.

Last season Appearances: 3 (2). Goals: 0. Rating: n/a.

Defenders

Wesley Brown

Born: Manchester, 13.10.79.
Height: 6'1". Weight: 11st 11lbs.
Previous clubs: Juniors.
Debut: 4.5.98 v Leeds (home PL) 3-0 Irwin, Beckham, Giggs; sub for David May.
Appearances: 106 (16). Goals: 1.

It was an indication of Wes Brown's stature in the club that, 21 games after injuring his ankle against Zalaegerszeg in the season's opening game, he was straight back in the first team. No waiting on the bench to see how things go, no protracted run-outs in the reserves to ensure there was no relapse. Just get back in the fray. And it was no coincidence that once Brown had returned, things began to turn around.

Quick, clever, hard, Brown is the most gifted home-grown defender since Paul McGrath – and brought up in the new puritan climate at Carrington, fortunately he displays none of

Wes Brown – on the ball (most of the time) with Ronaldo

the Irishman's thirst. Together with John O'Shea and Mikael Silvestre, he is at the heart of the most versatile defence in United's history; all three can play anywhere across the back line; all three are sprint-quick; all three are strong in the air; all three have ball control and passing range which belies the assumption that no defender's ambition extends beyond finding row Z. If you could slip a cigarette paper between them, of the three, because he is a local boy, Brown is the crowd's favourite, as the reaction to his debut goal proved; typical of a player of his class to open his account against Juventus in the Champions League.

In the first three years of his career, Brown's one serious failing was concentration. Almost every match he seemed prone to the moment of day-dreaming which undermines 89 minutes of unfettered concentration. Across 35 games last season there was barely one such aberration. It is called experience. It is called growing up.

But it helps if you are class in the first place. Sadly, the one thing class cannot insulate from is injury: and in the academic run-out against Everton he was carried off with a knackered cruciate, snapped when trying to stop Wayne Rooney heading for goal. The most difficult of injuries just as he was knocking on the door of greatness: no-one could suggest Wesley has had it easy. Then again, had he injured the same knee as last time, a recovery would have been doubly complicated and could have ended his career. There's still much hope for Wes.

Last season Appearances: 34 (1). Goals: 1. Rating: 7.5/10.

Rio Ferdinand

Born: Peckham, 11.7.78.
Height: 6'2". Weight: 13st 1lb.
Previous clubs: West Ham, Leeds (£30million, 30.7.02).
Appearances: 45 (1). Goals: 0.

Of all the players celebrating the Premiership triumph at Everton, it was Ferdinand who was the most wide-mouthed in excitement. Which was perhaps not surprising. Not only had he been nowhere near the sharp end of a trophy throughout his career, but there was a bit of personal relief swishing round: £30m is one heck of an albatross. To be the most expensive signing in English football history, to be the most expensive defender ever in the world, is not something easily forgotten. It sits on the shoulder nagging, the devilish sprite mocking mistakes, gnawing at self-confidence. To pop a Championship medal in his trackies after a season encumbered by all that baggage will have settled him down considerably. Now that's done, his body language seemed to be saying, at last I can get on with showing what I am really worth.

His choice of leisurewear might make Ali G look classy, but Ferdinand seems an amiable character – jokey, relaxed, unfussed. That belies a driving ambition which brought him to United in the first

Rio – he *really* wants to win

place. Harry Redknapp, the Portsmouth manager who, during his time at West Ham, nurtured Ferdinand through the ranks, says he cannot remember a player as hungry as the tall boy from Peckham. He was hungry to escape the estate where he was brought up, hungry to move on from West Ham to a trophy-winning club, desperate to get out of Leeds when it was clear he had been sold a pup. Now he is at United, he has got the trophy-winning business underway. Now he can get on with the next stage: improving his game.

Reckless as it might have been to make this analysis, at the World Cup last summer, Kieron Dyer said Ferdinand was the best player on show. Few fans will have voted for him as the best defender in the United team this season. Yet he has the potential. And while he has the will, United have the resources – including the most vital luxury of all, patience – to improve him. And while it might seem odd to spend enough to equip a medium-sized hospital on the unfinished article, look at what happens when – in the case of, say, Laurent Blanc – you sign the finished article. Ferdinand is for the future.

Last season Appearances: 45 (1). Goals: 0. Rating: 6/10.

Gary does his set piece

Gary Neville

Born: Bury, 18.2.75.
Height: 5'11". **Weight**: 12st 7lbs.
Previous clubs: Juniors.
Debut: 16.9.92 v Torpedo Moscow
(home, UEFAC) 0-0; sub for Lee Martin.
Appearances: 370 (23). **Goals**: 4.

If Gary Neville were a goalkeeper, he would have been shown the door at United after the derby. His was a horrible error that led to City's second goal: down on the touchline, he attempted to do the cynical, clever, Italian thing of talking the ball out of play even as your opponent bears down on you, breathing down your neck. But he lingered a bit too long in the act, was caught in possession and City scored. It was all the more unexpected a mistake because Neville's decision-making has been at a consistently high level throughout his career. For a man as Red-to-the-bone as Gaz, he will have known the consequences. They duly came. Months after that performance blues were still approaching him in Manchester to thank him for his generosity. Apparently they mainly do so in restaurants after they have spotted him going into the gents.

Still, he won't have worried about that as much as he worried about the immediate response to his folly within the United system. He was made the scapegoat for Maine Road failure, dropped publicly and unceremoniously for the next four games, the manager's words about those players who weren't up to it being shipped out to make way for those who are, ringing in his ears. That he came back against Liverpool was appropriate. And the message was clear: you have let down the fans in the second biggest local game of the season, don't you dare do it again in the big one. Typically of Neville, he didn't. He returned with his bustle and bristle at such full pitch he was voted the season's most hated opposition player by a Liverpool fanzine: from joke figure to hate figure, he was clearly doing something right.

The man who as much as anyone else has defined United's decade of dominance (focused, passionate and locally reared) was reckoned by Fergie still to have another five years at the top in him.

Last season Appearances: 35 (9). Goals: 1. Rating: 6.5/10.

Phil Neville

Born: Bury, 21.1.77.
Height: 5'11". **Weight**: 11st 13lbs.
Previous clubs: Juniors.
Debut: 28.1.95 v Wrexham (home, FAC) 5-2 Irwin 2, McClair, Giggs, og.
Appearances: 240 (69). **Goals**: 7.

When United faced Arsenal at Old Trafford in December, many Reds felt their stomachs occupied by a tight knot of fear at impending disaster. No Keane, Beckham, Butt or Scholes. On the bench May, Chadwick, Stewart. And in midfield, face to face with Patrick Vieira, who many consider the best midfielder in the world, Phil Neville. Arsène Wenger's smug assertion that the balance of power has shifted southwards was surely about to have a practical demonstration. Ninety minutes later the Stretford End could not stop singing about how 'Phil, Phil will tear you apart, again'. Neville minor was simply brilliant that day, first to every ball, harsh in the tackle and productive in possession: everything that was required. Vieira had looked ordinary in comparison, steam-rollered by an astonishing act of will.

Phil Neville – more than a match for Michael Owen

After that performance, you could sympathise with Phil's frustration at how the rest of his season unfolded. The Arsenal game was followed by a run of four successive victories with him in central midfield, in which eight goals were scored and none conceded. Yet as soon as the big guns were fit again, it was a case of thanks for your efforts, Phil, and see you at Moss Lane for the reserves. Demotion clearly rankled, and when Neville P was not even named on the bench for the away game against Spurs towards the end of the season, he stayed through the first half on the team bus, his pride apparently compromised beyond repair. However, come the conclusion of the league, Phil was there celebrating as enthusiastically as anyone. Which implies there was some clever man-management put into operation in the meantime, reminders that 35 starts in a season is hardly the return of a bit-part player, that these days it is a squad game and his value is immense, that anywhere else he might be in the starting eleven every week, but look who he would be lining up with.

At the time of writing Neville's future remains uncertain. For what it's worth, this guide would like to add its voice to those urging him to stay. If nothing else, we'd miss his great comedy step-over, worth the admission fee all on its own.

Last season Appearances: 35 (8). Goals: 2. Rating: 6.5/10.

John O'Shea

Born: Waterford, Ireland, 30.4.81.
Height: 6'3". **Weight:** 12st 1lb.
Previous clubs: youth system;
Bournemouth (loan), Royal
Antwerp (loan).
Debut: 13.10.99 v Aston Villa
(away WC) lost 0-3.
Appearances: 50 (18). **Goals** 0.

O'Shea – stepping up a gear

Midway through the second half of the home match against Charlton, the entire Stretford End kept up a single chant for more than ten minutes. An updating of the American civil war anthem, it went: 'When Johnny goes marching down the wing, O'Shea, O'Shea'. As United fans celebrated the title win that weekend, the main song in the pubs of Manchester was in recognition of Waterford's Mr Versatile. To hear such universal acclaim for a player who, before this season, had begun only five games in a United shirt was some assessment of the sort of season John O'Shea had at United. It was a season summed up in this statistic. In the Champions League quarter final first leg against Real Madrid, O'Shea was the only player on either side who had appeared in every previous game their club had played in the competition that season. Were it not for the untouchable Ruud van Nistelrooy, he would have been our choice of player of the year. That is how good he was.

In the last edition of the *Rough Guide* we asked a simple question of John O'Shea: when his time and chance came, would he have what was required to take advantage of it? If the implication was that he didn't, how wrong we were. And rarely can being proved wrong take on such a pleasurable hue. O'Shea was magnificent. From a fringe player he became not only central, but coveted by every other manager in the Premiership and a shoo-in for Andy Gray's team of the season on Sky. Suddenly, largely thanks to his emergence, a defence which had taken on a wobbly complexion, now looks one of the most potent in United's history, crammed with quick, lithe, infinitely skilful defenders. And what's more, they're all young.

The defining moment of his season came in an early Champions League game against Basle. Observers like Paul McGrath, who know what they are talking about, reckon his future is in the middle, but starting that game at centre back, he was caught out on a couple of early attacks. Swapped with Mikael Silvestre, he did not let what might have been construed as a public rebuke affect him, and played a blinder at left back, his pace and footwork adding a new flow and aggression to the side. After Basle, the leggy, coltish defender, wracked with indecision when he made his debut in the Worthington Cup three seasons ago, completely disappeared. In his place came a confident, aggressive, creative force, eager to attack on either flank, prepared to take opponents on, and with surprisingly nimble footwork for such a big man. What's more, he doesn't appear overawed by either occasion or reputation. Many reckon he might have a game broad enough eventually to take Roy Keane's place in central midfield, and as if to prove his versatility, he played in this position against Burnley in the Worthington Cup.

Last season Appearances: 42 (10). Goals: 0. Rating: 8/10.

Mikael Silvestre

Born: Chambrary-le-Tours, France, 9.8.77.
Height: 6'0". **Weight:** 13st 2lbs.
Previous clubs: Stade Rennais FC, Internazionale (£4m, 2.9.99).
Debut: 11.9.99 v Liverpool (away PL) 3-2 Cole, Carragher og 2.
Appearances: 174 (16). **Goals:** 3.

Silvestre – first name on the team sheet

In an era of rotation and squad play, Mikael Silvestre is as near to being a nailed-on certainty as you can get. Not only did he make more appearances than anyone else for the Reds this season, he was the only member of the first team not to start a single game on the bench.

After the Treble was secured in 1999, Sir Alex strengthened his squad by bringing in what he saw as a natural replacement for Denis Irwin. Others were not so sure. Because he was bought in rather than promoted through the ranks, it was forgotten how young Silvestre was when he first came to Manchester. As he laboured in his first season, unsure of the pace of the Premiership, up in the press box, several hardened cynics sneered that as Italian teams don't let their top talent go, he couldn't be the real thing. And the player himself – who has made all his international appearances in the middle of defence – wasn't convinced that his best position was out on the flanks. But Ferguson persevered, and got his reward. Silvestre's pace and adventure and crossing ability were never in doubt. And as his early youthful failings have been ironed out with experience, Inter's loss has increasingly looked a United steal, made all the sweeter since Sir Alex snaffled him from under Liverpool's noses, obliging Gérard Houllier to look else-where for recruits. Djimi Traore or Mikael Silvestre anyone? Yes, it is that good.

And after Ferguson finally accepted that Laurent Blanc's class could no longer compensate for a decline in physical gifts, the young Frenchman has even had his wish fulfilled, and now turns out more often in the centre than at left back. Indeed, so accom-plished has Silvestre become – his thirty-yard cross-field pass is as good as anyone's in the club, including Beckham and Veron – that when he falls from his lofty position of consistency, it shows. He was pretty woeful against Liverpool in the Worthington Cup Final, when he looked strained and indecisive. But even then his manager was reluctant to substitute him, hoping it was just the result of a muscle pull which he could run off. He didn't on that occasion: but with a player of his calibre, everyone knows there is always a next time.

Last season Appearances: 54. Goals: 1. Rating: 7.5/10.

Midfield

David Bellion

Born: Paris, France 27.11.82.
Height: 6'0". **Weight**: 11st 3lbs.
Previous clubs: Cannes,
Sunderland (fee to be decided
by tribunal, 1.7.03).
Debut: n/a.
Appearances: n/a.

Bellion: the new David on the wing

David Bellion's tortuous path to Old Trafford made David Beckham's will-he-won't-he departure for Real look speedy. Back in January, in the brief opening of the transfer window, United agreed personal terms to bring the quick, young winger down from the Stadium of Light. But Sunderland wanted more than the Reds were prepared to pay, the transfer negotiations spread well beyond the deadline, and, when he wasn't able to move, Bellion was thrown into a tailspin of depression that meant he did not turn out again for the Wearsiders again, instead returning to France to kick his heels. Sunderland's chairman Bob Murray fulminated against United for turning the player's head. United, meanwhile, bought him a house in Hale.

So will he prove worth all the fuss of the emotional tug-of-war? Well, Bellion is not so much quick as electric, he is hugely rated in France, and – so the theory goes – he has enough natural skill and flair to make everyone (well, everyone who watches for the football) to forget David Beckham ever played on United's right wing. True, he barely scored for Sunderland. But then, he was playing in the worst team in Premiership history. How he fares in the best is what counts.

Last season Appearances: n/a.

Nicky Butt – just give him the ball

Nicky Butt

Born: Manchester, 21.1.75.
Height: 5'10". **Weight:** 11st 5lbs.
Previous clubs: Juniors.
Debut: 21.11.92 v Oldham (home PL) 3-0 McClair, Hughes, og; sub for Paul Ince.
Appearances: 285 (68). **Goals:** 24.

During the last World Cup, Pele made the unexpected comment that Nicky Butt was his player of the tournament's first stage. Cue sniggers and sneers and the sound of mockery. Nicky Butt the best player in Japorea? Had Pele lost all touch with sanity? United fans, though, have known Nicky Butt's value for years: just because his face doesn't sell papers doesn't mean he can't play. He came back from the tournament, full of self-confidence, ready to take the place Alex Ferguson has always wanted him to seize – as first choice in the centre of midfield. And with his captain's hip problems, United needed him to do just that, his tackling and ball-retaining abilities vital. But then injury intervened. He too had suffered from his summer and needed surgery. It was as cruel to his personal development as it was to United's early season progress.

When Butt came back into the team, the sigh of relief was audible. Part of the reason why United conceded fewer goals than anyone else in the Premiership is the sort of selfless protecting and covering work he does in midfield: nobody spots that he is there, but he is sorely missed when he isn't. As a hairline retreating more rapidly than an Iraqi troop movement testifies, Butt is no longer a bright young prospect. He deserves his chance at the top table. But the kind of injury that comes with the territory of forever being prepared to put your body on the line for the team may well prevent him ever getting it.

Last season Appearances: 22 (7). Goals: 0. Rating: 6.5/10.

Luke Chadwick

Born: Cambridge, 18.11.80.
Height: 5'8". Weight: 10st 9lbs.
Previous clubs: Juniors.
Debut: 13.10.99 v Aston Villa (away WC) 0-3.
Appearances: 18 (21). Goals: 2.

There is nothing wrong with this boy's levels of optimism. When he was dispatched to Reading for the best part of a season's loan, he explained that he was looking forward to it. It might well kick-start his career, he thought. After all Matthew Upson had been called into the England side shortly after going to the Madjeski on loan. Chadwick in the England team? Optimistic indeed. In the end he didn't even make the Reading starting line-up for the play-off semifinal defeat by Wolves.

But still, the winger pillo-ried for his idiosyncratic face left us with one great memory of his time at Reading. After one of the games he played there, Alan Pardew, Reading's energetic manager, invit-ed the press into the dressing room to inter-view the players immedi-ately after the final whis-tle. As he sat there watch-ing the fourth estate move through, Chadwick shook his head and offered up this comment: 'it wouldn't happen at

Chadwick – looking beyond Old Trafford?

Old Trafford.' Unfortunately for him, brought up in the ways of Sir Alex, it looks as if he had better get used to how other managers operate. He doesn't look the obvious replacement for Goldenballs and is joining Burnley on loan for the season ahead.

Last season Appearances: 1 (4); goals: 0. Rating: n/a

Eric Djemba Djemba

Born: Douala, Cameroon, 4.5.81.
Height: 5'8". Weight: 11st 10lbs.
Previous clubs: Breweries of Cameroon, Nantes (£3.5–4.2m, 4.7.03).
Debut: n/a.
Appearances: n/a.

Djemba Djemba is precisely what the United squad need right now. The manager has taken a look at his core midfield options and realised that they are all ageing at the same time. A couple of years down the line, Keane, Scholes, Giggs, Veron and Butt will all simultaneously be passing their Premiership best – as would Beckham, had he stayed. Not wanting to wait until it is too late to rebuild, what Ferguson required was a young midfield prospect. Of the youth squad, only Darren Fletcher currently looks the business. But Cameroon's Djemba Djemba is a player who gets mentioned in the same breath as Roy Keane: a combative midfielder who the manager much admired when United played Nantes in the Champions League a couple of seasons ago.

Djemba Djemba – looks like he gets stuck in

Djemba Djemba came to Nantes as a 15-year-old, having been spotted, like many Francophone Africans, playing on rough local pitches by French club scouts. He went initally for a trial with Bordeaux, but Nantes slipped in, signed him and put him in their academy. Coached in France through his teenage years, he is in essence, a French footballer, though, unlike some of his compatriots, he chose to ignore the call of the cockerel and to play for his homeland in international competition. After debuting in the 2001 African Nations Cup, he was selected in the Indomitable Lions' squad for Japorea, though to his disappointment he didn't get a game out there.

Significantly, Djemba Djemba's footballing hero is Claude Makelele. Which says a lot: he has many of the unsung Madrid enforcer's physical attributes. Snappy in the tackle, endlessly competitive, he has real stamina. 'Everything I have achieved is by the sweat of my brow,' he claims, and watching him play you can only agree. As 19 yellow cards and two reds in 55 appearances for Nantes also attest, this is, too, a player of some commitment. Alongside Keane or Butt he will provide a formidable holding barrier, ideal in the new 4-2-3-1 formation Fergie is planning for the new season. The new Patrick Vieira? Only time will tell.

Last season Appearances: n/a.

Darren Fletcher

Born: Edinburgh, Scotland, 1.2.84.
Height: 5'11". **Weight**: 13st 0lbs.
Previous clubs: Juniors.
Debut: 12.3.03 v FC Basle (home CL) 1-1 (G Neville).
Appearances: 2. **Goals**: 0.

Darren Fletcher made two appearances for United last season, both in the Champions League. It is not a bad start to a player's career to have turned out in Europe before he has even seen action in the Worthington Cup, and testament to the potential of this graceful midfield schemer. A further compliment was paid to the 19-year-old most highly regarded in the youth system when he was replaced in the game against Basle by David Beckham. It was an appropriate switch. 'Darren reminds me of a young David Beckham,' the manager said after the game. 'He's slightly different as a player but still fantastic to have around. He's intelligent, works hard and has an engine comparable to Becks.'

Ferguson knows all about Fletcher. While other managers might prefer to buy ready-made from the continent, Fergie was putting in the hours to sell United to the player even when he was as young as 11.

Chased by Liverpool and Newcastle, the young Scotsman was hooked on the Reds after he was invited to Fergie Towers and given a cup of tea and a game of snooker. That's what you call investment in the future, and in Fletcher's case it could be worth millions.

Last season
Appearances: 2 (0).
Goals: 0. Rating n/a.

Fletcher – the boy most likely ...

Quinton Fortune

Born: Cape Town, South Africa, 21.5.77.
Height: 5'10". Weight: 11st 7lbs.
Previous clubs: Tottenham Hotspur, RCD Mallorca, Club Atlético de Madrid (£1.6m 1.8.99).
Debut: 30.8.99 v Newcastle (home PL) 5-1 Cole 4, Giggs.
Appearances: 34 (24). Goals: 7.

It must be a bit like being stuck in your own version of the film *Groundhog Day* for Quinton Fortune. South Africa's biggest footballing celebrity had a season that followed exactly the same pattern as the previous year: he started it recovering from injury, he was drafted into the first team to cover for lengthy absences of more elevated personnel, he performs creditably, full of running and charging and aggression, then he gets injured and rules himself out for most of the rest of the year, returning only for a brief cameo when the business of the season is all but concluded.

Intriguingly this time, Fortune's manager went out of his way to praise him even as the injury struck. In the press conference before the Arsenal game at Old Trafford, Fergie spent ten minutes briefing journalists on what a good player Fortune is, how his performance against Liverpool the previous week had been vital, how he was coming at last to the sort of fruition that had persuaded Terry Venables to bring him over to Spurs as a 14-year-old, boasting that he had landed the finest schoolboy in Africa. Ferguson knew at the time of his briefing that the player had fractured his leg in training and stood not a hope of playing against Arsenal and when this was discovered many of the papers used it as evidence of another Fergie mind-game scam, deliberately misleading his rival. But maybe there was something else at work: a desire to tell the player how much he rated him, in the hope it might help boost his morale during the recovery. It might have been enough to persuade the personable Fortune to stay on, for in May 2003 he signing a new extended contract that will keep him at the club until he's 30. Sir Alex keep saying how the South African is constantly improving, all Fortune needs is a change in er, fortune, and more first team chances.

Fortune – unlucky

Last season

Appearances: 8 (8).

Goals: 0. Rating: 5.5/10

Ryan Giggs

Born: Cardiff, Wales, 29.11.73.
Height: 5'11". **Weight:** 10st 12lbs.
Previous clubs: Juniors.
Debut: 2.3.91 v Everton (home, D1) 0-2; sub for Denis Irwin.
Appearances: 488 (56). **Goals:** 113.

The most decorated player in United history now has eight Champion-ship medals: only Phil Neal and Alan Hansen of the 1980s-dominating Liverpool side can match that haul in English football history. It must be some sizable display cabinet at his Lancashire mansion (or more likely, given his unswerving loyalty towards her, at his mum's place in Worsely). The last of those gongs, he says, is the one that gave him the most pleasure – and with good cause. In many ways, the arc of Giggs's season reflected that of the club as a whole. At the start he misfired, in the middle he was so out of sorts everyone was questioning whether the force was not now spent. Then from early spring came a building swell right back to top form, culminating in some of the most blistering performances seen for years, full of jinking, juggling, dummying mischief. No wonder he was smiling: as a way to prove your legion of doubters wrong, nothing could have been more satisfying.

There is a theory that Giggs's complicated private life (women, rather than drink have always been his Best-like Achilles' heel) was undermining his consistency for much of the autumn. And indeed he did start to play like a man relaxed once his first child had been born in the spring. Even so, never mind the press during his alarm-ing dip in form, the intemperate abuse he received from sections of United support (and by no means a tiny minority) was completely out of order. The many who said United could do without him and the sooner he moved on to an Italian club the better, simply do not know their football.

Sure, he made possibly the worst howler seen at Old Trafford in the Ferguson era when he missed an open goal against Arsenal in the Cup (having gone round everyone, it must be said). But ultimately

Giggs – at his best on the European stage

Giggs remains the man who makes the difference. No-one moves with the ball at such pace. No-one terrifies defenders like he does. No-one (certainly not English born) has a left foot as sweet as his. And few can match his versatility. It may have taken the players time to work it out, but Ferguson's 4-4-1-1 formation has transformed the way the team performs. Scholes, Solskjaer and Giggs have been given the opportunity to move all over the front line, leaving defenders completely at a loss. Giggs has loved this fluidity, switching, roaming, confusing. And never forgetting to run with the ball. How much longer he can do this remains to be seen. But when you are as committed a Red as Giggs and share your record with two Liverpool heroes, there will be no lack of motivation in looking for that ninth medal to add to his collection.

Last season Appearances: 52 (7). Goals: 14. Rating: 7/10.

In the money – United and the Rich List

For a club with a historical reputation for being parsimonious, it's little wonder some struggling Red legends envy the wages United pay out today. Back in the 1960s, household names had to beg for a quid a week rise out of Matt Busby; now members of the first team squad deal only in millions. The club have the highest wage bill in the Premiership (but are so rich that wages make up the lowest wage/revenue ratio of any outfit in any division) and when Madrid were first linked with **David Beckham**, it wasn't just the sharpest journalists who worked out that he is already paid more than Zidane or any other Globetrotter. Beckham earned £5m a year from his foot-

"That's two grand a minute, right?"

ball at Old Trafford, and made as much again from commercial endorsements. With £10 million a year topping up the current account, the Beckhams are thought to be worth £50m all in, and some marketing specialists have valued his brand at £200m.

Whilst the departing Beckham is the wealthiest young British sportsman, eight of his old United team mates made the *Sunday Times Young Rich List*. **Ryan Giggs** is reported to be worth £14m, and thanks to £4m signing on fees **Rio Ferdinand** and **Juan Veron** are probably worth £10m. **Nicky Butt**, **Gary Neville**, **Paul Scholes** and **Ole Gunnar Solskjaer** should have a good £6m, and **Ruud Van Nistelrooy**'s £3m a year wages mean that he can afford to pay the window cleaner to keep the view from his penthouse in Bowdon spotless. **Phil Neville**, meanwhile, gets by with a £4m fortune. You wonder how the poor lamb copes. Only six other footballers get a mention in the *Sunday Times* list, incidentally: Owen, Campbell, Fowler, Sutton, Heskey and Vieira. Though Wayne Rooney will not be going short of lollipops for long. **Roy Keane**, who didn't make the list on account of being over 30 and not being worth the £30m required to get a mention in the big boys' league, has an estimated £12m at his disposal.

But richer than all of his charges is **Sir Alex Ferguson**, with an estimated £30m fortune. Ferguson was a new entry in the 2003 *Rich List*, straight in at joint number 976 alongside Annie Lennox, Pete Townshend and Carl Fogarty – his income boosted by royalties from his bestselling autobiography, plus the phenomenal success of the racehorse Rock of Gibraltar, of which he is registered as owning half. Who would have thought it of a recalcitrant former shop steward from Govan?

Roy Keane

Born: Cork, Ireland, 10.8.71.
Height: 5'11". **Weight:** 12st 3lbs.
Previous clubs: Cobh Ramblers, Nottingham Forest (£3.75m, 19.7.93).
Debut: 7.8.93 v Arsenal (Wembley, CS) 1-1 Hughes.
Appearances: 379 (14). **Goals:** 46.

'The thought of being the next United manager would be fantastic. I'm hoping to take my coaching badges in the next year or two — but I think the current manager will be here for a few more years yet.'

Typical Keano, that. No false modesty, no beating about the bush, no wait-and-sees. Just a straight answer to a straight question. And the idea that has been floating around for a couple of years now appears to be solidifying in his mind. He would love to be the next United manager. And how the fans would love it if he were. How the press would, too. Keane means controversy. Because he speaks so straight, he makes himself hostage to a thousand headlines. No Shearer-style blandness for him, he goes straight for it, and what is so great about him, he never seems to baulk at the consequences, never seems to tone things down next time. One Irish Red suggested to the authors of this guide that after the World Cup controversy and the publication of his book last summer, Keane had divided his homeland like no other issue. To which the only response was: come on – more that the civil war, more than divorce, more than paedophile clergy, more than abortion, more than the euro? Seriously, came the reply: Keane was black and white – you were either for him or against him, there was no middle ground and the gap between the two camps was filled with bile.

It did no harm to sales of his autobiography, which shifted more copies on the island than any book except The Bible – it was a top seller across the water too. And talking of the book, in answer to all those cheap and easy gags that were prevalent at the time about Keano never actually getting round to reading his own book, it is worth pointing out that in fact he read it intently, making seventeen changes to Eamon Dunphy's first draft. Never once, though, did he

– or anyone else who read it in the early stages for that matter – think the Alf Inge Haaland stuff was remotely controversial.

In the meantime, before he becomes manager, full-time debating subject or merely spends his time walking what must be the fittest dog in Britain, there is life left in Keane the player. Which is more than many thought after he returned in early spring from an operation to correct a hip problem so severe he will probably need replacement surgery by the time he is 40. As he came back, there was

Keano – don't write him off

almost universal agreement in the press that he was spent as a force. He could no longer run as he did, which compromised the dynamism that is at the very core of his game. His only hope, was the consensus, was a retreat into the back four, where he could use his wonderful powers of reading the game and direct younger legs such as those belonging to O'Shea and Brown to do his running for him.

But, after a slow start, he did come back. And by the end of the season it was his bite and presence in midfield that eased the championship trophy back to its proper destination. Anyone who saw him run that decisive game at Highbury would have seen there was life in the old boy yet. 'As a player and as a competitor, the nearest thing I've seen in my lifetime to Duncan Edwards,' Bobby Charlton said of Keane the day after he had snapped and sniped at the Gooners' heels. Praise indeed.

Last season Appearances: 30 (2). Goals: 0. Rating: 7/10.

Kieran Richardson

Born: Greenwich, 21.10.84.
Height: 5'9". **Weight:** 10st6lbs.
Debut: 23.10.02 Olympiakos Piraeus (away CL) 3-2 (Blanc, Veron, Scholes); sub for Juan Veron.
Appearances: 3 (6). **Goals:** 1.

The future looks bright for Kieran Richardson

Richardson won the FA Youth Cup and made his first team debut in the same year: not a bad double for a player not yet 19. Not bad either to make that debut in the Champions League, substituting for Juan Veron, and to bag his first goal at the start of the Worthington's Cup run against Leicester. Plucked from the West Ham academy at 15, he is quick, skilful and has a hunger for goals. He is also cocksure, arrogant and walks with a gangster swagger. A bit like Paul Ince, then. The next couple of years when he comes increasingly under the control of Fergie could make for an interesting collision.

Last season Appearances: 3 (6). Goals: 1. Rating: n/a.

Paul Scholes

Born: Salford, 16.11.74.
Height: 5'7". **Weight:** 11st 9lbs.
Previous clubs: Juniors.
Debut: 21.9.94 Port Vale (away, LC) 2-1 Scholes 2.
Appearances: 297 (76). **Goals:** 101.

2002-03 was Paul Scholes's season. For a physically small player, he was a giant, hugely important to United. To score twenty goals might be considered sufficient contribution on its own to warrant the torrent of praise that came his way. But that tells only a fraction of the story.

The odd way the PFA members vote for their Player of the Season as early as February ensures that a late surge from a team such as the one United enjoyed this year goes completely unrecorded. Though Red players have benefited from this hasty voting system in the past (Teddy Sheringham, for instance, won the double playing award in 2001), last year it went against United as the professionals came to the preposterous conclusion that the best Premiership eleven of the season did not include Ruud van Nistelrooy. In fact there was only one Red in their premature choice: Scholes. Scholes always scores well with his peers – at Carrington he is rated as the best player at

Scholes – the man the Real Madrid players wanted, so they say

the club by many, and it was said that a straw poll in the Madrid dressing room suggested that he rather than Beckham should have been the target. One of the few United players who did not suffer a World Cup hangover (he was never quite at the party for England in Japan), he was brilliant all year, drifting into the box time unseen by opposing defenders to deliver a shot of awesome accuracy and power.

But Scholes is much more than just a goal-scorer. His range of passing, his ease of beating men in midfield, his ability to do virtually anything except tackle marks him out as the (almost) complete midfielder. The only mistake he made all season, when he gave the ball away on the edge area in Madrid, and which led directly to a Real goal, might have led less centred players to falter. But Scholes picked himself up and got on with the job of making amends by playing better and better as the season progressed. And what is so distinguished about him is that he does it all with such modesty and lack of noise. Not for him photo opportunities or public relations.

He admitted in a rare interview that he only has one commercial deal (with Nike). All that matters to him, he says, is playing football and winning. That is the kind of talk fans want to hear.

Last season Appearances: 46 (6). Goals: 20. Rating: 8.5/10.

Juan Sebastian Veron

Born: Buenos Aires, Argentina, 9.3.75.
Height: 6'3". Weight: 11st 13lbs.
Previous clubs: Estudiantes de la Plata; Boca Juniors; Sampdoria; Parma; Lazio (£28m, July 01).
Debut: 19.8.01 v Fulham (home PL) won 3-2 (Van Nistelrooy 2, Beckham).
Appearances: 75 (6). goals: 11.

The Veron conundrum continues. Last season the Argentinian played in two thirds of United's games, not a bad return, and he topped our own 'Man of the Match' table, exerting the prime influence over seven games. Some of his passing in those games bordered on the sublime and those who train with him claim that they are lucky to get the ball off him, so skilful is Veron. Yet he dropped away as the season progressed, unlucky with injury, sure, but when the final push towards the title came, when the manager selected those he considered constituted the team most likely to close the deal, did anyone really notice when Veron wasn't included? Did anyone think that he might have been more influential than Keane, Scholes or Butt? Or indeed Beckham, who gave way to him, badly lacking match fitness, in the big game at home to Real.

The whole point about Veron is that he was bought to make a difference in Europe. His was to be the extra dimension that would turn United from perpetual quarter-finalists into serial challengers. And at times in Europe this year he was very good indeed. Given the additional space to work things, he was in his element. Yet, in that Real Madrid game, his subtlety turned out to be significantly less effective in sixty minutes than the harem-scarem, up-and-at-em

Veron needs to run the show, but can he do that at United?

Beckham was in the half an hour on the pitch as his replacement.

Watching Veron play for Argentina in the World Cup there was a clue to his problem. In the game against Nigeria, there was one point where he took a free kick which he drifted in to the opposition area and was headed clear behind the goal line. He jogged over to take the resulting corner. When that too was cleared for a throw-in, guess who insisted on taking that? In between he shouted at his team maters, issued instructions, never stopped communicating. At United, with Beckham taking all the set pieces, with Keane in charge verbally, in any case slightly cowed by his lack of English, his role is reduced. He can't even get his hands on the throw-ins if Gary Neville is playing. The way he prefers to play, it is asking a lot of him to start dominating the opposition if he can't even dominate his own team.

Even so, it would be wrong, as Ferguson's critics do, to imply that Veron has no real purpose at United. Last season the team played more games than ever before. To have a player of his calibre in the squad, there to put in almost an entire Premiership's-worth of appearances, is of incredible value.

Even at £27m, though, his future United career is not assured, and as this book went to press, rumours of his impending sale to Chelsea were flying around, as Ronaldinho was supposed to replace him. If, as seems likely, that deal fails to come off, then Seba will have a major point to prove in the campaign ahead. Which may just prove good news both for the player and for the Reds.

Last season Appearances: 37 (4). Goals 6. Rating this season: 6.5/10.

Forwards

Diego Forlan

Born: Montevideo, Uruguay, 19.5.79.
Height: 5'8". Weight: 11st 11lbs.
Previous clubs: Independiente (£6m, 22.1.02).
Debut: 29.01.02 v Bolton Wanderers (Away PL) 4-0 Solskjaer 3, Van Nistelrooy. Sub for Ole Gunnar Solskjaer.
Appearances: 23 (39). Goals: 9.

When United were awarded a penalty against Maccabi Haifa in the Champions League home tie and Beckham declined the chance to take it, he once again demonstrated his mastery of PR. He handed the ball instead to Diego Forlan, and the cheer from the resultant conversion could have been heard in Leeds. There was, though, a degree of self-consciousness about the applause. Every fan there knew that for a striker, the young Uruguayan was rapidly becoming defined by his lack of goals, and there was a wry 'I was there' element to the cheering when he finally broke his duck. But no-one could deny that Forlan deserved his moment: he had worked tirelessly for breaks which just didn't seem to come his way. And after

Forlan – the captain's got his ear

that penalty, when he started to score proper goals that mattered, the note of indulgence began to disappear from the cheering as his contributions proved decisive against Villa and Southampton.

The match, though, that really changed attitudes was the one away against Liverpool. True, Jerzy Dudek was largely responsible for Forlan's elevation to folklore. And it helped that his origins had a neat rhyming symmetry. But the gusto with which 'He came from Uruguay/He made the Scousers cry' rang out in the United section at every game thereafter suggests that Forlan stepped over a vital mark at Anfield. He was no longer a cult because he couldn't score. He was the cult who did.

After that game, Forlan had a period where he couldn't stop putting the ball in the net. Maybe not quite at Van Nistelrooy's rates of return, but a lot better than, say, Dwight Yorke was managing at Blackburn. In the Dutchman's absence, he led the line with bravery and skill. Plus amazing work-rate: this is a forward who never stops running, never stops trying. Inevitably, when either Van Nistelrooy or Solskjaer are available, Forlan is going to find himself on the bench. Some might say he is unlucky to be behind two such players, unlucky that their presence means he will never be given an extended run in the side. But Forlan is 24, time is on his side. Having the chance to watch and learn from the bench the manner in which two masters set about their work, will help him add to his game. Give him the extra edge of subtlety to go with his coltish enthusiasm. If he develops as much as he has this season, we could be in at the start of something big.

Last season Appearances: 15 (30). **Goals:** 9. **Rating** 6/10.

Ole Gunnar Solskjaer

Born: Kristiansund, Norway, 26.2.73.
Height: 5'10". **Weight**: 11st 6lbs.
Previous clubs: Clausenengen FK, Molde (£1.5m, 29.7.96).
Debut: 25.8.96 v Blackburn (home, PL) 2-2 Cruyff, Solskjaer; sub for David May.
Appearances: 190 (121). **Goals:** 114.

Of the many David Beckham discussion points this season, the one which was the most bizarrely wrong-headed came in the aftermath of the home leg of the Champions League quarter final against Real Madrid. Steven Howard in *The Sun* reckoned that the demotion of Beckham to the bench had cost United the tie. Yet Alex Ferguson surely spoke for every match-going Red when he insisted that, whatever Beckham's qualities, it would have been impossible to select him ahead of Ole Gunnar Solskjaer, whose form in what had initially been an emergency role on the right side of midfield, had been so compelling. Critics might have scoffed at the idea, but those who had seen knew he was right. This is how good Solskjaer was this season: he was good enough to keep England's captain out of the side.

Look! Isn't that Becks on the bench?

Solskjaer's emergence as an advanced midfield player may have come about because of the injury crisis which denuded the squad in the winter. Ferguson may have anticipated only that the Norwegian's selfless attitude and work ethic would apply a serviceable bit of sticking plaster to the crisis. What he cannot have anticipated is the way in which the Gunnar's movement across the wings, his intelligence and his eye for goal would bring a new fluidity to the team. Watching the Reds with Giggs, Scholes and Solskjaer all swapping positions and roles at will, must give opposition coaches nightmares. Trying to plot a strategy to contain their movement is practically impossible: man mark and your defence will be pulled all over the place; mark zonally and huge gaps will open up for one or other of them to run into.

The way the three of them have supported Van Nistelrooy in the goal-scoring chart has enabled Ferguson to get away with being one striker light by the convention he himself established in the days of Cole, Yorke, Sheringham and Solskjaer. Indeed, if you want a testimony to the Norwegian, look at that list of names from 1999. Who would have bet that four years on he would be the only surviving member of the quartet at Old Trafford. But then who would have wanted it any other way? This is a very special player.

Last season Appearances: 40 (17); goals: 15. Rating: 8/10

Ruud van Nistelrooy

Born: Oss, Holland, 1.9.76.
Height: 6'3". Weight: 12st 13lbs.
Previous clubs: Den Bosch, Heerenveen, PSV Eindhoven (£19m 1.7.01).
Debut: 12.8.02 v Liverpool (Cardiff, CS) 1-2 Van Nistelrooy.
Appearances: 94 (7). Goals: 80.

There is a law in rock music called the difficult second album. It rules that after an explosive debut offering, artists find it excruciatingly hard to come up with a follow-up. The classic proof of the law is the Stone Roses, who spent longer than the Second World War labouring over their second album, only to be so disappointed by the result that they split up as soon as it was released. Ruud van Nistelrooy, it was reckoned by many, would suffer the footballing equivalent last term at Old Trafford. How could he follow a year in which he was top scorer in the Premiership, top scorer in the Champions League and PFA player of the season except with anti-climax? And it wasn't just media sneerers who were certain the Dutchman was heading for a fall. The otherwise admirable Sam Allardyce was blinded sufficiently by victory, after Bolton won at Old Trafford in September, to claim

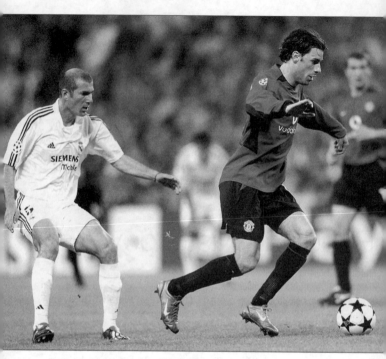

The two greatest players in Europe? Zidane watches Ruud

that Premiership defenders had got the measure of Van Nistelrooy, that this season he would struggle.

As Allardyce would cheerfully agree, if last season was a struggle for the player, then heaven knows what easy looks like. Records should normally speak for themselves, and Van Nistelrooy broke plenty of them this year: at a goal in every one and a quarter appearances, he is the most prolific Red ever; he scored the most goals by one player in a Champions League season; he scored in the last ten successive games of the season. But that barely does justice to him as a player. Watching him in action, the hunger he shows for goals, the work he puts in to get them, the joy he has from scoring them, is to realise that it is possible to become addicted to finishing. Van Nistelrooy simply can't get enough of scoring. He has admitted he is making up for lost time, compensating for those two seasons he lost to injury before his move to the Reds. He has admitted, also, that he feels an obligation to United and their manager who stood by him during that time. Most objective observers – and the manager himself – would reply that he long ago paid off any debt both emotional and financial – never in football history has a transfer fee as huge as his so quickly come to look a bargain.

Whatever drives him on, those who saw Van Nistelrooy in the flesh last season knew they had seen something unique. He may not have Eric's subtlety and intelligence, he may not have Denis's devilish streak, he may not be as smooth and athletic as Sir Bobby, but few can deny he is shaping up to be the greatest striker ever to wear a Red shirt. In a season that was characterised by incredible collective resolve, it might seem odd to single one player out for special praise, but if Ruud van Nistelrooy wasn't United's player of the 2002-03 season, then Sir Alex Ferguson is actually Kevin Keegan in disguise.

The only real question mark is over a striking partner. Solksjaer is becoming ever more the provider, playing wide, and Forlan, despite his cult status, is largely unproven. Ruud apparently wanted the Boss to bring in Patrick Kluivert to create the ultimate duo...

Last season Appearances: 50 (2). Goals: 44. Rating: 9.5/10.

On the bench

The seven players in this section following made fleeting appearances last season, most of them in the Champions League group phase games against Maccabi Haifa and Deportivo, when United had the group already sealed up. All will be pushing at the very least for a seat on the bench in the next campaign. And perhaps their ranks include the next O'Shea?

Mark Lynch

Defender   **Last season** Appearances: 1; career: 1; career goals: 0

A local-born defender from Wilmslow in the mould of Gary Neville, Lynch is quick and can play at right or centre back. Noted for his stamina, he likes to get forward and is a good crosser of the ball. With one year left on his contract, Lynch is likely to find that unless he really excels, it will be his last at Old Trafford.

Daniel Nardiello

Forward   **Last season** Appearances: 1 (2); career: 1 (1); career goals: 0

Son of the Coventry winger Donato Nardiello, this quick striker has found no difficulty making the progress from youth team to reserves, scoring a hat trick past Gary Walsh at Bradford this season. Nardiello is a classic goal poacher – his greed and skill were responsible for him being the top scorer in the reserves last season. Whether he makes the next leap remains to be seen for breaking into the Old Trafford forward from the stiffs is up there with marketing Middlesbrough as a tourist destination.

Jimmy Davis

Midfield/winger   **Last season** Appearances: 0

United's reserve player of the year, this youngster from Redditch made the bench at La Coruña. A strong right winger, he is comfortable on the ball and a mean crosser. Davis is rated by those who know – so much so that he signed a three-year contract in May. He has agreed a season-long loan at Watford for 2003-04.

Danny Pugh

Midfield   **Last season** Appearances: 2 (3); career: 2 (3); career goals: 0

A left-sided midfielder, Pugh was unlucky not to score a hat-trick on his debut in the Worthington Cup. He was there in the right place

Danny Pugh keeping exalted company – and against Juventus, too

at the right time for three cracking chances – unfortunately so was the Burnley keeper. The youngster from Cheadle Hulme has played centre back for the reserves, making use of his aerial prowess. Confident on the ball, Pugh has two years left on his contract.

Michael Stewart

Midfield   **Last season** Appearances: 1 (3); career: 7 (7) career goals; 0

Stewart had runs in the gentle wind-down at the end of the last two seasons but in the more pressing conclusion was not involved. Which probably says as much as you need to know about his long-term future at Old Trafford. Stewart is strong in the tackle and passes well. A sometime Scottish international, he irritated Sir Alex when he turned down a loan opportunity last season. At time of writing, Burnley have been making loan advances. He has two years left to run on his contract.

United's Feeder Clubs

Youth development has always been vital to United's success, and today the club cast their net far and wide through a series of five feeder clubs, or 'alliances,' as United prefers to call them.

Royal Antwerp (Belgium)

European Cup Winners' Cup finalists as recently as 1993, Royal Antwerp fell on hard times and were the first club to link up with United in 1998. The partnership, which was chosen partly because of Belgium's liberal immigration rules for non-EU workers, has proved mutually beneficial, with players like John O'Shea, Danny Higginbotham, Luke Chadwick, Kirk Hilton and Ronnie Wallwork all doing loan spells at Belgium's oldest club. Antwerp have profited from young talents in their team, and the United youngsters from experience in the Belgian first division and a different culture. Though probably the most advantageous aspect of the arrangement is that if United liked the look of a non-EU player, then he could be placed with Antwerp until he had qualified to play a Old Trafford.

IF Brommapojkarna (Sweden)

Don't try to pronounce it, just remember the name next time you play Scrabble. Brommapojkarna – based in a Stockholm suburb - are the largest football club in Scandinavia, with 180 teams (including 30 female sides) and 3,000 registered players on their books, from the age of seven upwards. Synonymous with youth development, the United relationship was forged when Bojan Djordic was purchased from the club. Old Trafford coaches have visited the club (which lists ex-Arsenal winger Anders Limpar as an employee) and young Swedish players have been on trail at Carrington.

FC Fortune (South Africa)

The link-up with Cape Town-based FC Fortune (named after local boy Quinton) was discontinued in 2001 with United not happy about the way the relationship was working out.

Oslo Øst (Norway)

Given United's incredible support in Norway (the Scandinavian supporters club has 22,000 paid-up members – most of them in Norway) and the number of players coming out of a country of just four million, it's understandable why United have a link-up with Oslo Øst (East). Øst were formed only in 2000, but boast excellent contacts throughout Norway. Like at Antwerp, United hope to use the club to polish players and with the Norwegian season being offset from the English one, it offers a chance of summer football for any Red players returning from long-term injury.

Paramatta Eagles (Australia)

Old Trafford's last Aussie, Mark Bosnich, was hardly a success, but that didn't put off United from linking up with Paramatta Eagles. Based in the west Sydney suburbs, Paramatta are United's youth development partners in Oceania. It's a good job they weren't from the neighbouring suburb – it's called Liverpool. Paramatta intend to attract the top young talent from Australia, New Zealand and Fiji between the ages of nine to sixteen into their academy. The best youngsters will be sent to Old Trafford for trials. Given that the Aussies are brilliant at most other sports, it's probably just a matter of time before they produce a harvest of talented footballers.

Shelbourne (Ireland)

United have a history of attracting fine talent from Ireland, but the flow has slowed in recent years, prompting a link-up with north Dublin club, Shelbourne. The initial relationship grew out of several pre-season friendlies between the clubs in the mid-'90s and Shelbourne aim to attract the best young Irish talent to the club. Shelbourne alert United to any players they should be monitoring, United send coaches over twice a year for specialised coaching and assessment of all Shelbourne's youngsters. The Shels benefit from higher standards all around, and United have early notice of any potential future stars.

Sporting Lisbon

In May 2003, United concluded a deal with Peter Schmeichel's (and Carlos Queiroz's) old club, Sporting Clube de Portugal SAD – aka Sporting Lisbon. The two clubs will work together on footballing matters, including youth development, scouting, training and player exchanges. United agreed a pre-season friendly at Sporting's new Jose Alvalade Stadium in August 2003 to celebrate the venture.

Walsall (England)

Despite terrace conjecture that Leeds are already a Reds feeder club, United announced a link up with an English club for the first time in summer 2003. First division Walsall have agreed a three-year co-operation agreement with United focused on a mutually supportive approach to youth development. United will provide assistance and expertise to Walsall in a number of areas including the development of an effective youth scouting network in the West Midlands area; coaching clinics, staffed by specialist United staff and attended by Walsall Centre of Excellence coaches; and the opportunity for Walsall's Centre of Excellence and Youth Scholarship players to visit the Carrington to enjoy some of its facilities, and play matches against their United counterparts. Staff from both clubs will meet on a regular basis to exchange ideas, and to ensure the support of parents.

Mads Timm: crazy name, crazy guy?

Mads Timm

Midfield/Forward

Last season Appearances: 0 (1); career: 0 (1); career goals: 0

The splendidly named Dane with a custard-coloured mop of hair is the most memorable member of the FA Youth Cup winning team. Thus far he has been limited to just eleven minutes of first team action as a substitute in Nicosia, but he's rated as having a good chance of making it by the men in padded coats at Carrington. Timm plays just behind front two, is quick and skilful and scored plenty of goals for the youth team. The only downside to his career so far has been that he keeps getting hamstring injuries.

The Back-room Boys

Sir Alex Ferguson

Manager. Joined United from Aberdeen, November 1986.

Ferguson never ceases to confound us. Each year the pattern seems to be the same, and each year we fall for it. But, as he gets older, the assumption is that, yeah we know we have been wrong before, but this time it really, really must be true. In the autumn, as United wobbled and Arsenal looked set to repeat their double of the previous year, driven on by a manager who appeared to have got everything right, the doubts in the media minds about Sir Alex's continuing powers changed to certainties. He was at last – a number of quite

Ferguson with Queiroz: now adversaries in Europe

sane and rational observers insisted – past it. He should have gone when he originally intended. Staying on will only dilute his legacy.

And, let's be honest, this was a view endorsed by many United supporters. Remember the plc AGM in November, when Ferguson turned up to answer questions from shareholders? The first speaker from the floor accused him of all sorts of things, including (and this probably annoyed a man who is at his place of work by 7.30 every morning) a dereliction of duty. United needed a clear-out, the anguished share- holder insisted, but Fergie was blind to what was required. He was wearing his nag Rock of Gibraltar's blinkers and he couldn't see that the biggest carthorse of the lot – Juan Sebastian Veron – had to be removed from the stables pronto. Fergie's initial amusement as he watched the man rant, quickly turned to thin-lipped contempt. The bloke was an idiot, he said, to much applause round the room. But at the time there were plenty who agreed with the dissident, even as he was escorted from the Old Trafford suite where the meeting was being held.

We should never have doubted. We have been here before, questioning the manager, only to be proven wrong every time. This time, he probably enjoyed dishing out the familiar lesson more than most. Because, as he took his list of managerial achievements to a surely now unassailable career record of 33 major trophies, he was not just proving his point to that doubter at the AGM. There was a more serious misapprehension that needed correction: the one which stated that Fergie's style of management was now obsolete, blown away by the cosmopolitan sophistication of men like Arsène Wenger and Sven Goran Eriksson. It irks Fergie, this comparison. Wenger is alleged to be the great professorial figure, but alongside Fergie's wide interests in horses, cookery, politics, music, fine wine and movies, the Frenchman looks obsessive and nerdish, a man whose pastimes do not extend beyond studying videos of German second division matches, an anorak who admits the only thing he has ever got out of six years living in London is a familiarity with the road between his house, Highbury and the Arsenal training ground. As for Sven, well, Fergie has rather more to him than an attraction to former weathergirls.

Alex makes an inspired substitution

The way in which Ferguson engineered the championship win this time around proved that he is still the master. While Wenger's classy-looking machine spluttered and choked to a halt, Fergie had his oiled to perfection, smoothly easing past in the last furlong. No wonder he regarded it as the most satisfying of the eight he has won at Old Trafford. Suddenly management gurus will be making room in their manuals for chapters on the vital motivational role of kicking boots about in the changing room.

His success this year has clearly rejuvenated the man. He has long looked north to Bobby Robson at Newcastle for a chronological guideline as to when he should pack it in. And since Sir Bob at 70 shows no sign of slowing down, Fergie, at eight years his junior, sees absolutely no reason even to think of doing so. And there is still the European Cup to be won again. This could go on for some time yet. So we might as well all get used to being proved wrong yet again.

And that goes for the Becks saga, too.

Mike Phelan

First team coach. Joined from Norwich City, July 1999. Played for the club 1989-94. **Appearances**: 126 (19). **Goals**: 3.

While it is impossible to imagine that a modest journeyman mid-fielder could play over 100 games for United these days, Phelan did precisely that in the pre-world domination days of the Fergie years. In that time he picked up FA Cup, Cup Winners Cup and League Championship medals, so few could question he was right to swap leading man status with Norwich for a bit part at Old Trafford – particularly given his elevation to assistant manager in the wake of Carloz Queiroz. His ever widening central parting and slightly-too-short shorts have been a fixture on the United bench for the past four years. And by all accounts, he is a very popular presence among the players at Carrington. Which mirrors his time in the dressing room, when he was renowned for leading his team mates on lengthy walks round the sights of towns they were visiting on European engagements. Something he might be up for reviving, now that Goldenballs is no longer in the tour-groups.

The bench: Swire, Ferguson and Phelan

Fergie's coaches: how they have performed

How crucial is the loss of Carlos Queiroz to Real Madrid? It's too early to tell, of course, but the statistics below (which tot up *all league games* under the five Ferguson assistants) show an impressive consistency in United's performances, with **McClaren** edging it on points from **Queiroz**. That said, Ferguson was generous last season in his praise not only of Queiroz but also first team coach, **Mike Phelan**, who has for the present taken on assistant manager duties.

Archie Knox (Nov 1986 to April 1991)
P 177   **W** 75   **D** 53   **L** 49   **Points won 52.35%**

Brian Kidd (May 1991 to Dec 1999)
P 296   **W** 175   **D** 79   **L** 42   **Points won 68.01%**

Steve McClaren (Dec 1998 to May 2001)
P 98   **W** 66   **D** 22   **L** 10   **Win rate 74.32%**

Jim Ryan (Aug 2001 to May 2002)
P 38   **W** 24   **D** 4   **L** 9   **Win rate 66.66%**

Carlos Queiroz (Aug 2002 to May 2003)
P 38   **W** 25   **D** 8   **L** 5   **Win rate 72.80%**

Tony Coton

Goalkeeping coach. Joined from Sunderland, August 1998.

Coton began his career at Birmingham City in the 1990s, where he was a leading member of a gang of players notorious for their hell-raising off-field behaviour. As close as England's third city could ever come to the rat pack, this group, including Mark Dennis and Robert Hopkins, made United's drinking team of the same time look modest teetotallers. Coton – and his liver -

Tony Coton, with Ferguson and Jim Ryan

survived his time there, and he went on to a distinguished career with Sunderland and City. He was even, briefly, on United's books, at Old Trafford on loan as cover for Peter Schmeichel, though he never got a run-out in the first team. Despite his past, these days he is about as likely to be discovered disorderly in a Manchester bar as Laurent Blanc is to win the Olympic 100m final. He spends his time instead wrestling with the various language difficulties in United's multinational pool of keepers. And that's just when he tries to penetrate Roy Carroll's accent.

Ricky Sbragia

Reserve team manager. Joined from Sunderland, November 2002

Despite the name, when Big Ricky talks he sounds about as continental as Bill Connelly. A Scotsman of Italian descent, he arrived from Sunderland midway through last season with a reputation honed after eight years working his way up through the coaching staff on Wearside. Not particularly distinguished as a player, he first entered United fans' radar as manager at York City, where he sold Jonathan Greening and Nick Culkin to Sir Alex.

The reserves are the most frustrating team to coach in the club: essentially there is no squad, players drift in and out, dropping down from the first team to recover fitness or form, and usually resenting the outing. Holes are plugged with juniors looking for a bit of experience. It means Sbragia is unable to plan from one week to the next, unsure who he will have available. Even so, next year with a full season in control, he will want to improve his results: mid-table in the reserve league isn't good enough.

Jim Ryan

Director of youth football. Joined from Luton Town, July 1990
Played for club 1965-70. Appearances 24 (3). Goals: 4.

If Jimmy Ryan was disappointed in being moved sideways after an unsuccessful year as assistant manager, he didn't show it. A long-time confidant of Sir Alex, the former Busby babe knew that he had only been there as a stop-gap anyhow. And he was also aware of the huge responsibility he was given in trying to put the United youth conveyor belt back together after the spluttering performance it had given over the past five years. If winning the FA Youth Cup and bringing over the man responsible for turning the French into world beaters – the fruits of his first year in charge – are just the start, then Ryan could go down in United legend. After all, as they have known at Old Trafford for generations, you win everything with kids.

The man they call Choccy

Brian McClair

Under 19s manager. Joined coaching staff from Blackburn Rovers, August 2000. Played for the club 1987-98. **Appearances**: 396 (72). **Goals**: 126.

The man with the best nickname on the staff, 'Choccy' was always a Fergie favourite. So when this maths graduate decided to pursue a career in coaching, it was likely he would end up under the United umbrella. He had an ill-starred spell as Brian Kidd's assistant at Blackburn, but Fergie didn't hold that against him and invited him aboard as soon as Kiddo was sacked from Ewood. This year he fulfilled the requirement of any coach of the Under-19s at the club and won the FA Youth Cup.

In his side he has potentially the best bunch of players since the now legendary class of '92. Goalkeeper Luke Steele, a £500,000 buy from Peterborough, is progressing well and said to be excellent on crosses. The left back Lee Lawrence looks a future star, David Jones has an improbably mature playing brain for one who looks so callow, and Chris Eagles has done well despite being lumbered with the title the new David Beckham. And the side's undoubted stars, Kieran Richardson and Mads Timm (see p.170 and p.186), have already been seen in the first team.

McClair's trophy-winning youth team – David Jones holds up the cup

McClair's major bugbear this season has been railing against the FA directive that insists players in a Premiership side's academy should live within 90 minutes' drive of the club. This is a law intended to both protect young children from ridiculous travel requirements and to stop big clubs hoovering up all the best talent in the land. McClair says it will prevent United from developing youngsters like Beckham, Best and Charlton, none of whom were raised within earshot of Carrington. Somehow or other, however, he has managed to circumvent the rule. Of the eleven players who started the Youth Cup Final triumph against Middlesbrough, only three hailed from Greater Manchester. The rest came from all over the country: in Richardson's case he had upped sticks with his dad from Greenwich and moved up north the moment United showed an interest in him when he was at West Ham. At United, where there is a will there is always a way.

Francisco Filho

Under-17s manager. Joined from the French FA, August 2002.

Manchester United may have established a blueprint of their own in the development of youth football back in the early 1990s, but there is little doubt the system was spluttering by the turn of the century. Alex Ferguson was particularly alarmed at the technical deficiencies of the players he was watching come through the academy. Where once he could rely on whole platoons of replacements spinning off the conveyor belt, only John O'Shea and Wes Brown had made the step up to the first team in seven years.

Now, there is nothing wrong with the facilities – the investment there has been huge. At Carrington, United's youth enjoy the same extensive range of pitches and kit as the first team; no-one in world football has better. Unless the nation's youth had suddenly forgotten how to play the game, there is nothing wrong with the raw material, either. Thus it was the coaches who paid the penalty of not living up to the high standards expected. Out went the raft of trainers brought in when Eric Harrison retired to spend more time with the Welsh national team and Jim Ryan was put in overall charge tasked with finding the best on the planet.

He went to the most obvious starting place, the French national setup in Clairefontaine and found the man responsible for developing virtually every French star you can think of, from Thierry Henry to Mikael Silvestre. And guess what: he turned out to be Brazilian. Seventeen years Francisco Filho had worked just south of Paris. Now he is in Manchester. He didn't get off to the best of starts (the Under-17 side finished a colossal 15 points behind City as runners-up in their league), but the results over the next few years could be interesting indeed.

Rob Swire

Physiotherapist. Joined August 1998

In an interview for the United website during the course of the season, Swire revealed that the bag he carries on to the pitch with him every time a Red player goes down injured does indeed contain not much more than a damp sponge. Which, given the wide variety of odd injuries he is expected to sort out, is refreshingly down to earth: if all anyone needs after the close attentions of Alan Shearer's elbow is a quick wipe with the sponge, then it is magic indeed. Swire leads a team of nine physios at United (the number has remained constant even though Ronny Johnsen has left the club) whose role is to pamper, preen and prepare some of the priciest limbs this side of Newmarket. If you are going to pull a muscle anywhere, Old Trafford is the place to do it.

Trevor Lea

Dietician. Joined United in 1993.

Most of Trevor Lea's work is done with the juniors, trying to inculcate them into good habits (pasta, plenty of fluid, Jaffa cakes and jelly babies at half-time) rather than the bad (chips, plenty of lager, Jaffa cakes and jelly babies during the match). One of the most fundamental changes in English football since the early 1990s has been in diet. Incredible as it may seem in a profession in which the body is the most vital piece of equipment, until then players were given very little guidance and education about what fuel would get the best out of their engine. While the players of today would have a light snack of pasta and an energy drink, George Best would eat a full steak lunch an hour before matches: it was thought that red meat would help his aggression (it actually sits in the stomach undigested and lead-weight heavy). Men like Lea have almost completely changed the mindset of football. And while most players don't have quite the paranoid attention to diet of track and field athletes, such a change in attitude (particularly to alcohol) is helping to prolong many a career.

😊 STOP PRESS: UTD'S NEW SIGNING

Kleberson

Born Jose Pereira Kleberson: Urai, Brazil, 19.6.79. **Height**: 5'8". **Weight**: 10st 1lb. **Previous clubs**: Atletico Paranaense (1.8.03, £5.5m).

You wait 125 years for United to sign their first Brazilian and then suddenly two come along at once. As we go to press, it seems that United have missed out on Ronaldinho, but bagged his compatriot, Kleberson. And what a satisfying bit of business. Sir Alex may not have his Brazilian duo for samba celebrations, but in Kleberson he has landed a class player for relatively small outlay – and put one over on Leeds at the same time. In early July, Peter Reid thought he had secured Kleberson for £3m, Atletico Paranaense being possibly the only club in the world right now in even more need of cash than Leeds. The United manager, sensing that Paranaense would bite his hand off for a couple of extra million, moved in quickly. 'Hijacked' was the term used in the tabloids. 'Sharp' is the word that would spring to mind for most Reds.

So what does £5m get you these days? Well, a World Cup winner for a start. And one whose contribution to lifting the trophy should not be under-estimated. Kleberson put in a lot of the fetching and carrying work through the tournament, and was an ever-present in the campaign. It was his run and pass, for instance, that Rivaldo stepped over so gloriously to allow Ronaldo in on goal to score the second against Germany in the final.

Kleberson is that rarity among Brazilian footballers: he was still playing his club football at home while starring for his country. Indeed, of the 2002 squad only he and the goalkeeper Marcos were South America-based at the time. Mind you, Kleberson had a particular reason for not joining the exodus of over 800 of his countrymen playing football professionally abroad: his girlfriend. He had to wait until she was 16 earlier this year, so that he could marry her, before he could countenance a move. It was this unusual clause in negotiations that stopped him joining Newcastle when the Geordies moved in for him during the transfer window last January. Once he was wed, he was clearly itching to expand his horizons. 'All people yearn for new conquests,' he said, when asked about the move to United. 'I have conquered everything with Atletico. I was champion of the Brazilian state and won the World Cup while representing the colours of Atletico.' So long as his teenage bride takes to life in northwest England, and the player settles in to his footballing rhythm with the Reds, this could be the buy of the summer.

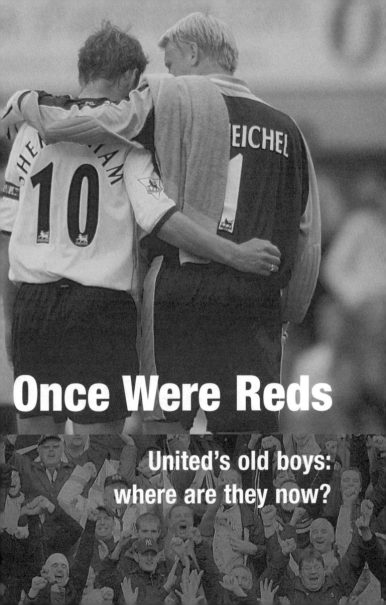

Once Were Reds

United's old boys:
where are they now?

That hair looks familiar — and he's trying to bend the ball over the wall — and isn't that Victoria in the stands? Why, it's David Beckham, having a run-out in Madrid. Yes, some one-time Reds remain easy enough to spot, but where are all the rest? Whatever happened to Mark Bosnich and Danny Higginbotham, or Peter Davenport, or Paul Parker, or that nice Paul Ince, and what the hell is Lee Sharpe up to in Iceland? If you're curious about football's twists of fate, this is the section you want.

We begin with departures last season, when David May finally said his farewells, Laurent Blanc hung up his boots, and Becks was dispatched off to the Bernabeu — followed, alas, by assistant manager Carlos Queiroz. Then we take in all the other Reds of note still playing football, from Birmingham to Bangor, or still involved in the game, managing, coaching, or talking a good game on radio and TV.

Last season's departures

David Beckham

Born: Leytonstone, 2.5.75
Height: 6'0". **Weight:** 11st 9lbs
Previous clubs: Youth Team product.
Debut: 23.9.92 v Brighton (away LC) 1-0 Wallace; sub for Andrei Kanchelskis.
Appearances: 356 (38); goals: 85

Sold to Real Madrid, 1.7.03; £21–25m (dependent on Champions League positions).

The Alice band, the boot in the eye, the fall-out with his manager, the way he was dropped to the bench for the Real Madrid game, the way he came off it to score twice, the world tour wearing white, the Barcelona presidential elections, the endless machinations involved in his on-off move to Madrid. It was almost a relief when the Real deal went public and we learnt he was going. Alex didn't want him. Player and manager hadn't spoken in two months. And so, no more (we hope) will Old Trafford witness those last-minute, perfectly bent free kicks.

Becks with Cantona, back when football was his big thing

Quite what Beckham thinks about it all – about the leaders written in serious newspapers about his image, his transfer, England's destiny – is anyone's guess. His wife – too often cast as a Lady Macbeth figure but in fact just a fluffy attention-seeker – seems to be amused by it all, frequently shown on TV thumbing through the tabloids giggling at the loopier stories. But how does a footballer retain his sanity in a world where his son has to be accompanied to nursery by two minders because of the very real threat of kidnap? And imagine what it must be like to sit down in front of the TV during one of the great historic moments of the decade, watching a bunch of excited Iraqis pulling down Saddam Hussein's statue in Baghdad and noticing that one of them was wearing a tee-shirt with your name across the shoulders. How bizarre is that? But we all saw that Iraqi wearing *Beckham* 7.

> *'We've got so many wider interests ... fashion, makeup. I mean, you think, yeah, football's great, and singing's great. But you've got to look at the bigger picture.'* Victoria Beckham

This is what Beckham's global reach has come to: like Michael Jordan (whose no 23 shirt he has adopted at Real) and Mohammed Ali he is a brand that has spread way beyond the parameters of his sport. Such is his marketing cachet, it was reported that Real Madrid were prepared to pay whatever it took to secure him. Or maybe they weren't. Or perhaps the fact they said they weren't was merely a smokescreen for their desperation. It all depended which of the thousands of newspaper articles you read about his impending move Spain-wards. Even Des Lynam joined in the fun, showing Becks mouthing the words 'there have been talks' to Gary Neville during the team huddle after the last home game of the season. Proof that he was on his way, reckoned Sir Desmond. Never mind that he might have just been responding to the Nev's question: 'any chance of the wife letting you out with the lads Tuesday night?'

Now, though, Becks has gone, taking his celebrity with him, selling shirts for someone else. In truth, it had been coming for some time. For at least three seasons, Fergie had been aware that the dressing room had wearied of the attendant nonsense of Beckham-mania. The manager was becoming alarmed that though the guy himself remains remarkably personable and decent, the baggage was beginning to poison morale. Roy Keane was the first to show the strain when he chucked the Posh/Becks wedding invite – complete with its instructions for guests to wear purple – in the bin. 'Nobody tells me what to wear to a wedding,' Keano snarled. Not a clever idea to marginalise the skipper.

Nothing matters more to Fergie than the collective will of his team, and so Beckham had to go. It might have been nice to discuss it with him first, but these days you have to book an appointment six months in advance just to ask the guy how he enjoyed his weekend. Predictably, many in the press, seizing any opportunity to slag him off, reckoned Ferguson a villain by for the ruthlessness of his action. The *Mirror* lambasted the manager in a front page editorial saying that his treatment of the England captain was a national disgrace. 'No way to treat a hero' was the headline. This from the very rag which had vilified the player after his return from France '98, kicking off its hugely irresponsible hate campaign with the headline: 'Ten heroes and one spoiled brat.'

Once they have choked back the bile produced by such hypocrisy, what United fans will want to know is this: does getting rid of Beckham represent a good bit of business for the club? Commercially, probably not. The transfer fee is good for a 28-year-old, but seems unlikely to cover the loss of merchandising. On the pitch, though, it's a more questionable matter. In our household, his departure was greeted with wailing and teeth-gnashing by the 14-year-old girl. Not because he was the best-looking player on the planet, but because she – as a regular Old Trafford attendee – reckoned he was so valuable to the team. 'Who'll take all the free kicks and corners now?' she said. Who will bend it like Beckham? In many ways, this is why he has become so celebrated: his contributions are the easily replayed, slo-mo, television moments. He is the perfect player for the edited highlights. But take him away, put Ryan Giggs on the dead ball, and will Becks really be that missed? Will results really be that affected if, without him, United can win 6-2 away at Newcastle and 4-0 at home to Liverpool?

"So, do you think they'll let me have the no 23 shirt, then?"

The season just past was typical Beckham: his free-kicks were as phenomenal as ever (the one against Everton in the last game of the season a work of art), he scored important goals from open play, and his passing was generally unimpeachable. There are few blue-arsed flies could match him for effort. But he didn't beat people running with the ball, he could be easily marginalised by a top full back (and Ashley Cole), and his tackling was sometimes alarming in its impetuousness. Some critics used the fact that he is not quite as dominant in a red shirt as he is when he plays for England as a stick to beat Sir Alex with, implying Fergie's old-fashioned methods don't get as much out of the player as Sven's sophisticated continental wiles. This misses the point that his role for United was different; for a start he had better players around him to take the strain. And the Red pattern of play required him to stick to the right flank more rigorously. Only time will tell, but Ferguson is usually proven right when he decides who is expendable, and many who have studied United closely these past couple of seasons see no reason why that record should change with this sale.

All this does not mean, however, that Beckham's contribution to the United cause in his decade with the club should be post-rationalised away as unimportant. The guy was brilliant, phenomenal. He was Red through and through and gave his all for the club. Sir Alex may well be right. But, Becks – we'll miss you – the beautiful free kicks, the whipped-in crosses, maybe even the haircuts.

LAST SEASON United appearances: 45 (7). Goals: 11. Rating: 7.5/10.

Laurent Blanc

Born: 19.11.65
Height: 6'4". **Weight:** 12st 8lbs.
Previous clubs: Montpellier, Napoli, Nimes, St Etienne, Auxerre, Barcelona, Marseille, Internazionale (free, 1.9.01).
Debut: 8.9.01 v Everton (home PL) 4-1 (Veron, Cole, Fortune, Beckham).
Appearances: 71 (4); **goals:** 4

Retired from playing at end of season.

If you wanted an explanation as to why, at the beginning of last season, Alex Ferguson decided it was worth paying a player who was clearly past it more than £2m to stay on for another term, it was there on the pitch after the Championship trophy had been lifted at Goodison. Laurent Blanc was pulled into the middle of the scrum of celebrating United players and thrown into the air like a crowd surfer at a rock concert. Then he was chaired in triumph on shoulders round the pitch, as if he were the very architect of victory.

That gave us a huge clue as to Blanc's influence. Certainly it wasn't on the pitch. If he had looked slow and apprehensive last year, this season he seemed to have ground practically to a halt. Sure, the sublime reading of the game, the timing, the ability to stick out a leg and make a crucial interception were all still there. But he was only really effective if opposing forwards ran straight at him. If he was obliged to chase or turn, he was in trouble. The moment the manager – always his most devoted admirer – realised it was finally over was at the Riverside, when Blanc was embarrassed by the Middlesbrough strikers in a performance which many thought at the time signalled the end not just of his career, but of United's Championship hopes. Yet clearly, as the reaction of his team mates showed, there was a lot more to the man.

Blanc – that's what he was paid for

On the training ground he was a huge influence: both Wes Brown and Rio Ferdinand have spoken eloquently about his ability to coax the best out of his defensive colleagues, describing playing alongside him as a masterclass in the art of stopping. Maybe Ferguson did indulge his romantic instincts by thinking that the player could defy chronology just as the manager had. Maybe he should have retired last year as he always intended to. But if his only contribution was to make Brown and John O'Shea even better players, then he was worth every penny spent.

LAST SEASON United appearances: 25 (4). Goals: 1. Rating: 5.5/10

The conductor: David May leads the European celebrations, Barcelona, 1999

David May

Born: Oldham, 26.7.70
Height: 6'4". **Weight**: 13st 2lbs.
Previous clubs: Blackburn Rovers (£1.2m, 1.8.95).
Debut: 20.8.94 v Everton (home PL). 2-0 (Hughes, McClair).
Appearances: 71 (4); goals: 4

Released at end of season.

Like a condemned prisoner on death row, May must have known one day the reprieve wouldn't come through from the governor. Every year he must have expected the chop, and every year he has clung on with superglue-like tenacity, his nails dug deep into the fabric at Carrington. Just 12 first team starts a season he has averaged over his lengthy United career, the very definition of the bit-part player. But these last four or five years, dogged by injury, much of his work has been in bringing the youngsters through the reserves, a thankless task which many bigger egos might have shunned. Besides, who can deny the grizzled old veteran his lingering testimonial at United? His celebrations at the Euro final in 1999 made him a legendary figure in Red folklore, loved for enjoying the moment with a relish few fans could have matched. Not bad for a childhood City fan.

LAST SEASON United appearances: 2 (2). Goals: 0. Rating: n/a.

Carlos Quieroz

Assistant manager. Joined United after parting company with the South African national team, June 2002. Left to manage Real Madrid, **June 2003**.

'No question, one of the best decisions I have made in my time at Old Trafford,' Alex Ferguson said of his recruitment of Carlos Quieroz. And if, as the manager has suggested, a large part of the responsibility for winning the title should be borne by the Portuguese coach, who could argue with that assessment? Certainly not Real Madrid, who, having sacked their manager Vicente del Bosque 24 hours after winning La Liga (and two Champions League titles in his four-year tenure), swooped on the United assistant as his replacement.

It seems that Ferguson regarded the loss of Beckham as, in large part, liberating for the club, but he will have seen Real's capture of Quieroz in a very different light. This was a crucial appointment for Ferguson: a man who had introduced new training methods to the squad, had insisted on their staying overnight in a hotel before every game, and, perhaps most important, a man who was at ease in English, French, Spanish and Portuguese. All in all, a perfect complement to Ferguson.

The signing of Quieroz had marked an interesting progression in assistant managers during Fergie's time at United, a progression which reveals a lot about his own development as a manager. He arrived from Aberdeen with Archie Knox in tow, an old-fashioned Scottish ranter, a hard-man soul-mate, brought up in the rough and tumble of league football north of the border. If Fergie was bad cop in the double act, Knox's role was to be badder. He motivated by passion, shouting was his major tool of communication. Then Knox returned to his roots at Rangers and Brian Kidd was brought in. An equally emotional fan of the game, Kidd was, however, considerably more open to fresh thinking about training methods. His restless search for new techniques across a huge variety of sports, made training an endless education for the players. After he left, Steve McClaren was equally absorbed in such developments, but took it to a new scientific level, a thoroughness which is evident in his success as a manager at Middlesbrough.

Carlos explains the Art of Defence

After the lull involving Jim Ryan – when Ferguson assumed there was no point replacing McClaren if he himself would soon be replaced – came Quieroz. Ferguson hoped his new assistant's continental experience (he was manager of Portugal's under-20 team which won the World Youth Cup in the early '90s, introducing players like Luis Figo and Rui Costa to the game) would add an edge to United in Europe. But by all accounts his influence was much closer to home: he helped turn a fragile wobbly defensive unit into the most parsimonious in the Premiership. On the training ground he encouraged the versatility and creative instincts of Brown, O'Shea and Silvestre while at the same time organising them into a much tighter unit. And he also championed the progress of Quinton Fortune, a player he had managed when South African national coach before the last World Cup.

It's going to be a hard act to follow.

Also released at the end of season

Lee Roche

Defender. Appearances 3 (2); Goals 0. **Youth Team** product. Loaned to **Wrexham**. Left for **Burnley** (June 03; free transfer).

Roche – off to Turf Moor

Bolton-born, the unassuming Roche looks like Spud out of *Trainspotting*. Luckily for his body, he plays football and doesn't knock about Edinburgh council estates indulging in the dangerous. He plays as a central defender or right back and reads the game well, but he found himself out of contract at the end of the season and being linked with a permanent move to various clubs, amongst them Blackpool and Bradford City, before finally settling on Burnley.

LAST SEASON United appearances: 2 (1); goals: 0. Rating: n/a

Youth players

At the end of the season, United also released 22-year-old Kirk Hilton, who had been a regular reserve but made no first team appearance; he joined Blackpool. Youth players John Cogger, Kalam Mooniaruck and John Rankin were also released.

Other former Reds still playing

Appleton – bad luck with the Baggies

Michael Appleton

Midfield. Appearances 1 (1). **Youth Team** product. Left for **Preston North End** 1997 (£500,000). Now at **West Bromwich Albion**.

Appleton's luck has not been auspicious. After just one full appearance as a Red in a league cup game, he left for Preston, before being snapped up by West Brom. But a cruciate ligament injury sustained in training truncated his involvement in Gary Megson side's rush for promotion last season. Worse, this year, with Albion enjoying life in the Premiership for just nine brief months, he was unable to join the party, with his knee still not right. At 27, he has the chance to make a comeback, but timing has rarely been so unfortunate.

Henning Berg

Centre Back. Appearances 79 (21). Goals 3. Signed from **Blackburn Rovers** Aug 1997 (£5m). Returned to **Blackburn Rovers** on loan Sept 2000, then permanently Jan 2001 (£1.75m). **Retired** at end of season.

Old Ice scored against United at Old Trafford in what was his last ever appearance there following the announcement of his retirement. As he skipped like a five-year-old round the turf, wide-eyed and wide-mouthed in celebration, it was difficult to know whether

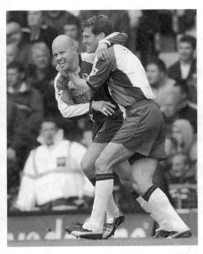

:Last hurrah: Henning scores at Old Trafford

his pleasure in netting for Blackburn was born of the poignant realisation that it was all over, or just the sheer astonishment of actually scoring. Not a regular threat in an opponent's penalty area, anyone wanting a memorial for Berg's United career should look to the other end of the pitch and remember the tackle he made in the European Cup quarter final in the treble year against Internazionale. With an Inter forward bearing down on goal in an apparently unstoppable surge, Berg, with clinical timing, stuck out a leg and not only dispossessed the player, but sent him sprawling and came away with the ball to initiate a Red attack. The forward concerned was Ronaldo. How we could have done with an intervention like that this season.

Clayton Blackmore

Midfield. United career 1983–94. **Appearances**: 200 (44). **Goals**: 25.

Affectionately known as 'Sunbed' by the Red fanzines because of his perma-tan, Blackmore these days splits his time between coaching Wales's youth teams and being roasted by whippy teenage wingers playing full back for Bangor City. The Phil Neville of his day, in many ways his versatility was his worst enemy – no-one could decide where to play him. A Welsh international, he returned to his roots after finishing his career at Middlesbrough and is still turning out for Bangor's former-Red, manager Peter Davenport.

Jesper Blomqvist

Winger. Appearances: 29 (9). Goals: 1. Signed from **Parma** July 1998 (£4.4m).
Released to **Everton** Sept 2001 (free transfer). Released by **Charlton** May 03.

In disgguise: Blomqvist with beard

You may have forgotten, but the man who gave David May the most traumatic evening of his career when playing for IFK Goteborg in the Champions League, was at Old Trafford for three long seasons. The irony was, the player bought as cover for the injury-prone Ryan Giggs was so susceptible himself. Still, he chose the right season to play in: the treble year. And even though, in pub quizzes about the 1999 Champions League final, his is the name most frequently forgotten from the starting line-up that day (he was replaced by Teddy Sheringham), he has the medal to prove it. He also deserves praise for fighting back to fitness enough to persuade Everton to give him a contract after he was released by United, though he failed to get a regular place there, nor at Charlton, who released him at the end of last season.

Mark Bosnich

Goalkeeper. Appearances 36. Signed from Aston Villa July 1999 (free transfer). Left for **Chelsea** Jan 2001 (free transfer). Currently out of contract.

Bozzer was last heard of seeking legal advice as to whether it was worth taking Chelsea to an employment tribunal for unfair dismissal. This arose after he was unceremoniously sacked the moment

90 minutes of glory: Bosnich keeping a clean sheet in Madrid

traces of cocaine were found in his system during a routine doping test; he was subsequently banned from football worldwide for nine months (he claimed his drink was spiked).

Last heard of, that is, in any sort of footballing context. Tabloid readers will have enjoyed endless tales about the Australian keeper brawling in swanky London nightclubs with his girlfriend Sophie Anderton, the former bra model (nice to be kept abreast of his activities). That and checking in to the Priory complaining of the debilitating effects of stress.

As football declines go, Bosnich's is one of the most precipitous in modern times, up there with Stan Collymore. And while sympathy should perhaps be reserved for those who are not in receipt of a £2m a year salary for sitting on the bench at Stamford Bridge, it is hard not to feel sorry for him as he self-destructs out of the game. Particularly as the tie with Real Madrid last season brought memories of the match in 2000 at the Bernabeu which was his finest 90 minutes in a United shirt. He was brilliant that night, big, brave and unstoppable, allowing United to come away with a 0-0. Everything you want in a keeper. That he played like that maybe only twice in his United career (the other occasion was in the World Club Championship in Tokyo when he was magnificent) is the biggest mystery of the most bizarre flop of the Ferguson era. Maybe the personality clash between player and manager was too extreme to be overcome. Maybe his appalling distribution ultimately undermined any confidence his defence had in him. Maybe the stifling arrogance which characterised his every turn was just a device to hide his sense of inadequacy. Whatever, his decline is a daily reminder that money and fame are no insulation against the effects of personal failure.

Grant Brebner

Defender. Appearances 0. Youth Team product. Left for **Hibernian** 1999 (free transfer).

Phil Neville's best mate, Brebner has become a permanent fixture in the two-horse race that is the Scottish Premier (how unlike the United/Arsenal spat in our own English league.) Unfortunately, Brebner is aboard the wrong horse. But nevertheless he enjoyed his best season yet as a Hibs player, even scoring a hat-trick against Dundee United in the club's cup run as he was pressed into emergency service as a forward.

George Clegg

Midfield. Appearances 0. Youth Team product. Left for **Wycombe** 1998 (free transfer). Now at **Bury**.

After featuring in the FA Cup semi-final three seasons ago as Wycombe took an unexpected march to the brink of the Millennium, the Wythenshawe-born, City-supporting Clegg returned closer to his roots with Bury where he was one of the Shakers' better performers in the push for promotion.

Andrew Cole

Forward. Appearances 227 (43). Goals 121. Signed from Newcastle Jan 1995 (£7m plus Keith Gillespie). Left for **Blackburn** Dec 2001 (£6m).

He can still do it ... Cole puts Blackburn ahead in last year's Worthington semi

For a player of such immense worth, Cole is a tortured soul. Where his striking partner Dwight Yorke is all grin and party, Cole scowls and broods. His latest spat has been with his manager Graeme Souness, whose decision to put the forward on the bench sent Cole into a tail-spin of depression. The two apparently sorted it out over a cup of tea, and, restored to the Blackburn side, he continued to score with the regularity which has put him right up there in the Premiership's all-time scoring records. Cole is a far better player than many give him credit for – a lithe, mobile striker who makes space for team mates as well as scoring himself. United fans look back on his six years at the club with great affection. Yet, when they survey Ruud van Nistelrooy in action, they know how much things have advanced.

Cooke – off with the Trawlers

Terry Cooke

Winger. Appearances 2 (6). Goals 1.
Youth Team product. Left for **Manchester City** April 1999 (£600,000). Now at **Grimsby**.

Cooke scored a sensational goal on his United debut, then almost immediately snapped his cruciate in a reserve game. Alex Ferguson believed that robbed him of his extra pace, though Joe Royle was prepared to pay David Beckham's salary for a month or so to take him to Maine Road. He starred in City's brief sojourn in the second division, but Kevin Keegan did not reckon him up to higher things. Next season he will be back in the division where he once shone, as Grimsby, his new club where he has been a regular all season, were relegated as the first's worst. That is, of course, if he has the luxury of a new contract at Blundell Park.

Jordi Cruyff

Midfield. Appearances 25 (17). Goals 8. Signed from Barcelona Aug 1996 (£1.5m). Left for **Alaves** Aug 2000 (free transfer).

Never in his father's class, Cruyff Jnr had a frustrating time at United. He would play in the Charity Shield, then get injured and not appear again until popping away a couple of goals in a meaningless end of season run-out. But he has flourished as elder statesman at the Basque club, Alaves, who had a good couple of years in La Liga, before being relegated last season. Jordi is now entirely hair-free, by the way.

John Curtis

Full back. Appearances 0 (9). Youth Team product. Left for **Blackburn Rovers** May 2000 (£1.5m).

FA Cup near-glory for Curtis, with Sheffield Utd

A strong-running defender, Curtis had his moment in the limelight during the putative take-over of United by BSkyB. The man the company wanted to run United was asked at a press conference to name the Reds' left back. He didn't know. Martin Edwards was asked the same question later in the day, and with his anorak attention to detail, not only gave the names of Denis Irwin and Phil Neville, but popped Curtis in there for good measure. In a sense it was understandable: Curtis was always a fixture at United from the day he arrived as the most pursued young player of his generation. But, as has often been shown by football, success as a kid is not necessarily replicated in adulthood, and Curtis has faded since his transfer to Ewood. Last season saw him out on loan to Sheffield United where, despite making a howler in the semi-final against Forest, he helped them to the play-off final.

Simon Davies

Midfield. Appearances 10 (10). Goals 1. Youth Team product. Left for Luton Town Aug 1999 (free transfer). Now at **Bangor**.

The tall Welsh international midfielder was another graduate of the 1992 Youth Team, and a Worthington Cup regular for several seasons. But, in a career which shows the narrow fractions which separate success from frustration, while his old team mate David Beckham enjoys wealth and celebrity undreamt of when the two were starting off, Davies is these days plying his trade for Bangor in the Welsh League.

The usually mild-mannered Dion takes issue with ... would you believe it, Robbie Savage

Dion Dublin

Centre **forward**. Appearances 6 (11). Goals 3. Signed from Cambridge Sept 1992 (£1m). Left for Coventry, Sept 1994 (£2m). Now at **Aston Villa**.

Dublin may have done what most football fans in the country would have loved to do when he nutted Robbie Savage during the Birmingham derby this season. But he was right to suggest in his mitigation in front of the FA's disciplinary committee that it was an action completely out of character. Dublin is a classic big centre forward, whose resilience is perhaps his most sizeable asset. After years suffering ill-fortune with injury (he even broke his neck playing for Villa) the veteran centre forward came back from a loan with

Millwall to enjoy one of his best seasons yet, putting himself about with customary bravery for the faltering Villa cause.

Darren Ferguson

Midfield. Appearances 22 (8). Youth Team product. Left for Wolves, Jan 1994 (£500,000). Now at **Wrexham**.

A candidate for management?

Having the most famous dad in football must have been a mixed blessing for young Darren at United. He had a couple of runs in the first team, notably in the 1992–93 Championship season, but lost his place through injury and never regained it. He didn't flourish at Wolves. However, he has found his niche running the midfield at Wrexham, and as captain cajoled the North Wales club to automatic promotion from the third division. Some of his finger-jabbing displays of temper at team mates' inadequacies as he pushed the side towards the next level suggest he may have inherited his character more from his father than his mother.

Keith Gillespie

Winger. Appearances 7 (7). Goals 2. Youth Team product. Left for Newcastle Jan 1995 (£1m make-weight in the Andy Cole deal). **Released** by Blackburn Rovers May 2003.

There was a time when many felt Keegan had a bargain when he took the winger in part exchange for Andy Cole. Not last season, though, when Gillespie found himself behind David Dunn and Damien Duff on the Blackburn flanks and was then held up in the tabloids once

Gillespie gets a hand-up from Henry

more as a poor example to us all when Michael Owen's gambling habits became public. he found himself released from contract by Souness at the end of term, but has been offered a chance to show his Premiership class by newly-promoted Leicester. At 28, it's not too late.

Shaun Goater

Forward. Appearances 0. Youth Team product. Left for Rotherham United Aug 1992 (free transfer). **Released** by Manchester City May 2003.

The Goat takes leave of Maine Road

The hungry goat was a legendary figure at Maine Road, a forward whose surfeit of spirit often compensated for his lack of skill. But he scored goals in whichever division he found himself after his transfer from Bristol City in 1998, and City followers warmed to the sort of whole-hearted commitment that would never be used to describe his direct replacement, Nicolas Anelka, or the Elk as he was known. Appropriate, really, elks and goats. While United employ gazelles, City prefer to put their faith in lumbering beasts prepared to forage on what few scraps are put in front of them. A mixed end of season for the Goat saw him released by City but honoured with an MBE for his charitable work.

Jonathan Greening

Midfield. Appearances 13 (13). Goals 0. Signed from York City March 1998 (£350,000). Left for **Middlesbrough** Aug 2001 (for combined fee with Mark Wilson of £3.5m).

Greening was a maddening presence at United, promising loads and delivering very little. But self-confidence was never a problem and he always maintained that if he were given a more prominent role, he would rise to the challenge. And to be fair, at Boro, under Steve McClaren who would have seen him in training every day at the

Greening – the jury is still out

Cliff and latterly Carrington, he has done just that. A regular in a Boro midfield bristling with highly paid foreigners, Greening's leggy runs have caused far more damage than they ever did at Old Trafford. When the Reds lost at the Riverside over Christmas, a defeat many observers at the time reckoned signalled the end of their involvement in the title, Greening was particularly good. Was every Red watching amazed at how much better he was than they all remembered? Yes. Would any have swapped him for any first team midfielder at Old Trafford? No.

David Healy

Forward. Appearances 0 (2). Youth Team product. Left for **Preston North End** Jan 2001 (£1.5m).

Healy scored five goals in his first seven internationals for Northern Ireland – more than his manager Sammy McIlroy managed in 88 outings during his own time at United. This scoring feat, however, was not replicated for the Reds: Healy appeared only twice, as a sub-stitute, for the first team. Clearly not someone over-endowed with patience, he once likened life in the United youth system to being a mushroom: you're kept in the dark and fed on shit. Without his mentor David Moyes at Preston, though, he has failed to maintain the promise of his early career there, and spent much of the season loitering on the bench. Wisely, whatever vegetable analogy he had for that experience, he kept to himself.

Danny Higginbotham

Defender. Appearances 4 (3). Youth Team product. Left for Derby County Aug 2000 (£2m). Now at **Southampton**.

Higginbotham turns it on for Strachan

Higginbotham had a couple of run-outs in Worthington Cup games, but never looked like jumping ahead of Phil Neville and Denis Irwin in the queue for the left-back position. Thus when Mickael Silvestre was signed, he knew his time was up. Two million pounds was typical of the business Ferguson does for the plc with his Youth Team. Higginbotham looked the part at Pride Park, so much so that as Derby's finances imploded, he was one of their few saleable assets. And he couldn't have picked a better season to switch to Gordon Strachan's Southampton, a side for once not struggling in the league. Even though he was cup tied and thus not eligible for the FA Cup final, Southampton's appearance there must have made him appreciate being at a club in decent health for next season.

Paul Ince

Success? It's all down to the Guvnor ...

Midfield. Appearances 272 (5). Goals 28. Signed from West Ham, Sept 1989 (£2m). Left for Internazionale July 1995 (£6m). Now at **Wolves**.

Dave Jones invested a lot in Paul Ince when he persuaded him to move to the Black Country in the close season. Not by way of a transfer fee – Ince was a free agent when Middlesbrough decided not to renew his contract – but with his reputation. Jones persuaded Wolves' long-suffering sugar daddy Jack Hayward that if he would bank-roll Ince's inflated wages, automatic promotion would be assured. It wasn't, but the guvnor and his team came good at last in the play-offs, and Wolves fans are now officially blissed out. As club captain, Incey performed with his usual mix of spike and arrogance that endears him to home supporters and enrages opponents. And though the delusion of grandeur which led him to insist on being called the guvnor grows ever more wearisome, his importance to the emerging United team of the mid-nineties cannot be denied, whatever his later Liverpool associations. His boots, with the moniker that so annoyed Alex Ferguson scrawled on the tongues, deserve their place in the club museum. Though sadly for him, however much he might consider himself still a force in English football, a museum will soon be the best place to consign his career.

Dogshit, Golden Bollocks and the Rest

It's hard to recall Paul Ince without his self-styled nickname, the 'Guvnor', coming into your mind; nor, indeed, once you've been told, his original United players' nickname – 'dogshit' – so-dubbed because 'he got everywhere.' And it seems likely there will only ever be one 'Golden Bollocks'. Here, then, is a role call of wit past and present from dressing room and terraces alike.

Baby-faced assassin Ole Gunnar Solskjaer.

Bamber Alan Gowling, then later Steve Coppell (as in Bamber Gascoigne, chairman of *University Challenge* – standard footballer's slang for any player with a university education).

El Beatle George Best (coined as a headline in the Portuguese press the day after his performance in the 5-1 away win against Benfica in 1965).

Black Pearl of Inchicore Paul McGrath.

Blind Venetian Massimo Taibi (quite possibly libellous as he doesn't come from Venice).

Bogota Bandit Charlie Mitten (after his ill-fated transfer to play for big money in Colombia).

Boleslaw Peter Schmeichel's real middle name.

Brujita (little witch) Juan Sebastian Veron (so named because his father – who played for Estudiantes in the 1968 World Club Championship against the Reds – was known as La Bruja, the witch).

Captain Blood Kevin Moran, also the Late Kevin Moran after his tardy tackle on Peter Reid in 1985 that led to him becoming the first player ever sent off in an FA Cup final.

Captain Marvel Bryan Robson.

Choccy Brian McClair.

The Crab Ray Wilkins (due to his propensity for passing the ball sideways; probably preferable to his nickname at Chelsea, Butch).

Dogshit Paul Ince – early appellation to describe his ability to get everywhere. For obvious reasons, he preferred to call himself the **Guv'nor**.

Dolly and Daisy Gary Pallister and Steve Bruce (a reference to their occasional old womanish lapses of concentration. Those two old women? Hell's Grannies more like).

Dracula Paddy Roche, a keeper terrified of crosses.

Dreadnought Alex Dawson (like the destroyers, except more indomitable).

Flash or **Big Ron** Atkinson.

Golden Bollocks What his wife admits to calling David Beckham.

Gunner Jack Rowley (a deadly marksman).

Hairdryer or **Taggart** Alex Ferguson (though to his face, it's strictly Sir).

Hayley What his team mates called David Beckham, after the *Coronation Street* character, who sports a dyed blond bob in a style not unlike the one he wore for much of his last season.

Happy Nobby Stiles (perfect name for someone who moaned for Britain)

Jaws Joe Jordan.

The Judge Lou Macari (he spent a lot of time on the bench).

The King (of the Stretford End) Denis Law.

The King (of Old Trafford) Eric Cantona

Lancelot Holliday Richardson Reds' keeper in the twenties – but with a moniker like that who needs a nickname?

Larry White Laurent Blanc.

Ledge Mark Hughes's dressing room nickname to describe his legendary status. **Double Ledge** Eric Cantona (as above only twice as much).

Merlin Gordon Hill (because of his allegedly magical qualities on the wing).

Old Brittle Bones Jimmy Delaney (rather injury prone).

Pancho Mark and then Stuart Pearson (possibly a reference to the first Pearson's luxurious tache, though Stuart P never wore one).

PB (Popular Bill) Bill Foulkes (somewhat sarcastic reference to his dressing room status).

Roadrunner David McCreery, a midfielder busy going nowhere.

Smiling Executioner Tommy Taylor (a cheerful finisher).

Sparky Mark Hughes (originally coined by Ron Atkinson as an ironic comment on his apparent diffidence in training).

Stroller George Graham.

Sunbed Clayton Blackmore (how else does he explain the perma-tan on Bangor City wages?).

Supersam Sammy McIlroy.

Swivel hips or **Snake hips** Eddie Colman (to acknowledge his deceptive body swerve).

The Tank Duncan Edwards.

Denis Irwin

Defender. Appearances 510 (18). Goals 33. Signed from Oldham Athletic Aug 1990 (£625,000). Left on a free transfer for **Wolves** Aug 2002.

Together with Paul Ince, Irwin was brought in to add a spine of experience to the permanently faltering Wolves side that would carry them to promotion. That the plot finally worked out seems no more than the due for this great Irish full back, who deserved a rip-roaring post script to his career. Not that Irwin had anything to prove, secure in the knowledge that he left Old Trafford with a display cabinet groaning under the weight of medals. Seven Championships, one Champions League, one Cup Winners Cup, one Super Cup, three FA Cups, one League Cup and a handful of Charity Shields were all secured with Irwin's calm, rational, dignified assistance. Not a player to feature in the pages of *Hello!* magazine, perhaps, but Irwin's utter reliability must have helped his manager sleep better at night. Whether he stays on at Wolves was, at the time of writing, a matter of discussion, although his fellow professionals thought highly enough of him to vote him into the PFA first division select XI last season. But whatever happens, unlike his Molineux colleague, he can be sure he will receive a hero's welcome on any return he makes to Old Trafford.

Irwin: distinguished service

Ronny Johnsen

Defender. Appearances: 128 (19). Goals: 8. Signed from Besiktas July 1996 (£1.5m).
Left on a free transfer to **Aston Villa** June 2002.

Poor Johnsen. How did his first season at Aston Villa go? Guess what: it was peppered with injury. In the case of Ronny Johnsen, statistics tell almost the entire story: 147 appearances over six years at Old Trafford. For a player of his calibre, it should have been at least double that. No manager would have left out a centre back as calm, skilled and brave. The problem was the Norwegian's physique. Apparently made of balsa wood, with cartilage

"Ouch!" Ronny warms up for Norway, with Ole and Steffen Iversen

and hamstrings constructed from frayed elastic bands, he was in the treatment room at Carrington so often they named one of the beds there after him. Still, when he left United for Villa Park, he took with him a unique record: he is the only player in football history to have made four successive trophy-winning appearances. How did he manage that? Well, he was there for each of United's treble-winning moments, trotting out for the league game which clinched the title, followed by the FA Cup and Champions League finals in 1999. Three games together clearly was too much for his body, and he did not turn out again until he came on as substitute in the game against Spurs in the spring of 2000, a match in which the title was won. It is a sequence he is unlikely to better at Villa Park, even if he were to stay injury free until the end of the next century.

Johnson doing the Forlan

David Johnson

Forward. Appearances 0. Youth Team product. Left for Bury 1995 (percentage of future fees). Now at **Nottingham Forest**.

Last year was probably the best season this quick little Brummie striker has enjoyed. A good chum of Ryan Giggs in the United Youth Team, Johnson was always reckoned full of potential, as he went first to Bury, then for big money to Ipswich, then on to Nottingham Forest. But his promise was never quite fulfilled and as Forest's finances imploded, Johnson was reckoned to be the most likely casualty of any cost-cutting clear-out. On Premiership money, he was farmed out on loan to Burnley to get him off the City Ground wage bill. The Turf Moor club couldn't afford to keep him, and he returned last summer to the East Midlands looking forlorn and mis-cast. But then he blossomed, becoming the first division's top scorer and taking the Forest player of the year award as he led Paul Hart's young team to the play-offs.

Andrei Kanchelskis

Winger. Appearances: 129 (29). Goals: 36. Signed from Shakhytor Donestk Jan 90 (£800,000). Left for **Everton** Aug 95 (£5m). released by Southampton in Feb 03 and now playing for **Al Hilal** in Saudi Arabia.

Happy times: Andrei and Choccy

During the Beckham transfer saga, the name of Kanchelskis was constantly served up as a reminder of how Fergie's previous ruthlessness resolved itself.

Back in '95 he was a player apparently at the peak of his powers, and many of us felt the manager had made a huge mistake letting the Russian flier go. His subsequent decline into obscurity proved how bang on the button the manager was. Let's be honest would any of us had known he was playing out a charade of a career, taking the oil money, if it wasn't for Beckham? It won't happen to Goldenballs, of course. But Kanchelskis is a reminder that life does go on for the rest of us once the big names leave.

Jonathan Macken

Forward. Appearances 0. Youth Team product. Left for Preston North End Aug 1998 (free transfer). Now at **Manchester City**.

A sharp-heeled, strong and quick-witted Mancunian forward, Macken had a brilliant couple of years at Preston, good enough to persuade Kevin Keegan to pay £5m to take him to Maine Road. He looked the business as City stormed out of the first division in 2002, scoring six goals in almost as many matches. Even when Keegan signed Nicolas Anelka, Macken must have thought he was

Can he put Fowler on the bench?

about to become a Premiership striker as he moved up the City striking order ahead of Paolo Wanchope and Shaun Goater. Injury, though, robbed him of the chance to prove himself the David Platt of his generation, the one whom United would regret letting go. A couple of substitute appearances long after City's season had spluttered to a pointless conclusion are all he has had to show for his time at the top. It might be thought the arrival of a potato-faced Scouser will have pushed Macken's chances back, but he has the pedigree to make it in the end. All he needs now is a bit of luck.

Pat McGibbon

Centre back. Appearances 1. Youth Team product. Left for Wigan July 1997 (free transfer). Now at **Portadown**.

A powerful Northern Ireland international centre back, McGibbon made the customary appearance in the League Cup back in 1995, before moving on. As Wigan rebuilt under Paul Jewell and stormed into the first division, McGibbon found himself on the outside looking in and was last heard of playing for Portadown back in his native territory.

Phil Mulryne

Forward. Appearances 4. Youth Team product. Left for **Norwich City** March 1999 (£500,000).

A stocky, bullish little forward, Mulryne has found himself in division one's marzipan layer – with a club not quite good enough to go up, but too good to go down. He scored in the play-offs two seasons ago, when Norwich were pipped at the last by West Brom, but found last season tougher altogether as the club failed to maintain the momentum many expected them to generate from that run. How long Delia Smith is prepared to use her cookery fortune to keep boiling the Canaries' eggs is presumably a question that Mulryne asks himself all the time.

Colin Murdock

Defender. Appearances 0. Youth Team product. Left for **Preston North End** 1997 (free transfer).

Nearly 200 appearances at Deepdale, but after thriving under David Moyes, the dependable Northern Ireland international has found himself not entirely central in new manager Craig Brown's vision. Expect him to move on soon.

Erik Nevland

Forward. Appearances 2 (3). Goals 1. Signed from Viking Stavanger July 1997 (free transfer). Returned to **Viking Stavanger** Aug 2000 (free transfer).

Big-time action for Nevland last season, against Chelsea

A second Ole Gunnar Solskjaer he was not: the Norwegian youth inter-national never got the run-out at Old Trafford many were expecting. Still, one of Nevland's few appearances in the first eleven, alongside Solskjaer, Berg and Johnsen, allowed the Norwegians – who make up the majority of United's biggest fan club, the Scandinavian branch – to boast that four of their fellow countrymen turned out for the team together.

Alex Notman

Forward. Appearances 0 (1). Youth Team product. Left for **Norwich City** Aug 2000 (£600,000).

It is an unexplained blip in the United youth system that, despite producing quality defenders and midfielders by the score, it has not thrown up a class centre forward since Mark Hughes. For a while Notman was thought to be the exception. The Edinburgh-born striker (one of the few Scots at a club that used to be packed with them) scored a hatful in the reserves, but was unable to make the step up. And he joined up at Carrow Road with another ex-United player, Phil Mulryne, where he was last seen playing on the right side of midfield.

Jovan Kirovski

Midfield. Appearances 0. Goals: 0. Joined the academy 95. Left for Dortmund 97. Now at **Birmingham City**.

Alex Ferguson was decidedly unhappy when work permit wrangles prevented him from keeping this talented young American at the Cliff in the mid nineties. He was snaffled up by Dortmund (how come they could employ Yanks?) and, after gaining his EU residential qualifications is back in England. Steve Bruce remembered him from his time at United and quickly brought him from Crystal Palace. Turned out twice against the Reds last season.

A card for O'Kane, watched by fellow ex-Red Wellens

John O'Kane

Defender. Appearances 5 (2). Youth Team product. Left for **Everton** Jan 1998 (£1m). Now at **Blackpool**.

Immensely talented, if somewhat wayward off the pitch, O'Kane never achieved the same level of self-disciplined consistency of his 1992 Youth Cup winning team mates. These days after brief spells at Everton and Bolton, he is to be found organising Blackpool's defence.

Kevin Pilkington

Goalkeeper. Appearances 6 (2). Youth Team product. Left for Port Vale July 98 (free transfer). Now at **Mansfield**.

Pilkington was observed playing this season for Mansfield – a side yo-yoing with monotonous regularity between the second and third divisions – where it was noted that he learned a lot from his time observing Peter Schmeichel at work. He bawled, yelled and, on conceding a goal, loudly blamed his defence. Presumably the red nose and bizarre Danish/Manc accent will come with time.

Karel Poborsky

Winger. Appearances 28 (19). Goals 6. Signed from Slavia Prague Aug 1996 (£3.6m). Left for Benfica Oct 1997 (£3m). Now at **Lazio**.

Karel may have trimmed his hair now he is in Serie A, but the man once called The Express Train still has not lived up to that goal, chipped over Peter Schmeichel's head, at Euro '96. Terminally inconsistent will be his epitaph and Reds will remember one brilliant performance against Leeds soon after he arrived and ponder the what-might-have-beens. Particularly the what-might-have-been had Fergie bought Poborsky's international colleague, the great Pavel Nedved, back in '96 instead.

Poborsky: the hair has gone

Paul Rachubka

Goalkeeper. Appearances 1 (1). Goals 0. Youth Team product. Sold to **Charlton Athletic** May 2001 (£200,000).

The one product which American soccer does well is goalkeepers: something to do with the combination of handling skills and physique honed through playing grid iron at school. Kasey Keller and Brad Friedel fly the stars and stripes in the Premiership and it was long thought that the Californian-born Rachubka would be the best Yank of the lot. At the back of a lengthy queue of keepers at Old Trafford, he tried his luck in south London only to discover the Irish do goalies too, and he has become understudy to the emerging Dean Kiely. Still, with Dave Beasant and David Seaman playing on deep into chronological injury time, he knows in his position at least, time is on his side.

Robins salutes the goal that saved his boss

Mark Robins

Forward. Appearances 27 (42). Goals 17. Youth Team product. Left for Norwich City Aug 1992 (£800,000). Now at **Rotherham**.

Nothing ages a United fan more than hearing that Robins – the rosy-cheeked prodigy whose goal against Nottingham Forest in the FA Cup may well have kept the boss in a job back in 1990 – being described as a grizzled old veteran. After his goals took Rotherham up to the first division, Robins found it harder breaching better defences, scoring only six times for the Miller men this season. For a while he was farmed out on loan to Bristol City, before being called back early by Rotherham manager Ronnie Moore to help in an injury crisis. In a recent interview he revealed that hardly a day goes by that he isn't stopped and thanked by Reds grateful for that goal and what it meant. Something which – no matter how ancient he becomes – nobody will ever forget.

Robbie Savage

Midfield. Appearances 0. Youth Team product. Left for Crewe Alexandra Aug 1994 (free transfer). Now at **Birmingham City**.

What is it about Robbie Savage? Marlet takes aim

Savage is about as popular as an outbreak of SARS in the claret half of Birmingham. During the season's last city derby, he was headbutted by Dion Dublin after tumbling somewhat theatrically after a tackle. Although the Welshman appeared to be the entirely innocent victim, his behaviour provoked what passes for a riot in Villa Park (a bloke in a baseball cap ran on the pitch and danced around him, throwing punches that missed by a good six feet). Needless to say, this immediately guaranteed him hero status among the followers of Birmingham City. Which is entirely typical of his career. Along with George Switzer, the only member of the 1992 Youth Cup winning team not to play in the first eleven at United, Savage's utter commitment to his team's cause, coupled with his ridiculous fop of blond hair, mean he is always singled out for opprobrium by opposition fans. And it is not just fans, it seems. When Leicester were relegated in 2002 and Savage put on the transfer list, he publicly voiced his doubts that anyone else would sign him: 'they all hate me,' he said. Be that as it may, the season he has had will have ensured he will be in demand for some time. For Birmingham he has been brilliant, largely responsible for the club defying gravity and staying up in the Premiership. He has been no less important in the great Wales revival. The fact that both campaigns have been conducted by former United players is, presumably, entirely coincidental.

Peter Schmeichel

Goalkeeper. Appearances 392. Goals 1. Signed from Brondby Aug 1991 (£500,000). Left for Sporting Lisbon July 1999 (free transfer). Retired from **Manchester City** in May 2003.

"Remember when I came up for that corner?'

When Schmikes celebrated a little too vigorously after City won the Maine Road derby, he set many a Red's teeth on edge. That coupled with his agitated condition the previous season when he got stressed with a United fan who invaded the pitch at Villa Park and merely wanted to shake him by the hand, has seen him re-assessed by Old Trafford regulars. No more hero, just a big red-nosed blue prat. While it is true there was little of Denis Law's dignified response when inflicting pain on old friends, and while he has never been the sort of person with whom you might wish to share quality down time, this fact remains incontrovertible: Schmikes was the greatest keeper in United history, the man whose huge presence anchored the team, a player significant enough to win games on his own. Plus he is the only Red keeper to score a goal in outfield play in modern memory. Also, as his behaviour at the derby confirmed, he is a competitive beast to the tips of his giant fingers. Not enough, though, to cushion him against the advance of time. Pushing forty, he retired at the end of the season, citing exhaustion. He has done that once before, when he left United for Sporting Lisbon after the treble. But this time, it seems he means it. After all, how long can anyone stand in City's goal before succumbing to exhaustion?

Lee Sharpe

Winger. Appearances 212 (50). Goals 36. Signed from Torquay United Aug 1987 (£185,000). Left for Leeds United Aug 1996 (£4.5m). Now at **Grindavik**, Iceland.

Since the Iceland season runs from May to September, Sharpe warmed up for his new club's UEFA Cup campaign by training at Bangor City. Quite how it came to this for a player who was first capped by England at 19, and won the PFA's Young Player of the Year Award in 1991, is one of football's mysteries. The words 'unfulfilled' and 'talent' are generally used in harness when discussing Sharpe. But the lad himself always seems remarkably relaxed and cheerful whenever he appears on those television documentaries about Fergie's temper. To his credit he has never taken the cash no doubt wafted under his nose to slag off his former mentor, perhaps recalling it was Ferguson's fatherly concern for him that guided him through a torrid time as the first teen star of the new United era, although that may change with the publication of a new autobiography. Whatever the rumours there may have been from that time, it was girls, he says now, that were always his weakness – Roy Keane reckons that nobody had more sway with the fairer sex than Sharpe. And he has been unlucky with his transfers (going to Leeds for big money just as Howard Wilkinson was

"Does something smell of fish?"

sacked, getting embroiled in the Bradford mess, being David Platt's only signing in the total disaster he made at Sampdoria). Still, spending a season failing in trials with Rotherham and Grimsby before fetching up in Iceland surely suggests his time is up.

Teddy Sheringham

One last Premiership swing for Teddy?

Forward. Appearances 98 (49 sub). Goals 46. Signed from Tottenham June 1997 (£3m). Returned to Tottenham May 2001 (free transfer). Released June 2003 and now at **Portsmouth** (free transfer).

Sheringham remains determined to defy all normal constraints of time, insisting to himself and his manager at Tottenham that he was worth another big contract at the end of last season. Glenn Hoddle, though, despite being a long-term admirer of Sheringham's guile and intelligence, desperately needed Teddy's enormous whack off the pay roll so that he can bring some youthful legs into his squad. He would only re-sign the player, he said, if Spurs achieved European qualification. And we all know what happened there. Sheringham tried to counter that with the suggestion that he did a better job this year than virtually anyone else in a club as always in a permanent state of transition. The stand-off between the two dulled Teddy's reputation among Spurs fans, and, judging by the lameness of his performance against the Reds at the tail end of the season, few White Hart Lane regulars mourned for long when he was released. United fans, of course, will long reserve a special place in our heart for Teddy and his Triple-winning goals and will give him an affectionate welcome if he visits with Portsmouth.

Jaap Stam

Centre back. Appearances 121 (1). Goals 1. Signed from PSV Eindhoven Jul 1998 (£10.75m); sold to **Lazio** Sept 2001 (£18m).

The big Dutchman remains the one sizeable question mark of the Ferguson era. True, he missed much of his first season in Italy through suspension following a positive test for nandrolone. True, in Mikael Silvestre, John O'Shea and Wes Brown, the future looks bright centre-back wise for the Reds. And true, usually playing out of position at right back, he has hardly looked the best defender in Europe as Lazio were mired in mid-table obscurity. But did Ferguson really need to let the brutally imposing Stam go? He may have been slowing marginally, but was Laurent Blanc really a better option? Especially since the £18m transfer fee, which was claimed to be an offer too good to be true has turned out to be exactly that: Lazio's perpetual financial crisis meaning the Old Trafford coffers are about as likely to see the cash as Major Charles Ingram is to get his cheque from *Who Wants to be a Millionaire?* Sadly, the suspicion hangs in the air that Fergie got rid of him through pique, angered by those derogatory comments in his autobiography. Indeed Gary Neville, described by Stam in the book as, along with his

Still big time: Stam deals with Shevchenko

brother, half of 'a busy pair of cunts', recently suggested that, given what happened to his former team mate, books aren't worth the grief.

Massimo Taibi

Goalkeeper. Appearances 4. Signed from Venezia Sept 1999 (£6m). Left for **Reggiana** July 2000 (£1m).

Taibi is every ABU's favourite keeper, his blunders keeping Nick Hancock chortling for a couple of seasons now. His unhappy few months in England have largely been forgotten. But he doubtless took one great pictorial memory back to Italy with him. The photograph of him at Anfield in his one and only fine performance for

the Reds, the snap in which he stands in the middle of a crowd of Liverpool players just in front of the Kop, casually in possession of the ball while the Scousers to a man hold their heads in their hands following a miss by Michael Owen, was this year voted the finest photograph in the first ten years of the Premiership.

Le Tiss's shot had just slid through his legs

Ben Thornley

Winger. Appearances 6 (8). Youth Team product. Left for Huddersfield Town July 1998 (free transfer). Now at **Blackpool**.

The Tom Cruise-lookalike winger had a couple of years in the north east of Scotland with Aberdeen before drifting back down to the northwest and joining up with the small colony of ex-United youth team players at Steve McMahon's Blackpool. Of the great '92 Youth Cup winning side, Thornley was reckoned by Ferguson to be the one who had the best chance of making the grade at Old Trafford. He was travelling with the squad on European matches in the 1993 season and made his debut before Paul Scholes. But a snapped cruciate ligament in a reserve team game against Blackburn in 1994 both slowed him and robbed him of his goal-scoring touch.

Michael Tonge

Midfield. Appearances 0. Youth team product. Left for **Sheffield United** July 2000 (free transfer).

Sheffield United's progress this season to the semi-finals of both domestic cup competitions and the first division play-offs has been largely dismissed as a triumph of spirit over skill, driven by manager Neil Warnock's uncompromising affection for the club. This

Tonge takes aim against the Scousers

overlooks Tonge's contribution, though, which allied commitment and drive with flair and quality. At times the young Mancunian looked a Steven Gerrard in the making, which is probably why Liverpool, against whom he scored a stunning goal in the Worthington Cup, have been sniffing round his availability. If he does become a Scouser, he would be well advised to keep his birthplace and first club to himself.

Raimond van der Gouw

Goalkeeper. Appearances: 47 (12). Signed from Vitesse Arnhem July 1996 (£200,000). Left for **West Ham** July 2002 (free transfer) and released in June 2003.

The former favourite of female Reds everywhere, Van der Gorgeous swapped life on the bench at the top club in the Premiership for life on the bench at one of the worst. Each week he has had to endure the sight of the least durable defence around leak goals from a position of utter powerlessness. Still, he has not entirely wasted his time. Some observers reckon that the improvement in David James's play last season was not entirely due to the amount of practice he got between the Upton Park sticks, and as much thanks to Van der Gouw's attentions in his role as the Hammers' goalkeeping coach. That said, he was one of ten players released at the end of the season, as West Ham attempted vainly to balance the books.

Ronnie Wallwork

Midfield. Appearances 10 (18). Goals 0. Youth Team product. Left for **West Bromwich Albion** June 2002 (free transfer).

Wallwork was the only major signing Gary Megson made after West Brom surprised most of the football world – themselves included – and got promoted at the end of the 2002 season. The club directors were anxious that,

A daytrip to Old Trafford for Wallwork

if they were to be relegated immediately they would not fall into the financial mess that ensnared Bradford, Coventry, Derby and Leicester. Unfortunately such a parsimonious approach to building a squad became a self-fulfilling prophecy and they were sent straight back down again. Which meant Wallwork's taste of the Premiership as a first team player was brief indeed.

Gary Walsh

Goalkeeper. Appearances 62 (1). Youth Team product. Left for **Middlesbrough** Aug 1995 (£500,000). Now at **Wigan**.

Walsh has always been generous to his old employers. Few who were there will forget his howler against the Reds at Valley Parade in 2001, when he kicked air in a manner even Massimo Taibi would find embarrassing, allowing Teddy Sheringham a free run in on goal. Well, last season he was at it again, keeping for Bradford reserves against the United stiffs at Moss Lane and picking a Danny Nardiello hat-trick out of the back of the net. Hard to reconcile that image with the young keeper Fergie rated so highly when he first arrived at Old Trafford, the player he once reckoned good enough to replace Peter Schmeichel in the Camp Nou in those dodgy far off days of juggling foreigner permutations in Champions League games. In the training session before that game, incidentally, Mick Hucknall was allowed to join in

The ever-generous Walsh

and scored a screamer past Walsh. Fergie preferred to rib the player mercilessly for it ('fancy letting a pop singer score past youse, son') rather than taking it as the omen many others thought at the time.

Danny Webber

Forward. Appearances 0 (1). Youth Team product. Left for **Watford** July 2003 (£250,000).

Webber impressed on loan at Watford last season, with his speed and sharpness. Sir Alex initially put a £1m price tag on him but he broke his leg, and left in the summer for a knockdown £250,000.

Richard Wellens

Defender. Appearances (1). Youth Team product. Left for **Blackpool** Aug 2000 (free transfer).

Wellens was never likely to progress far in the United system the moment he was convicted for drink driving not long after he had passed his test. But Steve McMahon snapped him up for Blackpool, where he has joined a list ex-reds enjoying the sea breezes.

Ashley Westwood

Defender. Appearances 0. Youth Team product. Left for Crewe Alexandra July 1995 (free transfer). Now at **Sheffield Wednesday**.

Getting a first team place is all well and good. But when it is with an outfit as limp as Sheffield Wednesday, there must have been occasions when Westwood pined for the comfortable obscurity of reserve team football at United. Still, he enjoyed at least one glorious moment: scoring the winner away at the first division champions, Portsmouth.

Mark Wilson

Midfield. Appearances 6 (4). Youth Team product. Left for **Middlesbrough** Aug 2001 (combined fee with Jonathan Greening of £3.5m).

A cloud hangs over Wilson's transfer from United, the allegation that he was forced out because he refused to sign for Jason Ferguson's agency central to Michael Crick's critical biography of Fergie. But whatever the reason for his going, the deal has not worked as well for Wilson as for his colleague Greening at Middlesbrough. Despite performing well against United in the Boxing Day victory at the Riverside, Wilson was last heard of on loan to Stoke at the scary end of the first division. His future does not look assured on Teesside.

Dwight Yorke

Forward. Appearances 119 (29). Goals 65. Signed from Aston Villa Aug 1998 (£12.6m). Left for **Blackburn Rovers** Sept 2002 (£6m).

Ruud van Nistelrooy reckoned during the season that there has never been a partnership in Europe to match Andy Cole and Dwight Yorke in 1999. And for that one glorious season, when everything the pair did turned to goals, Yorke should always be remembered at Old Trafford. Unfortunately his wilful behaviour towards the end of his time at United, together with his preposterous choice in girlfriends, and his over-fondness for Manchester's more brazen night spots, has

"You must know the club, man – just drop my name on the door...'

consigned him to the category of joke figure in the mind of most Reds. On the pitch he has done little to make anyone regret his departure: despite Graeme Souness's hopeful intentions, the reunion with Cole at Blackburn has not exactly had them partying in the Ewood stands like it was 1999.

And there are more ...

Other former United youth team products still playing include: David Brown (**Torquay**); Michael Clegg (**Oldham**); Ian Fitzpatrick (**Halifax**); Rhodri Jones (**Rotherham**); Sean McAuley (**Rochdale**); Neil Mustoe (**Yeovil**); Mike Pollitt (**Rotherham**); Andy Rammell (**Bristol Rovers**); John Thorrington (**Huddersfield**); Michael Twiss (**Chester**); and Paul Wheatcroft (**Singapore**).

Reds Managing or Coaching

It has been a mixed year for one-time Reds in the ever-turbulent managerial game. While Steve Bruce, Gordon Strachan and Mark Hughes have been making their mark at the top level, others have failed to progress, and – since the last edition of the book – no fewer than eight Reds have been evicted from the dug-out and forced to find paid work in a television studio: Viv Anderson, Gordon McQueen, Bryan Robson, Lou Macari, Joe Jordan, George Graham, Andy Ritchie and Stewart Houston.

Here is where the survivors are, as of summer 2003.

Daisy (or was it Dolly?) back at Old Trafford

Steve Bruce

1987–96. Appearances 407 (3). Goals 51.
Manager, Birmingham City.

The great captain of the first double winning side, Bruce carved himself a bit of a reputation as a managerial fly boy in his early days in the technical area: stays at Huddersfield, Sheffield United, Wigan and Crystal Palace were so brief there was barely time to stitch his initials into a tracksuit. But last season he found his spiritual home when he arrived at St Andrews and did the unthinkable: finally took Birmingham up to the promised land of the Premiership. What's more, after almost entirely rebuilding the side, he confounded the sceptics who made the Blues candidates for an immediate return, by steering them to safety long before the end of the season. So grateful were his employers, most of whom seem to have a history in soft porn, that he was promised a new contract to make him no longer the worst paid manager in the top division.

Chris Casper

1990-1998 Appearances 4 (3). Goals 0. **Manager, Team Bath**.

Chris Casper – son of Burnley's Frank – was the defensive heart of
the 1992 FA Youth Cup side, but could not dislodge Daisy and
Dolly (or May, Johnsen and Berg) at the back. When Jaap Stam
arrived, he finally moved permanently – to Reading, where he
enjoyed a first team place until injury brought a premature end to
his career aged just 27. But he emerged this season with real credit, taking the Bath University team to the first round of the FA Cup,
the first time since the Edwardian era that students had appeared
so late on in the competition.

Steve Coppell

1975–83. Appearances 395 (3). Goals 70. **Manager, Brighton.**

Coppell, who showed his common sense by taking one look at
Maine Road five years ago and walking out of the place, was managing Brentford at the start of the season. He was then brought in
by Brighton to keep them in the first division. Which was some task
as the Seagulls
were marooned
so deep in the
mire they need-
ed binoculars
to see the back-
sides of the
team in front.
That he nearly
succeeded was
one of the
managerial
performances
of the season.

Just three more points – Coppell begs for that bit extra

Peter Davenport

1985–89. Appearances 83 (23). Goals 26. **Manager, Bangor City**.

After it didn't work out for Davenport at Macclesfield, he headed west. Whatever John Fashanu, the preposterous owner of Barry Town might suggest, the League of Wales isn't La Liga. Nevertheless, Davenport has set up a little colony of former Reds on the north Wales coast, including Simon Davies and the still year-round chestnut-coloured Clayton Blackmore. Which suggests things might have been getting desperate.

Barry Fry

1962–65. Appearances 0. **Manager, Peterborough**.

A good mate of George Best when the two of them played in the United youth team, Fry – who never quite matched his chum on he field – has long been one of the noisier presences on the touchline. Anyone who thought he might have mellowed as he approaches his sixties would have been disabused by footage from a fly-on-the-wall camera inside the Peterborough dressing room last season. It was fantastic

"You're this f—ing far off the action..."

stuff, with Fry berating his central defender with such a stream of invective, you needed a copy of *Viz's Profanasaurus* just to keep up. And that was before he chucked a cup of tea over the player. No wonder the geezer has had three heart attacks. 'We all know we have to slow down,' he said during the course of the season. 'But we can't because we're all mad.' Vintage.

Terry Gibson

1985–87. Appearances 15 (12). Goals 1. **Assistant manager, Wycombe**.

Gibson was United's squarest player. Not in his fashion sense, but because, with probably the biggest backside-width-to-leg-length ratio in the history of football, he was shaped like a rectangle. Now he stands full square alongside his old Wimbledon team mate Lawrie Sanchez at second division Wycombe Wanderers.

Mark Hughes

1983–86; 1988–95. Appearances 448 (14). Goals 162. **Manager, Wales.**

Now greying and dignified, Sparky has almost single-handedly revived Welsh football. Playing in front of passionate crowds at the Millennium stadium, his boys have stormed to the top of their Euro 2004 qualification table, threatening to become the first Welsh side since 1958 to make it to an international tournament. So respected has he become, he was said to be targeted by his old boss to replace Carlos Queiroz. But he chose to stay at Wales, where, assisted by his former United youth team mentor Eric Harrison, he has extracted such astonishing perform-

Thumbs up as Wales miraculously beat Italy

ances from his collection of journeymen, many observers reckon his side could take England. Mind you, they are all Welsh observers.

Jim Leighton

1988–92. Appearances 94. **Goalkeeping coach**, **Aberdeen**.

The hapless bandy-legged Leighton, the first of a long line of United keepers leading straight to Fabien Barthez who didn't quite satisfy their demanding master, didn't appear for the first team again after his mistakes in the 1990 Cup Final. But he completely rebuilt his career in Scotland and played until the end of the 1999–2000 season. He now puts out the jumpers for goal posts on Aberdeen's training ground.

Ian Wright equalises for Palace – and Leighton's career is in nose-dive

Brian McClair

1987–98. Appearances 396 (72). Goals 126. **U-19s coach**, **Manchester United**.

Choccy is back in the United fold again, after a brief dalliance with Kiddo at Blackburn. (See previous chapter).

Sammy McIlroy

1971–82. Appearances 390 (28). Goals 71.
Manager, **Northern Ireland**.

World Cup glory seems a long shot for Sammy

McIlroy has shown enormous perseverance as he has tried to make something of the pig's ear that is Northern Irish football. Largely bereft of talent, he must look across the water to what Mark Hughes is doing with Wales to wonder what, with a bit of resources and focus, a small footballing nation might achieve. Until then, don't expect him to be gracing the finals of any major tournaments. Not when his team haven't apparently scored since the last time he himself slipped on a green shirt.

Paul Parker

1991-95. Appearances 136 (4) Goals 1. **Manager, Billericay Town**.

As right back in the first double winning side, Parker was quick, sharp and talented, but he was one of the less celebrated players, and as soon as Gary Neville arrived on the scene, with the class of '92, he was on his way. He flitted around the London clubs before taking up a managerial post in the Ryman League, and these days is often seen in the Old Trafford press box, with a mobile phone pressed to his ear. Presumably on the blower to Keano's agent, checking whether he would be available for a move to Essex.

Steve Paterson

1976–80. Appearances 5 (5). **Manager, Aberdeen**.

Remembered by Reds with long memories as possessing a quality perm in the seventies, Paterson has not had a great season personally at Pittodrie. Brought in to replace the Dane Ebbe Skovdahl as

254 ◀ ONCE WERE REDS

manager of the Dons, a man who himself was partial to a drop of Scotland's national drink, Paterson found himself plastered all over the Scottish tabloids after admitting that he too spent most of his time seeking refuge in the bottle. His problems became public after one occasion when he didn't turn up for a Dons' game. He blamed a stomach bug, but when local tittle-tattle revealed that he had been away on a binge in several city centre bars, he came clean. He kept his job after undergoing treatment but for how long is debatable. And to think, this was a club once led by Alex Ferguson.

Mike Phelan

1989–94. Appearances 126 (19). Goals 3. **First team coach**, **Manchester United**.

Phelan is another of the first wave of Fergie veterans back beside him on the bench, and when Carlos Queiroz left, he took the reins as assitant manager/first team coach. (See previous chapter).

The next England manager

David Platt

1983–85. Appearances 0. **England U-21 coach**.

The one that got away from the Youth Team (his departure still gives Eric Harrison sleepless nights), Platt has never suffered from a deficit of self-confidence. Despite a modest record in club football with Forest and Sampdoria (where modest is a kind description of his ill-starred tenure) the man who once took a year out to study managerial techniques has failed to qualify for the European Under-21s tournament with perhaps the most talented bunch of players since the days of Beckham, Scholes and Butt.

Still, he reckons he will be a shoo-in for the big job when Sven Goran Eriksson resigns. So at least someone is happy.

Jimmy Ryan

1965–70. Appearances 24 (3). Goals 4. **Director of youth football, Manchester United**.

Contemporary of Law, Best and Charlton, Jimmy Ryan has become a United fixture – see previous chapter.

Alex Stepney

1966–78. Appearances 535. Goals 2. **Goalkeeping coach, Burnley**.

For a while in the relegation season of 1973–74, Stepney was the club's leading scorer (he took the penalties). At time of writing the long-serving Red is at Turf Moor, though quite how long he will be there after his keeper let in seven at home against Sheffield Wednesday, a side already relegated, we will have to wait and see.

Strachan – he's looking a lot happier

Gordon Strachan

1984–89. Appearances 195 (6). Goals 38. **Manager, Southampton**.

Easily the most entertaining manager in the Premiership, the quick-witted, ever-humorous Strachan has at last begun to show signs of fulfilling his huge potential in management. After presiding over Coventry's first relegation from the top flight in 37 years, many assumed his days in the dug-out were over. But Southampton saw something in him, and have been proved right. For the first time in living memory, the Saints were not in the Premiership relegation reckoning. Plus they reached the FA Cup final for the first time since 1976 (not that anyone remembers that occasion).

Not quite the boyhood dream job ...

Chris Turner

1985–88. Appearances 79. **Manager, Sheffield Wednesday**.

Signed by Big Ron and sold by Fergie, Turner shared one attribute with Fabien Barthez: he was short for a keeper. After an ill-starred time at Leyton Orient, when he was assistant manager and featured in a fly-on-the-wall documentary that became a by-word for managerial incompetence, Turner made his name at Hartlepool. So impressed were the bosses at Hillsborough by the way he took the northeast club to the brink of the second division, they persuaded him to come back to the club he supported as a boy and once played for. He arrived too late to affect any change in the Owls' hopeless league position, and next season will be managing in the same division as Hartlepool.

The Old Gaffers

It's not only players who leave Old Trafford, of course. United had five managers between Sir Matt and Sir Alex.

Wilf McGuinness

Manager, 1969–70.

McGuinness is well-known as a radio pundit, corporate hospitality host and after-dinner speaker in the northwest, telling gags about his ill-starred tenure as manager after Matt Busby ('I knew I'd done

The year in which Wilf lost all his hair

a rick when I dropped Bobby Charlton,' is his favourite line, 'You'd have thought I'd declared nuclear war').

Frank O'Farrell

Manager, 1971–72.

O'Farrell lives a quiet retirement in Torquay, refusing all media requests for interviews about his time at Old Trafford.

Tommy Docherty

Manager, 1972–77.

The Doc is one of the most in-demand speakers in the country: although well into his seventies, his diary is so crammed with engagements that you have to book him at least a year in advance. Though he can always find time for a quick radio interview to claim Fergie is finished. Still married to Mary Brown, who acts as his secretary, he has mellowed into a jovial gag-cracker, delighted to be earning more money now than at any time in his long managerial career.

When Tommy met Mary

The wild ones: Sexton and Sven

Dave Sexton

Manager, 1977–81.

Sexton was never one for the limelight, wilting visibly under the intense heat of interest at Old Trafford. 'If you said, 'Good morning' to him, he'd go out the room and check', is Tommy Docherty's favoured analysis of his successor's style. After managing Coventry for a time, the studious, careful Sexton joined the England coaching set-up and can still be seen aiding Sven Goran Eriksson.

Ron Atkinson

Manager, 1981–86.

Ron Atkinson now devotes all his time to media work, though many Sheffield Wednesday and Coventry fans were under the illusion he was a full-time pundit when he was officially manager of their club towards the end of his career in the dug-out. A brilliant television and radio presence, he has introduced a whole new lexicon into coverage of the game. He was granted a profile in the prestigious *Observer Sports Monthly* magazine during the course of the season, which mocked him up to look like Shakespeare and claimed he had contributed almost as much to modern English as the Bard. Talk about the Hollywood ball.

The Assistants

Brian Kidd

1967–74. Appearances 255 (9). Goals 70. Coach/Assistant Manager 1991–98.
Assistant Manager, **England**.

Much as they tried to pin the blame on their side's decline on Kiddo, Leeds fans now know the horrible mess their club is in is due to figures far more ridiculous, notably Peter Ridsdale. But for a time, the idea that Kiddo was a Red fifth columnist, out to sink Leeds from the inside, was current on the Elland Road terraces. It was a conspiracy theory United fans cheekily enjoyed stirring with loud renditions of 'Kiddo is a Red' on every visit to Elland Road. Kidd's bottomless reserves of loyalty have now been extended to three managers at Leeds: after David O'Leary went, there was Terry Venables, then Peter Reid, who gave him his cards (plus £500k – a Yorkshire tradition) at the end of the season. Still, at least Kidd could take comfort that his qualities were recognised by Sven Goran Eriksson, after he was called into the England set-up following the departure of Steve McClaren.

Archie Knox

Assistant Manager 1986–91.

Archie Knox arrived as assistant manager with Alex Ferguson from Aberdeen, where the pair had formed a sort of chalk and chalk partnership. If anything, Knox is even more abrasive and angry than his mentor, and his outbursts of temper were legendary at United. With an odd sense of timing, he left on the night of the Cup Winners Cup final, just as the team he had helped forge was on the brink of something big. He went to Rangers, his first love, where he teamed up with Walter Smith, whom he followed to Everton on a lucrative contract. Not many tears were shed among Goodison faithful when he and the excitement-free Smith made way for the altogether more charismatic and together David Moyes. Now retired.

Steve McClaren

Assistant Manager. Arrived from Derby County 1999. Left to manage **Middlesbrough**, June 2001.

McClaren and Kidd: the old assistants face up

The ever-ambitious McClaren almost made the first big mistake of his managerial career last summer when he shook on a deal to become the next manager of Leeds United. When Boro's chairman Steve Gibson heard of the impending departure of the man who had brought some good sense to a club drifting badly under Bryan Robson, he acted quickly and scuppered the deal. How McClaren must have lived to thank him, well out of the shambles at Elland Road. It was seen by some as Gibson's revenge on him when McClaren was forced to relinquish the England position he so enjoyed during the season. But if the two are no longer seeing eye to eye, and if Boro never quite lived up to the early promise of the season when the Champions League beckoned, at least he remains in employment and his pay cheques don't bounce.

Talking Reds

If you have worn a Red shirt and can string a few words together, then there is a career in the media waiting for you. For some this may not account for anything more than the occasional fifty quid, for others (such as the great Eamon Dunphy) it has turned into a career more elevated than their time playing.

The big time

Eric Cantona would be a dream pundit to have alongside someone like Motson for big games, but, alas, our man has too much taste. However, he did have his own show for the World Cup: the **Nike** prison-ship tournament, which he MC'd, chest puffed out as of old, to a fine Elvis remix soundtrack.

In the absence of Eric on the co-commentary front, we have to make do – especially for United games – with ex-gaffer Big Ron Atkinson (see previous section) and his homespun wisdom on **ITV**.

Just as much fun, especially during Ireland's 2002 World Cup campaign, when he was sent home after arriving for work 'tired and emotional', are the now perhaps historic RTE appearances of Eamon Dunphy – George Best's mate in the juniors, though he never made a first-team appearance at United. Dunphy doesn't need RTE, however, as he is a top writer, dividing Ireland with his book with Roy Keane.

Garth Crooks, another player whose career at Old Trafford was not his finest hour, is an interviewer on sport and politics at the BBC.

Sky punditry

Paddy Crerand – Red through and through

Sky TV is a decent pension plan for former Reds. The following have been spotted sitting alongside Richard Keys on matchday:
Pat Crerand – every Red's favourite one-eyed commentator, a one-man fan's zone.
Brian and Jimmy Greenhoff – the Phil and Gary of their day, and about as enlightening.
Denis Irwin – clearly they don't pay him enough at Wolves.

Lou Macari – always happy to give a comment to help pay those legal costs he incurred when he sued Celtic for wrongful dismissal.
Paul McGrath – a lovely bloke, we all agree, and, alas, also a regular talking head on programmes about football and alcohol.
Stuart Pearson – said what many of us reckoned after the derby showing, which rattled many a cage in the corridors at Old Trafford.
Bryan Robson – still treading water after his removal from Boro.

Sky Soccer Saturday regulars

George Best – bravely returned to work after his liver transplant.
George Graham – it's easy to be right from the studio, though to be

fair, gorgeous George thought he was right wherever he was.

Gary Pallister – always looks self-conscious in those one-eared headphones.

Frank Stapleton – never quite sure which of his old employers to support, United or Arsenal.

Other pundits

Arthur Albiston – Piccadilly radio's man at the match.

Gary Bailey – apparently the Des Lynam of South Africa, though without the tache.

Joe Jordan – hardly recognisable with those teeth.

Mickey Thomas – now entirely hair-free presence on Century FM.

Ray Wilkins – genetically programmed never to say anything negative about anyone.

Reds are here, Reds are there...

Here's news of other Reds we've kept tabs on. If you know what any other ex-Reds are up to, we'd like to expand this section in next season's Rough Guide, so please email *uws@dial.pipex.com*

Warren Bradley Winger on the fringes of the Busby Babes; runs *Legends*, the Manchester United old boys association.

Martin Buchan Elegance personified at centre back. Now an executive at Puma and was seen – snowy of hair these days – presenting Paul Scholes with an award on the pitch at the Fulham home game.

Raphael Burke A man reckoned by Ryan Giggs to be the best youth team player of his generation. Works at Bristol City youth academy and is a born again Christian.

Phil Chisnell The last player to go from United to Liverpool. For his sins, now makes malt loaf in Urmston.

Dave Gardner Former youth player of the Beckham era. A partner in Jason Ferguson's Elite agency, he occasionally turns out for Altrincham. Still good enough mates with the likes of Ryan Giggs to swap partners (this season Giggs had a child with Gardner's former girlfriend).

John Gidman Scouse full back in the Big Ron era. Lives near Malaga with a Spanish air stewardess, where he plays a lot of golf and tennis.

David McCreery Busy supersub in the Docherty era. Now an agent in Newcastle.

Ralph Milne Fergie Flop. A publican in Bristol.

Kevin Moran Maniacally brave centre back. Works for Paul Stretford's Proactive agency in Wilmslow.

Willie Morgan Big-haired Busby signing. Runs a golfing corporate hospitality company.

Remi Moses Midfielder so hard you wouldn't even look at him. Keeping busy as a landlord in Moss Side.

Jesper Olsen Tricky winger. Also works for Paul Stretford's Proactive agency in Wilmslow.

David Sadler Centre forward in the 1968 team. Runs a corporate hospitality firm in Hale.

Ian Storey Moore A potential great cut down by injury. Now a bookie with a shop near the City Ground in Nottingham.

Arnie Sidebottom Utility defender under Tommy Docherty. Shifted sports to become bowling coach at Yorkshire cricket club, where one of his charges is his son, Ryan.

Graeme Tomlinson Bright hope as a striker until he broke a leg on loan. Released by Exeter last season, he now makes a living as a DJ.

Ian Ure Arsenal man brought in unsuccessfully to shore up the defence in the latter days of Matt Busby. Works as a social worker in Glasgow.

Neil Webb Elegant midfielder turned pie-eater. Now a postman in Reading.

Norman Whiteside Folk hero. Works as a podiatrist for the PFA when he's not enjoying a pint of Guinness.

Please keep off the pitch

Defense de marcher sur l'herbe

Das betreten des rasens ist verboten

Prohibido pisar la hierba

Évietaro camminare sull erba

Old Trafford

A Rough Guide to the
Theatre of Dreams™

Tickets ★ Matchdays ★ Around the Stadium
Stadium Tour and Museum ★ A Swift Half

When Old Trafford *staged the 2003 Champions League final between Juventus and Milan, it vindicated a decade of near continuous investment that has seen the stadium develop into one of the finest on the continent. If there's any criticism of the imposing mass of grey steel on the fringes of the vast Trafford industrial park it's that the 67,800 seats are still too few to cope with the insatiable demand for match tickets. United were the best supported team in Europe in 2001 and 2002, but lost the title to Real Madrid in 2003 on account of the Spaniards having eight thousand more seats. Yet if Old Trafford grows any taller, there will be even less natural light – already a major factor, along with Manchester's grey skies, in a pitch that needs to be relaid midway through each season.*

Still, that's for the groundstaff to worry about. For fans – whether following the Reds, or England, or here for a Cup game – a first glimpse of the stadium is always a thrill. And when there's no big event on, the ground and museum are usually busy, even in the post-Beckham world.

Following is a guide to the Old Trafford experience, beginning, of course, with getting in to see a game. For details of getting to the ground and parking, see the next chapter.

5 reasons why we love Old Trafford...

1. It's the biggest club stadium in Britain.
2. It's a beautiful cavity of redness on the inside, with every seat afforded an unobstructed view of the pitch.
3. The long-term foresight of the development – not for United running tracks or stands that bear no resemblance to each other. It's a football stadium in the truest sense of the word.
4. It may not be the biggest stadium in Europe, but in terms of furnishings and other supporter facilities like televisions in the concourses, it's the best.
5. The neon 'Manchester United' sign, the Busby statue, the Munich clock, the Museum. It's these details that add to the tradition and international reputation of the stadium. That, and all the memories...

... and 5 reasons why we don't...

1. It's still not big enough to satisfy demand.
2. If it's leg-room you're after, you get more on a bus.
3. There's a dearth of decent pubs and restaurants in this location on the edge of an industrial estate.
4. Putting an executive section in the middle of the Stretford End, previously the vocal heartland of United support, was a shockingly bad idea.
5. The grass won't grow in winter.

Anyone got a ticket ...?

When United met Arsenal at Highbury in April, the announcement
of the crowd figure – 38,164 – produced no end of mockery from
the travelling Reds. They knew the significance of the figure, 30,000
lower than the average United gate. It is this stadium capacity at Old
Trafford that is United's biggest financial advantage: £1m a home
game more than Arsenal's receipts from the turnstiles – which
means over the season, enough to pay for Ruud van Nistelrooy. For
all its merchandising, sponsorship and television money, gate
receipts still provide the largest chunk of United's income. Indeed,
the latest figures available reveal that in the six months to 31 January
2003, commercial activity brought in £22.8m and media income
£26.8m, while in through the turnstiles came a whopping £42.9m.

With its extended capacity, the moan that it is impossible to get
hold of a ticket for a home game has become a slightly hollow one.
True, spares for the big games are harder to come by than a Gary
Neville goal. But anyone can become a member at the start of the
season and members who apply for tickets on a regular basis receive
a fair number (if not all) of the tickets they request. You don't always
need to book far ahead, either: matches against lesser teams, and
midweek or Sunday games, don't tend to sell out immediately.

Tickets for away games are a very different issue (see p.309).

Ways and means: home tickets

To apply for tickets, you have to be a member of the club (see p.387
for details). As part of the membership package, you receive a book-
let of application forms for all Premiership games. There are around
20,000 seats available in this way; the rest are reserved for season-
ticket holders (for which there is a long waiting list).

To apply for members' tickets is straightforward: you fill out the
relevant form, send it off with an SAE and cheque or credit card
details six weeks before the game for which you wish to apply, and
wait. A couple of weeks later, you will either receive a fat envelope
(good news) containing tickets, or a thin one (bad news) with a let-

ter from club secretary Ken Merrett thanking you for your support and suggesting you try again next time. It appears to be a genuine lottery: some members seem to get tickets every time, others are less lucky. By the law of averages, someone has to miss out.

Around half of United season-ticket holders are signed up to a deal where they automatically receive cup tickets. The rest will decide if they want to attend a particular cup game and exercise their right to a ticket in the weeks before the game. The rest of the tickets are available to members in the same way as league games.

Most FA Cup and European games tend to sell out fast. However, a few of the lesser European games go on open sale in the weeks before the games – as do League Cup games – if you fancy a look at the juniors.

For details on tickets for all home games, call the United ticket information line: ☎0161 868 8020.

High Fives with the manager: the best seats in the house

Supporters' club tickets and trips

Another way of securing a ticket is through your local branch of the supporters' club (see p.388); they order in blocks and may have spares available. Supporters' clubs are particularly useful if you live away from Manchester, as most branches also organise cheap trips to home matches. The Oxford and Banbury branch, for instance, charges only £11 for the round-trip from Oxfordshire to Old Trafford, while the London branches offer reduced fares on the trains (if they're running). Despite the club encouraging Mancunians to join the membership scheme rather than form a supporters' club, more supporters' clubs are now opening in and around Manchester. These can be a source for tickets, too.

Executive packages

Tickets to United home games are also offered as part of executive packages, through United's commercial department (☎0161 868 8200) and various travel agents. Prices and packages vary, but for around £140 you will typically receive a meal in one of the many restaurants at the ground, a decent match ticket, car parking space, match programme and access to the museum. Or you can go for broke with the platinum club – a cool £400 for the above, plus a chance to stroll round the pitch, unlimited champagne and a pre-match bevvy with Norman Whiteside or another ex-player. The 'cheaper' packages tend to sell out fast for the bigger games but the club has been known to advertise packages for lesser games. The club has come in for some criticism as many of these packages end up being touted on the Internet and they have cut down the number of companies they supply tickets to.

Despite discouragement from the club, privately run ticketing companies know that it's not illegal to buy executive packages and sell them on, often at highly inflated prices. If you browse the Internet you'll find numerous offers, some with accommodation included (perhaps at the part-United-owned *Golden Tulip Hotel* opposite the ground). Prices vary hugely according to the game and where the company is based. Irish companies can be good value; US

Ticket touts

Despite perennial clampdowns, matchday tickets are traded regularly on the black market outside Old Trafford – and in particular around the approach road, Sir Matt Busby Way. Undercover police look out for ticket touts but seem as likely to arrest and charge United fans, selling a spare ticket for a game. It's a bit hit and miss.

Before home matches, the touts are not hard to track down – they tend to sweep through the crowd advancing on the stadium, saying: 'anyone need tickets, I'll buy or sell'. Most touts conduct the transaction in reasonable faith but it goes without saying that this is an illegal activity and is not covered by standard consumer legislation: if the ticket turns out to be forged or the tout legs it with your cash, you just have to swallow hard.

Simple rules of supply and demand dictate ticket prices from the touts. For Liverpool, Arsenal or a big European match, prices will be at their most expensive and can exceed £100 a ticket. Saturday games, too, tend to be expensive. But for a midweek European game or a Premiership fixture against moderate opposition you can usually pick up a ticket for little over face value. You can also find tickets on the Internet auction site *ebay.co.uk* – though this again is an area that the club are trying to crack down on.

Of course, you could always try at the ticket office first, as some tickets are returned on the day of the game.

ones tend to charge a pretty hefty premium. But there are no rules: you need to shop around. The website *lastminute.com*, in particular, is always worth monitoring for deals.

Matchdays

Most matchday fans approach the stadium along Sir Matt Busby Way (previously Warwick Road). The sheer number of people filling the road in a slow procession to the ground is a spectacle in its own right, as are the unofficial 'swag' stalls selling badges, scarves, souvenirs and T-shirts celebrating a recent victory with a cheeky slogan or a United hero, or slagging off Liverpool, Leeds or City. There are stands offering to paint your face in United colours – popular with a surprising number of adults as well as kids – and

Legends, featuring Ashley Grimes

fanzine sellers dispensing *United We Stand*, *Red News* and *Red Issue*. You can buy the official match programme from red cabins along the route.

Fast food, inevitably, is also much in evidence, with pies and chips to the fore. Where Chester Road meets Sir Matt Busby Way the parade of shops includes Lou Macari's – a fish-and-chip shop once owned by the great Luigi himself – and the prominent Legends, a chippie with a café and off-licence inside, plus a huge mural of United's star players of yesteryear. As you stare at the players, trying to name them all, you might wonder what that character in the Leo Sayer wig is doing among the Bests, Charltons and Whitesides. It can't be Ashley Grimes, can it? Well, yes. One of Ashley's mates owns the place and decided to include the curly mopped ex-Red alongside more famous counterparts.

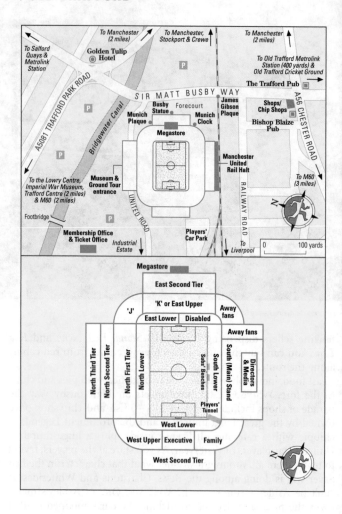

The heart and soul of Salford

Around the stadium

Approached from Sir Matt Busby Way, Old Trafford is a majestic sight – the glass and steel portico of the East Stand towering above, visible for miles across Salford, calling the faithful to worship. Sir Matt himself is there, his statue perched halfway up the glasswork, looking down on the throng pouring into that vital hub of the new football economy: the United Megastore.

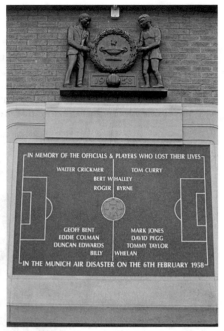

The Munich plaque

There are two poignant reminders of the Munich air disaster outside the stadium. The Munich clock – stopped forever at the time of the disaster – stands above the ticket office, while a plaque dedicated to those who lost their lives is built into the wall of the new glass-fronted East Stand. At the opposite end of the stadium, outside the players' entrance at the Stretford End (you'll see their cars before you see the entrance) is a good-looking plaque dedicated to the memory of Sir Matt Busby. This was organised and paid for by supporters following the great man's passing in January 1994.

If you're a completist, you can spot three more plaques around Old Trafford. One is inside the North Stand to commemorate its opening by UEFA's Lennart Johansson, another in the museum to commemorate its opening by Pelé. A third is outside on Sir Matt Busby Way, by the corner of the ground on the bridge over the

Liverpool to Manchester railway, in memory of the former United chairman James Gibson who saved the club in the 1930s (see History).

In 2002, the club also unveiled a statue of Denis Law, the original King of the Stretford End. Its location, on the concourse of the second tier, means it is accessible to only 6,000 United fans. Nevertheless, it was a noble gesture and perhaps one which should be repeated to honour other United greats.

Sir Matt still presides

The Megastore

Back in 1992 United appointed a man called Edward Freedman to look at the club's merchandising operation. Having overseen Tottenham's commercial activity, he was shocked at what he found: the souvenir shop's mail order department, for instance, consisted of just two people answering the phone and packing the orders, and when they wanted to pack orders they'd take the phone off the hook. One of Freedman's first moves was to open a 5,000-square-foot supermarket-style Megastore in a warehouse behind the Stretford End. It was an immediate and huge success.

Whilst the new store and merchandise operations – with their Fred the Red babygros – seemed crassly offensive to many fans, as the profits rolled in the operation became the envy of every other football club from Barcelona to Bayern Munich. United never looked back, replacing the original Megastore with one three times the size when the new East Stand opened in 2000.

The Megastore, and its rows of checkouts, is packed on a match-day and busy throughout the year, especially in school holidays. There's a printing facility for shirt lettering (Van Nistelrooy 9 is a pricey item) and a household-worth of United branded goods to choose from. The store is a first call for many visiting tourists and overseas supporters and even the hardcore fans, these days, accept its role in keeping United's financial muscles flexed.

Since Nike took over the shirt sponsorship – and with it control of the merchandise operation – the store has undergone an overhaul. A sheen of Nikeworld slickness has been glossed on, and the leisure wear is significantly more stylish than in the pile 'em high, sell 'em cheap days of Freedman and Umbro. Profits, too, are thought to have increased, and the Megastore's value to the bottom line of United plc – reckoned to be upwards of £100,000 a home match – is not underestimated by the board. How cheesed off the accountants must have been when UEFA insisted the shop remained closed on the day of the Champions League final.

Of the cash flying through the tills, Beckham accounted for 57 percent of all player-specific merchandise sold and his departure will be a major short-term loss. But others are catching up: O'Shea is very popular with the Irish, while Van Nistelrooy is frequenting the back of ever more shirts, despite the financial implications of his name. Intriguingly, despite the efficiency of the operation, the Megastore had no Championship-specific merchandise ready when United won the league in 2003 for the 15th time. Which allowed the swag men operating down the Warwick Road to clean up with their 'We've got our trophy back' number.

Memorabilia

Memorabilia fans might like to make a quick detour at the start of Sir Matt Busby Way to check out a trio of matchday outlets along the parallel Partridge Street (by the *Bishop Blaize* pub). The largest of these is Red Star Sports – a crowded shop that stocks official merchandise as well as badges and programmes, and has a good collection of fanzines, badges, books and videos, all decently priced. To its side is a cabin which also sells old programmes and, behind that, in a garage, is Tony's stall, which sells boxloads of programmes and United-related books.

The Red shirt – carried with pride

The stadium tour and museum

Even on a non-matchday, Old Trafford is a top attraction: so much so, in fact, that just down the road stands a Salford tourist information centre (a concept that seems to have escaped from stand-up comedy). But it is good to report that visitors – wide-eyed Scandinavians, Japanese and Malaysians, and Reds from every part of Britain – are not ripped off for their devotion. There is plenty more on offer than an empty pitch.

The State of the Pitch

Often compared with barren arctic tundra in the 1980s, Old Trafford's pitch gradually improved and by the mid '90s was one of the best in the country – a green oasis throughout the season. But problems started again with the building of the giant North Stand in 1995. Such was the height of the 25,000-seater monolith that it cast a longer shadow and affected Old Trafford's microclimate so much that pitches began to be relaid as frequently as Ronny Johnsen picked up an injury. Almost. The new, higher, East and West Stands which were built in 2000 exacerbated the problem, while Manchester's excessive rain hardly helped either. Nor, according to Sir Alex and other critics, did allowing big rugby games to be played on the pitch mid-season.

Revolutionary attempts using grass from Australia and Kentucky have been tried to stop the winter disintegration from lush to mush, but ultimately, given the towering stands, whichever pitch is laid at Old Trafford, it never receives the ideal amount of sunlight or wind, and fans have reluctantly become used to the pitch being ripped up and replaced once or twice each winter.

Whether he had had enough of this or not, Keith Kent, United's groundsman for over a decade, left tending the worms at Old Trafford to try his hand at an even bigger stadium, Twickenham, last season. He was replaced by another Keith – Porter - who was a groundsman at Carrington. We wish him well. He'll need it.

The stadium tour

The United stadium tour lasts around 90 minutes with a chance to visit such out-of-bounds places as the corporate hospitality areas, the law court-like press conference room and the directors' box. The guides, who take around groups of up to thirty people at a time, are invariably chirpy and upbeat. True, some of their patter seems targeted at 8-year-olds ("and who's the captain of the club? That's right, it's Mr Roy Keane"), but nobody could gainsay their enthusiasm.

And there are real points of interest on the tour you would never get to see otherwise: the pads of discarded chewing gum in the manager's dug-out, the home dressing room's Jacuzzi (the visitors are obliged to make do with a couple of showers), or the players' lounge with its honours board detailing every capped United player on the wall opposite the bar (which, incidentally, serves no alcohol immediately after matches). The guides are hot on trivia, too. Those who have been on the tour will never be troubled again by such pressing United quiz questions as: Who was the first international from a country outside the British Isles to play for the Reds? (Answer: Nicolai Jovanovic, for Yugoslavia in 1980.)

The museum

The stadium tour begins in the club museum, which you can visit on its own if you prefer. Deep in the bowels of the North Stand, this is a brilliantly curated attraction, chock-full of fascinating archive material. Naturally, the players feature heavily. There are shirts, caps and tro-

phies galore belonging to any number of heroes, including an original pair of George Best's side-laced purple and black Stylo Matchmaker boots, manufactured a good 25 years before Nike caught onto the idea. Fans, too, are commemorated, most notably by a tailor's dummy mocked up to resemble the typical member of Doc's Red Army back in the 1970s – decked out in denim, every inch of it covered in United badges and patches, with scarves knotted around wrists and neck.

There's poignancy, here, as well. The Munich air crash is recalled in headlines of the day; a plaque was installed in memory of the three construction workers killed building the vertiginous stands of the new Old Trafford; and

The trophy is back

Inside Old Trafford: the three Ps

Much of the catering at Old Trafford is, as Roy Keane famously hinted, geared to corporate packages and their hospitality suites. If you're one of the majority privileged enough not to be watching football from one of these executive facilities, your choice inside the ground is essentially a crowded steel and breeze-block bar in one of the underbellies of the stands. They're nothing special.

However, for most fans, the vital elements of matchday catering are still the three Ps: a pint, a pie and a piss. Two prongs of this essential trinity are well attended to at Old Trafford. There are plenty of toilets, and quite decent pies (reasonably priced at £1.50). But pints? Well, beer is served at most games (certain European ties are designated alcohol-free for the masses), but, oddly enough, United haven't cracked how to dispense it – at least at half-time. By the time you've got to the bar and had your can of lager poured into a plastic glass, you're missing the action. And you can't take it with you. Any alcohol has to be consumed away from a view of the pitch.

there is a section dedicated to Sir Matt, including some of the tributes that formed an impromptu shrine spreading across the stadium forecourt for a fortnight after he died in January 1994. And, if you wondered what happened to the rest of the material from that shrine – the scarves, the shirts, the newspaper collages – it was stuffed into the hollow centre of the statue to the great man at the front of the stadium.

The museum has regular special exhibits so that fans are enticed to return. An exhibition devoted to the glorious treble year was well received last season, as was one dedicated to Ryan Giggs in his testimonial year.

On the subject of museums, the new Imperial War Museum (see following chapter), just ten minutes walk from the North Stand, has been an unlikely beneficiary of all those lunchtime kick-offs. Rather than wrestling with the traffic jams that fur up all arterial roads after the game, many a family party has spent the post-match afternoon enjoying its magnificent architecture, stunning audio-visual displays and the best roof-top angle on Manchester from its vertiginous viewing platform. The double whammy of match and history is an intoxicating one. And entry is free.

The Red Café

United's own Red Café, hidden away above the museum in the North Stand, feels in many ways an extension of the museum, stuffed as it is with memorabilia. If you have an appetite for more framed mementoes, and fancy watching a United video while you eat, then here's your place. If you're over 10, you probably won't thrill to the food, which is standard American fare – burgers, chicken wings, potato skins – served by waiting staff dressed in United kit. And outside matchdays, it's not very full.

Stadium tours (including museum entry) take place daily 9.40am–4.30pm. There are no tours on matchdays. Prices: £8.50 (adults); £5.75 (juniors, OAPs, concessions); £23.50 (family: 2 adults, 2 juniors). Advance telephone booking on ☎0161 868 8631 is strongly recommended.

Old Trafford Museum is open every day 9.30am–5pm; on matchdays, it closes 30 minutes prior to kick-off. Prices: £5.50 (adults); £3.50 (juniors, OAPs, concessions); £15.10 (family: 2 adults, 2 juniors); under-5s free.

Around Old Trafford: a swift half

Old Trafford is located on the edge of Trafford Park – one of Europe's biggest industrial estates and an area not renowned for its public houses (or anything much else). But getting a pre-match, or post-match, drink is not a problem, either for locals, who meet at pubs along the way, or for the coachloads of supporters' clubs, who tend to have long working relationships with local landlords. The Lowry Outlet mall in the Quays has a couple of new generic bars that are a ten- to fifteen-minute walk from the stadium over the impressive new canal bridge.

For the uninitated, here are some of the more popular pubs near to the ground.

The Trafford ▶ Chester Road (at the top of Sir Matt Busby Way)
The nearest pub to the ground, this gets very noisy and busy on a matchday, with fans enjoying the freedom to do things they are no longer allowed to do in the stadium, such as standing up and singing. Plus there's a big screen to take in previews and highlights.

Floating high – a European night at Old Trafford

Bishop Blaize ▶ Chester Road
This Wetherspoons pub is the place to go for a pre-match sing-song, usually led by the resident conductor, Peter Boyle. It has good-value beer, food and service, and matchday bouncers stop it getting too hectic.

Sam Platts ▶ Trafford Wharf Road
Modern pub overlooking the Manchester Ship Canal. Members only on match-days. IMUSA and Shareholders United members meet upstairs for a drink before the game.

The Gorse Hill ▶ Chester Road
A big Victorian pub on the A56 into the City Centre, frequented by locals and supporters' club branches on matchdays. Good beer, pool tables, TV screens. 10 mins walk from the ground.

The Tollgate ▶ Seymour Grove

Opposite Trafford Bar metro station 10mins walk from the stadium. Again, popular with supporters' club branches and locals alike.

The Quadrant ▶ Kings Road

Near to Lancashire Cricket Ground, the 'Quaddy' used to be a big hangout of the Babes. Tommy Taylor had an understanding with the publican who would quietly refill his glass under the counter with gin while he had a bottle of tonic on the table. 15mins walk to ground.

Trafford Hall Hotel ▶ Talbot Road

Basement public bar underneath a hotel of the same name near the Trafford Bar metro. Good pint of Stella. Fills up quickly. The bar, that is, not the pints.

Trafford Park Hotel ▶ Trafford Park

Huge pub in the industrial estate, 10mins walk from the stadium. Full-size snooker table. Popular with branches. Good for parking.

Old Pump House ▶ Salford Quays

Good-looking canalside pub. Busy on a matchday.

Hanarahans ▶ Salford Quays

Theme bar offering good food and several TV screens. Situated amidst a clutch of new American diners. 10mins walk from the ground.

Manchester

A Rough Guide to to the city
(just in case you need it)

Around Town ★ Getting there ★ Accommodation
Restaurants ★ Pubs & Clubs

Manchester's stock is at its highest level since the industrial revolution. If the Commonwealth Games brought attention and appreciation from the remnants of the British Empire that still envelop a quarter of the world's population, then the staging of the 2003 European Cup final boosted the image of the city on the continent. Italian fans, whose knowledge of Manchester was based on their geography teacher's assessment that the north of England was industrial, grey and forbidding, were surprised not to find Lowryesque landscapes, but a vibrant, self-confident city with a European feel. That it coincided with one of the few sun-filled days that constitute a Mancunian summer was down to divine intervention.

The Italians witnessed a Manchester that has changed beyond recognition in the past decade. Madchester may have been mooching in the early 1990s, but the city was the epitome of industrial decay and urban blight. But that was then… If you want to gauge the new Manchester then stand on the sleek footbridge over the Ship Canal in Salford Quays. On one bank is the Lowry, on the other the new Imperial War Museum, two buildings as daring and articulate as the Guggenheim in Bilbao. Beyond is Old Trafford's North Stand, the biggest stadium structure in Britain. It's apt, because United beat at the heart of the reinvented Manchester and the club's importance to the city's profile cannot be understated. After all, if there was no Old Trafford then there would have been no European Cup final to stage.

Apparently some people who come to watch the Reds each fortnight don't come from Manchester. So, if you are a Red from Oxford, Oslo or Osaka, next time you are in the city, take time to look beyond the Megastore and check out a few of the places in the pages following…

Manchester: so much to answer for

That's the boast on the T-shirts and why not? As well as being home to the world's greatest football team, Manchester was the birthplace of the industrial revolution and the place where the atom was first split and the world's first computer built.

More recently, Manchester has been a dominant force in British music and club culture. And, during the last decade, it has seen a genuine city renaissance, with new galleries, restaurants, museums and shops fired up by its bids for the Olympic Games, its hosting of the 2002 Commonwealth Games and, in no small part, the phenomenal success of United. Ironically, the IRA bombing of the city centre, in June 1996, also made a major contribution to the new Manchester. The bomb killed nobody – some kind of a miracle, considering 80,000 people were evacuated – but destroyed much of the city's more unattractive shopping areas. Seven years on, substantially rebuilt, the city centre is a much better place with new civic squares and bold new stores – *Harvey Nichols* has arrived, much to the relief of half of Cheshire (and most of the city's Premiership footballers). The buzz is tangible.

In truth, of course, the boom has not reached all parts of the city and for all the talk of 24-hour party people (as the best and funniest film ever made about the city coined its denizens), Manchester simply isn't happening for much of the week. The Commonwealth Games was intended to kick-start the regeneration of East Manchester, yet huge swathes of the metropolitan area remain blighted with poverty, crime and drug dependency. But in the centre, at least, Manchester is very much the face of New Britain.

Around town

If you don't know Manchester, take some time to explore some of the sights, new and old. The Manchester visitor centre in the town hall offers free maps of the city centre and, like every newsagent, sells the *City Life* listings magazine. Equipped with these, and an umbrella, you're ready to roll.

Spin City

Whilst Mancunians are proud of their city, Manchester isn't always perceived positively elsewhere. To some who have never visited, the city conjures images of satanic mills and back-to-back terraced houses whose flat-cap wearing occupants dream of an inside toilet. We'll forgive them for confusing our city with Bolton.

The 2002 Commonwealth Games and 2003 Champions League final helped change perceptions of Manchester for the better. The Commonwealths were a resounding success and boosted Manchester's international image, and whilst it's City rather than United who will benefit from their legacy as they move into the new 48,000-capacity City of Manchester stadium, a Manchester that is perceived positively will aid United when it comes to attracting top continental stars who, according to one *Times* writer: "currently look from their coaches with horror at the northwest's industrial environs" on their away-day trips to United. New buildings, museums, shops, hotels and fancy street furniture mean that the city is as scrubbed up as the former cotton warehouses turned into expensive apartments.

Old Trafford, too, is already regarded as a footballing citadel by many Europeans, but it needs further redevelopment to be compared with the very best: Nou Camp, Bernabeu and San Siro. On a different level, City's new stadium may receive the plaudits for its architecture, but it doesn't compare to Old Trafford, in size or stature. United fill the ground each week and if it weren't for the limited 68,000 capacity, the club would be the best supported in Europe. As it stands, Real Madrid, Barcelona and Borussia Dortmund all have bigger stadiums and slightly higher average attendances. The latter are expanding theirs still further for the 2006 World Cup. Is it time that United did the same?

Around Salford

You could do no better than to start at Salford Quays, just down the road from Old Trafford (and an easy place to visit after a lunchtime game). Here, the £96m lottery-funded Lowry Centre was established around a huge collection of paintings by L.S. Lowry – a City fan, apparently, but creator of the definitive images of the North's industrial cityscapes. The galleries are free, and there are theatre-concert halls (a top place to see bands and stand-up comedy), temporary exhibitions and cafés in the complex.

On the opposite banks of the Manchester Ship Canal is the Imperial War Museum for the North, designed by acclaimed architect Daniel Libeskind and opened in July 2002. This distinctive building is made up of three shards of fractured steel which represent the world's conflicts on land, sea and in the air. Entrance to the museum is free. There's also a new outlet shopping mall next to the Lowry, all within a fifteen-minute walk of the stadium.

Who would have imagined a Salford Tourist Office? But here's the new view

Off to the city centre

In the centre, it's worth a wander around the revamped shopping areas, panning out from Deansgate, and a look at the great Victorian Royal Exchange building. Opposite here is a new glass (an important ingredient in modern Manchester's make-up) building built by the site of the '96 bomb. It was initially the world's biggest M&S,

although half the building is now occupied by Selfridges and its captivating food hall. Meantime, a *Harvey Nichols* store is opening in the base of the No.1 Deansgate building opposite, a glass tower of expensive apartments, some of which have been purchased by United players as city centre bolt holes.

Nearby, in front of the Triangle shopping centre, is Exchange Square where visiting European fans are usually entertained before a match. Opposite the neon-covered Printworks cinema and leisure complex (where the young Brooklyn celebrated his birthdays, and many players bring their kids along for private cinema showings) is Urbis, a striking, sloping glass structure. Opened in 2002, Urbis (£5 for adults, £3.50 concessions) is a museum about cities of the world, comparing Manchester with São Paulo and New York amongst others. It's highly interactive and innovative, but unlike Manchester's other new attractions, visitor numbers haven't been as impressive as expected.

By the side of Urbis is Cathedral Gardens, a new public space (Manchester's industrial heritage means that it doesn't have enough of these) with a water feature that's a great spot by the city's Cathedral for a picnic...when the weather's good.

Perhaps the grandest building in Manchester in the Town Hall, the neo-Gothic Victorian pile north of the Houses of Parliament. Free tours take you around the inside on a Wednesday and Saturday. United used to celebrate Cup wins on the balcony outside until safety fears, due to the crush in Albert Square, led to a simple open-top bus procession around the city.

The John Rylands Library on Deansgate is another classic piece of Victorian Gothic (free guided tours). And, if you still have time to kill, there's the Museum of Science and Industry in Castlefield and the Manchester Museum and Whitworth Art Gallery on Oxford Road.

Finally, the enlarged Manchester City Art Gallery which opened in 2002 on Mosley Street contains works by Constable, Turner and Gainsborough. A new twentieth century art section contains Hockney and Freud – but not, sadly, any canvasses by the locally revered Cantona. Again, admission is free.

Getting to Manchester

Although you might not always think it, stuck on an approach road to Old Trafford, or arriving behind schedule on a delayed Virgin train, Manchester has some of the best transport infrastructure in the country.

TRAINS Located on the northeast fringe of the city centre, **Piccadilly train station** has been spruced up beyond recognition. There's an hourly connection direct with London Euston (2hr 40min in theory and due to be trimmed in the near future once the sleek new fast trains are allowed to run at full pelt) and direct links to most other UK cities. Liverpool and Leeds are both less than an hour away. For timetable and fare information, call ☎08457 484950.

   Local trains have an extensive network serving the 2.3m people of Greater Manchester, and Old Trafford has its own stop on matchdays, trains disgorging passengers directly into the South Stand (very useful when it's raining). Some of these trains start from Crewe, but all pick up passengers at Stockport and Manchester Piccadilly and Oxford Road stations. Four trains return in the ninety minutes following matches. For local rail (and bus) information, call ☎0161 228 7811.

COACHES **National Express** (☎0900 808080) coaches arrive at the city's Chorlton Street bus station, which received a long-awaited make-over in time for the Commonwealth Games. It is a two-minute walk from the terminal to the Metrolink station (see opposite) at Piccadilly Gardens.

FLIGHTS **Manchester International Airport** (☎0161 489 8000) is the UK's biggest outside London and has direct flight connections with most major European cities, half a dozen US destinations, and regular London links. However, despite recent introduction of the low-cost BMI baby, it still doesn't offer the same choice of budget destinations airlines as Liverpool, to the frustration of many of United's Euro travellers. The airport is linked by a direct 25-minute train service to Manchester Piccadilly, the city's main railway station (see above). Or you can get a taxi direct to Old Trafford for around £14.

DRIVING The Old Trafford area gets pretty clogged up on matchdays, but even in a car you can normally clear the area in thirty to forty minutes. The biggest problem is **parking**, both in central Manchester and around the ground (see below).

   Driving to Old Trafford is fairly straightforward:

City of trams – and the sun always shines

Approaching Old Trafford from the south along the M6, leave at junction 19 and take the A556 (signposted Airport), then the M56 (signposted Manchester) and M60 (signposted Stretford). Leave the M60 at the junction 7 for Stretford and follow signs for A56 Manchester. Old Trafford is two miles from this junction and you can see the huge stands from the motorway.

From the north on the M6, leave at junction 21a, and take the M62 (towards Manchester), joining the M60 at junction 12 (signposted Stretford). Leave the M60 at junction 7 as above.

From the west, take either the M56 or the M62 and follow the instructions above.

From the east, take the M62 (as above).

PARKING AROUND THE GROUND Most **car parks** around Old Trafford are owned by the club and are reserved for some of the 7,000 fans who eat a meal in one of the many corporate hospitality facilities before a game. If you're not on for that, then look out for the makeshift car parks you pass along the way in. Some of these are organised by school PTAs who boost funds with the pro- ceeds, others by local 'entrepreneurs'; they range in price from £3 to £5. Of course, the closer you park to the stadium, the longer it will take you to get away at the end of the game. However, the recent stadium developments and increase in capacity were matched by new and improved roads around Old Trafford and better public transport.

Another alternative is to park in **Altrincham** or **Sale** and take the tram to the ground.

GETTING AROUND: TRAMS, BUSES AND TAXIS Manchester's excellent if pricey **Metrolink tram system** runs on two lines, both of which serve the city centre and have stops within a half mile of Old Trafford: these are **Old Trafford station** on the Bury–Altrincham line and **Exchange Quays station** on the newer Manchester–Eccles line. Matchday trams are crowded but they are frequent enough to cope. A new introduction has been the free Metroshuttle buses which link the main rail stations and Metrolink stops in two circular loops around the city centre. Best of all, they're free.

Trams have taken most of the custom from **city buses**, but there are still plenty of buses between the ground and the city centre, too. Bus routes hub from the Piccadilly bus station.

Manchester's **black taxis** aren't overly plentiful: count yourself lucky if you get one at throwing-out time or after a game. A yellow rooflight means they're available to be flagged down in the street, or you can call one on ☏0161 236 5133 or ☏0161 236 9974. A cab costs about £4 from the city centre to Old Trafford and £13 to the airport.

Accommodation

When Manchester made its bid to host the 2000 Olympics, the London press mocked the city and its facilities – with some justice, as the best hotel was a *Holiday Inn*. But over the last few years cranes have sprouted on the city's skyline, and the city has gained a host of excellent accomodation, with its first five-star, Rocco Forte's waterfront *Lowry*, soon to be joined by a *Radisson Edwardian* in the historic Free Trade Hall. There are also dozens of new chain hotels and refurbished office buildings that have been converted into hotels. Even United have got in on the act, with a themed three-star hotel, the *Golden Tulip*, opposite Old Trafford, and another, *The Tulip Inn*, opposite the Trafford shopping centre.

It has reached the point that an oversupply of rooms seems on the horizon, but you still have to book early to stay over for a United home game. If you have problems, try the city's visitor information centre ☎0161 234 3157, or accommodation credit card booking line ☎0161 234 3169.

Hotel prices below are for a double room for two people, and, where stated, include breakfast. They were current as of mid-2003.

Budget (under £60)

Bishopgate Premierlodge ▶ Lower Mosely St; ☎0161 237 9955; 147 Rooms; £46 B&B
Excellent-value budget rooms in a handy location, opposite the Midland hotel, above *Henry's Bar*, and with a nearby tram stop for Old Trafford.

Castlefield YMCA ▶ Liverpool Road; ☎0161 832 7073; 48 Rooms; £59 B&B
The YMCA is these days a modern(ish) three-star hotel, convenient for Old Trafford and the regenerated Castlefield bars. A plaque in the hotel commemorates the Babes who died at Munich and who were YMCA members.

Holiday Inn Express ▶ Salford Quays; ☎0161 868 1000; 120 Rooms; £38.50 B&B
A useful budget choice ten minutes' walk from Old Trafford, and ideal for the Lowry and Imperial War Museum, with decent rooms, and a bar.

Ibis ▶ Charles Street; ☎0161 272 5000; 126 Rooms; £35 B&B
Another great-value budget choice near Oxford Road and the fine *Lass O'Gowrie* public house, a favoured haunt for thirsty Reds. (If this hotel is full ask them for the number of their second Manchester hotel on Portland Street.)

Manchester Conference Centre ▶ Sackville Street; ☎0161 955 8000;
134 Rooms; £47 room only; £65.50 B&B
Three-star hotel with a restaurant and bar. Convenient for village bars and Piccadilly station.

Mitre Hotel ▶ Cathedral Gates; ☎0161 834 4128; 32 Rooms; £50 B&B
Refurbished guesthouse set in Manchester Cathedral grounds.

Old Trafford Lodge ▶ Talbot Road, Stretford; ☎0161 874 3333; 68 Rooms; £42–£47 B&B
A smart new hotel with rooms overlooking Old Trafford cricket pitch. There's car parking – and it's only five minutes' walk to the football.

Premierlodge ▶ Victoria Bridge Street; ☎0870 700 1488; 170 Rooms; £46 B&B
A new conversion occupying ten floors in a city centre tower block. Rooms on the upper floors have great views.

Premierlodge ▶ River Street; ☎0870 700 1490; 200 Rooms; £46 B&B
A brand-new budget hotel in the developing 'City South' area close to Deansgate Lock bars.

Travel Inn ▶ Oxford Street; ☎ 0870 242 8000; £49.95 B&B
Budget option in a new hotel/pub/bar development. Close to Chinatown and Oxford Road station.

Travelodge ▶ Blackfriars Street; ☎ 0161 834 9476; 181 Rooms; £49.95 B&B
This newish hotel on the banks of River Irwell is a minute's walk from the city centre.

Tulip Inn ▶ Trafford Centre; ☎ 0161 755 3355 121 Rooms; £49.50 B&B
This newly built mock Georgian pile is part-owned by United. It's bang opposite the Trafford Centre – Britain's largest out of town shopping centre – and Old Trafford is a five-minute drive away.

Walkabout ▶ Quay Street; ☎ 0161 817 4800; 20 Rooms; £44.95 B&B
Part of huge and very busy Australian bar/pub/club complex.

Mid-range to expensive (£60–£150)

Britannia Hotel ▶ Portland Street; ☎ 0161 228 2288; 225 Rooms; £75–£105 B&B
This garish four-star hotel was used for a David Beckham fashion shoot for *Arena* magazine. It's a popular stopover for Irish Reds, so is usually good for a singsong in the bar after games.

Britannia Sachas ▶ Tib Street; ☎ 0161 228 1234; 223 Rooms; £75–£105 B&B
This big, brassy chain hotel is a favourite with visiting Scandinavian supporters – perhaps the big stuffed bear in reception makes them feel at home.

Copthorne Hotel ▶ Salford Quays; ☎ 0161 873 7321; 166 Rooms; £99 B&B
This four-star hotel, five minutes' walk from Old Trafford and the Salford Quays Metrolink, is popular with visiting UEFA officials.

Golden Tulip Hotel ▶ Old Trafford; ☎ 0161 873 8899; 111 Rooms; £80 B&B
United part-own this three-star hotel – located bang opposite the stadium – and unsurprisingly it's United-themed. There's a well-rated Gary Rhodes (now who did he play for?) signature restaurant.

Jurys Inn ▶ Great Bridgewater Street; ☎ 0161 953 8888; 265 Rooms; £61–£75 B&B
An excellent-value, large, new three-star hotel in a superb location for current nightlife hotspots. Rooms can sleep three adults.

The Lowry ▶ Chapel Wharf; ☎ 0161 827 4000; 164 Rooms; £120–£185 room only
Manchester's first five-star hotel has established itself with wealthy visitors as the city's top hotel and with local folk who like to be seen in its bars and Marco Pierre White signature restaurant. Giggs has been there a few times, they say.

Malmaison ▶ Piccadilly; ☎ 0161 278 1000; 200 Rooms; £82.50–£115 B&B
This trendy and popular boutique hotel near Piccadilly station occupies the splendidly renovated Joshua Hoyle building, which itself replaced the old Imperial Hotel, birthplace of the Professional Footballers' Association. It's a characterful hotel and a good alternative to the chains.

Le Meridien ▶ Victoria & Albert, Water Street; ☎ 0161 832 1188; 156 Rooms; £85–£125 B&B

Another chain refurb – not very enticing, though there's a novelty in your room's name and wall photos – each has been designated a Granada TV production. You might hope for *Coronation Street* but end up with *Dig It*, the afternoon gardening show. Views over the murky Irwell and the Salford tower blocks in the distance.

The Midland ▶ Peter Street; ☎ 0161 236 3333; 303 Rooms; £107 B&B

Before *The Lowry*, this was perceived as Manchester's finest hotel. The best suite was home to Fabien Barthez for five months following his arrival, and his girlfriend Linda Evangelista was regularly spotted slipping out on a shopping trip. Registering not quite so high on the celebrity monitor, Phil Neville had his wedding reception here, Posh'n'Becks once ate Christmas lunch here, and Martin Buchan works out in the gym.

Novotel ▶ Dickinson Street; ☎ 0161 235 2200; 164 Rooms; £55–£139 B&B.

New upper mid-range chain hotel in central location close to Chinatown, the village and Oxford Road.

The Palace ▶ Oxford Street; ☎ 0161 288 2222; 252 Rooms; £99–£149. B&B

Another impressive conversion: this time of the wonderful grade II listed former home of Refuge Assurance. It is a good central location, and the hotel's grand ballroom has been used to host several United testimonials. Apparently, the players like the unusually large dance floor.

The Princess ▶ Portland Street; ☎ 0161 236 5122; 85 Rooms; £65 B&B.

This three-star, in another recently converted Victorian listed building, is well positioned for the many bars of the Canal Street area, and Chinatown too.

Renaissance ▶ Blackfriars Street; ☎ 0161 835 2555; 200 Rooms; £90 B&B (£75 room only)

Four-star hotel in a fine location for shops and Deansgate bars. Good-value weekend rate popular with fans.

Rossetti ▶ Piccadilly; ☎ 0161 247 7747; 61 Rooms; £105 B&B.

Stylish new hotel in an old Victorian textile factory headquarters. Close to Piccadilly station, rooms are all designer furniture and prints. The basement bar served as the venue for the players' 2002 Christmas party. The bar takings weren't low.

Thistle Hotel ▶ Portland Street; ☎ 0161 228 3400; 205 Rooms; £50–£143 B&B

Great-value rooms if you can get them in this four-star hotel which used to overlook Piccadilly Gardens but now faces a new anodyne office building.

Away from the centre

If you are driving to Manchester, or the hotels in town are booked, you might consider staying out in the suburbs of Altrincham, Didsbury or Worsley (each of which are 20–25 minutes' drive from Old Trafford, and have pubs and restaurants), or out at the airport.

Britannia Country House ▶ Didsbury; ☎ 0161 434 3411; 255 Rooms; £49–£65

A three-star hotel with a health club and popular nightclub.

Cresta Court ▶ Altrincham; ☎0161 927 7272; 138 Rooms; £56.50
Altrincham is convenient for the M6 south, so this three-star hotel can be a good halt on an Old Trafford trip.

Eleven Didsbury Park ▶ Didsbury; ☎0161 448 7711; 14 Rooms; £79.50 B&B
A stylish, friendly boutique hotel in a fine Didsbury townhouse. If full, ask about a newer sister establishment, *The Didsbury House Hotel*.

Novotel Manchester West ▶ Worsley; ☎0161 799 3535; 119 Rooms; £55 B&B
The name doesn't conjure much but this is a good-quality, three-star hotel in Giggs's mates' territory.

Radisson SAS ▶ Manchester Airport; ☎0161 490 5000.; 360 Rooms; £89 B&B
New four-star deluxe hotel out at the airport.

Waterside ▶ Didsbury; ☎0161 445 0225; 46 Rooms; £55
A three-star hotel with a health club, overlooking the River Mersey.

Restaurants

Manchester has long had a decent stock of Indian and Chinese restaurants but until the late-1990s it had no culinary reputation to speak of. That has all changed. The city has got serious about eating and genuinely cosmopolitan in its tastes. Following is a choice selection of restaurants you might want to try after a game. You could also eat at many of the café-bars listed in the section following, particularly those around Deansgate Lock, the Village and the Printworks.

City centre

It's in the city centre – from Piccadilly to Deansgate – that Manc's restaurant scene is booming. Many are chain establishments, but dotted among them are a number of good, idiosyncratic places and the odd celebrity-chef venture. The city centre is also home to Manchester's Chinatown, complete with dragon arch.

Armenian Taverna ▶ Albert Square ☎0161 834 9025.
Filling *meze* platters (for vegetarians too) bring in many, who then find they wish they'd plumped for a halibut kebab or grilled spring chicken, or one of a dozen other mighty main courses. Closed Mon. Moderate.

Café Istanbul ▶ 79 Bridge Street ☎0161 833 9942.
Delicious Turkish dishes, including a great *meze* selection, and an extensive wine list (including a powerful Turkish red). Closed Sun. Inexpensive to Moderate.

Dimitri's ▶ 1 Campfield Arcade, Deansgate ☏ 0161 839 3319.
Pick and mix from the Greek/Spanish/Italian menu (good for vegetarians), or grab a sandwich, an arcade table and sip a drink (everything from Greek coffee to Lebanese wine is on offer). Moderate.

Le Petit Blanc ▶ 55 King Street ☏ 0161 832 1001.
The best place in the city for reasonably priced French cooking is Raymond Blanc's mid-range brasserie operation – classic and regional dishes range from fish soup to a roast poussin off the *à la carte* menu or good-value, three-course, *prix fixe* for around £15. Real food for children, too. Moderate.

Little Yang Sing ▶ 17 George Street ☏ 0161 228 7722.
Celebrated basement restaurant (forerunner to the larger *Yang Sing*) where the emphasis is on *dim sum*, rice or noodle dishes, and down-to-earth Cantonese cooking, with lots of choice under £8. Moderate.

Livebait ▶ 22 Lloyd St, Albert Square ☏ 0161 817 4110.
Beautifully fresh fish in a lovely restored building, though since even the fish and chips are around £12 a plateful you'll probably have to try and exercise some restraint. Expensive.

The Market Restaurant ▶ 104 High Street ☏ 0161 834 3743.
One of the city's hidden treasures, this is a very relaxing spot for dinner. The changing menu throws its Modern-British weight around in adventurous, eclectic fashion. Reservations essential. Open Wed–Sat dinner only. Expensive.

Penang Village ▶ 56 Faulkner Street ☏ 0161 236 2650.
You soon get the idea – Malay village scenes on the wall, a traditional fishing boat as centrepiece – but this friendly Malaysian joint backs up the decor with tasty, authentic dishes. *Ayam percik* (barbecued chicken with a mild curry sauce), beef rendang, veg curry, and the good *roti* bread are all recommended. Closed Mon. Moderate.

Reform ▶ King St, Spring Gardens ☏ 0161 839 9966.
The city's great and good have adopted *Reform* as their pet restaurant, revelling in its oh-so-glamorous Venetian-Gothic exterior and spiffy French-inspired food – the late-opening bar is a see-and-be-seen experience too. Closed Sun. Expensive.

Simply Heathcote's ▶ Jackson Row ☏ 0161 835 3536.
Massive, minimalist dining rooms operated by Lancastrian chef Paul Heathcote. Mixes Mediterranean and local flavours, so expect updated working-class dishes alongside the parmesan shavings. The set lunch/early-bird menu is one of the city's best deals for food of this stature. Expensive.

Stock ▶ 4 Norfolk Street ☏ 0161 839 6644.
Superior Italian cooking (the fish is renowned) and a serious wine list. It's housed in the city's old stock exchange, hence the name. Closed Sun. Expensive.

Tampopo ▶ 16 Albert Square ☏ 0161 819 1966.
Basement noodle bar with long benches and a fast turnover. Noodle dishes are Japanese, Thai, Malaysian or Indonesian with most dishes under £7. Inexpensive.

Wagamama ▶ The Printworks, Corporation St/Withy Grove ☏ 0161 839 5916.
An outlet of the Japanese noodle bar chain. Portions are generous, though with communal seating at long tables and zippy service, this is more of a quick-bite spot than a place to linger over dinner. Inexpensive.

Wong Chu ▶ 63 Faulkner Street ☏ 0161 236 2346.
Simply the best of the budget Chinatown eateries, this no-frills, paper-tablecloth joint serves up enormous portions of Cantonese staples. Highlights are the deep-bowl noodle soups or piled-high rice-and-meat plates, at bargain prices. Inexpensive.

Yang Sing ▶ 34 Princess Street ☏ 0161 236 2200.
The *Yang Sing* is one of the best Cantonese restaurants in the country, with thoroughly authentic food, from a lunchtime plate of fried noodles to the full works. Stray from the printed menu for the most interesting dishes; ask the friendly staff for advice, who will pick a banquet for you (from £20 per head) if you prefer. Moderate to expensive.

Rusholme – Currynation Street

Rusholme, a couple of miles south of the city centre close to where Maine Road stands/stood (demolition is imminent), is a half-mile of glittering, neon-lit Indian eateries is worth crossing town for after a game. Known locally as Currynation Street, **Wilmslow Road** and its adjoining streets are home to fifty or so Indian restaurants. Competition ensures quality and value, and several places stay open until 3am.

Darbar ▶ 65–67 Wilmslow Road ☏ 0161 224 4392.
Award-winning Asian food in plain but friendly surroundings. The chef's special (he's been voted Manchester's Curry Chef of the Year twice) is *nihari*, a slow-cooked lamb dish, while other home-style choices appear on Sundays. Take your own booze. Inexpensive.

Punjab Sweet House ▶ 177 Wilmslow Road ☏ 0161 225 2960.
Superb all-vegetarian Indian restaurant, specializing in *dosas*, *thalis* and special sweets. Inexpensive.

Sanam ▶ 145–151 Wilmslow Road ☏ 0161 224 8824.
One of Rusholme's earliest arrivals, now thirty years old, the *Sanam* serves all the usual dishes plus award-winning *gulab juman*. Drop by the takeaway sweet and snack centre on the way home. No alcohol allowed. Inexpensive to moderate.

Sangam ▶ 13–15 Wilmslow Road ☏ 0161 257 3922.
The ever-expanding *Sangam* can do no wrong – great curry-house classics, every time, and a nice café-bar for a drink, too. Moderate.

Shere Khan ▶ IFCO Centre, 52 Wilmslow Road ☏ 0161 256 2624.
Big brash Indian brasserie with stylish (ie uncomfortable) chairs and a wide-ranging menu strong on *karahi* and *biryani* dishes. Moderate.

'That's the large takeaway *mejillones* for David, then, with beans ...'

Pubs and clubs

Manchester's nightlife enjoys a reputation for innovation and style, as celebrated in the *24 Hour Party People* film of 2002. Fuelled by liberal attitudes to licensing and late-night clubs, the number of licensed late-night premises in the city rose from 160 in 1996 to more than 500 now. This is doubtless a major reason why the city attracts the biggest student population in Europe – over 40,000 at last count. Many long-distance United fans rarely stray beyond the hotel bar for a post-match drink, which is a shame, for this is a city for partying, irrespective of football. Speaking of which, visiting fans and journalists are often surprised that – unlike, say Glasgow – there aren't any specific Red or Blue watering holes. Local fans, after games, fetch up everywhere and anywhere although the pubs near Old Trafford became the focus for celebration after Leeds beat Arsenal for United to win the league.

We've divided the city centre into rough geographical sections, reviewing some of the most popular places. For bars immediately around Old Trafford, see p.282.

Castlefield

This canalside district features handsome brick-built warehouses re-generated into expensive apartments and bars. Its popularity increases exponentially on the one or two non-rainy days which constitute a Mancunian summer.

Atlas ▶ 376 Deansgate.
Despite a rebranding, Atlas remains an ever-popular, glass-fronted bar under a railway arch between Castlefield and Deansgate Lock. Terrace for summer drinking.

Barca ▶ Catalan Square.
Red enthusiast Mick Hucknall originally owned a slice of the action at this bar/restaurant tucked into restored railway arches. It's less trendy these days, but the patio makes it worthwhile on summer nights. There's a sign by the door requesting ordinary drinkers not to badger famous patrons for autographs. Yeah ... they wish.

Dukes ▶ 92 Castle Street.
Large, modern bar with pub feel, recently extended due to popularity. Its two forecourts are ideal for summer drinking. Superb cheese platters.

The Ox Hotel ▶ Liverpool Road.

Manchester's listings magazine, *City Life*, has voted this Pub of the Year in recent years. It's a traditional pub with splendid decor, friendly staff, and good food.

White Lion ▶ Liverpool Road.

A well-run pub with fine ales and classic United prints in the back. Barge trips to home games are organised from here by the Red landlord a unique experience and, given the queues for the trams, not a bad way to travel to the game.

Deansgate Lock

This bar-filled development, opened in 2000, is a tad pretentious but hugely popular, with half a dozen bars, and a *Comedy Store* club, housed in state-of-the-art railway-arch conversions. Initially trendy and a touch pretentious, the Locks have become more raucous and mainstream, although *Sugar Lounge* still brings the celebrities in.

Loaf ▶ Deansgate Lock.

Loaf started out as Manchester's celeb spot, with huge queues at the weekend frequently bypassed by Dwight Yorke and his more socially inclined team mates who, you sense, weren't coming here to appreciate the minimalist design. It has remained busy, justifying the huge investment in the place by brewer Bass.

Sugar Lounge ▶ Liverpool Road.

In the last year the minor celebs that frequent Manchester at night (*Coronation Street* and *Hollyoaks* actors) shifted along to *Sugar Lounge* for the privilege of being both seen and over-charged at the bar. The most famous post-match visit of the year was that of United fan Angus Deayton, who launched his 'cocaine-fuelled sex binge with hooker' bid for glory here, while City had their end of season players' do here in 2003. Oddly enough, it's also not a place for real ale buffs.

Revolution, Fat Cat Café, Bar Baa, Lock, Aqua ▶ Deansgate Lock.

These bars in between *Loaf* and *Sugar Lounge* have their devotees, too. And Angus might have done well to wander into *Aqua* for a beery late night session with a decent Indie music soundtrack.

Deansgate/Peter Street

A rash of new pubs and bars have opened up in this central area in recent years. Groups of young lads and ladies get drunk and dance the night away with more abandon than in other areas.

Brannigans ▶ Peter Street.

A sign outside says, 'eating, drinking and cavorting'. It isn't wrong. *Brannigans* will never be described as cool but it doesn't pretend to be. Do not enter unless you're prepared to make a fool of yourself on the dance floor.

Circle Club ▶ Barton Arcade

Private members' club – although the United players who go in this cool bar don't seem to have many problems on the door. It's a relaxed place with good DJs and strong links with Manchester's media, musical and arty types.

Life Café ▶ Peter Street.

A vast new venue with regular live music acts as diverse as the Inspiral Carpets and Puressence to 1980s throwbacks. Packed at weekends.

The Living Room ▶ 80 Deansgate.

The celebrity bar in Manchester for 20-30 somethings. The Beckhams were frequent visitors, as are many of the United players who kept returning to celebrate the league Championship come May. Given its trendy status and slightly low-key location between less refined establishments, *The Living Room* is surprisingly unpretentious. The food is good too, but what gives this place real class and cachet is that it once banned Manchester City players because they couldn't behave properly.

Moon Under The Water ▶ Deansgate.

The largest pub in Manchester on a stretch of Deansgate which features a huge number of bars. Cheap ale. No music.

Sports Café ▶ Quay Street.

Large, bright sports theme bar with lots of screens showing everything from football to Alaskan hockey. Part of the chain that started on London's Haymarket.

Teasers ▶ Deansgate.

This American-style sports bar, with scantily clad attendants, is part of the Great Northern warehouse developments and close to *Bar 38*, a multi-screen cinema.

Walkabout ▶ Quay Street.

A rambling, multi-level Australian theme bar with excellent live music and lots of swaying arms.

Village People

The Village

Some of Manchester's best bars are to be found in the 'Village' – which, despite its name and fame (as home to the BBC series *Queer as Folk*), isn't exclusively gay. Chains like *Bar 38* and *Slug and Lettuce* jostle for attention with more individual places such as …

O'Shea's ▶ 80 Princess Street.
Just out of the gay village at the junction with Whitworth Street, this is usually packed with a mixed crowd. Frequent live music and good Guinness. This was the venue for United's players' Christmas do a couple of years ago.

Prague V ▶ Canal Street.
This two-floor, industrial-looking bar features top DJs playing loud dance sounds. It is open late, and often has queues at weekends.

Piccadilly/Northern Quarter

The busy Piccadilly area is currently being smartened up – and not before time. Further out, the self-styled Northern Quarter is trying to become an arty, cutting-edge enclave amidst run-down warehouse land.

Circus Tavern ▶ 86 Portland Street.
A tiny, real-ale Victorian drinking hole with two small rooms barely big enough to hold a football team.

Cord ▶ Dorsey Street.
Bohemian, trendy and slightly cliquey bar for media/arty types who obsess over life's major issues: like whether they've done their trainer laces the right way.

Wetherspoons ▶ Piccadilly.
This large chain pub is popular with United fans after a match. Cheap drinks and no music, unless you count the chants.

Oxford Street area

The area west of Oxford Street has seen a major regeneration with a new concert hall and shiny office blocks.

Briton's Protection ▶ 50 Great Bridgewater Street.
Another recent Pub of the Year winner, this is an exquisitely finished, traditional ale house, with a tiny garden, next to *Jurys Inn*. Good beer in cosy surrounds.

Kro Bar ▶ Oxford Road.
An independent bar – bright, airy and trendy – and thus unlike most of the student hangouts around this area opposite the university.

Kro 2 ▶ Oxford Road.

Newer, sister establishment of *Kro* housed in the National Computer Centre closer to the city centre. Glass-fronted with a courtyard for summer drinking, and friendly door staff. *City Life* Bar of the Year for 2002.

Lass O'Gowrie ▶ 1 Charles Street.

A traditional pub which brews its own beers. Popular with students and nearby BBC workers.

Peveril of the Peak ▶ 127 Great Bridgewater Street.

Despite now being surrounded by glitzy new developments, 'The Pev' and its glazed Victorian tilework remains a Manchester real-ale favourite. Cantona even popped in once to play table football.

Rain Bar ▶ 80 Great Bridgewater Street.

Pub of the Year in 1999, but it could so easily have been bar of the year. Downstairs is dark and set in wood like a traditional local whilst upstairs is a light café-bar environment with a canalside terrace outside.

Cross Street shopping area

Manchester's central shopping area, ripped apart after the 1996 IRA bomb, has some interesting hostelries, new and old.

Corbieres ▶ Half Moon Street.

Strictly speaking, this is a basement wine bar, but it's a defiantly lively one, with probably the best jukebox in Manchester. Or is that the world?

Mr Thomas's Chop House ▶ 52 Cross Street.

This long, thin Victorian watering hole has a beautiful exterior, a very mixed clientele, and excellent food.

One Central Street ▶ 1 Central Street.

Decent DJs, industrial décor and leather booths in this trendy basement bar. Busy at weekends for those who like to dress up and dance.

The Printworks ▶ Withy Grove.

A vast new entertainment complex with differently themed bars on various floors and a newer nightclub, *Lucid*. The Canadian hunting lodge bar is particularly authentic. See it to believe it.

Reform ▶ Spring Gardens.

Occupying the lavish first floor of probably the most beautiful building in Manchester, *Reform* has long been a show-off bar/restaurant for footballers and *Coronation Street* stars. Tends to attract an older crowd now. It is open late.

Sinclairs ▶ New Cathedral Street.

Moved twice since the Second World War, this fine pub with its olde worlde decor has now happily settled by the cathedral.

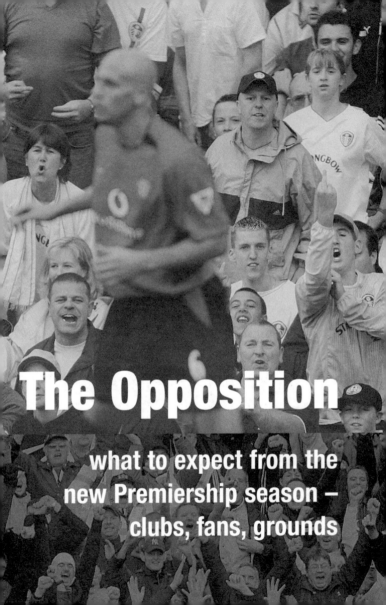

The Opposition

what to expect from the
new Premiership season –
clubs, fans, grounds

Who would have thought that United's stiffest opposition last season would come from Bolton Wanderers and Manchester City? Yet those were the bogey teams, United picking up just one point out of six from each. This year, of course, there might be more of a challenge from the French national team at Arsenal, where the manager doubtless expects another unbeaten season. And then there are trips to Fratton Park and Molineux (it's been a long time), and Leicester's new Walkers Stadium, to look forward to. Not to mention the City of Manchester Stadium, publicly funded to help the Blues catch up a bit.

Over the next few pages we assess the new season's Premiership opposition, and advise on how to get tickets for away games, how to get to opposition grounds, and where to enjoy a swift, trouble-free, pre-match half once you are there.

Getting to away games

Tickets for United away games are gold dust. In these days of all-seater stadiums, almost every Premiership ground is filled with season-ticket holders or priority-booking members. Away clubs are offered small allocations of tickets, either 10percent of capacity or 3,000, whichever is the smaller, and if you fail to get one of these you're basically at the mercy of the **touts**. And not only that: if you are going anywhere halfway popular, you'll be sat among ranks of home supporters, turning out for perhaps their only time in the season with one common goal – to see United lose. It doesn't always make for a great day out, although seeing as no team won more away games than United last season, there are often compensations.

A few years ago, it was possible to apply for tickets for most away games through the opposition club's ticket office – even at places like Anfield or Stamford Bridge. But unless fan-less Wimbledon return to the Premiership (bit of a long shot, that), this is no longer an option, except perhaps for Carling Cup run-outs.

Membership tickets and travel

United are generally allocated **3,000 away supporters' tickets** for each away game in the Premiership, the exception being Blackburn where 7-8,000 tickets are generously offered up. Fans wanting away tickets must apply six weeks in advance through the Old Trafford membership office (see p.388). The distribution of these tickets was a sore point throughout last season as, in an attempt to be more transparent in the way they went about the task, the club decided to issue tickets through a completely random ballot. To **enter the ballot** you had to have been a season ticket holder who had been to all the non-Premiership home games, too. Around 19,000 fans met that criteria and an average of 3,300 fans applied for 2,000 tickets (the other 1,000 went to executive box holders, sponsors and players), so most applicants were therefore successful. But for games like the Manchester derby or Liverpool away, far greater numbers applying meant that many fans who had not missed a game for years were turned down or 'chubbed'.

After persistent criticism, the club have agreed to change the system for season 2003-04. Loyalty will now be taken into account and around half the tickets will be allocated to those who applied for every away game last season. Some tickets will still be allocated to season ticket-holders who don't go to every away game, however, so that away tickets don't just go to a closed shop of hardcore fans. You know what the end result will be? The same faces in the same away ends, just as it has been for years.

United's official **travel arrangements** for fans are organised by the membership office (℡0161 868 8450). For **domestic away** trips, the club organises coach travel although most fans prefer to make their own way to games. The fanzines *United We Stand* and *Red Issue* have jointly run executive coaches to away games for ten seasons now (℡0161 748 0670 for details; 24hr answerphone).

European games

For **European away trips**, United's membership office organises two forms of travel: an executive package and a regular package (often a straight 'day'-return). **Match tickets** are guaranteed with these although the trips tend to be on the expensive side compared with those offered by independent travel operators. Many fans book with **independent operators** – often fans – who advertise through the local media and on the Internet.

Arsenal

Premiership position (2002-03): 2nd. Last season: *Dec* Utd 2 Arsenal 0 *April* Arsenal 2 Utd 2. United's 10yr record: *Home* W6 D2 L2 *Away* W2 D4 L4.

'I know it will be difficult for us to go through the season unbeaten. But if we keep the right attitude, it's possible that we can do it. It was done by Milan in Italy (in 1992) and I can't see why it's shocking to say that we can do it this season. Every manager says it. Do you not think that they say something similar at the start of the season at Manchester United or Chelsea or Liverpool? They think exactly the same, but they don't say it because they're scared of looking ridiculous. If we lose, people will turn to me and say: 'You have a big mouth.' But I can only be honest.' **Arsène Wenger, Sept 2002.**

Unfortunately for Arsène, his pretensions to remain unbeaten were a flight of fancy up there with Michael Knighton's plan to get Carlisle in the Premiership. By the end of the season, Arsène's Arsenal had lost six league games and their European charge saw them limp no further than the last sixteen. So much for the 'We'll be back again in May' chants that Gooners sang at Old Trafford in February. Unless, of course, they were offering to return the Premiership trophy personally.

Not a lot for the Prof to smile about: Whinger and Ferguson after last year's 2-2 decider

Whilst it's amusing to mock Arsenal and Wenger's failure to credit United with winning the league (in complete contrast to United fans who were generous in their praise for Arsenal last season) they are our closest domestic rivals and were responsible for some of the best football seen in the league last season. And though many a Red wearies of his unrelenting bleating, Wenger remains an outstanding coach, working on a budget a fraction of that available to Sir Alex. The only surprise will be if the fierce rivalry between the best two teams in the country isn't renewed in 2003-04. Oh, and until Arsenal get themselves a decent ground, finding a ticket for the away match will remain as hard as ever.

Highbury Avenell Road, London N5 1BU. ☎ 020 7704 4040. Capacity 38,500. Away allocation 2,800 (Clock End/West Stand Lower).

Bite to eat *The Exquisite* offers half-price food and wine before 7pm and the *Moonshine Café* serves a great fry-up, both on Blackstock Road; *Golden Fish Bar* in Gillespie Road offers, you've guessed it, top-class fish'n'chips.

Swift half *The Auld Triangle*, St Thomas's Road; *Arsenal Tavern*, Blackstock Road (don't wear colours); *The Drayton Park*, behind the away end, is a popular haunt for visiting fans, as is the *World's End* at Finsbury Park.

By car From NORTH M6, M1 and exit at junction 2. Follow signs for City. After Holloway Road station (6¼ miles) turn third left into Drayton Park, after ³/₄ mile turn right into Aubert Park and second left on to Avenell Road. From SOUTH at London Bridge follow signs to Bank of England, then Angel. Turn right at traffic lights towards Highbury roundabout on to Holloway Road, and third right into Drayton Park. Then as from north. From WEST M4 exit at Junction 1, take A315 towards Chiswick, left after 1 mile to M41, then A40 (M) to A501 ring road. Turn left at Angel then as from south.

Parking On street only and very restricted at that. Best option is to park near Caledonian Road or Bounds Green, either side of Arsenal tube station on the Piccadilly Line.

By bus Victoria coach station, then Victoria Line tube to Finsbury Park.

By rail Euston station, then Victoria Line to Finsbury Park or Piccadilly Line to Arsenal station.

Aston Villa

Premiership position (2002-03): 16th. Last season: *Oct* Utd 1 Villa 1 *March* Villa 0 Utd 1. United's 10yr record: *Home* W8 D2 L0 *Away* W6 D3 L1.

And we thought Tottenham Hotspur had perfected the undignified art of mediocrity. If anything, it is Villa who truly excel in this area. When he's not playing tennis, chairman Doug Ellis remains the central character at Villa Park. Whilst he's invested wisely in the stadium (and named a stand after himself, naturally) he remains largely unpopular among fans who cite his reluctance to spend big money. A touch unfair, as he has spent big money. Unfortunately, as the not inconsiderable outlay of £10m on Juan Pablo Angel and £6m on Bosko Balaban prove, Villa have also honed the craft of buying malfunctioning foreigners.

Ellis has his enemies – Graham Taylor was said to be so sick at the way the club was run that he resigned – but the chairman who cheerfully calls him-

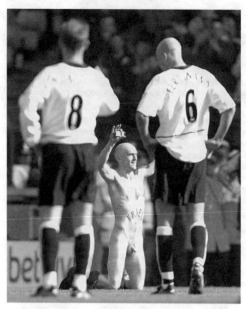
You get a different kind of fan at Villa Park

self 'Deadly Doug' has not allowed 'his' club to be encumbered by debt. And his critics, the Villa fans, are not beyond reproach. They may well fill the ground for the visit of United or Birmingham, but there are always thousands of empty seats when smaller clubs show. Villa fans would counter such a point by questioning the football they are served up, and it is true that the team won just one away game in the league last season. Dressing room morale has barely been measurable these last couple of years, as a convoy of players have left claiming that the club lack ambition. In which case the arrival of David O'Leary could be interesting. Not short of ambition at Leeds, how he functions at a club unwilling to mortgage the future on the never-never remains to be seen.

Villa Park remains an away day favourite with Reds, partly because of the many happy memories conjured from previous visits, partly because it usually means three points. Yes, Villa have a truly awful record against United: the last twenty league meetings have resulted in 14 wins for United, 5 draws and just one defeat. And some Villa fans consider United a truer rival than their neighbours from Small Heath. Perhaps it's about time they checked out the league table.

Villa Park Trinity Road, Birmingham B6 6HE. T 0121 327 5353. Capacity 42,500. Away allocation 3,000 (North Stand).

Bite to eat Villa Fish Bar on Manor Road is handy from Witton station; otherwise try the Aston Lane Fish Bar on the corner of Aston Lane and London Road; for a taste of the West Indies (or, in contrast, a full English breakfast) call in at *Silver Sands Caribbean Takeaway* on Witton Road; on the novelty tip, sample a Villa balti inside the ground… but only once. Post match, get a cab to the Balti Triangle of Moseley, Sparkhill and Sparkbrook.

Swift half Near Witton station, *The Harriers* and the *Yew Tree* are decent pubs for away fans, as is the *Witton Arms*; Broad Street is Birmingham's 'golden mile' for pubs, including the *Sports Café*, *Key Largo*, *All Bar One*, *Tiger Tiger*, *The Figure of Eight* and *Bakers*.

By car From NORTH exit M6 at junction 6 (Spaghetti Junction) on to the A38 (M) Aston Expressway towards the city centre. Take first exit right on to Victoria Road. At roundabout take right exit into Witton Road for Villa Park. From SOUTH take M1 to junction 19 then M6. Exit at junction 6 then as from north. From EAST M42 to junction 8. M6 heading towards Birmingham then as from north. From SOUTHEAST at the end of the M5 the road divides, keep left and follow signs for London M1 M40 on to M6 eastbound. Exit junction 7 or 6 and as from north.

Parking Car parks at Aston Villa Leisure Centre on Aston Hall Road and Brookvale Road at the junction with Tame Road. On-street parking is restricted around the ground.

By bus Take #7 from outside Marks & Spencer in city centre to the ground – you'll know when you're there by the queue of claret and blue.

By rail From Birmingham New Street take a local train to Witton station, it's a two-minute walk from ground, or Aston station, 10 minutes away.

Birmingham City

Premiership position (2002-03): 13th. Last season: *Dec* Utd 2 Birmingham 0 *Jan* Birmingham 0 Utd 1. United's 10yr record: *Home* W1 D0 L0 *Away* W1 D0 L0.

Steve Bruce's first season as a Premiership manager was an undoubted success. Charged with the task of avoiding a rapid return to the first division, Birmingham were never sucked into the relegation morass proper, although there was a nervous period around the time United beat them twice when it looked as if their season might end in tears.

Birmingham's two derby victories over Aston Villa, although marred by merry mayhem on and off the pitch, made their return to the top flight for first time since 1986 very sweet. There was something comical about keeper Enklemann's mistake that led to a Birmingham goal, mind. Finishing above Villa cemented Bruce, the ex-Red's, popularity – and went someway to him being awarded a new, much improved contract.

The nature of Birmingham's owners has often meant a higher profile than a similar sized club given the prominence of a lady, Karren Brady, and two parties who made much of their money through soft porn: the Gold brothers and David Sullivan. Although derided by some, Birmingham's owners are popular with the people that matter to them, the fans, and they can maintain their claim that under them, the fortunes of Blues have been transformed. After all, this was the club who were knocked out of the FA Cup at home to non-league Altrincham whilst still an old first division club in 1986. In front of 6,000.

Since that nadir, three sides of St Andrews have been completely rebuilt, although the demolition of the antiquated main stand has been put on hold, the club preferring to invest in playing personnel with the aim of establishing themselves in the Premiership. By signing players of the quality of Zidane's best mate Christophe Dugarry, that prospect looks more rational than it did a year ago.

St Andrews Birmingham B9 4NH. T 0709 111 25837. Capacity 30,200. Away allocation 4,000 (Railway Stand).

Bite to eat *McDonald's* is two minutes from the ground on Bordesley Park Road; a flourishing Chinatown in the city centre and balti shops galore on A34 route into the city; *Fat Terry's* hotdog stand near Kingston Road; plenty of chip shops along Digbeth.

Swift half Avoid most pubs around St Andrews, but for the determined check out *The Ibis Hotel*, Bordesley Park Road or *The Brewer and Baker* on Camp Hill; otherwise head for city centre and New Street.

By car From NORTH exit M6 at junction 6 on to A38 (M) for Birmingham city centre. Exit at 2nd junction and bear left at the roundabout, following signs to Birmingham City FC. From SOUTHEAST exit M40 at junction 3A on to M42 northbound. Exit at junction 4 and turn left at roundabout on to A34. Continue over 4 roundabouts (the road becomes A41) to Camp Hill Circus roundabout. Take 3rd exit on to A4540 Sandy Lane. Follow signs for Small Heath and Bordesley Green for ground. From SOUTHWEST M5, M42 and exit at junction 3a. Follow signs to The North, B'ham East, North and Central to M42 then as from southeast.

Parking St Andrews Street behind the garage but get there early. From Bordesley Circus roundabout, follow signs to Ring Road North and M6 into Watery Lane, first left into Adderley Street – there's an industrial area with plenty of unrestricted parking. Side streets off Coventry Road.

By bus From Birmingham New Street take #15, #15a or #17 along Coventry Road. Despite the maze of subways, it really is quicker to walk.

By rail Birmingham New Street, then see above for buses.

Blackburn Rovers

Premiership position (2002-03): 6th. Last season: *Dec* Blackburn 1 Utd 0 *April* Utd 3 Blackburn 1. United's 10yr record: *Home* W6 D2 L0 *Away* W4 D2 L2.

Blackburn could never be described as a thriving metropolis, but as a bolt hole for ex-Reds who can no longer quite cut it at Old Trafford, the town's football club can represent a convenient move. Its proximity to Manchester means that many of their players can spurn the dim lights of Blackburn and stay rooted in the leafier reaches of the northwest, and thanks to a lavish trust fund set up by their ex-benefactor Sir Jack Walker, financial remuneration is seldom an issue. To suggest that the likes of Cole and Yorke are only at Ewood for mercenary reasons is unfair though – manager Souness has crafted a team good enough to reach the UEFA Cup for the second year running, a team good enough to beat both United and Arsenal last season.

The very existence of Blackburn Rovers in the Premiership is usually good news for Manchester United. United receive almost twice as many tickets for Ewood Park than at any other club and the short trip through the East Lancashire time warp is one of the most popular of the season. By being the only team to beat Arsenal home and away last season, Blackburn aided United's title win – a gesture which saw manager Souness bestowed a decent bottle from the impressive wine collection Chez Ferguson.

Already one of the longer-serving managers in the Premiership, Souness is genuinely happy working at club not sidetracked by financial pressures and therefore focused on football. This stability has allowed Blackburn to pursue their vision, which, according to chief executive John Williams, is about consolidating and being competitive with a wage bill much smaller than the biggest clubs. Blackburn have achieved this, for only United, Arsenal and Chelsea lost fewer games than them last season. Yorke and Cole's proficiency in front of goal needs to be rediscovered if they are to continue improving, though: only the relegated teams scored fewer goals at home than Blackburn.

Ewood Park Blackburn BB2 4JF. T 01254 671666. Capacity 31,500. Away allocation 8,000 (Darwen End).

Bite to eat Opposite the ground on Bolton Road visiting fans can gorge themselves at the *Mother Riley Café*, or there's a 'walk-thru' *McDonald's* at Ewood Triangle.

Swift half *The Fernhurst* on Bolton Road is close to the away end and is popular with United fans; *The Ewood Park*, *The Ewood Arms*, *The Aquaduct*, *The Moorings*, *The Angel*, *The Brown Cow* and *The Waters Edge* are all within a short stroll of the ground.

By car From NORTH leave M6 at junction 29 and join M61. At first exit join M65 and head east to Blackburn. At junction 4 join A666 Blackburn. Ewood Park is well signposted and about 1 mile away on the right. From SOUTH exit M6 at junction 29 for M65. Head east to Blackburn then as from north. From WEST from M6/M62 or M60 join M61. Exit at M65 and head east. Then as from north or south. From EAST from Yorkshire, either B6234, A56 Haslingden bypass or the Skipton Road, join M65 and head west. Then as from north, south or east. Alternatively, if coming direct from Manchester, take M60, M61 and follow signs for Bolton when the road splits near the start of the M61. Stay on A666 Blackburn Road through Darwen to ground.

Parking Behind *The Fernhurst* in the Youth Aid car park off Albion Road; Albion Mill car park on Albion Street; industrial estate car parks on Branch Road. All within a stone's throw of the stadium.

By bus Blackburn Central bus station is next to the railway station. Services #3, #3A, #3B, #46, #346 all go from Blackburn to Darwen. Ewood Park is about 1$\frac{1}{2}$ miles along the route.

By rail Direct trains from Manchester Victoria to Blackburn. The ground is a couple of miles from the station.

And you get a different class of ball boy at Ewood

Bolton Wanderers

Premiership position (2002-03): 17th. Last season: *Sept* Utd 0 Bolton 1 *Feb* Bolton 1 Utd 1. United's 10yr record: *Home* W1 D1 L2 *Away* W2 D2 L0.

Despite their cheek by jowl co-existence, Manchester United and Bolton Wanderers are as different as Mancs and Yonners. Mancunians sneer at their flat caps and pie image, but Boltonians are proud of their Lancashire roots so you can understand why integration of the town from Lancashire into the new borough of Greater Manchester in 1974 was not popular. Unlike Sam Allardyce, the town's heroic adopted son.

Under 'Big Sam', Bolton somehow manage to stay in the Premiership where economics would dictate that a bigger club snaffle their position. Whilst you wouldn't necessarily like to use a toilet cubicle after him, Allardyce is a shrewd man and with no money to spend on transfers due to his club's precarious financial position, he excels in two areas. First, he scours the European leagues for possible targets, then he convinces class players like French World Cup winner Youri Djorkaeff to join the club. Selling Bolton Wanderers to Djorkaeff or Jay Jay Okocha must be like selling rice to the Chinese. Difficult. Secondly, patently aware that his squad is not as strong as rivals, he makes use of sports psychologists, physiotherapies and dieticians. Players are attuned to the powers of positive thinking, a sensible diet and injury prevention. Check out Bolton's injury list – or lack of it – for the results. It's easy to deride his techniques as easily as Allardyce laments the £50m lavished on the admittedly stunning Reebok stadium – 'We've not even got our own training ground and yet we built a monument when we needed a football stadium,' Allardyce told this writer last year – but they work.

Bolton remain the only English club to have a better record against United than vice versa, and the four points they took off the Reds last season not only improved that record further, but was the difference between staying up and going down. With a growing confidence, who would bet on Bolton repeating their now routine heroics next season?

Reebok Stadium Burnden Way, Bolton BL6 6JW. T 01204 673601. Capacity 27,400. Away allocation 4–5,000 (South Stand).

Bite to eat *Stuart's Bakery* near the station on Newport Street for pies, pastries and rolls; *Mahoney's Pie Shops* inside the ground.

Swift half Most of the pubs around the ground are home-only and United fans are not popular in these parts.

Allardyce – not a man to meet in the queue for the toilets

By car M60 then M61 s/p Preston (ignore Bolton signs) to junction 6, turn right at round-about into Burnden Way.

Parking Parking at stadium – follow signs – £6 and 30-minute wait to get out. Victoria Road, off the Chorley New Road or restricted spaces on Lostock Industrial Estate, Lostock Lane.

By bus #539 runs twice an hour from Bolton station to the ground.

By rail The Reebok has the new Horwich Parkway halt by the ground. Direct trains from Manchester and Salford Crescent.

Charlton Athletic

Premiership position (2002-03): 12th. Last season: *Sept* Charlton 1 Utd 3 *May* Utd 4 Charlton 1. United's 10yr record: *Home* W3 D1 L0 *Away* W3 D1 L0.

Two thirds of the way through last season, when the Valiants looked like they might qualify for Europe, the Italian sportspaper *Gazzetta dello Sport* did a feature on the club, calling them the 'English Chievo'. Although meant as a compliment, the description didn't do Charlton justice, for unlike the tiny team from a Verona suburb, Charlton boast a rich history. And in recent years, the club have grown intelligently, sticking with a prudent, yet ambitious, business plan and a manager who knows the club better than anyone.

Just being in existence as a football club is an achievement for those Charlton fans who saw them homeless and nearly hopeless in the late '80s (the directors are said to throw a party every year upon reaching 40 points – a figure usually good enough for Premiership survival). Meantime, the newer converts to Alan Curbishley's evolution have come to expect Premiership survival and mid-table security, if not more. But if Charlton's

THE OPPOSITION ▶ 321

greatest problem to stem from their development is divided expectations, then they have relatively little to be concerned about.

Curbishley has played a major part in the success, his eye for young players a vital attribute given the small size of his squad. With Charlton progressing to the FA Youth Cup semi-final (where they went out to United), the future looks bright in this department.

The Valley, which once boasted the largest terrace in football – and a Who concert that everyone of a certain in age in London claims to have attended – may be a pain to get to from the north, but travelling Reds won't experience the animosity received at other clubs. It is usually full to its 26,000 capacity and the club are looking at expanding the stadium further to meet demand. Hopefully that would mean a bigger allocation for away fans because at the moment, it's easier to get a straight answer on the future of the nearby Millennium Dome than to get a ticket for this one.

The Valley – usually good for three points, but not much chance of a ticket

The Valley Floyd Road, London SE7 8BL. T 020 8333 4010. Capacity 26,500. Away allocation 2,000 (Jimmy Seed Stand).

Bite to eat A top all-day scan can be had at the *Valley Café* opposite Charlton station; *Seabay Fish Bar* in Floyd Road will cater for cod needs.

Swift half *The Antigallican*, just seconds from Charlton station, is the main away fans pub; *The Bugle Horn* in Charlton Village (right out of the station up Charlton Church Lane); *Charlton Liberal Club* welcomes away fans for small entry fee at the door.

By car ALL DIRECTIONS exit M25 at junction 2 and follow A2 towards London for 10 miles. When A2 becomes A102 (M) Blackwall Tunnel approach road, take A206 Woolwich Road towards Woolwich. Ground is on the right.

Parking Around the ground is no-go unless you want your motor towed away. Best bet is Thames Barrier car park near *The Antigallican* pub or book in advance with the club for space at Fossdene School.

By bus From North Greenwich tube take #161, #472 or #486.

By rail Euston station and Jubilee Line underground to North Greenwich or Northern Line tube to London Bridge, overland to Charlton station.

Chelski

Premiership position (2002-03): 4th. Last season: *Aug* Chelsea 2 Utd 2 *Jan* United 2 Chelsea 1. United's 10yr record: *Home* W2 D5 L3 *Away* W4 D4 L2.

All change for Chelsea this summer. Or Chelski as they are now known. A billionaire Russian oil man called Roman Abramovich bought out Ken Bates's holding stake in the company, which meant the Santa lookalike cleared £19m personally from the deal. All from an original £1 stake. And there are some people who claim there is no money in football.

Abramovich, apparently the 46th richest man in the world, though don't ask too many questions about where that fortune came from, acquired the most indebted club in the Premiership: £90m in hock, a loan which requires £7m a year to service. When you consider that Bates was paying the third choice goalkeeper Mark Bosnich £40k a week, and that fellow outcast (although for non jazz-salt reasons) Winston Bogarde is still on the same amount, you begin to understand why a) Bogarde can afford to commute from Amsterdam and b) how the debt accrued in the first place.

But, bizarrely, they have been rewarded for that financial madness. Money is pouring in, every player on the continent is now officially a Chelsea target, and unless Abramovich has some Machiavellian plan to sell the ground and relocate the blues to Minsk, they could finally issue the Premiership challenge they have long dreamt of in the Bates era. Unlike their main London rivals Arsenal, Chelsea have completed the costly redevelopment of their stadium, a pad that sits on a sizeable tract of land worth considerably more than if it was in Blackburn. With average gates of 40,000, and the

Reds on the left, Russians on the right

highest ticket prices in Britain, they have the basis to progress. And, as their celebrations proved when they came fourth last year, they are in the Champions League.

Despite Forlan's injury time winner last January, Chelsea boast a better record at Old Trafford than any other team. Maybe it was that stat which helped to draw Abramovich's eye and wallet over to West London. Now all he has to do is keep shelling out to realise the ambitions of Chelsea's (often deeply unpleasant) Home Counties based, fans.

Stamford Bridge London SW6 1HS. T 0891 121011. Capacity 42,449. Away allocation 3,086 (East Stand Lower).

Bite to eat Uncle Ken's eateries in the grandiosely titled Chelsea Village: *Arkles*, *Fishnets* and *King's Brasserie* – all pricey. Usual fish'n'chips and kebab shops around the ground. For upmarket eateries try King's Road.

Swift half *Slug and Lettuce* and *Bootsy Brogan's* on Fulham Broadway (near Fulham Broadway tube); *The Blackbird*, Earls Court tube. Otherwise, in true Peter Osgood style, treat yourself to an overpriced cocktail or fancy foreign lager up the King's Road. Don't wear colours, mind.

By car From NORTH and EAST M6, M1, M25 and exit at junction 15. Take M4 which becomes A4, following signs to Central London. Over Hammersmith flyover, still on A4 (Talgarth Rd) and take 2nd available left-hand turn into Earls Court Road.

Go past Earls Court station to next major junction and straight across into Redcliffe Gardens. At next traffic lights, turn right into Fulham Road and Stamford Bridge is about 1/2 mile on right-hand side.

Parking Underground car parks at the ground as part of Ken's west London white elephant if you arrive before 2pm. And are willing to pay £15 for the privilege. Otherwise, some pay-and-display spaces around ground and off King's Road.

By bus #14 from Tottenham Court Road, #211 from Waterloo to Hammersmith, or #11 from Liverpool Street station.

By rail Euston, Victoria Line to Victoria and change to District Line, direction Wimbledon, for Fulham Broadway. Turn left out of station and ground is 200 yards away.

Everton

Premiership position (2002-03): 7th. Last season: *Oct* Utd 3 Everton 0 *May* Everton 1 Utd 2. United's 10yr record: *Home* W10 D0 L0 *Away* W8 D1 L1.

The Everton fanzine When Skies *Are Grey* regularly publishes details of where players have been spotted around Liverpool and until last season, it contained the usual, predictable, footballer haunts. Kevin Campbell would be down the Albert Dock in a trendy eatery (that's what cool restaurants are called these days); Mark Pembridge would be buying designer labels in *Wade Smith* and Duncan Ferguson would be seen leaving hospital. Then this kid Wayne Rooney came onto the scene and before long, hawk-eyed Evertonians had him in their sights with reports of him…hanging around with mates on his mountain bike by the local shops. There's something so brilliantly innocent about Rooney's story that even a *Roy of the Rovers* scriptwriter would dismiss it as being unrealistic. The photos of his bedroom only add to the tale – showing the room of a typical Everton mad teenager on a Liverpool housing estate, proof that he's living out his dream.

Before David Moyes turned the club around from the pitiful nadir under Walter Smith, Everton were arguably the most predictably depressing team in the Premiership, a long way from that mid-'80s side who never had the chance to truly test itself against the finest on the continent, largely because of events involving despised Liverpool fans at Heysel. That still rankles.

Everton were never the same again. Playing in an ageing home, their failure to invest in players meant they missed the boat when Sky's money flushed through English football and within years, their 'Big Five' tag was but a memory. Managers were hired and fired, players bought past their prime and those who did flourish, like Jeffers and Ball, were sold to balance the books as Everton floundered.

Under Moyes, surely the manager of the year if that trophy wasn't given to the title winners, Evertonians now have reason to believe again…despite their appalling recent record against United. One word of warning though: Everton fans don't take kindly to any suggestion that Moyes is merely serving his apprenticeship at Goodison before taking one the big one as Sir Alex's successor. However true that might be.

Rooney and Moyes: the new regime

Goodison Park Liverpool L4 4EL. T 0151 330 2300. Capacity 40,260. Away allocation 3,075 (Bullens Road).

Bite to eat Chippies, pie shops and cake outlets galore on County Road. Tea and cakes at St Luke's church on the corner of Gladwys Street – honestly. Normal home-game pies and the like in ground.

Swift half *The Spellow* on the corner of Gladwys Street, *The Blue House* at the Park End and *The Winslow*. *The Arkles* (see Liverpool) is okay for Everton games.

By car From NORTH exit M6 at junction 23 and follow signs to Liverpool A580 for 10 miles. Pass under M57 and after 3^{1}/2 miles turn left on to A5058 then right into Utting Avenue (signposted Liverpool FC, Everton FC). Go under railway bridge and turn right at crossroads into Priory Road. Car park is on the left. From SOUTH exit M6 at junction 21a on to M62. Take junction 6, turn right at roundabout on to M57 until junction 4. Turn left at roundabout on A580 for 2 miles, left on to A5058 and then as from north.

Parking Stanley Park car park – 1,000 spaces, and easier to get in when United play Everton than Liverpool.

By bus The #19 runs from Queen's Square to Walton Lane; #20 from St Thomas Street along Spellow Lane.

By rail Regular services from Manchester Piccadilly to Lime Street. From Liverpool Lime Street walk to Central station and catch an Ormskirk or Kirkby train. Get off at Kirkdale and follow the crowds.

Fulham

Premiership position (2002-03): 14th. Last season: *Oct* Fulham 1 Utd 1 *March* United 3 Fulham 0. United's 10yr record: *Home* W2 D0 L0 *Away* W1 D1 L0.

Mystery and uncertainty continue to envelop Fulham Football Club. The official line, which hasn't been wholly consistent, is that the club are still looking at ways of redeveloping Craven Cottage whilst lodging elsewhere – which at the moment means QPR's Loftus Road. Ground-sharing with nearby Chelsea, a more logical proposition, has been discarded for the moment. But such statements have been undermined by talk that the prestigiously located Cottage could be turned into luxury flats after local NIMBYs objected to proposals to redevelop the ground. Fans are confused. On one hand, after years of struggle they're getting to watch Premiership football and such talents as Malbranque and Boa Morte, yet on the other, they feel as though the club could go bust if its benefactor, the phoney Pharaoh Mohammed Al Fayed, pulled out.

'If Al Fayed was driven away by angry supporters, then I cannot see how the club will function with astronomic wage bills and no home,' reckons Matt Boisclair from the Fulham fanzine *There's Only One F In Fulham.* 'His popularity is no longer what it was – we haven't sung his name for a while. He does still go to every home game, although he hasn't paraded the pitch swinging his scarf over his head for a while.'

Another key figure Fulham fans will get used to not seeing by the side of the pitch is their highly rated ex-manager Jean Tigana, whose contract was not renewed at the end of last season. He's been replaced by ex-player Chris Coleman, a popular personality with the fans and players, but one lacking in managerial experience. Fulham's future depends on Al Fayed's commitment. And that doesn't inspire confidence.

Loftus Road (temporary ground share with QPR) South Africa Road, Shepherds Bush, London W12 7PA. T 020 7384 4710. Capacity 19,300. Away allocation 3,000 (School End).

Bite to eat Uxbridge Road offers travelling Reds possibly the widest variety of the season, from cafés, burger bars, fried-chicken outlets and chippies to Caribbean, Indian, Chinese, Thai and Lebanese restaurants.

Swift half *The Fringe and Firkin* on Goldhawk Road offers an eclectic mix of backpackers, woollybacks and pseuds; *Moon on the Green* on Uxbridge Road serves decent food but turns its nose up at football shirts; *The Springbok* on South Africa Road is the away pub, but get there early.

By car From NORTH M6, M42 and M40 into London where it turns into A40. Exit at junction signposted White City and Harlesden. Turn right off the sliproad, under A40 flyover into Wood Lane and take a right at the first lights into South Africa Road. Ground is on the left. From WEST exit M4 at junction 4b and stay in lane for Watford M1, Oxford M40 on to M25. Exit at M40 eastbound. Then as from north. From SOUTH from Hammersmith roundabout take exit with Lloyds Bank on corner and follow Shepherd's Bush Road to Shepherd's Bush past *Fringe and Firkin* on the left, on to Wood Lane. Pass BBC Centre and turn left at lights on to South Africa Road.

Parking BBC car park in Wood Lane costs £5. On-street parking is scarce.

By bus From Victoria coach station take District Line tube to Hammersmith – direction Ealing Broadway or Richmond – then #293 bus. Or change on to Hammersmith & City Line for Goldhawk Road or Shepherd's Bush – 15-minute walk to ground.

By rail Turn right out of Euston station, walk 300 yards to Euston Square and catch Hammersmith & City Line to Shepherd's Bush. Alternatively, take Northern Line from Euston south to Tottenham Court Road and change on to Central line westbound until White City. From here it's a five-minute walk.

Leeds United

Premiership position (2002-03): 15th. Last season: *Sept* Leeds 1 Utd 0 *March* Utd 2 Leeds 1. United's 10yr record: *Home* W7 D3 L0 *Away* W4 D2 L4.

2002-03 will go down as one of the worst seasons ever in the history of Leeds United. A team that played in the semi-finals of the European Cup as recently as 2001 was torn apart and the club only narrowly avoided relegation. If there was jaw-dropping shock at just how in debt Leeds United were, there was little sympathy in Manchester as Leeds' financial problems reached a head. Under immodest chairman 'Publicity Peter' Ridsdale – the football equivalent of Mr Micawber – the club gambled on future success by borrowing money to buy a plethora of established stars. It was money they couldn't afford to pay back when things didn't go to plan.

The moderately successful – as he should have been after spending so much – David O'Leary was sacked in the summer of '02, to be replaced by the cliché-rich cockney charmer Terry Venables. Despite Leeds insisting that players like Ferdinand and Woodgate wouldn't be sold, both left the club for rivals, Ferdinand following the likes of Jordan, McQueen and Cantona by moving to Old Trafford…prompting the 'Leeds are our feeder club' song from Reds.

Venables lasted eight months after alienating much of the Elland Road support (Very Terribles, they nicknamed him), partly by criticising his own players in his *News of the World* column. He was replaced by Peter Reid –

Rio can always sure of an affectionate welcome back at Elland Road

hardly a manager in demand after his time at Sunderland. But it was Reid who steadied the club to avoid relegation – and earned himself a longer contract. At the end of the season Leeds fans suffered the ultimate in ironies: the victory over Arsenal which secured their Premiership (and possibly future) existence gifted their hated rivals in red the title. How that one was enjoyed in Manchester.

Ridsdale eventually stepped down in the face of intense pressure (though when he was borrowing with reckless abandon there was little complaint on the terraces, everybody loved his 'ambition'). What a cost that ambition came at: some of the financial madness of his regime sent a shudder down the spines of every Leeds fan. £500,000 a year on private planes for directors, £500,000 a year still being paid to Robbie Fowler, even though he had been sold to City, £200 for the yellow and blue tropical fish in Ridsdale's office. Despite offloading half of their best players to pay for the folly, Leeds still have a huge £79m debt and are under pressure to sell yet more. Whatever happens at Elland Road, the future doesn't look anything like as bright as it did two years ago.

Elland Road Leeds LS11 OES. ☎ 0113 226 1000. Capacity 40,204. Away allocation 3,500 (South Stand).

Bite to eat *Cracked Egg Café* on Elland Road does a decent all-day breakfast; *United Fisheries* is the chip shop favoured by most regular patrons of LS11 – get there early to avoid the queues.

Swift half *The Grove* near the station; *The Old Peacock* on Elland Road; *The Britannia* on Top Moor Side and *Bull's Head* in St Matthew's Street both in Holbeck, five minutes from the ground; in town head for the *Corn Exchange* and juicers such as *Norman's*, *Oporto* or *The Elbow Rooms*. Be wary of wearing colours in city centre and even more so near the ground.

By car From NORTHWEST and WEST exit M62 at junction 27 on to M621 direction Leeds. Take junction 2 and first left A643 on to Elland Road. Ground is on the right. From SOUTH and EAST at end of M1 keep in lane for Manchester M621. Exit at junction 2 then as from northwest and west.

Parking Visitors' car park at the ground or on industrial estate on Low Fields Road.

By bus Leeds run matchday shuttle bus from Neville Street to the ground, £1 return. Come out of railway station, across car park and down steps. The buses are on the right under railway bridge.

By rail From Leeds station, see above. Otherwise, it's a half-hour walk.

Leicester City

Promoted as first division runners' up. Last season: n/a. United's 10yr record: *Home* W4 D2 L1 *Away* W5 D2 L0.

When United last played Leicester in the league, in April 2002, the whole ground – club officials, the lot – stood up to sing 'Stand Up If You Love Leicester'. There was a resigned feeling about Filbert Street then, a sense that the club were going down and weren't quite sure when they would be returning. Leicester were heavily in debt and whilst the investment into the new 32,500-capacity Walkers Stadium (think Southampton or Middlesbrough with blue seats) was brave, the ground hadn't been built to entertain Grimsby or Stoke.

The pessimism was justified when Leicester went into administration and the future of the club looked bleak, especially when it was revealed that the Foxes board were anything but wise in paying Denis of the same name £35,000 a week. Wise was injured for much of his first season, but burnt off some of his excess energy by assaulting a team mate at the start of his second. If any good came from the assault, it was that it enabled Leicester to sack him and his vulgar wage. A new consortium which included Gary Lineker took control and all associated with Leicester soon had reason to feel more sanguine. Despite relegation and selling Robbie Savage, Gary Rowett and Matt Piper, average attendances rose by 10,000. And all because, thanks to their highly rated young manager Mickey Adams, Leicester fans had a winning team. Without a considerable budget, the straight-talking Yorkshireman has thrived, creating a siege mentality at the club. And his accomplishments have been tangible when compared with the fortunes of Derby and Ipswich, the two other relegated clubs last season. Leicester were promoted after coat-tailing Portsmouth for much of the year.

However, the euphoria of promotion will be tempered by the reality that life in the Premiership for a club still with creditors will be as tough as last time. If they can somehow stay up this season and Adams continues his evolution, there's no reason why they can't repeat the mid-table finishes that Martin O'Neill made the norm. Let's just hope that on their return to Old Trafford they don't produce performances as turgid as those perfected during the Celtic manager's time.

Walkers Stadium Filbert Way, Leicester LE2 7FL. T 0870 0406000. Capacity 32,500. Away allocation 3,000 (Northeast corner).

Bite to eat Head to the city centre for a curry.

Swift half *The Wyvern* (57 Grandby Street) is close to the train station and is a must for real ale fans, *Morgan's Sports Café* (Belvoir Street) built into the ground floor of the *Grand Hotel* offers big-screen sports.

By car From NORTH or SOUTH, exit M1 at junction 21 (M69). Follow signs for city centre via A5460 for 3 miles, turn right into Upperton Road, over the bridge and first right on Western Boulevard. The stadium is on the right. The club's official website *lcfc.premiumtv.co.uk* contains a handy AA route-planning facility.

By rail BR London Road and stadium is five minutes' cab ride or a 20-minute walk.

Liverpool

Premiership position (2002-03): 5th. Last season: *Dec* Liverpool 0 Utd 2 *April* Utd 4 Liverpool 0. United's 10yr record: *Home* W5 D2 L3 *Away* W4 D2 L4.

In 1990, Liverpool boasted 18 league championships to United's seven. Thirteen years later and Liverpool are still on 18, whilst United are just three behind with 15 titles. The once seemingly unassailable total is being caught quicker than a Scouser in...(insert your own stereotypical Scouse joke here).

Liverpool's demise from Kings of Europe to mediocre underlings has, unfortunately for them, coincided with United's lofty ascendancy. But unlike the Scousers, United have capitalised on the success, strengthening their financial muscle each season. As Liverpool have been hampered by a 44,500 capacity ground whose future remains undecided, United have accelerated into a different financial league by expanding Old Trafford on a regular basis and playing commercial trailblazers to the point that United now shop at the top people's store – and Liverpool still buy from *Littlewoods*.

United's strike force meet and greet the Anfield stewards

However – to dismiss Liverpool as washed-up has-beens is as bright as the Happy Mondays' musician who once spiked their coach driver's drink with acid before an overnight journey. Liverpool are still a far bigger club than Arsenal, for example, with a global following second only to the team their fans despise, the champions of England from the right end of the East Lancashire Road. And for United fans, the trip to Anfield remains one of the most eagerly awaited of the season – an outing that contains all the edge, passion and vitriol that you'd expect from a longstanding enmity between two teams whose cultural and social influence extends far beyond their city boundaries. What we're saying is this: we despise each other and wouldn't have it any other way.

What amuses many Reds is that there's an entire generation of young people who can't remember Liverpool winning the league, although they've been spared the hirsute perma perms of the Anfield Rap brigade. That wasn't quite how Scousers intended it to be when they unleashed their 'form is temporary, class is permanent' banner in 1992…

Anfield Liverpool L4 OTH. T 0151 260 8680. Capacity 44,500. Away allocation 3,000 (Anfield Road).

Bite to eat Several chippies and takeaway shops on Walton Breck Road. Normal home-game pies and the like in ground.

Swift half *The Arkles* on the corner of Anfield Rd is a big pub that is full on match-days but entry isn't advisible. Mancs aren't the most popular species around L4 – or L-anything for that matter. There's a few decent pubs around Anfield like *Breckside* on Walton Breck Road, but again, drinking in one of them isn't suggested. Find a quiet pub in the city centre or head back to Manchester.

By car From EAST: M62 until the end of motorway then turn right on the A5058 into Queens Drive. After approximately 3 miles turn left into Utting Avenue. After 1 mile turn right into Anfield Road for Liverpool FC. The Stanley Park car park is 200m before Anfield Road and away coaches park up just off Utting Avenue.

Parking Use Stanley Park car park – 1,000 spaces, secure and cheap. Failing that, street parking isn't a problem near where the away coaches park, just be prepared to toss a coin into the hands of a young scal to 'mind yer car mister'.

By rail Manchester Piccadilly to Liverpool Lime Street every half hour. From there, it's an unadvisable 30-minute trek, a taxi or a bus.

Manchester City

Premiership position (2002-03): 9th. Last season: *Nov* City 3 Utd 1 *Feb* Utd 1 City 1. United's 10yr record: *Home* W4 D1 L0 *Away* W4 D0 L1.

United fans sneered at Kevin Keegan's assertion that a top six finish was realistic last season but chants of: 'City's coming up but they're going straight back down' were muted when it became clear that the Blues were capable of beating the best in the Premiership. Like United. The less said about the 9/11 the better, but United's outstanding run against the neighbours had to end sometime. And given that City don't do trophies, it would have been cruel to deny them their moment in the rain. No doubt they'll add another star to their shirt to commemorate the victory…

Despite improvements on the pitch, City's ability to crumble from within has not deserted them and last season saw their genuinely popular chairman

David Bernstein resign amidst suggestions of a boardroom rift about the future direction of the club. A faction forming around the manager wanted to continue bringing in big-name, big-nosed players like Fowler and Schmeichel, others preferred a period of austerity given the repercussions of reckless overspending at Elland Road. Either way, City's finances appear as interesting the manner in which they qualified for European competition for the first time in a long time (by coming near the top of the fair play league, prompting bizarre suggestions from Blues that United and City could meet in the final of the UEFA Cup). It might be better if they stopped day-dreaming and starting learning the realities of foreign travel, such as the fact that one-year passports are no longer issued, that there is a single currency and that East Germany has ceased to exist.

Fuelled by the enthusiasm of a move to possibly the best-looking ground in the country, the 48,000-capacity City of Manchester stadium, City fans are rightly optimistic about the future. United fans will look forward to a trip to the new ground, after all, it has been largely paid for using their money –

Keegan: he loved it last season, he really loved it

from the tax payers of the city of Manchester.

But with everything going relatively and uncharacteristically well with Manchester's second club, Bernstein's bitter departure reminded everyone that it's only a matter of time before the next catastrophe.

City of Manchester Stadium Rowsley St, Manchester M11 3FF. T 0161 232 3000. Capacity 48,000. Away allocation 3,000 (South Stand).

Bite to eat See our Manchester guide.

Swift half There are countless old-time working-class pubs – many frequented by Reds – near the City of Manchester stadium. Publicans are delighted at the prospect of increased trade from the new stadium and ex-City player Mike Summerbee has even purchased the closest pub to the ground on Rowsley Street, renaming it *Summerbee's*. *The Crossroads* and *Mary D's* stand nearby, facing each other on Grey Mare Lane. *The Derby Arms* and *The Grove* (the latter owned by Mancunian brewers Holts) are just along on Ashton New Road and the pub formerly known as *The Church* is now *The Blue Moon* (complete with garish laser blue makeover) on Clayton Lane. *The Stadium* (formerly *The Cricketers*) on Bradford Road has also been clad in gaudy laser blue. Whether United fans will drink in these pubs, or on the northern fringes of the city centre a 20-minute walk away, remains to be seen, although it's doubtful we'll be in a rush to *Summerbee's*.

By car With no parking available round the ground, the car's not such a great idea. Best advice is to park in a city centre car park and walk east straight down Great Ancoats Street to the stadium.

By bus Buses #216, #217, #230–237, X36 and X37 will take you close.

By rail The stadium is about 20-25 minutes' walk from Manchester Piccadilly.

Middlesbrough

Premiership position (2002-03): 11th. Last season: *Sept* Utd 1 Boro 0 *Dec* Boro 3 Utd 1. United's 10yr record: *Home* W6 D1 L2 *Away* W5 D2 L1.

When Juninho first joined Middlesbrough, London's *Evening Standard* newspaper was aghast, all but suggesting that life for the diminutive Brazilian would be better in an impoverished Rio *favela* than the industrial Teesside town. The coverage was cutting, arrogant and snobbish, for which the newspaper later apologised. Middlesbrough has never pretended to rival Paris as a tourist attraction – has never pretended to rival Hartlepool for that matter – but locals should have seen the comments as a compliment of a kind, proof that the town's football club had entered the radar screen of football consciousness. Proof that they had potential to matter.

Today, Middlesbrough are established Premiership performers, although given the money that chairman Steve Gibson has lavished on his hobby horse, there's a nagging feeling that they should have achieved more. Hero that he was at Old Trafford, long-time manager Bryan Robson may have succeeded in attracting big-name players slightly past their best (and therefore with little re-sale value) like Ravanelli and Boksic, but considering the vast amounts of his chairman's money spent, his team disappointed.

When the fans' patience finally snapped in 2001, Robson was nudged aside, eventually making way for another ex-United employee, Steve McClaren. McClaren had been content in Manchester but thinking that his boss Sir Alex Ferguson was about to leave, he decided to do likewise. He wasn't short of offers – West Ham must still be regretting his rejection letter – and it's unlikely that he regretted his decision to leave.

In these cash-tight times, McClaren enjoyed the luxury of spending nearly £20m, largely on younger, hungrier players than the type Robson went for. His signings seemed to be an instant success and by October '02, Boro sat in third, before falling away; they eventually finished a moderate 11, with just 12 pints picked up away from home all season. However, with teams like Charlton doing just as well on a fraction of the budget, there will always be pressure on McClaren and his team to do better.

Cellnet Riverside Middlesbrough TS3 6RS. T 01642 877745. Capacity 35,100. Away allocation Most clubs get 2,800 – United get around 1,000 (South Stand).

Bite to eat Basically it's burger vans and more burger vans along the chilly dockside trek. Downtown Middlesbrough doesn't offer much better.

Swift half Away fans are welcome at *The Cornerhouse*, below Middlesbrough station and *Yates Wine Lodge* near the bus station but drinking in the town isn't advisible; *The Bridge* on Bridge Street East is an okay small pub only five minutes from the ground.

By car From SOUTH exit A1 (M) at signpost Thirsk A168, Teesside A19 on to A19 for 32 miles. Turn right on to A66 Middlesbrough bypass for 3 miles until first roundabout. Turn left into Forest Road, the ground is straight ahead. Conversely, head straight into town and park up. From NORTH approaching town on A19, cross River Tees and turn left on to A66 Middlesbrough bypass. Then as from south. From WEST leave A1 (M) at junction 57 on to A66 (M), then as from south.

Parking Street – or should that be 'verge' – parking near the stadium.

By bus #36, #37 and #38 go from central bus station to North Ormesby, a short walk from the ground.

By rail Change from GNER East Coast mainline at Darlington for Middlesbrough station, 1 mile from the ground. Leave station from back exit, follow the crowds right along Bridge Street East, past *The Bridge* pub and swing right into Windward Way which, as the name suggests, offers a fairly blustery walk to the stadium.

Newcastle United

Premiership position (2002-03): 3rd. Last season: *Nov* Utd 5 Newcastle 3 *April* Newcastle 2 Utd 6. United's 10yr record: *Home* W6 D4 L0 *Away* W4 D3 L3.

After the mediocrity endured under previous incumbents Dalglish and Gullit, Newcastle have undergone a quiet revolution under the septuagenarian Sir Bobby Robson, who has imposed a rare stability within the club. At the start of the 1990s, Newcastle's state was akin to the plight of

Tyneside's great ship yards: desperate. A second division club at the wrong end of the table, gates dropped as low as 10,004 for one game, and Kevin Keegan was greeted as the saviour when appointed manager in 1992. Keegan's Newcastle, bankrolled by Sir John Hall's money, excelled. Premiership status was reclaimed playing attacking football, St. James's Park was rebuilt and by the start of 1996 the Geordies looked likely champions…until they saw a 12-point lead overtaken by United.

Seven years on, and Newcastle still haven't won the Premiership. In fact, the Geordies have not won a major domestic trophy since they lifted the FA Cup…in 1955. And they haven't been champions since 1927.

Knights like these: retirement and pensions advice from Sir Bobby

After Keegan resigned, Daglish and Gullit actually took the club into reverse, racking up huge debts and when Bobby Robson replaced the dreadlocked Dutchman in 1999, Alan Shearer was not even in the team. Robson has guided Newcastle to a second successive crack at the Champions League and whilst money has been lavished both on the stadium and new players, with average gates from regular full houses of 52,000, the Mags are the second best supported club in England and have substantial buying power. Where Dalglish and Gullit squandered, Robson has cleverly invested in young talent like Craig Bellamy, Lomano Lua Lua, Jermaine Jenas, Kieron

Dyer, Laurent Robert and the admittedly dim-witted Jonathan Woodgate. Every single one of them looks – to borrow a Geordie phrase – a canny buy. Though reuniting Woodgate with his old *Majestick* chum Lee Bowyer may not have been Sir Bob's brightest move.

Still, with all that talent at his disposal, all the old boy needs to do now is win a large, shiny, silver object. They're known as trophies, for any Geordies reading.

St James's Park Newcastle NE1 4ST. T 0191 261 1571. Capacity 52,193. Away allocation 1,800 (northwest corner of Sir John Hall Stand).

Bite to eat Stowell Street is handy for St James's and features a variety of decent Chinese restaurants and takeaways; *Café Sol* in Pink Lane is good for bocadillos to butties; *Eat Out* on Westgate Road promises the usual mix of burgers, kebabs and pizzas.

Swift half Head for the Quayside for any number of pubs and clubs; *Free Trade Inn*, City Road is a short cab ride from the station; *Rafferty's* on Pink Lane is walkable from Newcastle Central.

By car From NORTH exit A1 on to A167 Ponteland Road towards city centre. After 1½ miles at fourth roundabout turn left on to Jedburgh Road, right on to Grandstand Road and left on to A189 Ponteland Road which becomes Barrack Road. Carry on until roundabout. St James's is on the left. From SOUTH turn off A1 (M) at junction with A184. Carry on and bear left on to A189. Go over Redheugh Bridge, straight over roundabout and on to Blenheim Street until you meet Bath Lane. Turn left into Bath Lane, right into Corporation Street and left at the roundabout into Barrack Road. The ground is on the right. From WEST take A69 towards city centre, go past Newcastle General Hospital and at traffic lights turn left into Brighton Grove. After 70 yards turn right into Stanhope Street, then into Barrack Road.

Parking On-street parking and council-run car parks around the ground.

By bus Gallowgate bus station is ¼ mile from the ground.

By rail Newcastle Central railway station is ¾ mile from the ground. The Metro runs every 3 to 4 minutes to St James's station.

Portsmouth

Promoted to the Premiership as first division champions. United's 10yr record: n/a.

Fulham aside, if the foundations of any Premiership club are built on a questionable base then it's at Portsmouth. Not for Pompey a 30,000 stadium and a large established match-going fan-base which seems to be the prerequisite of Premiership survival, but the whims of a benefactor, the chairman Milan Mandaric, who has given this grand old club a quite unexpected stab at the big-time. The trouble is, the club aren't quite ready for it, with their revenue is limited by the 19,000 capacity Fratton Park, a pre-war relic that has not been top division standard since Portsmouth were England's top team. Fifty years ago.

If Mandaric were to pull out, then the club would be unable to pay the wage bill. This, after all, is a club which has to rent its training ground from the university. In Southampton. But to be too negative is to detract from the excellent job that old potato face Harry Redknapp has done. (Mrs R, incidentally, must be a bit of a stunner to produce an offspring capable of marrying Louise.)

Last season, Redknapp and his still sprightly sidekick Jim Smith surprised many by building the strongest side in the first division without paying big transfer fees. Whilst the wage bill climbed quickly, they still persuaded established Premiership players like Paul Merson and Steve Stone to take a pay cut and moulded them with inexpensive but largely unproven rising stars like defender Matthew Taylor, midfielder Nigel Quashie and forward Svetoslav Todorov. Starting with eight debutants on the first game of the season was a gamble, but it clearly paid off.

Portsmouth have the potential to match neighbours Southampton for crowds, but potential is a phrase bandied about too readily in football and the reality is that Pompey will surprise many if they are not involved in a relegation battle. And as Reds who travelled there for the cup games in '89 and '95 will testify, there are better away days than ones which involve a five-hour road journey followed by 90 minutes in an open stand. Still, it's different.

Fratton Park Frogmore Road, Portsmouth PO4 8RA. T 023 9273 1204. Capacity 19,500. Away allocation undecided but likely to be only 1000–2000 (in the uncovered Milton End, or Intercash Stand).

Swift half *Mr Pickwick's* and the *Brewers Arms* in Milton Road. Families and those in search of hot food should head for *The Good Companion* on the Eastern Road, about a third of a mile before the junction with Milton Road. Other notable boozers include *The Rutland Arms* in Francis Avenue.

By car Follow A3(M) on to A27, exit on to Eastern Road (A2030) towards Southsea. The ground is up ahead where the road meets Milton Road (A288).

Parking If you're early enough, your best bet is on-street. Turn off Goldsmith Avenue (the A2030 main road south of the ground) to find a network of side streets.

By rail Fratton Station is served by most, but not all, trains running from London Waterloo to Portsmouth. From the station, it's a 10-minute walk to the ground along Goldsmith Avenue. Come out over the footbridge, turn left when you hit the main road, and go left again into Apsley Road.

Portsmouth get a preview of United in last season's FA Cup clash

Southampton

Premiership position (2002-03): 8th. Last season: *Nov* Utd 2 Southampton 1 *Feb* Southampton 0 Utd 2. United's 10yr record: *Home* W9 D1 L0 *Away* W4 D1 L5.

They may have failed to wise up to the fact that releasing an appalling Cup final song is up there with saying you admire H from Steps, but Southampton have been quick learners under Gordon Strachan. Perennial relegation strugglers throughout the 1990s, many Saints fans still can't believe how they stayed in the Premiership with the weighty handicap of the tiny, antiquated, Dell home – and more managers than the civil service. When, under Graeme Souness, 'George Weah's cousin' (a hoaxer who could barely trap a ball let alone play in the Premiership) was introduced as a substitute, only to be substituted minutes later, it summed up Southampton's attitude. Anything was worth trying, so as long as they stayed up. However, in 2001, after twenty years in the attempt, Southampton moved into a new home, the 32,000 capacity St Mary's stadium. Finally, the club attracted the kind of attendances and revenue that had become the Premiership norm. And in Strachan they enlisted a manager as feisty and determined as his former mentor, a gentleman by the name of Ferguson.

The Saints' upper-crust chairman Rupert Lowe was regarded with suspicion at first, yet alongside Strachan, they run a club with a strong work ethic and excellent team spirit, seemingly bereft of big names and bigger egos. They are a real business, too. Southampton cut their wage bill by 45percent in 2002 and were one of the few Premiership teams to declare a profit – £3.3m on a turnover of £38m – partly because rather than lavish money on ageing fringe players from bigger clubs, they source emerging talents from far and wide. James Beattie may be the top scorer who attracts more attention than any Saints player since the ever loyal Matt Le Tissier (still 'Le God' to fans) but behind the front man is a team of underrated and gutsy performers like Swedish attacking defender Anders Svensson and fleet-heeled Fabrice Fernandes. New signings David Prutton and ex-Red Danny Higginbotham will only compliment more established players like England international Wayne Bridge, Claus Lundekvam and the impressive Finnish keeper Antti Niemi. The comedy value hasn't entirely disappeared, mind – the Saints paid £3.5m for the often-injured Ecuadorian international Augustin Delgado for whom they should consider a tagging device, so frequently do they lose track of his whereabouts.

Southampton won't win the league, but success is relative, and reaching Europe is definitely an accomplishment. That and being a rare example of a football club that's gaining respect on and off the field.

Saints' Anders Svensson on the trail of Ruud

Friends Provident St Mary's Stadium St Mary's, Southampton SO15 2XH.
T 0870 220 0150. Capacity 32,000. Away allocation 3,200 (Northam Stand).

Bite to eat Plenty of choice in and around the station or you could try one of the
pies sold at the various outlets around the impressive new stadium.

Swift half Arriving by train, most away fans will probably go in *The Victory* opposite
the station. Around the corner in Commercial Road is *The Rat & Parrot* and dead
opposite is a converted church called *Café Sol*. *The Giddy Bridge*, a large
Wetherspoons pub in London Road, *The Prince of Wales*, *The Bevois Castle* and
The Station all welcome away fans too. But these aside, Southampton is pretty
poor for a night out.

By car From NORTH follow A34 or M3 until it meets M27. At Eastleigh head off on
A33 sliproad marked Southampton. Go straight over roundabout into Upper Avenue,
left at next roundabout and straight until big roundabout. Take 2nd exit, stay in left-
hand lane until Six Dials junction. Go over Northam Railway Bridge and turn right into
Britannia Road. From WEST exit M27 at Junction 3 and join M271 southbound. Turn
left at roundabout to join A35 towards city centre. Continue on West Quay Road
(shopping centre is on the left) until roundabout. Go straight across towards Town
Quay, Isle of Wight ferry terminal on right-hand side. Follow one-way system round
park then turn left into Canute Road. At main set of traffic lights with Ocean Village
on the right, turn left and up to roundabout. Go straight over into Albert Road North,
this becomes Marine Parade, St Mary's is on the left. From EAST exit M27 at junction
7 and turn left on to A334 (Charles Watts Way). At next roundabout take 2nd exit into
Thornhill Park Road which becomes Bitterne Road East then Bitterne Road West. Go
over Northam Bridge with Meridian TV studios on the right, at next set of traffic lights
turn left into Prince's Street (Prince of Wales pub on corner) round into Millbank Street
and straight on into Belvidere Road. St Mary's is on right-hand side.

Parking Public car parks are scattered 10–20 minutes' walk from the stadium.

By bus St Mary's free shuttle bus from opposite railway station. Match tickets come
with free return park-and-ride bus tickets specifically for away supporters. It's situated just off M27 at junction 8 and is clearly signposted from motorway exit. It takes
about 20 minutes and they line up waiting after the match has finished.

By rail From Euston take Northern Line to Waterloo and mainline train to
Southampton Central – it takes about an hour.

Tottenham Hotspur

Premiership position (2002-03): 10th. Last season: *Sept* Utd 1 Spurs 0 *April*
Spurs 0 United 2. United's 10yr record: *Home* W9 D1 L0 *Away* W6 D1 L3.

Only a decade ago, Tottenham were classed as one of the big five teams in the
country, and their visit regularly drew one of the highest crowds of the season

to Old Trafford. True, they were never genuine title contenders, but they seemed to exude a sophisticated metropolitan confidence matched by attractive football and big name stars that continued the tradition of the original glory, glory club. Despite their not winning the league since 1961, top players wanted to join Tottenham and when Paul Gascoigne chose the club over United there wasn't the surprise that there would be today if a player chose N17 over M16. Off the field, Tottenham exceeded United with commercial acumen: as recently as 1991 Tottenham had a higher revenue from merchandise than United. No wonder Martin Edwards borrowed their commercial maverick Edward Freedman to turn things round at Old Trafford.

Hoddle demonstrates his new Reiki Healing program

But that was then. Whilst fans may still believe that Tottenham's rightful place is amongst the big teams, the reality is that they've become a pallid imitation of their former selves. As their rivals down the Seven Sisters Road push United for honours, Tottenham flounder along as mid-table certainties, their fans ever hopeful of a change in fortune, resolutely loyal as they fill their ground to its 36,289 capacity most weeks. After another season of adding negligible value to the Premiership, fans have started to question the man they once saw as their prodigal son, manager Glenn Hoddle. Some think he should stay, others that he has lost the dressing room and should be off – which is the sum of Tottenham's existence for much of the last decade: internal conflict and strife.

United have an excellent recent record against Spurs, which may partly explain why tickets are so hard to come by for the Tottenham away. It's certainly not because Reds want to see the spluttering Cockerels, in their own right.

White Hart Lane Bill Nicholson Way, 748 High Road, Tottenham N17 0AP. T 08700 112222. Capacity 36,289. Away allocation 2,480 (South Stand).

Bite to eat The hike along Seven Sisters Road takes you past any number of Turkish, Indian, Italian, Chinese and Greek restaurants, plus the usual fast-food chains.

Swift half *The Railway Tavern*, White Hart Lane; *O'Mara's*, Tottenham High Road; *The Beehive*, Stoneleigh Road; *The Park*, Park Lane; *The Two Brewers* and *The Victoria*, Scotland Green.

By car From NORTH from M1 (A1 at junction 2/3) or M40 (A40 at junction 1) join A406 North Circular eastbound until you hit Edmonton junction. Take sliproad signposted Tottenham to A1010, Fore Street. Continue 1 mile and ground is on the left. From SOUTH go through Dartford Tunnel on M25 and exit at junction 31, turning left at roundabout on to A13. Exit at North Circular A406 and continue until you see sign for Tottenham, Brimsdown A1055. Follow signs for 1½ miles until you pass Tesco on the left. Filter right at lights into Leeside Road and straight on into Brantwood Road, turn left at T-junction into Tottenham High Road. White Hart Lane is on the left.

Parking Like the match tickets, parking is pricey. If you can't find a spot on a neighbouring street, try Gibson Business Centre at the junction of White Hart Lane and Tottenham High Street.

By bus Victoria coach station, Victoria Line to Seven Sisters and bus #259 or #279 to ground. Or 25-minute walk.

By rail Euston then Victoria Line to Seven Sisters or Tottenham Hale.

Wolverhampton Wanderers

Promoted via the play-offs. United's 10yr record: n/a.

The reality of promotion took time to register with ripened Wolves' benefactor Sir Jack Hayward. Minutes after the final whistle of the play-off final, the Bermuda-based tax exile who has pumped tens of millions of pounds into his hometown club – with an up until then doubtful return – opined to the Sky cameras that he hoped Wolves would be going to Old Trafford and Highbury. Failing the aforementioned clubs going bust between now and next season, he doesn't need to hope, for strange as it seems, Wolves are heading back to the top flight for the first time since 1984.

Wolves seemed destined to follow Manchester City up from the first division in 2002 until their promotion bid floundered badly in the last few weeks of the season. It didn't help that Black Country rivals West Brom boing-boinged past them to take the automatic promotion spot. And frustrated with a series of near misses, fans called for manager Dave Jones to resign midway through last season, calls which became muted as they reached the play-offs, beating Sheffield United 3-0 in the final.

Much is made of Wolves' support, and whilst it's true that 50,000-plus crowds were the norm at Molineux during the 1950s when the club won three first division titles and became pioneers in European competition, in the '80s they played fourth division football to 5,000 crowds and were close to going out of existence until the goals of Steve Bull hauled the club back up the league ladder.

Playing in a modern 28,500 capacity stadium with trademark old-gold seating, Wolves have the potential to stay in the Premiership, especially if Sir Jack fulfils his promise once more to dip his hand into his deep pockets. Although how long two of their promotion-winning stars, Denis Irwin and Paul Ince, will hang around is, at the time of writing, unsure.

Molineux Waterloo Road, Wolverhampton WV1 4QR. T 01902 655 000. Capacity 28,525. Away allocation around 3000 (in either John Ireland Stand or Jack Harris Stand).

Swift half No shortage of pubs but they're not welcoming to away fans. Best local bet is probably The Great Western at the station, with real ale on tap; or, if you're driving, try family-friendly pubs *The Moreton Arms* on the A449 Stafford Road, or *The Spread Eagle* on the A4123.

By car Molineux, just off the Wolverhampton ring road, is hard to miss. Coming from the NORTH, EAST or SOUTHEAST, exit M6 at Junction 10A, taking A449 into Wolverhampton. Approaching the town centre, take the third exit at the Five Ways roundabout onto Waterloo Road – the ground is half a mile along on the left, signposted 'Molineux Centre'. From SOUTHWEST, exit M5 at Junction 2 and take A4123 into Wolverhampton. Follow this road until the Snow Hill Junction, and turn right onto the ring road; Molineux is signposted to the right.

Parking Very limited – but there are several multi-storeys in Wolverhampton town centre, no more than a 10-minute walk.

By rail Direct train services run from Manchester, Liverpool and London-Euston, and there are frequent links with Birmingham New Street. From Wolverhampton station, proceed along Lichfield Street, and right into Stafford Street. The ground is a little way up on the left, the other side of the ring road.

The History

Heathens to Heroes

**Heathen beginnings ★ Early days in the League
War, corruption and decline ★ The Busby Era
★ Pretenders ★ Arise Sir Alex**

In truth it wasn't the greatest of orations, not *Winston Churchill or Martin Luther King. Not even up there with a Robin Cook resignation special. But when Sir Alex Ferguson stepped on to the pitch at the end of Manchester United's last home game of the 2002-03 season, he said everything that needed to be said. After the waves of affection, gratitude and respect had stopped washing down in his direction from the stands, Sir Alex could not resist one last dig at his rival Arsène Wenger. 'We've not won anything yet,' he said, which was factually spot-on at that moment. 'To do a lap of honour today would not be appropriate. But I just wanted to say that everything that has been achieved this season has been down to the players. They have been fantastic.'*

Fantastic indeed. Just a day after Ferguson had delivered his speech, the players were crowned as Premiership champions when Arsenal lost at home to Leeds. That has been the way of the season's climax since the arrival of the Premier League: television schedules rarely allow the crowd in the stadium on the day to celebrate a title win, and match-going Reds had to wait more than a week to sing 'we've got our trophy back. But in the end nobody much minds. It is winning that counts. Even if you learn about the victory, as Sir Alex did this time round, at your young grandson's birthday party. After he had helped himself to a last Cadbury's chocolate finger, the manager emerged from the party to announce that the 15th Championship of United's history was the most satisfying he could recall. A man acutely aware of the achievements of the past, he reckoned it would go down in Red history because of the way it was achieved, because of the way an excellent and at times rampant rival was hauled back and overtaken. But most of all because of what those players he acknowledged on the Old Trafford turf had done to achieve it.

Sheringham, Solksjaer ... they always score. Barcelona, 1999

Ferguson touched on the essence of the club in his short speech. It is the **players** that count. It is the players who are Manchester United. It is the players whose efforts twice a week thrill and frustrate, it is the players who accumulate the trophies, it is the players in whose reflected glory the millions who call themselves United fans bask. And, over the decades, what players we have seen. In any list compiled of the greatest in British football history, there would be at least a dozen men who have worn Red in the top fifty. At least three would be in the top five. And one – George Best – would be at the very top.

The odd thing is, through the generations a certain ethos has been passed down. Though **Billy Meredith**, **Duncan Edwards**, **George Best** and **Ryan Giggs** belonged to eras that didn't even overlap, you get the feeling that if some way could be found to bring them all together at their peak to play in the same side, they would immediately be on the same wavelength. This is the United way, one formulated over the years. It is a mix of skill and graft, effort and grace, style and substance, all bundled up with a refusal ever to accept that a cause is lost.

It was never better exemplified than on the night of **26 May 1999**. That night, the manager, **Alex Ferguson**, had given up hope. He had offered a prayer or two, but he had resigned himself to the fact he was not destined to take his Manchester United back to the summit of European football. His place in the history books looked set to include the phrase runner-up. He was not alone in being gloomy: 50,000 Reds supporters inside Barcelona's Camp Nou stadium knew it was over. The several million followers of the United cause across the planet were set to change channels. Manchester United, with a double in the locker, were not, after all, to land the treble – it was, as the commentators had long told us, an impossible ambition. **Bayern Munich** led with seconds to go of the Champions League final of 1999, a game with little to distinguish it except the fierce free kick with which Mario Basler had given the Germans the advantage in the fifth minute. Already the steel-grey ribbons denoting Bayern's change colours had been tied to the handles of the biggest piece of silverware in world football. Lennart Johansen, the UEFA president, was on his way to the pitch side to hand out the medals. And George Best, too upset to watch his team fail at the last, had left the stadium for what was in those days his favoured place of refuge: a hotel bar.

But the players, they knew different. With the clock on the Camp Nou's giant screens showing that all 90 minutes had been spent, **Teddy Sheringham** scored an equaliser nobody watching thought would ever come. Seconds later, with the Bayern players visibly buckling under the weight of disappointment, United won a corner. David Beckham teased it into the box, Sheringham nodded on and there was **Ole Gunnar Solskjaer**, swivelling, twisting, looping the ball into the Germans' net.

Seldom can a night's football have been celebrated like this one was. In a joyous communion, players and supporters alike stayed on in the stadium for what seemed like hours as the cup was lifted time after time to a roar which never diminished. All night, apparently dazed by what he had seen, Alex Ferguson could only repeat his stunned observation over and over: '**football: bloody hell**'.

Alex should have known. Not just under his shrewd guidance but always, that was the way United players had always approached their task: the **comeback** has long been their staple. Indeed, in a sense, the last ten years, with their climax in that wonder season of 1999, have been the exception in the long history of Manchester United. Sustained success has never been the pattern before, rather it has been a stumbling lurch between feast and famine, cock-up and glory. And United players always had that extra sparkle that made them stars, the glint in the eye that others could not match. The modern United may have become the biggest soap opera in British sport, in an era when David Beckham's latest haircut demanded first airing on national news bulletins. But you wonder what would today's media have made of the match-fixing conducted by Edwardian Reds, of the club's near bankruptcy in the 1930s, of the United captain leading a national players' strike in 1910, and of the air crash in **Munich** in February 1958 – the awful night that marked the beginnings of the United legend.

Heathen beginnings

There was no hint of the substance to come at the beginning. The club of Edwards, Whelan and Taylor, of Law, Best and Charlton, of Cantona, Hughes and Giggs, had an inauspicious birth. Unlike many football clubs, there was no church connection in United's foundation. Although many have identified the Reds as Manchester's Catholic club, with a romantic affiliation to Glasgow Celtic, there was no hint of that in the early days.

In fact, this was a reputation that did not develop until the early 1950s, when Matt Busby, the fiercely devout west of Scotland

Newton Heath 1892–93

Catholic, made no secret of his **religious loyalties**. By the 1960s observers would talk of the tide of priests washing through the South Stand on matchdays. And when Frank O'Farrell, Tommy Docherty and Dave Sexton – Catholics all – followed Busby into the manager's office, it seemed as though a connection with Rome was a prerequisite for the job. But the last two managers – Big Ron Atkinson and Alex Ferguson – are Protestants by birth, non-sectarian by inclination. With Busby's death all hint of the club's supposed RC heritage disappeared. In truth, even before the great man died, the boardroom at Old Trafford had been infected by a new religious fervour: the worship of money.

Far from being God-botherers, United started as a bunch of Heathens. It is a historical irony, given the organisation's position at the vanguard of converting football into big business in the last decade of the twentieth century, that the club was established as a working men's recreational society. It was the lads of the **Lancashire and Yorkshire Railway**'s carriage and wagon department who, in **1878**, got together to play football at their **Newton Heath** works. Soon nicknamed the Heathens, the railwaymen played in yellow-and-green halved shirts with laced-up collars (a style briefly resurrected in 1993 as a money-spinning heritage item). In a hint of what was to come with a certain notorious grey kit more than a century later, despite their gaudy attire, the railwaymen weren't always able to pick each other out on the pitch, thanks to an almost permanent fug of soot and steam billowing on to their North Street ground off the adjacent railway track. Still, they managed to find each other sufficiently often to develop something of a reputation locally, winning their first trophy, the **Manchester Senior Cup** in 1886.

Already by then, the club had broadened its horizons beyond the employees of the railway. Anyone could be a Heathen. And by **1890**, ambition had really taken grip: the team applied to join the new Football League. They had no success. Instead they were tempted in to the **Football Alliance**, a short-lived alternative to the league. Within three years the League had amalgamated with its rival (in the same way a shark amalgamates with a sprat) and Newton Heath were in the big time, voted into an expanded first division; **Ardwick**, their principal Mancunian rivals and soon to take the name **Manchester City**, were at the same time placed in the second division. Thus was the local pecking order established early on.

Early days in the league

By 1893, when they joined the **Football League**, the Heathens had moved away from the smoke of North Street. Not that their change of environment was much more conducive to good football. So appalling was the pitch at their new **Bank Street ground** that it cost them a record. A 14-0 romp over Walsall Town Swifts on 9 March 1895 was declared void because the visiting club secretary took the precaution of making an official complaint about the state of the playing surface before kick-off.

Even in those early, unregulated, days of league football, it was a costly business running a club. Players did not come cheap, and, with just gate receipts and the occasional transfer fee to rely on, only the successful made money. After an initial spurt of excitement, Newton Heath were not successful, soon lurking in the lower reaches of the league's second division, and by 1902 the club was declared **bankrupt**, owing £2600, much of it to their own chairman who had run out of patience bank-rolling operations.

Harry Stafford, the club's full back, took it upon himself to raise the money to keep them going and when he bumped into a local brewer called **John Davies** (allegedly when Davies stopped to admire his dog) he wondered if he might effect a rescue. The booze baron bought the club, cleared its debts and, to declare a fresh start, suggested a change of strip – to red and white – and a new name. Manchester Celtic was dismissed as an idea, Manchester Central sounded too much like a railway station. But, at a special meeting organised for **26 April 1902**, everyone present agreed that a director called Louis Rocca had a good idea when he proposed Manchester United. Or, at least, that was the tale Rocca dined out on for the next half century.

Ernest Magnall's Red and White Army

By the turn of the century, tactics, training and an aggressive will to win had replaced the hearty corinthianism of football's origins on the playing fields of the public schools. And at United, in **1903**, they found a man who epitomised the new way of football thinking. **Ernest Magnall**, called the club secretary, but in effect United's first team manager, was a fitness fanatic, who drove his players with real ruthlessness. His methods paid off, his team were promoted to the first division, where, under his guidance, they won the **Championship** twice, as well as the **FA Cup**. In between cycling from John O'Groats to Land's End, Magnall found time to philosophise about his calling. In the *Manchester Evening News* he once waxed lyrical: 'A great intricate, almost delicate and to the vast majority of the public, an incomprehensible piece of machinery is the modern up-to-date football club.'

Magnall was helped enormously in his endeavours by **Manchester City imploding** up the road. In 1904, City won the FA Cup, but in order to do so they breached the league's regulations on paying

United, 1911–12; Ernest Magnall is on the right (in the hat)

Billy Meredith, the first United superstar

United's Managers

J. Ernest Magnall	1903–12	Sir Matt Busby	1945–69
John Bentley	1912–14	Wilf McGuinness	1969–70
John Robson	1914–21	Sir Matt Busby	1970–71
John Chapman	1921–26	Frank O'Farrell	1971–72
Clarence Hilditch	1926–27	Tommy Docherty	1972–77
Herbert Bamlett	1927–31	Dave Sexton	1977–81
Walter Crickmer	1931–32	Ron Atkinson	1981–86
Scott Duncan	1932–37	Sir Alex Ferguson	1986–present
Walter Crickmer	1937–45		

players: astronomical figures of up to £7 a week were handed over.
For such a heinous crime, the entire playing squad was banned fo.
turning out ever again for City, and from any football for a year.
Magnall bided his time, let the sentence be served, then signed up
several City men, including the brilliant Welsh winger **Billy
Meredith**, the Ryan Giggs of his day. In **1908**, Meredith led his new
team to the **league title**, the following year they took the **FA Cup**
against Bristol City and, on their return from Crystal Palace, paraded it through the streets of Manchester before a crowd of 300,000
(299,999 of whom presumably made the day trip up from
Basingstoke).

Such enormous potential sparked an idea in chairman John
Davies's head. In **1910**, he moved the club from Bank Street to a new
stadium in Trafford Park, which would take up to 100,000 supporters. Although without an official title, the place soon became known
as Old Trafford and was christened with a game against Liverpool.
Not that the players seemed that impressed by their new workplace,
they promptly lost the inaugural match. Then **Charlie Roberts**, the
team captain, who was also head of the Professional Footballers'
Association (formed in a Manchester hotel) led a brief **strike** after
the management attempted to sack any player joining the union.
Roberts, together with Meredith and a bunch of other players,
began to train elsewhere, calling themselves '**The Outcasts**'. Within
days, Davies and the board caved in, recognised the union and the
players were back.

Inspired, perhaps, by their show of strength, another **league win** was recorded in **1911**. But, in a hint of what was to happen with United managers across the decades, Ernest Magnall's relationship with his chairman was growing strained. Money divided the pair: Magnall wanted more and Davies, crippled with debt after building the ground, didn't have any spare. Thus in 1913, the manager resigned and stropped across town to join Manchester City, a revenge the Moss Side club had been itching for since Magnall pinched their players a decade before. Still, it took them a while to prise the great Meredith away. It wasn't until 1921 that the fans' favourite, now well into his forties, left United for City, to take up the position as player coach, all hint of his life ban from Maine Road apparently forgotten.

War, corruption and decline

The **First World War** cut a swathe through English football, killing off players by the dozen. A whole company of footballers, who stuck together in the trenches just as butchers, bakers and factory workers did, were wiped out at the Somme.

Perhaps it was not surprising in a time when death was imminent, that other values seemed to head out of the window. United, for instance, faced with relegation, needed a victory against Liverpool in the last game of the **1915** season. They duly achieved it, 2-0, but the referee had been suspicious of the attitude of both teams. And when a local bookie revealed that several players had placed big wagers on just that result, an inquiry was launched. It concluded that collusion had taken place, and **life bans** were initiated. But frankly, with the war on, nobody seemed to notice.

The league resumed hostilities in 1919, and by then, the Reds were not exactly thriving. Already financially holed below the water, gates plummeted as the football took a sorry turn. Without Magnall, then Meredith, managers such as **Clarence Hilditch** and **Herbert Bamlett** (a former referee, for goodness' sake) presided over a steady decline. By the time Davies died in 1927, the patient was in a parlous condition.

After two more years of depression, the fans demanded action. A document was presented to the board by the newly formed **United Supporters' Club** proposing five things: a new manager; a better scouting system; the signing of quality players; the election of five shareholders to the board; the raising of funds through a new share issue. How things don't change: the board ignored every proposal. So the supporters voted for a **boycott** of a home game against Arsenal on 18 October 1930. It was

only a partial success: some 23,000 turned out. But such was the abject display of the players, losing the match 1-2, they probably wished they hadn't. As anyone attempting a fans' boycott will know, however principled the motives in a strike, the best way of ensuring no-one pays to watch a club is if it plays crap football. United duly obliged and soon only a handful of die-hard Reds were rattling round Old Trafford on matchdays as the combined effects of a useless team and the Great Depression sent average crowds plummeting below 4,000.

Before long the debts were mounting higher than the roof of the North Stand: £30,000, a phenomenal sum in those days, was owed. With the team marooned in the lower reaches of **Division Two**, the club was poised on the edge of oblivion, refused credit at the bank, with the mortgage holders of Old Trafford seeking to foreclose. Step forward the next significant figure in the club's history: the businessman **James Gibson** agreed to pay off the debt in return for a seat on the board. Gibson, not a football fan, but a loyal Mancunian keen not to see a symbol of local pride disappear, provided the financial security which saw the Reds reclaim their place in the top division just in time for war to intervene again.

The Busby era

When the German forward Uwe Rossler turned out for Manchester City in the early 1990s, a big selling T-shirt outside Maine Road suggested that 'Uwe's granddad bombed Old Trafford'. Located in the heart of an industrial estate, it was a fair chance the stadium would take a stray **Luftwaffe bomb,** and while it may have been a libel on old Herr Rosler to suggest he was responsible, whoever did it reduced the place to a dust heap. James Gibson, surveying the mess, wondered if he had the energy or commitment to begin the rebuilding process. What he required, he told the chairman of the supporters' club as they stood in the rubble, was a manager who would take over responsibility for more than just team affairs: he wanted a boss.

Matt Busby had been a half back with Manchester City and Scotland before the war, who spent his active service in the RAF. Gibson approached him before the Football League had resumed, through the all-round fixer Louis Rocca. The pair liked each other's ideas. Busby was signed

Busby at City

up on **15 February 1945**, and would join up at Old Trafford as soon as he was demobilised. Gibson did many things for United to deserve his commemoration by a plaque on the railway bridge behind the Stretford End, but offering Matt Busby a five-year contract was by far the most significant.

Reconstruction

Before becoming a footballer, Busby had been a mining engineer in the same west of Scotland coalfield that produced Bill Shankly, Jock Stein and a host of other Scottish greats. That experience, plus his wartime service, forged many of Busby's theories of **teamwork**. In both environments, he learned that a team was only as good as its weakest member: lives literally depended on being able to place absolute trust in your mates.

At Old Trafford (well, **Maine Road**, which, at an annual rental of £2000 was where the Reds played until their home was rebuilt), Busby immediately constructed resourceful teams both on and off the pitch. On it, he was lucky to inherit some good players: **Johnny Carey**, his leader on the pitch, **Henry Cockburn**, **Johnny Morris**, **Charlie Mitten**. Off it, he brought in his old chum **Jimmy Murphy** to oversee the reserves and juniors and the wheeler-dealer **Louis Rocca** was given the job as chief scout.

In the early days of his tenure, Busby was not the genial presence he became in his retirement. Tough, flint-eyed, demanding, he expected as much of his players a he did of himself. His presence transformed the club: they finished runners-up in his first season in charge and in **1948**, they beat Blackpool 4-2 in what many regarded as the finest **FA Cup**

United 1948
FA Cup Final
v. Blackpool 4-2
Jack Crompton
Johnny Carey
John Aston
John Anderson **1**
Allenby Chilton
Henry Cockburn
Jimmy Delaney
Johnny Morris
Jack Rowley **2**
Stan Pearson **1**
Charlie Mitten
Manager: **Matt Busby**

final yet. A dying James Gibson thanked Busby for delivering his deepest wish.

Busby cared enormously for his players, but generous with his (or anybody else's) cash, he was not. By 1950, as he refused his players the illegal under- the-counter bonus payments that many clubs indulged in, the team was beginning to break up: Morris went to Derby, **Mitten**, famously, to Colombia and an unheard of annual salary of some £2,500. Busby was also ruthless with those who did not share his utter dedication to the cause: when Mitten returned from Bogota after only a year, hoping to revive his Red career, the manager not only refused to forgive and play him, but maintained his registration so he would find it impossible to play anywhere else.

Duncan Edwards

The Busby Babes

But Busby could afford to be hard. He knew the job his back-room staff were doing with MUJAC – the **Manchester United Junior Athletic Club**. The Busby aim was to produce home-grown talent, who not only understood his method on the pitch but would follow his vision off it: United footballers, not mercenaries.

The remnants of the 1948 team, though, was special enough to see Busby through to his first **league title** in **1952**, which by now could be paraded round a repaired **Old Trafford**. They were already bolstered by a couple of MUJAC graduates, and rapidly more and more began to appear in the team. By now, with Louis Rocca finally retired and **Joe Armstrong** in control, the scouting operation had become a national business, unearthing talents such as **Bobby Charlton** from the northeast and **Duncan Edwards** from the Midlands. The boys were brought to Manchester, placed with a willing network of landladies and groomed for the task that lay ahead of them.

In 1951, the *Manchester Evening News* journalist Tom Jackson, seeing **Jackie Blanchflower** and **Roger Byrne** in action, reputedly coined the phrase the Bubsy Babes. Busby never really liked the term, thinking it spoke of a naivety lacking in his youthful charges. But whatever the nomenclature, these were a special bunch. From its inception in 1953, the junior team built by Jimmy Murphy and his coaches Bert Whalley, Bill Inglis and Tom Curry, won the **FA Youth Cup** five times on the bounce. The future had been seen. And everyone liked what they saw.

Busby became known for his pre-match instruction to his teams '**just to go out there and enjoy themselves**'. But the work which allowed them to do so had been done long before the dressing room. This was a team coached in the continental methods of passing and moving, while most of English football was mired in the complacent assumption that the old approach was the only approach. They had strength at the back, power in the middle and a ruthless finishing up front. Plus the added ingredient: whether it was out of respect, fear or gratitude, every player was willing to sweat the extra few pints for Busby.

In **1956**, a side largely made up of youth-team graduates won the **league title** by 11 points from Blackpool. **Dennis Viollet** scored 20 league goals, but across the country the name on most lips was that of **Duncan Edwards**, soon to be an English international and only just 18.

Into Europe

As winners of the league, United were invited by UEFA to participate in the **European Cup**. In their wisdom and foresight, the FA, fearful of the loss of bureaucratic control and certain anyhow that

United 1958

**The Munich Team
v. Red Star Belgrade**

Harry Gregg

Roger Byrne
Eddie Colman

Duncan Edwards
Bill Foulkes
Mark Jones

Bobby Charlton
Dennis Viollet
Tommy Taylor
Albert Scanlon
Kenny Morgans

Manager: **Matt Busby**

nothing could be learned from mixing with foreign types, had banned the previous year's champions, Chelsea, from accepting the invitation. They tried to do the same to United, but Busby, desperate to see how his side measured up to the world's best, held up two fingers to the authorities.

Playing evening games at Maine Road (fitted with massive floodlights even then), United the next season began their European affair with a staggering 10-0 win against the Belgian champions Anderlecht. A joyful run in the competition was ended by the mighty **Real Madrid** in the semi-final, but Busby saw enough to be hooked on the competition and to encourage the club that this was the one that mattered. He had another go in the **1958** season, after winning the **league** once more and almost making it a double, losing the FA Cup final only after the goalkeeper – Ray Wood – suffered what would be today regarded as criminal assault by an Aston Villa forward.

Munich

That 1958 European season has repercussions even today. The facts are these: on **6 February**, returning from a 3-3 draw in Belgrade that earned the club another semi-final in the Champions Cup, the United team plane crashed after refuelling at Munich airport. Twenty people died as the plane spun off the runway, including seven players – **Geoff Bent**, **Roger Byrne**, **Eddie Colman**, **Mark Jones**, **David Pegg**, **Tommy Taylor** and **Liam Whelan**. The colossus **Duncan Edwards** was to die later in hospital. Club officials **Walter Crickmer**, **Tom Curry** and **Bert Whally** died too. As did eight journalists including **Tom Jackson** (who minted the Busby Babes term) and the former Manchester City goalkeeper **Frank Swift**. Their names are commemorated on a plaque in the press lounge at Old Trafford. The players **Johnny Berry** and **Jackie Blanchflower** survived, but, because of injury sustained, never resumed their careers.

The team that died so young had given a glimpse of what they could achieve, but without ever realising their potential. What could they have done had they lived? Won the European Cup? Very likely. Might their English contingent have lifted their country to success in the World Cups of 1958 or 1962? Maybe. Would Duncan Edwards have been there at Wembley in 1966, the skipper instead of Bobby Moore? Perhaps. Part of the poignancy of their early death was the endless speculation of pondering what might have been. Yet, in the very act of being destroyed, they were preserved forever young, without decline, without ageing, never to be broken up. In dying it was the team that never palled.

And the huge public sympathy which engulfed United after the crash transformed the club from essentially a regional operation into one of national, even **international consequence**. All over the planet, people with no knowledge of where Manchester even was, began to follow the team's fortunes. After the disaster, everyone wanted United to win for the lost boys. As their manager still lay in a Munich hospital critically injured, the bit part team of youth players, reserves and hasty purchases lost in the European semi-final to Milan. But apparently driven by destiny, they reached the **FA Cup final** that year, only to be beaten again, this time by a Bolton team who felt almost crushed by the weight of opprobrium bearing down on them for daring to win.

The crash made United a different proposition. Even now, followers of United's fiercest rivals – Leeds, Manchester City, Liverpool – express their dislike through the deliberate iconoclasm of refusing to respect the victims of the tragedy. They come to Old Trafford wobbling their arms about pretending to be crashing aircraft and calling the local followers 'Munichs'.

The dream of Europe: Charlton, Best, Law...

For the next ten years, indeed for the rest of Busby's tenure at Old Trafford, the Munich crash informed everything. Busby, racked with guilt that his ambition had killed his boys, initially wanted no more of Europe or even of management. But **Jimmy Murphy**, absent from the crash because he was on duty as the manager of the Welsh national squad, persuaded him the best epitaph for the team would be to win the European Cup.

It took Busby as long to fulfil that destiny as it did to drive his team into a position to compete in the first place. And for the first five years, many wondered if he would ever achieve the dream. According to his biographer Eamon Dunphy, Busby was a detached, lonely figure in those early months after the crash, unable to work out how he would ever repeat his trick of team management. He found it hard to motivate the collection of the bought-in and the second-rate that constituted his squad, wondering often to Murphy if they would ever find another Byrne or Edwards out there.

It wasn't until the **1963 FA Cup** was won, that a side looked as though it was beginning to gel. Backed by the new chairman (and effectively club owner) **Louis Edwards**, a butcher who had made a fortune out of

United 1968
European Cup Final **v. Benfica** 4-1 (aet)
Alex Stepney
Shay Brennan Tony Dunne
Nobby Stiles Bill Foulkes Pat Crerand
George Best **1** Brian Kidd **1** David Sadler Bobby Charlton **2** John Aston
Manager: **Matt Busby**

Sir Matt and his squad with the European Cup, 1968

contracts to supply meat for school dinners, Busby had at last made some shrewd buys in the transfer market: **Pat Crerand** had come from Celtic, **David Herd** from Arsenal and the King himself, **Denis Law**, returned to England after an unhappy exile in Turin. Adding to the Munich survivors **Bill Foulkes** and **Bobby Charlton**, plus a chippy midfield enforcer in **Nobby Stiles**, this was some side being forged. And when the youth system threw up a talent every bit as good as anything that emerged in the fifties, the Ulsterman **George Best**, Busby was back in business.

Off the pitch, too, things were looking up. Busby, who had always enjoyed the company of Manchester money, suggested to Edwards that a way should be developed to encourage the rich to spend their cash at United. When the North Stand was rebuilt as the first cantilever structure in British football in 1963, it was Busby's idea that it should include **executive boxes** for the wealthy. Unwittingly, the father of United was also the progenitor of a whole industry of sporting corporate entertainment.

In **1965** the **league** was won, allowing another stab at Europe (in those far off days, only the champions took part in the Champions

Cup). Despite Best's brilliant performance in the quarter final against Benfica, a game which saw him christened 'El Beatle' and begin his long battle with the consequences of fame, the Reds were beaten again in the semi-final, this time by Partizan Belgrade. After winning the league in 1967, when the performances of the great triumvirate of **Law, Best and Charlton** added another veneer of gloss to the club's mythic condition, Busby had another go.

Ten years on from Munich, United at last reached the final, after crash survivor **Bill Foulkes** had scored the winner against Real Madrid in the semi. The final was to be held at Wembley. Law was in hospital, his leg suspended in traction, and the opposition **Benfica**, led by the great Eusebio (then reckoned the finest player in the world after Pelé), were not there to make up numbers. But fate suggested United had to win the **1968 European Cup** – and they duly did, 4-1, after extra time, with goals from Charlton (two of them – one almost uniquely with his head), Brian Kidd (on his 19th birthday), and a glorious individual effort from George Best. The tears that flowed that night – from Busby, from Charlton, from several million fans around the globe – were the tears not just of glory but of a club exorcising their ghosts, fulfilling their destiny.

Pretenders to the throne

Glorious as it was, Busby's European Cup victory cast a shadow for years to come. It is often said that when the newly knighted **Sir Matt Busby retired** in **1969**, he left an ageing team. This was not the point: yes Foulkes, Charlton, Crerand, Brennan and Law would not see 30 again, but **Stepney**, **Dunne** and **Stiles** at 28 were in their prime; **Aston**, **Kidd**, new buy **Willie Morgan**, and **Best**, the finest player Britain has ever seen, still had years left in them. The problem was that the entire drive, the ambition, the aim of the club, had been to conquer Europe for Busby and the boys of '58. And once it had been won, the purpose was gone.

Naturally, it was not easy to follow Sir Matt. But (and this might be the lesson from history that those arguing about Alex Ferguson's future have failed to take into account) the men chosen for the job could likely not have undertaken it whether the old man had been on a desert island, never mind upstairs, willing to offer avuncular advice. The first nominee, **Wilf McGuinness**, lost his hair in the attempt; his successor **Frank O'Farrell** came with modern ways from Leicester and took the Reds to a couple of cup semis. But neither had the range, the man-management skills, the aplomb, to do what was necessary. And it did not help either of them that **George Best**, after carrying the team more or less single-handed for three post-1968 years, wondered what the point was and began going absent without leave.

Enter the Doc

When **Tommy Docherty**, the third post-Busby manager, arrived from his post in charge of the Scotland team to take control of United in 1972, the 1968 hangover was at its most pervasive. Best had become a liability, Law and Charlton were nearing the end of their careers: Charlton retired at the end of the Doc's first season, Law was sold on to Manchester City. But in truth the entire club was living on reputation. In his second season in charge, **United were relegated**.

Five seasons on from winning the Champions Cup, the Reds were engaged in Division Two fixtures with Hull, Cardiff and Bristol Rovers. But Docherty was energetic in his reconstruction and, in a romantic echo of the Busby Babes, rebuilt the side around a swashbuckling, carefree collection of youngsters. **Steve Coppell** and **Gordon Hill** rampaged down the wings, **Lou Macari** and **Sammy McIlroy** (the last player signed by Busby) scuttled around the middle, while the immensely cool **Martin Buchan** was such an efficient defender, he ensured keeper Alex Stepney, by now the only survivor of '68, could keep his reputation intact.

Meanwhile, off the pitch, **Doc's Red Army**, as the supporters styled themselves, laid waste to market towns across England. English football had entered its hooligan period and, everywhere, lads could prove themselves harder than their peers by professing an affection for United. Matchday coaches brought Reds up from Bournemouth, Basingstoke and Bangor – distance was a mark of pride, back then. Liverpool might have been winning all that was on offer but United were glamour. Even in their season in Division Two, the Reds had the highest home gates of any team in England.

On the field, the team's momentum was swiftly restored. Promotion was won at the first attempt, and bouncing back up into Division One there was incautious, premature talk of a double as the boys reached the FA Cup final (they lost to Second Division Southampton) and finished third in the league. In 1977, the Reds won the **FA Cup** and the first trophy in nine years was placed in the Old Trafford cabinet. As he danced round Wembley with the lid of the cup perched on his head, the Doc looked unassailable, the true heir of Busby. But that night, at the winners' banquet, he revealed to Louis Edwards that he was having an affair with Mary Brown, the wife of the club physio. Edwards told him not to worry, it was a private affair and there was no reason it need affect his working relationship. However, within the month, **Docherty was sacked**.

To anyone inside Old Trafford, it was not such a shock. The Doc had made enemies at every level, going about the removal of dead wood with a relish many thought pathological. Long servants of the club

United 1977
FA Cup Final
v. Liverpool 2-1
Alex Stepney
Jimmy Nicholl
Brian Greenhoff
Martin Buchan
Arthur Albiston
Lou Macari
Sammy McIlroy
Steve Coppell
Jimmy Greenhoff **1**
Stuart Pearson **1**
Gordon Hill (David McCreery)
Manager: **Tommy Docherty**

Really going places – the Doc leads the 1977 FA Cup celebrations

had been ruthlessly removed, and good, honest professionals treated with what they regarded as a lack of dignity. Many of those the Doc crossed – notably Pat Crerand, Willie Morgan and Denis Law – still had the ear of the club's *éminence grise*, Sir Matt. And they took the opportunity offered up by the Mary Brown affair to take revenge. It was Crerand who broke the news of the relationship to his former manager, now club president. 'What's he done this time?' was the great man's weary response. 'What's he done?' the ever sardonic Morgan would put it succinctly. 'He's only sending the first team physio on away matches with the reserves so he could shag his missus behind his back.'

New faces: Sexton, Martin Edwards and Big Ron

Louis Edwards had had enough of personality managers. So with Docherty gone he recruited the personality bypass **Dave Sexton**. The former Chelsea manager took his side to a Cup final, brought in **Joe Jordan**, **Gordon McQueen** and **Ray Wilkins**, gave a first start to the rampaging **Kevin Moran**, even managed to win his last seven league matches in charge. But the board were probably right, he wasn't a United manager.

The new chairman, **Martin Edwards**, had taken over in 1980, after the death of his father, Louis, who was at the time under intense media investigation over alleged business corruption. Edwards Jnr was alarmed at the way the Manchester public was voting with its feet. Attendances were deteriorating rapidly: after the 60,000 crowds of the Doc's day, Sexton's tedious soldiers were regularly drawing in 40,000. Reversing his father's strategy, Edwards reckoned what the club needed was a big man in charge to reinvigorate the place. **Ron Atkinson** fitted the bill – although he was allegedly Edwards's fourth choice after Jack Charlton, Jock Stein and Bobby Robson. Still, many Reds remembered the swaggering way Atkinson's West Brom side had walloped Sexton's United 5-3 at Old Trafford and felt at last here was a man to restore Old Trafford's tradition for swash and buckle.

Atkinson produced the best United side since '68. With **Bryan Robson** (brought from West Brom) at its heart, **Paul McGrath** at the back, and **Norman Whiteside** terrifying allcomers, there were times when the Reds really seemed to be heading back to the top.

They won the **FA Cup** in **1983** and **1985** and, in between, stormed through Europe to reach the Cup Winners Cup semi-final. But that was Big Ron: a **great cup manager**. The long haul of the league seemed beyond him.

Atkinson was also not much of a man for administration and forward programmes, happy to wave a chequebook as and when required. He concentrated his energies exclusively on the first team (or at least those he called his golden circle), encouraged them to have a laugh, to think of themselves as special, to bond over a beer. The rest of the club he left largely to its own devices. He was lucky that his old mate

United 1985
FA Cup Final
v. Everton 1-0 (aet)
Gary Bailey
John Gidman
Paul McGrath
Kevin Moran *sent off*
Arthur Albiston (Mike Duxbury)
Gordon Strachan
Bryan Robson
Norman Whiteside **1**
Jesper Olson
Mark Hughes
Frank Stapleton
Manager: **Ron Atkinson**

Big Ron's big men: McGrath, Robson and Whiteside pick up the 1985 FA Cup

Eric Harrison was doing the business in the youth section, bringing **Mark Hughes** and **Clayton Blackmore** through for the first team.

Big Ron wasn't overly interested in that side of things – and his greatest error turned out to be his not paying enough attention to **Mark Hughes**, who had stormed his way into the first team, and seemed intent on winning the league on his own in the 1985–86 season. Top of the table come Christmas, United were looking as if this would at last be their year, after a nineteen-year gap. Hughes was not in Big Ron's inner circle and his contract was due to expire at the end of the season. Just at the moment when Atkinson should have been most focused on his new star and the league campaign, he had a call from Terry Venables at Barcelona, offering £1.8m for Hughes. Instead of offering a top contract to the player, Big Ron and chairman Martin Edwards, who was then looking for a buyer for the club, sanctioned the sale. Worse, they agreed Barcelona's terms, which were to keep the deal secret to the end of the season so as not to worry Barcelona's already full quota of foreign players. Hughes promptly lost his form, morale fell apart, and the Reds' championship campaign was fatally injured.

Atkinson might have considered himself unlucky when Edwards sacked him as his team floundered early in the following season. But the fact of the matter is, the club needed a new broom. It needed someone with the passion, the energy, the drive to reconstruct it. In short, just like James Gibson back in 1945, what Edwards needed was a Matt Busby.

Arise Sir Alex ...

'My greatest challenge is not what's happening at the moment, my greatest challenge was knocking Liverpool right off their fucking perch. And you can print that.'   Sir Alex Ferguson, 2002

It was Bobby Charlton, by now a director of the club, who recommended **Alex Ferguson**, the manager who had so successfully challenged the dominance of the Glasgow teams while managing Aberdeen. Ferguson, who recalled how his mentor Jock Stein had always regretted turning down the Old Trafford job, jumped at the chance to move south. He was in his new office the day after Big Ron had left. And, ominously for some of his new charges, he was not impressed that he could smell the after effects of the old manager's leaving party lingering on some players' breaths.

As messiahs go, Ferguson was slow to show himself. As Edwards tried to sell the club to a comedy would-be purchaser called **Michael Knighton**, who went on to turn Carlisle United into the force they are today, Ferguson's expensive buys refused to gel. Three years into his regime, all he had to show was the departure of a few terrace favourites – **Whiteside**, **McGrath** and **Strachan** – and an edgy, unhappy media persona, forever looking for a get-out clause for failure. In Old Trafford's scoreboard end for the visit of Crystal Palace to mark his third unsuccessful year in charge, a banner was unfurled: 'Three years of excuses, ta-ra Fergie'.

It would be nice to report that the editors of this guide were able to see beyond the general consensus, but the newly emerged **fanzines** were firmly of the opinion that he was not up to the job. The fans were dismayed that he had removed their favourites (Whiteside and McGrath) without replacing them. Not for the first time, we were to be proven wrong by the manager's apparently reckless decision-making over players.

Sir Bobby Charlton always maintains that Ferguson's position was never even discussed at boardroom level in those dark days of autumn 1989, and Martin Edwards maintains that he had never had considered a replacement. However, if Fergie's future was not an issue in the boardroom, that was about the only place it wasn't. Certainly the media was convinced defeat in the FA Cup away to Forest in January 1990 would signal the end of his reign. But Mark Robins famously got the winner, and the team went on to win the **FA Cup**, and suddenly it all began to fall into place.

The bright side of life

The next season, 30,000 delirious Reds danced in a Rotterdam downpour to signal triumph in the **European Cup Winners Cup** over Barcelona – both goals scored by the returning hero **Mark Hughes**, Ferguson's wisest early purchase. From then on, a benevolent circle seemed to be constructed. Of course there were blips: the 1992 league title went to Leeds after nerves seemed to paralyse the dressing room. But once Ferguson's first **league title** was won in **1993**, thanks mainly to the inspired signing of the Frenchman and second King of Old Trafford, **Eric Cantona**, a mental barrier had lifted. 'Always Look On the Bright Side of Life,' sung the fans, its irony vanishing by the day.

The breakthrough: Alex and Sir Matt with the European Cup Winners Cup (1992), and Eric lifting the first Premiership trophy (1993)

Twenty-six years it had taken to reclaim the title, and, with Sir Matt smiling down from the directors' box, a dynasty had at last been constructed. Two driven Scotsmen, similar in background and outlook, had taken United to the top. What had happened in between their reigns was forgotten, their epochs merging into one as old Busby heroes mingled in the Championship-winning party with the new Fergie's fledglings. Busby died six months later, content that glory had been restored.

New money, new business

United's victory in the first ever **Premiership** meant the club was perfectly poised to take advantage of the **new money** being thrown at the game. With Sky TV and its cheerleaders in the popular press shouting the game up constantly, football became our new version of Hollywood, its practitioners feted and garlanded. Munich, the 1968 team, the Red Army of the 1970s – all played their part in building the United brand. But it was the merchandising operation of the 1990s that finally exploited it. By making it easy to buy into the dream through a business-driven souvenir department, United found themselves sitting on a mint.

Martin Edwards, who once believed the only way he could make money out of the club was to sell out (and had been willing to do so to Michael Knighton for an unbelievable £12m), suddenly appreciated the irony that if he wanted to become seriously rich, he should stay put. As United floated on the **stock market**, the funds were released for a **redevelopment of the ground**, meaning that ever

Eric and his charges – another team goal, by the look of things

more paying customers could clack through the turnstiles on matchdays, supplying yet more money.

In the autumn of 1998, the media imperialist **Rupert Murdoch**, through his BSkyB operation, bid £623m for the club. While the board accepted the deal and expected it to be rubber-stamped, for many fans it was a commercial move too far. Why did Murdoch want the club? It was purely for his own corporate ends. Besides, the move questioned one fundamental tenet of footballing faith: whose club was it? Organised, articulate, determined, the fans rallied and fought the bid, eventually seeing it stopped by a government who would never had moved against it had the supporters not acted. Interestingly, even without Sky's backing, the club kept on growing, and by January 2000 was valued on the stock exchange at over £1bn.

United 1994
FA Cup Final
v. Chelsea 4-0
Peter Schmeichel
Paul Parker
Steve Bruce
Gary Pallister
Denis Irwin (Lee Sharpe)
Andrei Kanchelskis (Brian McClair **1**)
Roy Keane
Paul Ince
Ryan Giggs
Eric Cantona **2**
Mark Hughes **1**
Manager: **Alex Ferguson**

Fergie's Fledglings

None of this financial growth would have happened without **Alex Ferguson**. He achieved success by much the same methods Busby had used: energy, determination, will to win, delegating to a good back-room team, and an ability to imbue a respect in his charges that was close to fear. Plus he had an eye for a player, in particular the kind of young man who had the extra stiffness of resolve to make it in the circus that Old Trafford had become. He recognised it in Cantona, for instance, where the player's previous managers saw only madness. He saw it also in Keane, Giggs and Beckham.

Most of all, he understood how to construct a team able to do the business on the pitch. In **1994** he won the club's first ever **league and FA Cup double**, with a squad of power, skill and aggression

United's Trophy Cabinet

European Champions Cup
Winners 1968, 1999

European Cup Winners Cup
Winners 1991

Football League Division One
Champions 1908, 1911, 1952,
1956, 1957, 1965, 1967
Runners-up 1947, 1948, 1949,
1951, 1959, 1964, 1968, 1980,
1988, 1992

FA Premiership
Champions 1993, 1994, 1996,
1997, 1999, 2000, 2001, 2003
Runners-up 1995, **1998**

Football League Division Two
Champions 1936, 1975
Runners-up 1897, 1906, 1925,
1938

FA Cup
Winners 1909, 1948, 1963, 1977,
1983, 1985, 1990, 1994,
1996, 1999
Defeated finalists 1957, 1958,
1976, 1979, 1995

Football League Cup
Winners 1992
Runners-up 1983, 1991, 1994, 2003

Inter-continental Cup
Winners 1999

Uefa Super Cup
Winners 1991

FA Charity Shield
Winners 1908, 1911, 1952,
1956, 1957, 1983, 1993,
1994, 1996, 1997
Joint holders 1965, 1967,
1977, 1990

FA Youth Cup
Winners 1953, 1954, 1955, 1956,
1957, 1964, 1992, 1995, 2003

(his warriors, he called Schmeichel, Robson, Hughes, Cantona, Ince and Keane). As it happened, the eleven that beat Chelsea 4-0 in the Cup Final that season played together only twelve times, winning the lot, scoring 23 goals and conceding only two. They can lay claim to being the most successful side in United history, and they were a template for each of the Ferguson teams that followed: competitive in midfield, murderously quick on the counter-attack, and imbued with a never-ever-say-die attitude.

Ferguson's comparison with Busby became more pronounced in the next team he built, which was constructed largely of **players from the youth system**. In the summer of 1995, the Boss felt confident enough in his new generation to let Ince, Hughes and Kanchelskis go. Again many could not see his method, but he was proven right with another **double in 1996**, this time based around the brilliant FA Youth Cup-winning team of 1992. Enter 'Fergie's Fledglings' – and the new England line-up of **David Beckham**, the **Neville brothers**, **Nicky Butt**, **Paul Scholes**.

In the big time

By now United had become a completely different proposition from the listless under-performers Ferguson inherited. When he made purchases they would be the top players in the world, such as Fabien Barthez, Juan Sebastian Veron, or the player who could become the greatest buy of his tenure, Ruud van Nistelrooy. Watching these players strut their stuff in the myriad colours of the new United it seemed impossible to believe this was once the club that gave house room to Ian Ure, Wynn Davies, Ted MacDougall, Mickey Thomas and Ralph Milne.

There was, inevitably, a downside to this continued success. United became **loathed as much as loved**: 'Stand up if you hate Man U' for a time the unofficial national anthem. And every minor crisis was worked up into a cataclysm by a press that could sell copies off every mention of the club. If Eric Cantona went walkabout on a gobby fan's chest, or David Beckham turned out for England wearing Tupac Shakur's hair, or Roy Keane went against all previous precedent and wrote a truthful autobiography, it was major front- as well as back-page news. But the players, rewarded with a handsomeness their forebears could never dream about, never seemed to be affected by the nonsense off the pitch. And, for Ferguson, the one final point of

United 1999
European Cup Final v. Bayern Munich 2-1
Peter Schmeichel
Gary Neville
Jaap Stam
Ronnie Johnsen
Denis Irwin
Jesper Blomqvist (Teddy Sheringham **1**)
Nicky Butt
David Beckham
Ryan Giggs
Andy Cole
Dwight Yorke (Ole Gunnar Solskjaer **1**)
Manager: **Alex Ferguson**

The legion of honour

With four knights and a whole raft of Os and Ms, United are as decorated a club as any in football. Here is a list of all those who have partaken of the Queen's hospitality, with David Beckham (and one-time United player Shaun Goater) the latest in line. Why the great Denis Law is not among the honourables, only those at Buckingham Palace can say. Come on, Your Maj, give the King a gong.

Sir Matt Busby, CBE 1958;
  knighted 1968
Sir Bobby Charlton, OBE 1969;
  CBE 1974; knighted 1994
Sir Walter Winterbottom, OBE 1963;
  CBE 1972; knighted 1978
Sir Alex Ferguson, OBE 1984;
  CBE 1995; knighted 1999
Sammy McIlroy, MBE 1986
Bryan Robson, OBE 1990

Ray Wilkins, MBE 1993
Gordon Strachan, OBE 1993
Jim Leighton, MBE 1998
Mark Hughes, MBE 1998
Garth Crooks, MBE 1999
Nobby Stiles, MBE 2000
Peter Schmeichel, MBE (hon) 2001
Harry Gregg, MBE 1995
David Beckham OBE, 2003
Shaun Goater MBE, 2003

comparison with his great predecessor came right on that crazy night in **Barcelona** when – on Matt Busby's birthday (he would have been 90) – Bayern were beaten at the last, and the **European Cup** returned to Old Trafford.

Regime change? No thanks

As always it is the future that is the most interesting part of the United story. And for the manager, it is all that matters. But Ferguson knows to achieve things in the future you need to draw on the lessons of the past. And history did provide him with one stark message that May night in 1999. He remembered the way that, following the Reds' first victory in the European Cup, things had gone into decline at the club, how the ambition had seeped away. Because of the understandable emotional baggage tied up with finally fulfilling Sir Matt's dream in 1968, a full stop seemed to be drawn under the place: psychologically everything had been achieved, destiny had arrived. And what was the result of that mindset? Within four seasons, United were relegated, a shambles. That wasn't going to happen under Fergie's stewardship, and two more championship trophies were popped into the cabinet in the years following the treble as he refused to allow the energy and focus of the operation to be dissipated.

Even so, in Europe, United couldn't quite get it right. Ferguson had expected his team to dominate the competition in the way that Milan, Real, Ajax and Liverpool had in the years immediately after winning it. However, the **Champions League** is a much harder competition to win than the old European Cup, when a fortuitous draw serving up some Belgians, Danes and Poles could slip a team into the semi-finals before anyone had really noticed. That said, Fergie's United always qualify through even the toughest of groups for the quarter-finals, sometimes with ease, often with style. There, though, a mental curtain seems too often to descend: three times since winning the trophy they have

All Time Top United Appearances

Top Twelve United Appearances In All Competitions

1. Bobby Charlton	1956-73	759	249
2. Bill Foulkes	1952-69	688	9
3. Ryan Giggs	1991-	544	113
4. Alex Stepney	1966-78	539	2
5. Tony Dunne	1960-73	535	2
6. Denis Irwin	1990-02	528	33
7. Joe Spence	1919-33	510	168
8. Arthur Albiston	1974-88	485	7
9. Brian McClair	1987-98	471	127
10. George Best	1963-74	470	179
11. Mark Hughes	1983-95	467	163
12. Bryan Robson	1981-94	461	99

Top Twelve United League Appearances

1. Bobby Charlton	1956-73	606	199
2. Bill Foulkes	1952-69	566	7
3. Joe Spence	1919-33	481	158
4. Alex Stepney	1966-78	433	2
5. Jack Silcock	1919-34	423	2
6. Tony Dunne	1960-73	414	2
7. Ryan Giggs	1991-	382	79
8. Jack Rowley	1937-55	380	182
9. Arthur Albiston	1974-88	379	6
10. Martin Buchan	1972-82	376	4
11. Denis Irwin	1990-02	368	22
12. George Best	1963-74	361	137

been beaten in the last eight, once by Bayern, twice by Madrid. In 2002 they did manage to progress to the **semi-finals**, only to be knocked out by the German one-season wonders, Bayer Leverkusen.

Barthez, Veron, Ferdinand, Van Nistelrroy ... but something's missing (and it's not just Becks)

Ferguson did his best to graft into his squad what he describes as 'that little bit of guile and know-how' required in Europe. The operation has not been cheap: at £7m, **Fabien Barthez** has not been the successor to Peter Schmeichel everyone hoped, at £30m **Rio Ferdinand** is not the finished article, **Juan Sebastian Veron** cost £28m, and has only occasionally dazzled. True, for £19m, **Ruud van Nistelrooy** is heading towards being the best pound for pound bargain in United history. But even his astonishing tally of European goals have not been enough to propel the team beyond the last four. A mark of how hard it is in Europe is that, in the same period as Fergie has lavished £70m in the transfer market, **Real Madrid** have spent twice as much assembling their globetrotter side. And in 2003, that still wasn't sufficient to lift the trophy.

It was the conundrum of cracking Europe that persuaded Ferguson to make unquestionably the biggest decision at the club during the post-Barcelona years. On 5 February 2002, he reversed a long-standing **commitment to retire**. In the months prior to his volte-face, Peter Kenyon had been linked with virtually every big name in the game and – according to Michael Crick's Fergie biography – had shaken hands with Sven Goran Eriksson to take over. But in the end, when it came to finding a successor, everyone (or almost everyone) was delighted to land the best man for the job: Fergie himself.

Last season he was clearly re-invigorated by the challenges ahead. The word he used most frequently is 'fresh'. And the pictures of him smiling next to the Premiership trophy in May, not to mention **offloading David Beckham** in a very public act of rebuilding a successful team, looked like those of a man set fair for the long haul. It is an attitude which in

All Time Top United Scorers		
Top Seasonal Scorers – All Competitions		
01. Denis Law	1963-64	46
02. Ruud van Nistelrooy	2002-03	44
03. Denis Law	1964-65	39
04. Ruud van Nistelrooy	2001-02	36
05. Tommy Taylor	1956-57	34
06. Billy Whelan	1956-57	33
David Herd	1965-66	33
08. Dennis Viollet	1959-60	32
George Best	1967-68	32
10. Brian McClair	1987-88	31
11. Jack Rowley	1948-49	30
Jack Rowley	1951-52	30
Denis Law	1968-69	30
Top Seasonal Scorers – League Only		
01. Dennis Viollet	1959-60	32
02. Jack Rowley	1951-52	30
Denis Law	1963-64	30
04. Bobby Charlton	1958-59	29
05. Denis Law	1964-65	28
George Best	1967-68	28
07. Jack Rowley	1946-47	26
Billy Whelan	1956-57	26
09. Sandy Turnbull	1907-08	25
Tommy Taylor	1955-56	25
Ruud van Nistelrooy	2002-03	25
12. David Herd	1965-66	24
Brian McClair	1987-88	24

turn has infected the players. In the 2001–02 season, when Arsenal took the Premiership, as Ferguson himself admits, the all-pervading sense of the end of an era undermined the collective will. The very philosophy that he himself had instilled of always looking to the next challenge had been questioned: how can you do that when you don't know what the future holds? In his admirable attempt to create an orderly succession by giving such a long notice period, Ferguson did the precise opposite. Next time he makes a decision to retire, he has said, he will just go.

But that won't be for some time yet. The next few years will still be the Fergie years. Which means United fans can continue to look forward with optimism. Domestically, where will the challenge come from? The answer is pretty straightforward. **Liverpool**, despite beating the Reds in the Worthington Cup, fizzled out early as Championship contenders, and will continue to do so until they rid themselves of an all-pervasive defensive approach. **Chelsea** have developed greater consistency under Claudio Ranieri, enough to qualify for the Champions League. Though not enough to win the title. **Newcastle**'s huge stadium has allowed their magnificent old manager to buy in a whole squad of exciting players young enough to be his grandchildren. But the major rivals will remain **Arsenal**, whose players on their day are as good as any. And it remains the job of United's squad to ensure that day does not come round too often.

As for Europe, well, at least since the **2004 Champions League** final is to be held in Gelsenkirchen, a German town with which United has absolutely no historical connection, there will be no lazy talk of destiny. This time, more than ever, the players know that history is at their feet. Which is precisely where they want it.

The Directory

of all things red

Membership ★ Supporters' organisations
Manchester United plc ★ Media ★ On the Net
United books and videos

In June 2003, in the unlikely surrounds of the Kazakhstan desert, the British space craft Beagle 2 was launched in the direction of Mars. If it arrives as scheduled on Christmas Day, its aim is to discover if there is life on the earth's closest planetary neighbour. Followers of Manchester United (and there are bound to have been a couple on the space programme, for it is based in Milton Keynes) could have told them how much is happening on the Red planet. It is swarming with life. There are, according to received opinion, about ten million people worldwide who call themselves United fans — even in United's post-Beckham world. It's a larger group than many European states, and has a whole network beyond the business of football matches: supporters' organisations, shareholder action groups, Websites, fanzines, matchday songwriters, and of course the plc that controls the club. The satellites of the Red planet: that's what this Directory is about.

Club membership

Over the summer, United's membership scheme was re-vamped under the branding 'One United' – or to put it another way, the prices went up. Last season costs had been frozen at the previous year's level of £18 for adults, £12 for juniors. This time around it is £22/£14 (though with a £2 discount for existing members). With 110,000 or so members, it doesn't take an accountancy genius to work out this is a handy little earner for the club. That said, you do get a bit more for your money: a much improved *Official Manchester United Yearbook*, and a rather handy *Rough Guide to the Premiership* with the low-down on the opposition, a members' magazine, plus various other perks – discounts at the megastore, a chance to enter competitions for Champions League away travel packages, an opportunity to meet your player of the season, and free entry to reserve matches at Moss Lane and Old Trafford (just flash your membership card at the turnstile).

Most importantly, full membership gives you the right to enter the ballot for home match tickets (see p.269 for details). Although, this summer also saw the launch of a non-match members package which confers 'all the benefits of membership' but not the chance to apply for tickets. This is for United fans who don't manage to get to matches, or for season ticket holders who want the extras.

To apply for membership, contact: The Membership Office, Manchester United Football Club, Old Trafford, Manchester M16 0RA. ☎0870 442 1994. Or you can become a member online through the Website: *www.manutd.com*.

Supporters' organisations

The first United supporters' organisation was born in the financial crisis that threatened the club during the 1920s. A group of fans, alarmed that the team they loved was crumbling before their eyes, formed an association and lobbied for action. Today their successors are as busy as ever, keen to promote and encourage their own vision of the Red thing.

Supporters' clubs

Many fans join their local United official supporters' club as a way of getting match tickets en bloc and transport to the ground. Supporters' clubs can be particularly useful if you live away from Manchester, as most branches organise cheap coach trips to home matches, and the London branches offer reduced fares on the trains. The supporters' clubs are well managed by Barry Moorhouse in the membership office (see opposite) and they are detailed at the back of the *Official Yearbook* and at *www.manutd.com*.

Useful United numbers

Old Trafford switchboard ☎0161 868 8000	Manchester United soccer schools ☎0161 643 5955
Textphone ☎0161 868 8668	Megastore ☎0161 868 8567
Ticket office ☎0161 868 8020	Membership and supporters' clubs ☎0161 868 8450
Season-ticket holder ticket line ☎0161 868 8010	Museum and Tour Centre ☎0161 868 8631
Man Utd Radio ☎0161 868 8888	MUTV ☎0870 848 6888

There are supporters' club branches in most corners of the UK, and over a hundred dotted around Ireland, where Red support crosses sectarian divides. Tiny villages both north and south of the border boast clubs, which organise regular meetings amongst members as well as travel to Old Trafford. These are grand days out. If you ever find yourself at Manchester or Liverpool airports (the budget airlines mainly use Liverpool), the day after a big game, it will invariably be full of bleary-eyed Irish fans returning home.

The biggest individual supporters' club, however, is the Scandinavian branch. Formed in 1981, this operates out of Bergen in Norway and has around 23,000 members across the region. It produces an excellent full-colour glossy magazine and its merchandising operation alone has several full-time staff. The Malta branch is well established, too, with an impressive clubhouse, and every summer a couple of first team players are only too happy to spend a week on the Mediterranean island mixing with supporters. Gary Neville seems particularly enchanted with the place and has even bought a property on the island.

Well-established supporters' club branches also operate out of South Africa, the USA, Switzerland, Australia and the Far East. United have recently opened official *Red Café-Megastore* combinations in Singapore and Kuala Lumpur with the hope and expectation that supporters will watch televised games from there and presumably buy a T-shirt with their burger while they do so. More local supporters' club branches have opened in and around Manchester in recent years, too, going against the previous trend of encouraging local supporters to travel direct from Old Trafford.

United may claim to have the most fans, incidentally, but we don't have the most fan clubs: Barcelona, Real Madrid, Bayern Munich and Juventus all boast four times as many supporters' clubs as United, although some are little more than a group of mates watching the game down at a local bar. For supporters' club details, call the Membership Office on ☎0161 868 8450.

Disabled supporters (MUDSA)

There are more than 1500 members of Manchester United Disabled Supporters Association (MUDSA) and 104 dedicated spaces in the Old Trafford disabled fans' stand. Simple maths suggests demand way outstrips supply. Philip Downs, of MUDSA, has the tricky task of trying to accommodate as many disabled fans as he can. It works like this. Disabled fans need to be club members. You apply for membership in the standard way (see previous pages), and put the disabled association as your branch: automatically you become a member of MUDSA. To attend matches, you need to apply for a telephone ballot, by ringing the number below. 'The system has evolved over a number of years,' says Downs. 'In the past, season passes were issued, but that meant no-one else got a chance. So over the years we have stopped issuing season passes. We try to operate a one-in-three matches rotation system.'

Currently, wheelchair users and blind fans are not charged for tickets, neither are their helpers. There is further accommodation for 40 ambulatory disabled, who are charged a nominal sum. What would help is more space, but Downs is realistic that this might not be available. 'According to the green book guide, Old Trafford should have 250 disabled spaces,' he says. 'But I would rather have 104 Rolls Royces than 250 Reliant Robins, with no disrespect to Del Boy. There are many issues involved in a disabled position beyond just finding a space; there's parking, there's access, there's the view, and United have got everything right bar the numbers.'

Which is something disabled fans discover trying to follow United to away games: at Blackburn, for instance, there are more spaces, but they are right round the perimeter of the pitch, leaving wheelchair

Hello, Hello, We are the Busby Boys ...

Old Trafford often gets slagged off as 'the theatre of silence'. Yet Simon Inglis, a man who has visited (and written about) every stadium in Britain, and who as a Villa fan is almost by definition a football neutral, rates Red supporters top of the league. 'I have to tell it how I see it,' he says, 'and on my last three visits, I've been impressed by the volume and the variety of songs from the United fans. Most fans have a catalogue of five tunes, but United fans seem to be genuinely original and witty.' Praise indeed – and much of it should be directed at indie DJ and cheerleader Peter Boyle, who dishes out his songsheets in pubs around the ground, and leads first, cautious renditions of such gems as *'Neville, Neville'* (to Bowie's *'Rebel Rebel'*).

Boyle, of course, has quite an established canon of songs to build on. Long-time favourites like *'The Pride of All Europe'*, *'Glory, Glory Man Utd'*, *'We Are The Busby Boys'*, *'U-N-I-T-E-D, United are the team for me'* and *'We Love United, We do'* receive frequent airings, while the most popular song last season was a re-worked old Stretford End classic: *'Take me home, United Road, to the place where I belong, to Old Trafford, to see United, take me home United Road.'* There's a variation, too, in honour of **Señor Veron**: *'He's a genius from Argentina, Juan Sebastian Veron.'* Pushing it in the popularity stakes is another old number: *'I see the Stretford End arising, I see there's trouble on the way, don't go out tonight, fight for the red and white, I see there's trouble on the way.'*

It's perhaps the spontaneous songs, though, which offer the most amusement. Liverpool's **Phil Thompson** is an unlikely award winner for being the subject of most terrace ditties, nosing ahead of Alan Shearer and Arsène Wenger. *'Get those nostrils off the pitch,'* sang Reds at Anfield, and *'Big nose, what's the score?'* was added after Diego and Dudek had contrived to give United the game. Then there was: *'Who put the ball in the Scousers' net, half of f***ing Europe.'* And talking of **Scousers**, one of the many magic moments in the Real Madrid tie at Old Trafford came when **McManaman** was recalled to the bench to 20,000 fans belting out, to the tune of 'Blue Moon', *'Re-serve, you're just a f***ing reserve, you're just a f***ing reserve.'* **City** get frequent mentions too: *'This is how it feels to be City, this is how it feels to be small. This is how it feel when your team wins nothing at all'*, sung to the tune of 'This Is How It Feels' by the Inspiral Carpets, kicked off last year's return of the Blues to big-time action.

Player-specific praise-songs remain the staple, from the now seemingly old ones like *'Gary Neville is a Red, he hates Scousers'* to new uplifting hero tunes like: *'When Johnny goes marching down the wing, O'Shea, O'Shea ... When Johnny goes marching down the wing, the Stretford End will always sing, we all know that Johnny will score a goal'*, or the full back's partner's upbeat *'We've got Wesley Brown'* (to 'Knees up Mother Brown').

'Who put the ball in the Germans' net?' Altogether now ...

Rightly, though, **Ruud van Nistelrooy** gets the most singing. These days he scores so much that the most common acclamation is the *'Ruud–Ruud–Ruud'* boom, that sounds almost like a boo as it echoes around the ground. But in more leisured moments, *'Ruud van Nistelrooy, tra, la, la, la, la'* – to that bizarre '70s chestnut 'Brown Girl in the Ring' – still gets aired. And, whether he's playing or not, few matches go by without a 'Blue Moon' chorus or six of *'Kea-no, there's only one Keano'*, as well as a *'Tra la, la la, Keano'*. Talking of not playing, of course – Ruud and **Keano** notwithstanding, **Eric** is still the most sung-about icon: *'Ooh-aah Cantona'*, of course, to the tune of the Marseillaise, and if it's anytime near Christmas, *'The Twelve Days Of Cantona'*.

Giggs, having notched up 500-odd appearances, has had a string of songs, moving down the years from the Robin Hood ditty, *'Ryan Giggs, Ryan Giggs, running down the wing,'* to the Joy Division-inspired *'Giggs, Giggs will tear you apart'* – a song which has had a semi-ironic spin-off as *'Phil will tear you apart'* in honour of **Neville P**. And then there's a spot of funk, as you'd expect, from **Nicky Butt**'s variant on KC and the Sunshine Band's *'Baby Give It Up'*, while **Scholes**, a no-nonsense lad, gets 'Kumbiyah', the old Christian camp-fire staple: *'He scores goals galore, he scores goals, Paul Scholes he scores goals'*. **Solskjaer**'s exploits in the Camp Nou are still celebrated in *'Who put the ball in the Germans' net'* and when feelings are fond, we roll out *'You are my Solskjaer, my only Solskjaer'*. **Forlan**'s sudden journey to cult-scorer has also been honoured, with 'Diego, woah, Diego, woah, he came from Uruguay, he made the Scousers cry' – a 'Volare' variant that Gooners sing to the less worthy Vieira.

Finally, for whatever reason, no Beckham songs truly caught on aside from the occasional 'Only One David Beckham' acclamation. But perhaps the boy will fare better in Spanish.

Those United classic songs in full:

The Pride of All Europe

'We are just one of those teams that you see now and then,
We often score six but we seldom score ten,
We beat 'em at home and we beat 'em away,
We kill any bastards that get in our way.

'We are the pride of all Europe, the cock of the north,
We hate the Scousers, the Cockneys of course (and Leeds)
We are United without any doubt, we are the Manchester Boys,
Na, na na, na, na, na, na, na, na, na, na, na…'

The Banks of the River Irwell   To the tune of: 'The Halls Of Montezuma'

(Chorus)
'From the banks of the River Irwell
To the shores of Sicily,
We will fight, fight, fight for United
'Till we win the Football League…

'To hell with Liverpool,
To hell with Man City (They're shit!)
We will fight, fight, fight for United
'Till we win the Football League'.

By Far The Greatest Team   To the tune of: 'The Wild Rover'

'And it's Man United
Man United FC
We're by far the greatest team
The world has ever seen!'

Glory Glory Man United

To the tune of: 'Glory! Glory! Hallejulah'

'Glory, Glory Man United,
Glory, Glory Man United,
Glory, Glory Man United...
And the Reds go marching on, on, on...'

If You Know Your History

'Oh, it's a grand old team to play for,
Oh, it's a grand old team to see –
And if, You know, Your history,
It's enough to make your heart go woh, oh, oh...

'We don't care what the City fans say,
What the hell do we care,
For we only know,
That there's gonna be a show,
And that Man United will be there!'

Hello, Hello

'Hello! Hello! We are the Busby boys!
Hello! Hello! We are the Busby boys!
And if you are a City fan surrender or you'll die,
We all follow United!'

Eric ...

'What a friend we have in Jesus,
He's our saviour from afar,
What a friend we have in Jesus,
And his name is...CANTONA...
Ooh Aah CANTONA'

... and the previous king

'Son of a Fisherman from Aberdeen,
Played for his country when only eighteen,
His football magic is a sight to see,
As he leads United on to victory,
(Chorus)
Denis, Denis Law,
King Of The Football League.

users with poor views and vulnerable to hasty clearances. Not that many United wheelchair users will get the chance to sample away grounds. Pressure on tickets is even greater than at Old Trafford, not least because, as facilities are shared, home fans turn out in larger numbers when the Reds are in town.

MUDSA lobbies for disabled rights throughout the Red planet and recently challenged representatives of the board as to why MUTV does not have subtitles for the hard of hearing. Too expensive was the shoddy reply from the richest club in world football.

Contact: MUDSA, PO Box 141, South DO, Manchester M20 5BA; ☎ 0161 434 1989.

Independent Supporters' Association (IMUSA)

IMUSA (Independent Manchester United Supporters' Association) is a political voice for United fans. There is little doubt that without IMUSA and shareholders' group Shareholders United (see p.401) the club would now be a subsidiary of Rupert Murdoch's BSkyB empire. From the moment the takeover was announced back in September 1998, IMUSA, led by its articulate spokesman Andy Walsh, was in there, organising resistance, lobbying government, generally refusing to accept what so many observers reckoned was the inevitable.

But the victory over BSkyB, achieved in April 1999, did not signal the end of the association. Formed back in 1995 to fight for United fans' issues, there is still much work to be done. One of IMUSA's current campaigns, for example, is for a return to 3pm Saturday kick-offs. The traditional rhythm of matchday attendance, the group believes, has been disrupted by television schedules. Away kick-offs at midday entail prohibitively early starts or expensive overnight stays; home starts at the same time are not much better for those living a distance from the ground. More to the point there is a sense that this is just the start of the way in which the requirements of the armchair fan will gradually take precedence over those who actually turn up and support their team.

Frankly, it is hard to see how IMUSA can win this one, with the Premiership plans for greatly expanding the number of televised games, but perhaps the campaign will have some moderating influence.

IMUSA's other gripe has been with the distribution of away tickets, which seem increasingly to favour the corporate supporter. In fairness to the club, there has been movement here. Indeed, since the arrival of Patrick Harverson as Communications Director and Peter Kenyon as Chief Executive, there has been a much greater willingness on the part of the hierarchy to listen to its customers. Both have attended IMUSA meetings and spoken.

Talking of which, IMUSA is not just about Red politics. Socialising with those of a similar dedication is part of the point, and the branch meetings in Manchester and beyond are much more about having a good chinwag than whinging. The London branch, incidentally, meet monthly in the Princess Louise pub in Holborn, which is where the song 'Flowers of Manchester' had its first airing.

Details of IMUSA memberships from IMUSA, PO Box 69, Stretford, Manchester M32 OUZ; *marks@breathemail.net*; or *www.imusa.org*.

Fans Forum

Set up in 2000, in the spirit of glasnost following the appointment of Peter Kenyon as chief executive, United's Fans Forum is the formal conduit of communication between the club and the fans. Members are drafted on to the forum by various sections of supporters, and meetings take place regularly (with a decent buffet laid on, apparently). You can tell how seriously the club takes the forum as all the minutes are available on the official website and summarised in the match programme.

But all is not quite hunky or dory. Some members of the forum want all representatives to be democratically elected (the SU representative already is), but there was resistance from some quarters and the club were reluctant to push the idea. Plus, there are current disputes over the hot issue for match-going fans of the allocation of away tickets.

The Development Association

Younger fans may wonder what the office between the programme sellers and the woman painting faces on Sir Matt Busby Way is all about. Well, it houses the United Development Association, a long-standing organisation founded back in the 1960s, based around the principle of supporters raising money to improve the stadium and its facilities. Fund-raising activities include pools, draws and the Cash Dash, the half-time handout conducted by a celebrity which most fans miss because they are queuing up at the bar. Over the years, hundreds of thousands have been raised by the association for the ground development and selected charities. It is a commendable idea, supporters helping out the club they love (and being rewarded, if they are successful at selling draw entries, with free match tickets). Cynics, on the other hand, might question the need for a highly profitable plc to extract yet more money from fans to do their work for them.

Information on becoming a sales agent from ☏0161 868 8600 or on the club website: *www.manutd.com/trafford/devassociation.sps.*

Association of Former Players

Now in its eighteenth year, the Association of Former Man Utd Players raises cash for various charities and produces an aptly titled magazine, *Legends*, featuring interviews with ex-players (magazine subscription £12 a year). The group also organises an annual dinner at Old Trafford at which stars from the past meet up to swap stories and bathe in the glow of shared memories.

The club have warmed to the association's cause in recent years and they now have an office inside Old Trafford and boast a membership of 260 former players. Anyone who stepped out for the first team can join, but as the secretary Warren Bradley notes, the more recent departees – the Jonathan Greenings and Mark Wilsons, not to mention the likes of Bosnich, Taibi and Stam – have not yet snapped up the opportunity. 'You don't get hit by the nostalgia bug until you've retired,' Bradley says.

Contact/subscription: Association of Former Man Utd Players, PO Box 92, Old Trafford, Manchester M16 9XW.

Manchester United plc

In 1991, United's then-chairman Martin Edwards masterminded the flotation of the club on the London Stock Exchange in order to raise finance necessary to redevelop the Stretford End. The flotation substantially changed the way the club was governed. As a plc rather than a private company, the club was subject to much greater transparency. For example, anyone can pay a visit to Companies House in London and discover that in the twelve months to July 2002 United's small army of employees were paid a total of £70,812,000. Which makes the club's average wage about the highest of any company in the country.

The move to plc status also brought more scrupulous accounting rigour, professional financial management, and a new business dimension to the club: each year a portion of the profit is handed over to shareholders as a dividend, instead of being ploughed back for the purchase of new players and upgrading facilities. A little ironically, this financial thankyou for their investment has meant that in the ten years since flotation more than five times as much has left the club's coffers in the way of dividend payments than was raised in the first place.

If you want to keep a grip on what's going on, then the best thing to do is buy some shares. Like 30,000 other fans.

Shareholders

What fun and games there have been in the City this past year, trading in Manchester United shares. *The Observer* reckoned back in March that the real soap opera at Old Trafford had nothing to do with Fergie's furies or Ryan Giggs being ostracised by team mates for his courting habits, or the will-he-won't-he-go-to-Spain soap opera that was David Beckham. No – it was all to do with who owns shares. A whole raft of rich men climbed aboard the United bandwagon over the year, many of them snapping up the shares sold by the disgraced Martin Edwards (see box on following page).

Among the arrivals was Malcolm Glazer, the owner of the Tampa Bay Buccaneers, this season's Super Bowl champions, who took 2

The strange case of Martin Edwards

A couple of months before Manchester United played Juventus in the second group stage of the Champions League in 2003, both clubs lost long-standing chairman. In Turin, as Gianna Agnelli was laid to rest, banners were unfurled in his honour, fans wore black arm bands and tears rolled unashamedly down from the Stadio Delle Alpi's stands. The man who owned the three pillars of Italian life – Fiat, Ferrari and Juve – Agnelli was often described as Turin's royalty – widely loved and universally respected. United's chairman, **Martin Edwards**, was by

contrast, slipping away from the Old Trafford boardroom, his head hung in shame after being held to ridicule in the *News of the World* over allegations of hookers, slappers and a proclivity for peering under the cubicle doors in ladies' lavatories at Old Traffford. This was not behaviour tolerable for a plc board member, and he was pressured into resigning, severing his ties by selling his last tranche of shares – a sale which precipitated an excited rush in the City. As consolation, he was bestowed the largely honorary position of club president – a title last held by Sir Matt Busby.

The popular view of Edwards among United fans is that he used his inherited position as the club's main shareholder purely for self-enrichment. He never invested a penny of his own money in the club, he tried on three occasions to sell his (and our) birthright to wholly unsuitable predators (Maxwell, Knighton, Murdoch) and his communication with his customers was aloof at best. Yet he deserves a bit more credit than that. The magazine *When Saturday Comes* used the opportunity of Edwards's departure to publish an article suggesting he was the architect of United's success in the past decade, depicting him as an administrative genius who revolutionised football. This is clearly over-egging the case, but it must be stated that Edwards left United in a hugely healthier position to when he first joined the board. And leaving the personal enrichment aside, he is also an undoubted United fanatic, a man who has seen almost every game of his adult life, read every single book published about the club, and could wipe the floor in any Red trivia contest.

As a business player, Edwards's talent was to delegate effectively. He never pretended to be anything more than a back-room operator. No Ridsdale, Fayed, Ellis or Bates-style delusions of grandeur for him. Instead, he brought in people who knew what they were doing and stuck by them through the bad times. If only for the recruitment of Alex Ferguson he deserves lasting credit. He also presided over the expansion of the stadium into the biggest in the country, and managed to do so without landing the club in a penny of debt.

percent, while the same number was snapped up by John de Mol, the Dutch television magnate, whose company, Endemol, makes *Big Brother*. What this means for United is not altogether clear. It may be just a case of extremely rich men spotting an opportunity to become even richer, as the cost of United's shares plummeted along with the general havoc in the stock market (have you seen the state of your pension recently?). In January 2000, each share cost slightly north of £3.80 a piece. In January 2003 they briefly touched 99p. Yet the club, as the figures printed elsewhere point out, remains in not so much rude as quite disgusting health. Which means those with money to flash about reckon that the shares are criminally under-valued. Hence the keenness to move in.

More intriguing, however, is the presence on the share register of a collective of Irish billionaires known as the Coolmore mafia, a group supposedly led by the owners of the Coolmore stud in County Kerry, JP McManus and John Magnier, who through their offshore company Cubic Expression have acquired 8.65 percent of United's 260m shares. Their mate Harry Dobson, a Scots mining magnate, bought up 6.5 percent via his company Mountbarrow Investments, and another good buddy, Dermot Desmond, the majority shareholder in Celtic and owner of the London City Airport, bought 1 percent in March. So together, the celtic tigers own 16 percent of the Reds, significantly more than BSkyB's 9.95 percent. What makes it intriguing is that the Coolmore boys,

Coolmore man, John Magnier

through a shared obsession with racing, have become good friends with Sir Alex Ferguson after they were introduced by his biographer Hugh McIlvanney. Every time the chums are seen dining together, the theories begin to circulate that the Irish boys intend a takeover, with Fergie installed as chairman. Then in summer 2003 there were rumours of a falling-out, and City talk of a possible takeover of the club in consequence.

Accountants' corner

Chelsea's Russian money aside, last year was a miserable one for football finance. Eleven of the 92 league clubs drifted into administration at some time during the season. And others – Leeds, for instance – have been able to continue trading thanks to their banks' indulgence. Technically they are more skint than Poland. Manchester United, though, march to a different financial beat as one of only three profitable clubs in the Premiership.

Perhaps the most staggering thing about the latest set of accounts released by Manchester United plc can be found in the table under the heading 'Bank overdraft'. Here there is entered a simple figure of £0.00. In a world where debt threatens to extinguish more than 10 percent of our clubs at any moment, United, despite undertaking a £120m property development programme over the past six years, despite paying a British record fee for Rio Ferdinand, despite not yet receiving most of the money due for the sale of Jaap Stam not to mention Real's poxy Beckham instalments, are completely debt free.

Here are some more details from the latest set of accounts, for the six months up to January 2003.

Gate receipts: £42,906,000
Media revenue: £26,862,000
Commercial and merchandise: £22,806,000
Total turnover: £92,574,000
Profit before tax: £31,128,000

For context, United's profits in the last six months are more than the paper value of Leeds (or half a dozen other Premiership clubs).

All this, of course, will have little effect on the vast majority of United shareholders. Most shareholders (as opposed to the holders of most shares) have no idea what the current value of their investment is, don't read the *FT* and do little more than raise a snigger at the bank when they go to pay in their annual dividend cheques. Most Red shareholders are fans, in it for the sentiment not the money. At the last count 22,602 shareholders own 1,000 shares or less (or 1/260,000th of the overall action).

Shareholders United

'Shareholding Manchester United fans who care more about their club than their dividends' is the Shareholders United mission statement, to be found on the homepage of their Website. And that sums

Who's in charge of United: the board directors

The departure of **Martin Edwards** (see p.399) was the most significant change on the board of directors in 2003 as he accepted the position of club president. His departure left the board firmly in the hands of professional finance men, with a few more football-oriented members to assist them on the 'Football Board' which considers transfers and other ball-related activities.

The following directors constitute the **board of MU plc**:

Roy A. Gardner, senior independent non-executive director. Age 57. Joined board in 2000. Chief executive of Centrica plc, non-executive director of LaPorte plc, president of Carers' National Association, chair of Employers' Forum on Disability. Previously group finance director of British Gas plc, and MD of GEC-Marconi.

Peter F. Kenyon, chief executive. Age 48. Joined Utd in 1997. Previously chief operating officer of Umbro International.

David A. Gill, group managing director. Age 45. Joined Utd in 1997. Previously finance director of First Choice Holidays plc.

Amer M. Al Midani, non-executive director. Age 45. Joined 1991. Interests in the hotel and leisure industries; not currently a director of any other company.

E. Maurice Watkins, non-executive director. Age 60. Director since 1991, on the club board since 1984. Senior partner in James Chapman and Co, solicitors to the MU group. One of the club's major individual shareholders.

Ian F. R. Much, independent non-executive director. Age 58. Joined board in 2000. Chief executive of De La Rue plc. Previously chief executive of T&N plc.

Philip E. Yea, independent non-executive director. Age 47. Joined board in 2000. Senior executive of Investcorp. Non-executive director of Halifax Group plc and Leica Geosystems AG. Previously group finance director of Diageo plc.

Sir Bobby with Bill Foulkes and Pat Crerand

Nick Humby, group finance director. Formerly with Pearson TV.

The **football board members** are Kenyon, Gill and Watkins, together with:

Sir Bobby Charlton, former player, 1956–73, still holds the record for appearances and goals scored in a United shirt.

R. Les Olive, former player (he made two lleague appearances as emergency goalkeeper in 1952) and club secretary 1958–88.

J. Michael Edelson, Manchester businessman.

it up. This is a collective of fans who see shareholding as a way both to secure the long-term independence of their club and to use as a lobbying tool to pursue supporter interests. Founded as Shareholders United Against Murdoch at the height of the battle to stop BSkyB taking control of the club, SU now boasts well over 850 members – and growing. SU members ask awkward questions at the AGM, they have a representative on the Fans' Forum, and they generally appreciate that the way to this club's soul is through its dividend.

Membership of SU costs £10 a year, and for that sum each member receives a share in United every year they pay up. All members are sent a quarterly newsletter, *United Shareholder*, a publication that broke the news that Martin Edwards is paid a salary of £100,000 a year, plus a company Merc, for two days' work a week (if you wondered, Peter Kenyon is on £325,000 plus a BMW, and his deputy David Gill earns £225,000). Plus, during an interview for the mag, this ringing endorsement from Sir Alex was elicited: 'Shareholders United can only be good for the game. I urge United fans to get involved.' There is a Shareholders United/IMUSA social before every home game in *Sam Platt's* pub.

Membership details from: PO Box 30766, London WC1E 7NW. Or visit the website: *www.ShareholdersUnited.org.*

United Media

Beckham may be history, but it seems unlikely that United will henceforth be ignored on the front and back pages of the UK and world media. But, of course, we fans need more than that – in fact, we need different from that. The 'Anyone But United' attitude infects so much press coverage of the club, from its players to the plc, that it's a relief to read, listen to, or view media with a clear Red-sightedness. Here, then, is a round-up of what's available.

United Review: the matchday programme

After several years of stagnating, with sales slipping faster than Sunderland, United Review, the United matchday programme, received a welcome revamp this season. Out-sourced to the publishers Haymarket, the venerable old programme was suddenly worth reading. Indeed, it was more or less a magazine, and a lot better than anything on the newsstands. Every week there are two or three features which slip away from the standard agenda of player interviews and match reports (both of which, incidentally, are well handled) and provide some real insight. A feature on United players in America in the seventies, for instance, was a gem. As was a piece recalling why Lou Macari decided on United instead of Liverpool when he had the chance to join either back in the 1970s (something to do with knowing true glamour when he saw it). All of which, coupled with a thoughtful use of archive and museum stock, make

it the country's top programme.

There are some, of course, for whom the programme has long been about more than just a good read. For Iain McCartney, a Scot who travels down from Dumfries to every home game, the programme is a vital part of his interest in the club. McCartney is the chairman of the United Programme Collectors Club, a group which numbers some 260 diehards, hailing from across the globe, who exchange information on rare and valuable *Reviews* and other United memorabilia. McCartney says, 'The Red Star Belgrade away, prior to Munich, is your Penny Black of United programmes. I guess one in good condition would be worth about £2000 these days. I was always led to believe that there were only a couple of dozen printed, but at every auction there seems to be one cropping up.' He has one, of course, as he does that other rarity, Wolves home in February 1958, which was printed but never distributed after the match was postponed following the Munich crash.

For info on the United Programme Collectors' Club, send an SAE to: 7 Cartha Road, Lochvale, Dumfries DG1 4JB.

MUTV

MUTV – the club's United-dedicated television channel – is the only major loss-making branch of United activity. For the last two seasons they have screened first-team matches in full 48 hours after the game; subscriptions have increased, but not at the rate the club had hoped for. However, the real take-up (and indeed the reason why the club and its partners Sky and Granada invested in the project in the first place) will come when first-team matches are shown live. Following the demise of ITV Digital, observers of the scene believe the time is not far off when clubs themselves, rather than leagues or associations, control their own broadcasting rights. United, therefore, will be perfectly poised to take advantage of individual bargaining.

In the meantime, MUTV serves a daily ration of re-runs of old and (sometimes) classic games, phone-ins on United issues when all fans' views are given the oxygen of publicity, live reserve-team games, and highlights of training sessions (up there with paint drying as a spectator sport). Oh – and the chance to see a whole bunch of one-time Reds talking a good game.

MUTV is available through Sky Digital, NTL or Telewest Digital packages at an additional £5.99 per month. Subscription hotline: ☏0870 848 6888.

Man Utd Radio

Broadcast on 1413AM, within a five-mile radius around Old Trafford on a matchday, Man Utd Radio is safe and predictable – and a little boring. There's match commentary and pre- and post-match interviews but the club line is toed at all times and any criticisms are severely tempered. Alan Green it is not.

United magazine

The *United* magazine (£3.20) sells 40,000 copies a month – a fair number for a football magazine, but a third the number it was doing at its peak when the market was more buoyant. Its official status means that it tends to be quick to praise and slow to criticise but the magazine has good access to the team's stars (it makes a generous payment to the players' pool) and is far better produced than rival club magazines.

The magazine, together with its poster-based stablemate for young fans, *Glory Glory Man United* (£1.75; monthly), is published under licence by the Future Network.

Fanzines

Red fans were slow to produce their own fanzines, not really picking up on the craze until the late 1980s, but these days United boasts arguably the best-written lot in the country. On matchdays, the walk down Sir Matt Busby Way is soundtracked by young lads yelling out their mantra, imploring passers-by to pick up the latest copy of their fanzines, of which there are three regulars, appearing each month in the season.

Red News (£1.50). The original United fanzine, this was started by Barney Chilton, a Cockney Red. Humorous in tone, its dense type always has something worth reading, including good gossip and cartoons.

Red Issue (£1.50). The sharpest and most scurrilous United fanzine. It is full of clever and vitriolic attacks on rival teams, conspiracy theories and caustic wit. Plus good features on upcoming European destinations.

United We Stand (£1.50). Hard to venture an opinion on this as it is edited by Andy Mitten – co-author of this book – and has the other co-author as a columnist. So we suggest you buy a copy and make up your own mind. In fact, while you're at it, why not buy one for a mate as well?

United on the Net

Type the words 'Manchester United' into Google and around 1.5m website links will come up. These include the major sports sites such as www.football365.com (which you can bookmark to United for news, reports and stats) and http://football.guardian.co.uk (which posts reports from *The Guardian* and *The Observer*), as well as a dozen or so fanzine and supporters' organisation websites. The best of these are detailed below.

Banners
www.cwalton19.fsnet.co.uk/BANNERS.htm

This specialist site has pictures of lots of the banners currently hanging over the edge of the second tier of the Stretford End. Indeed, it was through the site that much of the money to make them was raised.

IMUSA and Shareholders United

`www.imusa.org`   `www.ShareholdersUnited.org`

These two pressure groups run their own sites, useful for picking up the latest information on fan campaigns and general news and gossip. IMUSA's also includes access to the innovative fans Webring, which enables computer-based fans to leapfrog from Red site to Red site.

m-u-f-c

`www.m-u-f-c.co.uk`

Another well-established independent site with a decent message board, offering plenty of forthright opinions from matchgoing Reds.

Manchester United

`www.manutd.com`

When manutd.com – the club's official site – was revealed to be the most visited website in China, United's share price hit its all-time peak. That was back at the height of dotcom frenzy, and ensured that the plc's value struck £1bn for the first time. The reason for the market excitement was the thought of the mail-order possibilities – turning the Megastore into an international mint, and perhaps even adding live web action. But that hasn't quite come to pass on this dreadful, ploddy site, that tends to crash home computers. It is due to be relaunched during the 2002-03 season – and not before time. Nevertheless, for those wanting up-to-date ticket information it is the first web port of call, and many members use it to apply for match tickets online.

Manchester United are better and best ever

`http://www.kokwee.net/manutd.html`

Put together by a clearly loopy United fan in Thailand, Kok Wee, this is an example of a fan site on the extreme frontiers. A red carpet floats across the screen, and below Veron with extended head are bizarre match reports ('they play like fast and score like monkey's eat bananas'), and a Ryanshrine ('All Bowel to Ryanshrine'). He likes Liz Hurley, too.

Red Café

`www.redcafe.net/home`

Redcafe.net is a well-designed site, as you'd expect from its host, the *totalfootball* web network. Though the news is up to date, both it and the match reports are taken from the Press Association and thus lack some of the rawness and passion of contributions to other sites. It is not short on clichés, though.

Red Issue

www.redissue.co.uk

As befits its origin as the spikiest fanzine, Red Issue has perhaps the most rabid message board of any United site. Now hosted by the FootyMad network, it's hugely popular, updated daily and worth visiting for an unadulterated Red view of the world

Red News

www.rednews.co.uk

Red News includes an archive of articles, features and columns which first appeared in the fanzine. The site has a comprehensive daily news round-up.

Red Org

www.Red11.org

Finally, depressing proof of the ageing process can be gleaned from this site (which used to go under the name of *mufc.simplenet*). Its superlative stats section has everything the anorak could need, including information on ticket prices since 1960. And it is true: when the older member of this guide's editorial team first went to Old Trafford, you could indeed go through the turnstiles, buy a programme and still have change from 50p. Bet you're glad you logged on for that news.

United Online

www.UnitedOnline.co.uk

This is an amalgam of several United sites, run by Polar Internet. It is an excellent source of regularly updated news, comment and stats, useful and very nicely designed.

United We Stand

www.uwsonline.com

Hosted by the *Rivals* network (along with 91 unofficial club sites), UWS's regular contributors add new stories every day and match reports from a fan's perspective from every away end. The site also has two lively message boards – although the ABU attracts, as the name suggests, bitter rival fans and their inane bleatings. Then there's a section by UWS's own Robert Brady, which is as conventional as Morrissey, as witty as Coogan.

United books

Ever since 1930, when George Hunter put together *Football's Funny Side*, a collection of anecdotes from Old Trafford, publishers have been knocking out books about Manchester United. Just about every player

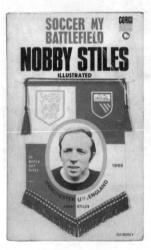

worth his salt has 'written' an autobiography, though very few have come up with anything worth reading. Still, for every ten of *Ryan Giggs: My Story* or *Nobby Stiles: Soccer My Battlefield* there is an occasional gem. Following is a starter kit recommended for any self-respecting library of United tomes.

Many of these books are out of print but specialist bookshops, such as *Sportspages* in St Ann's Square, Manchester (☎0161 832 8530; also at Caxton Walk, 94/96 Charing Cross Rd, London WC2H 0JG; ☎0207 240 9604), might be able to help you track down copies. *Sportspages* Manchester also stocks plenty of United ephemera, and both branches carry all of the United fanzines.

Reference and history

Lance Bellers The Unseen Archives – A Photographic History of Manchester United (Mustard, 1999). A bargain-priced doorstop of a book, compiled from the *Mirror* library, mixing action shots with 'story' photos of stars with cars, George Best swinging, Denis Law as Santa, etc. All in all, irresistible, and well worth seeking out.

Michael Crick Manchester United: The Complete Fact Book (Profile Books, 1999). In many ways, if you were going to restrict your United library to one book, this, as the Stone Roses would put it, is the one. A mink coat among footballing anoraks.

Garth Dykes The United Alphabet (A&C Polar, 1994). Quite some work: an encyclopaedia of every player to step out in Red, from the earliest days through to the early Ferguson-era. An updated edition would be gratefully received.

David Meek Official Manchester United 100 Greatest Players (Man Utd Books, 2001). As picked by supporters in a poll conducted by *United* magazine. Satirical types managed to slip Ralph Milne in there. And presumably there will have to be an entire re-count of the poll to accommodate Ruud van Nistelrooy.

Ivan Ponting The Red Army (Hamlyn, 2000). This is a hard-to-resist browse: an illustrated coffee-table book of profiles of all the players who have represented United at club level since the 1950s. It includes complete career statistics and a photo of every player.

Jillian Somerscales, et al The Official Manchester United Illustrated Encyclopaedia (André Deutsch, 1999). An excellent, lavishly illustrated reference work, full of fascinating detail.

Tom Tyrrell and David Meek The Illustrated History of Manchester United 1878–2000 (Hamlyn, 2000). This history of United from the most prolific pair of Red authors (Meek alone must be responsible for half the books on United available through *amazon.com*) features a good array of features spreads and stats, running to the end of the 1999–2000 season.

Official Man Utd Colouring Book (André Deutsch, 2002). The editors of this book's favourite.

Following the Reds

Adam Brown and Andy Walsh Not for Sale: Manchester United, Murdoch and the Defeat of BSkyB (Mainstream, 2000). Biased, passionate and rightly jubilant insiders' account of the battle to keep the club out of the clutches of the world's biggest media imperialist.

Barney Chilton et al If The Reds Should Play in Rome or Mandelay (Juna, 1997). Affectionate, warm-hearted account of what it is like to follow the lads around the world.

Terry Christian Reds in the Hood (André Deutsch, 1999). He may have once sent the nation into a fury as presenter of *The Word*, but as this book proves, Christian is a true and loyal Red, growing up in the shadow of Old Trafford in the 1960s and '70s.

Michael Crick and David Smith Manchester United, Betrayal of a Legend (Pelham, 1989). As he is the first to admit, none of what Crick prophesied about the imminent decline of United has come to pass. Nevertheless, this controversial book remains a cracking tale of jaw-dropping boardroom greed. For a continuation of the story of Football and Big Business in the past decade (a story inevitably featuring United in large part), For Love or Money (Boxtree, 1998) by Alex Fynn and Lynton Guest is another compelling read.

Tony Hill If the Kids are United (Victor Gollancz, 1999). A genial, gentle tale of a United fan growing up in the Thatcher-devastated Nottingham coal-fields.

Stephen F. Kelly (ed) Red Voices (Headline, 1999). An anthology of memories from United fans across the generations.

Richard Kurt Dispatches from Old Trafford (Sigma Leisure, 1996); The Red Army Years (Headline, 1997); Red Devils (Prion Books, 1998). Kurt, the acerbic *Red Issue* columnist, is one of the funniest and most prolific observers of United over recent decades. *Dispatches* gathers his early *Issue* columns; *Red Army Years*

(with Chris Nikeas) is a fan's eye view of United in the '70s; *Red Devils* is a hugely entertaining rogues' and rebels' gallery, from strikeleader Billy Meredith to 'Bogota Bandit' Charlie Mitten to the Edwards family and 'sex-god' Lee Sharpe.

Jim White Are You Watching Liverpool? (Heinemann, 1994). A journalist-fan's account of United's 1993–94 double season. Doubles? Once a rarity, bit of a common-place now.

Players and managers: biogs

Richard Adamson Bogota Bandit: The Outlaw Life of Manchester United's Penalty King (Mainstream 1998). The extraordinary story of Charlie Mitten, the man who took the money in South America, and paid for it with his career. An appalling way to treat a hero. It couldn't happen now, of course.

George Best Blessed (Ebury Press, 2002). Not the first Bestie autobiography, but given his health problems recently, for a time it threatened to be the last. The title is a deliberate riposte to the old chestnut about chucking it all away.

Michael Crick The Boss: The Many Sides of Alex Ferguson (Pocket Books, 2002). Crick's biography of the man with the plan is not easy reading for faithful Reds. Turning a forensic investigative approach on to a football figure – probably for the first time – Crick has unearthed many a detail about the greatest manager in English football history's way of doing business that you might rather not know. Nonetheless, a respect for the man shines through and, superbly researched, it is compelling stuff.

Eamon Dunphy A Strange Kind of Glory (Heinemann, 1991). Although this reads as embittered at times, it is a never less than intriguing biography of Matt Busby – by a modest player (he never made it at United) who did good as a writer.

Alex Ferguson with Hugh McIlvanney Managing My Life (Hodder/Coronet, 1999). Alex's life story lays good claim to being the best football autobiography ever – pulsating, acerbic and beautifully written ... and that's just the introduction. A deserved bestseller.

Roy Keane Keane: The Autobiography (Michael Joseph, 2002). No book has sold as many copies as this in Ireland since the Bible. Seriously. Keane and his World Cup shenanigans divided the island, and his autobiography was published with perfect timing into the teeth of all that walk-out publicity. His ghost writer Eamon Dunphy exorcised many of his own demons through the voice of Keane in the book: assaults on Mick McCarthy and Jack Charlton had the whiff of revenge about them. Talking of which, the reminiscences of that revenge assault on Alf Inge Haaland were pure Keano. 'Take that you ****': not since Princess Anne was in her pomp can asterisks have appeared with such frequency on the front page of newspapers. As you might expect of Keane, though, there is a lot more to it than just a few headlines. An exemplary autobiography, the best yet of a United player.

Richard Kurt Cantona (Pan, 1996). Kurt plays Boswell to Eric's Dr Johnson. Don't expect criticism, but the insights are worth the ride.

Joe Lovejoy Bestie: A Portrait of a Legend (Sidgwick & Jackson, 1998). Warts and all tale of the great man – and in Bestie's case the warts are in the Oliver Cromwell class.

Iain McCartney Duncan Edwards (Temple Nostalgia Press, 1999), Roger Byrne – Captain of the Busby Babes (Empire Publications, 2000). Edwards and Byrne were the heart of the Busby Babes and both lost their lives at Munich. McCartney has talked to family, friends and contemporaries for these affectionate portraits of two United legends from an era when footballers were woefully underpaid.

Brian McClair with Joyce Wooldridge Odd Man Out (André Deutsch, 1997). McClair became an unlikely Old Trafford cult towards the end of his time as a player in the 1990s – and he was ever the odd man in the dressing room – a footballer with a desert-dry sense of humour who considered becoming a maths teacher, and was a regular churchgoer.

Jaap Stam Head to Head (HarperCollins Willow, 2000). Repackaged with a photo doctored to make Jaap and Fergie look like Griff Rhys Jones and Mel Smith, nose to nose, this is the largely dull autobiography that rumour has it cost Stam his United career. Still, in his short time with the Reds he learned some interesting vocabulary in the dressing room. Calling the Nevilles a 'busy pair of cunts' was something of a descriptive masterstroke.

Norman Whiteside My Memories of Manchester United (Britespot, 2003). If legend is to be believed, these will have been pretty foggy by the morning after. Still, Big Norm is a good value storyteller, and particularly entertaining about the huge cultural change that came over the club when Alex Ferguson arrived.

Jim White Always in the Running: The Manchester United Dream Team (Mainstream, 1996). Eleven characters in search of a team, profiled by the co-author of this book. Clearly a corker, then.

United videos and DVDs

There are an awful lot of 'Manchester United' videos – especially if you browse one of the Internet merchants where you'll find every issue of the old bi-monthly *Manchester United Official Video Magazine* – a record of recent games lumbered with MUTV-calibre sub-features that won't bear repeat viewing. And that's something that, sadly, goes for an awful lot of the other United video product. However, there are certain items that these authors are glad to have seen and would not willingly dispatch to the school jumble ...

Historic

The Official History of Manchester United FC (BBC). This was put together in 1988, so it's the pre-Alex glory years. But it can't be beat for history, with proper emphasis on all the right events, great BBC footage, and ever-amazed commentary from John Motson.

Soccer Legends: Law, Best, Charlton (BBC). Another class BBC production, with lots of action, and good interviews, on United's truly legendary trio from the 1960s.

The Manchester United Family Tree (BBC). The Family Tree is a history of the not-so-good times, 1968–93, but it's a great bit of viewing, with brilliant contributions from those who were there – notably Willie Morgan's acid comments on Tommy Docherty.

Manchester United in the 70s (VCI), Manchester United in the 80s (VCI). Looking back, it's amazing to see how underachieving United could be. Yet at the time it seemed like glory, and the players heroes. And then that Alex Ferguson came along ...

The Alex years

Champions: Manchester United 1992–93 The Official Review (VCI). The first league title in 26 years and Alex's first classic team with Cantona, Hughes and Giggs to the fore. Magic.

The Double: Manchester United 1995–96 The Official Review (VCI). This was the year of Eric's real greatness, and the year of Beckham, too, when United showed they could win it all with kids.

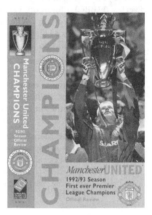

United in the 90s (VCI). Thrill to Alex's first dozen trophies – up to the glorious conclusion of the treble. Look, there's Brian McClair... and how could we ever forget Mike Phelan?

The Pride Of All Europe (VCI). A 2002 compilation, featuring United's European achievements, with particular focus on the Champions League. Action covers up to end of the '02 season.

The Treble: Manchester United 1998–99 The Official Review (VCI). Can it ever get better than this? If you want one video (or for more features, including Alex's comments on each game, one DVD) of United in the 1990s, here you go: Giggs's wonder-goal against Arsenal in the FA Cup (and Schmeichel's penalty save before it), and those extraordinary games in Turin and Barcelona. That we should live through such times ...

The 2002-03 Review: We've Got Our Trophy Back (VCI). A pleasing season review of the season past, released on video and DVD. The DVD comes with a bonus disc, The Premiership Years, presented by Sir Alex as he guides fans through United's first ten years of Premiership football.

300 Premiership Goals (VCI). Nothing subtle about this: if it's goals you want, it's goals you get. Sometimes, though, after a long night at the pub, nothing else will do…

Classic games

1968 European Cup Final: Man Utd 4 Benfica 1 (BBC). Anyone born in the 1950s or earlier probably still finds this the most memorable match in United history. It wasn't a classic but it meant everything, it had goals from Charlton and a cracker from Best, and tears all round. Commentary is terrific, too, with Kenneth Wolstenholme assisted by Walter Winterbottom.

1985 FA Cup Final: Manchester United 1 Everton 0 (BBC). Moran off, Whiteside's goal and Motty in ecstasy ('When the history of this player is written, where will they start?'). Magnificent.

1999 The Italian Job: Juventus 2 Manchester United 3 (VCI). The match many Reds reckon their best ever – along with highlights from the home leg and the two games against Inter in that wonderful spring.

2001 Premier League: Manchester United 6 Arsenal 1 (VCI). A handy reminder that Arsène's mob are not the all-conquering sporting gods their cheer-leaders would like us to believe. 1-6 to the Arsenal anyone?

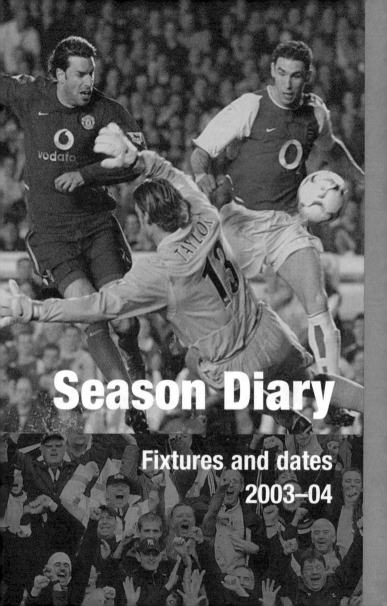

Season Diary

Fixtures and dates
2003–04

Monday August 4

....

Tuesday August 5

....

Wednesday August 6

....

Thursday August 7

....

Friday August 8

....

Saturday August 9

....

Sunday August 10
Utd v Arsenal **FA Community Shield (Millennium Stadium, Cardiff)**

....

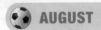

Monday August 11
1971 A vital day for the modern United: Roy Keane is born in Cork.

Tuesday August 12

Wednesday August 13

Thursday August 14
1980 Ray Wilkins becomes the club's biggest ever purchase, when he arrives from Chelsea at a cost of £825,000.

Friday August 15
1993 Roy Keane makes his debut against Norwich (a) after signing for a British record £3.75m from Nottingham Forest.

Saturday August 16
Premiership season kicks off

Utd v Bolton Premiership

Bolton are United's current bogey team, with one win, one draw and two defeats over the past two seasons.

Sunday August 17
1989 Michael Knighton proudly announces he has bought the club from Martin Edwards for £10m. But he never had the money and the deal collapsed two months later.

2002 On the opening day of the league season, Ole Gunnar Solskjaer scores his 100th goal for United in a 1-0 win over West Bromwich Albion.

Monday August 18

1962 Denis Law scores on his debut against West Brom.

Tuesday August 19

1998 Dwight Yorke becomes United's most expensive signing – £12.6m from Aston Villa.

2001 Ruud van Nistelrooy becomes the first United player since Ole Gunnar Solskjaer in 1996 to mark his debut with a goal, and the 88th scoring debutant in club history.

Wednesday August 20

Euro 2004 Qualifiers include: Serbia and Montenegro v Wales. **International friendlies include:** England v Croatia (Portman Road); Norway v Scotland; Ireland v Australia.

Thursday August 21

Friday August 22

1999 Nick Culkin makes the shortest ever debut by a United player. Coming on as a sub against Arsenal at Highbury, he plays for twelve seconds. He has not appeared since.

Saturday August 23

2002 Ryan Giggs joins Solskjaer in the United centurions' club by scoring in the 2-2 draw at Chelsea.

Newcastle v Utd **Premiership (Sky, 12.30pm)**

Sunday August 24

1949 United play their first game back at Old Trafford after it had been rebuilt following bomb damage during the War. Charlie Mitten scores the first goal in a 3-0 win over Bolton.

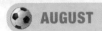

Monday August 25

1996 Ole Gunnar Solskjaer becomes the first United substitute to score on his debut, after signing for £1.5m from Molde.

Tuesday August 26

Wednesday August 27

1955 United field their youngest team ever, with an average age of 22 years 106 days. The babes are: Wood, Foulkes, Byrne, Whitefoot, Jones, Edwards, Webster, Blanchflower, Lewis, Viollet and Scanlon.

Utd v Wolves **Premiership (Sky, 8pm)**

Thursday August 28

Friday August 29

Saturday August 30

Southampton v Utd **Premiership**

Sunday August 31

 **SEPTEMBER** 2003

Monday September 1

Tuesday September 2

Wednesday September 3
1892 United's first league game – as Newton Heath – away at Blackburn. Rovers win 4-3.

Thursday September 4

Friday September 5

Saturday September 6
1998 Rupert Murdoch's BSkyB corporation makes £575m bid for control of Manchester United. But it doesn't work out after referral to Monopolies and Mergers Commission.

Euro 2004 Qualifiers include: Scotland v Faroes; Ukraine v N. Ireland; Macedonia v England; Italy v Wales; Rep of Ireland v Russia.

Sunday September 7

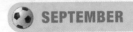
Monday September 8

....

Tuesday September 9

....

Wednesday September 10

Euro 2004 Qualifiers include: Germany v Scotland; N. Ireland v Armenia; England v Liechtenstein; Wales v Finland.

....

Thursday September 11

....

Friday September 12

....

Saturday September 13

Charlton v Utd **Premiership**

....

Sunday September 14

1966 Worst ever result in the League Cup: 1-5 away at Blackpool.

....

Monday September 15

....

Tuesday September 16
UEFA Champions League Group Stage Match 1

....

Wednesday September 17
UEFA Champions League Group Stage Match 1

....

Thursday September 18
1958 Albert Quixhall signs from Sheffield Wednesday for a then-record British fee of £45,000.

2002 Diego Forlan finally scores for United, from the penalty-spot, on his 27th appearance for the club since his signing in January 2002 (though most of those games were as a late substitute).

....

Friday September 19
1956 United record their best ever result in Europe, when they beat Anderlecht 10-0 at Maine Road in the European Cup. It is their first appearance in European competition.

....

Saturday September 20
1926 United manager John Chapman is suspended from football by an FA enquiry. To this day no explanation has been given, and Chapman never managed the club again.

....

Sunday September 21
Utd v Arsenal **Premiership (Sky, 4.05pm)**

....

Monday September 22

. . . .

Tuesday September 23

1992 David Beckham makes his debut in the League Cup tie against Brighton.

. . . .

Wednesday September 24

. . . .

Thursday September 25

. . . .

Friday September 26

1984 Bryan Robson scores the fastest goal in United history, when he opens the scoring in a League Cup tie against Burnley after twelve seconds.

. . . .

Saturday September 27

Leicester City v Utd **Premiership**

. . . .

Sunday September 28

. . . .

Monday September 29

2001 United win 5-3 at Tottenham Hotspur, after being 3-0 down at half-time. It's thought to be the greatest comeback, mathematically, in United history. In 1910 United were losing 3-0 at Newcastle but won 4-3.

....

Tuesday September 30

UEFA Champions League Group Stage Match 2

....

Wednesday October 1

1981 Ron Atkinson signs Bryan Robson for a new British record £1.5m. On the same day in 1995, Eric Cantona makes his return after suspension and scores in a 2-2 draw with Liverpool.

UEFA Champions League Group Stage Match 2

....

Thursday October 2

....

Friday October 3

....

Saturday October 4

Utd v Birmingham **Premiership**

....

Sunday October 5

....

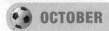

Monday October 6

1956 Bobby Charlton scres twice on his debut – against Charlton Athletic.

....

Tuesday October 7

....

Wednesday October 8

....

Thursday October 9

....

Friday October 10

1921 John Chapman becomes United manager.

....

Saturday October 11

Euro 2004 Qualifiers include: Scotland v Lithuania; Greece v N. Ireland; Turkey v England; Wales v Serbia and Montenegro.

....

Sunday October 12

....

Monday October 13

1999 Rotation! The United team which starts the Worthington Cup tie against Aston Villa does not include a single player who began the previous game at Chelsea.

....

Tuesday October 14

....

Wednesday October 15

1892 United's record league win, 10-1 against Wolves.

....

Thursday October 16

....

Friday October 17

....

Saturday October 18

Leeds v Utd **Premiership**

....

Sunday October 19

....

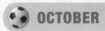 **OCTOBER**   **2003**

Monday October 20

Tuesday October 21
UEFA Champions League Group Stage Match 3

Wednesday October 22
1980 Garry Birtles makes his debut. A record £1.25m purchase from Nottingham Forest, the centre forward becomes the butt of many a joke after failing to score in his first 25 league appearances.

UEFA Champions League Group Stage Match 3

Thursday October 23

Friday October 24
1956 Goalkeeper David Gaskell becomes the youngest ever player to appear in the United first team at the age of 16 years, 19 days.

Saturday October 25
Utd v Fulham Premiership

Sunday October 26

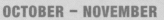
Monday October 27

Tuesday October 28

2000 At 34 years and 208 days, Teddy Sheringham is the oldest man to score a hat-trick for United, when he nets three times in the Premiership against Southampton.

Worthington Cup Third Round

Wednesday October 29

2002 Mads Timm plays for eleven minutes as a substitute in the 3-0 defeat at Maccabi Haifa, which currently gives him the second shortest United career on record (after Nick Culkin's 7.5 seconds at Arsenal in 1999).

Worthington Cup Third Round

Thursday October 30

1996 The forty-year record of never losing at home in European competition goes west (or, rather, east) as United lose 0-1 to Fenerbache of Turkey.

Friday October 31

Saturday November 1
Utd v Portsmouth **Premiership**

Sunday November 2

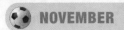

Monday November 3

1894 First ever Manchester league derby. Newton Heath win 5-2.

Tuesday November 4

1951 An article in the *Manchester Evening News* about the debuts of Jackie Blanchflower and Roger Byrne uses the phrase 'Busby Babes' for the first time.

UEFA Champions League Group Stage Match 4

Wednesday November 5

1986 Alex Ferguson appointed manager.

UEFA Champions League Group Stage Match 4

Thursday November 6

Friday November 7

Saturday November 8

Sunday November 9

Liverpool v Utd **Premiership** (Sky, 4.05pm)

Monday November 10

....

Tuesday November 11

....

Wednesday November 12

....

Thursday November 13

....

Friday November 14

....

Saturday November 15

2000 David Beckham becomes the fifth United player to captain England, following Bobby Charlton, Bryan Robson, Ray Wilkins and Paul Ince.

....

Sunday November 16

1998 United announce link-up with Belgian feeder club Royal Antwerp.

....

Monday November 17

....

Tuesday November 18
1980 Luke Chadwick born in Cambridge.

....

Wednesday November 19

....

Thursday November 20

....

Friday November 21

....

Saturday November 22
Utd v Blackburn **Premiership**

....

Sunday November 23

....

Monday November 24

....

Tuesday November 25
UEFA Champions League Group Stage Match 5

....

Wednesday November 26
UEFA Champions League Group Stage Match 5

....

Thursday November 27

....

Friday November 28

....

Saturday November 29
1973 Ryan Wilson, son of the rugby player Danny, born in Cardiff. He later takes his mother's maiden name of Giggs.

....

Sunday November 30
1999 United beat Palmeiras of Brazil 1-0 to win the World Club Championship in Tokyo.
Chelsea v Utd Premiership (Sky, 4.05pm)
Euro 2004 Draw for Final Tournament **(kicks off in Portugal, June 12, 2004)**

....

Monday December 1

Tuesday December 2
Worthington Cup 4th Round

Wednesday December 3
Worthington Cup 4th Round

Thursday December 4
1937 Jack Rowley scores his first goal for United. He scores his last a full seventeen years later on January 12 1955.

Friday December 5
World Cup 2006 Draw for Qualifying Competition

Saturday December 6
Utd v Aston Villa **Premiership**

Sunday December 7

Monday December 8

....

Tuesday December 9
UEFA Champions League Group Stage Match 6

....

Wednesday December 10
UEFA Champions League Group Stage Match 6

....

Thursday December 11
2002 Ruud van Nistelrooy's two strikes against Deportivo La Coruna bring his tally to 20 goals for United in the European Cup, overtaking Andy Cole's club record of 19.

....

Friday December 12
1992 Eric Cantona makes his debut against Norwich City, at Old Trafford; United win 1-0 with a goal from Mark Hughes.

....

Saturday December 13
Utd v City **Premiership (Sky, 12.30pm)**

....

Sunday December 14

....

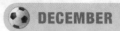

DECEMBER

2003

Monday December 15

. . . .

Tuesday December 16

Worthington Cup Quarter-finals

. . . .

Wednesday December 17

Worthington Cup Quarter-finals

. . . .

Thursday December 18

. . . .

Friday December 19

1972 Frank O'Farrell sacked as manager, three days after United lose 0-5 at Crystal Palace.

. . . .

Saturday December 20

Tottenham v Utd Premiership

. . . .

Sunday December 21

1907 In the home match against Manchester City, Sandy Turnbull becomes the first man ever to be sent off while playing for United.

. . . .

Monday December 22

Tuesday December 23

Wednesday December 24

Thursday December 25 *Christmas Day*

Friday December 26 *Boxing Day*
Utd v Everton **Premiership**

Saturday December 27
1920 United record their biggest crowd at Old Trafford – 70,504 for the game against Aston Villa.

Sunday December 28
Middlesbrough v Utd **Premiership**

Monday December 29

1970 Wilf McGuinness is sacked after only eighteen months in charge of the club. Matt Busby returns from retirement to take charge.

Tuesday December 30

1972 Scotland boss Tommy Docherty appointed manager.

Wednesday December 31

Thursday January 1 *New Year's Day*

Friday January 2

Saturday January 3
FA Cup Third Round

Sunday January 4

Monday January 5
1932 Bill Foulkes born. The Munich survivor plays a record 61 consecutive cup-ties for the Reds between 1954 and 1967.

Tuesday January 6

Wednesday January 7
Bolton v Utd **Premiership**

Thursday January 8

Friday January 9

Saturday January 10
Utd v Newcastle **Premiership (likely Sky kick-off/date change)**

Sunday January 11
1957 Bryan Robson born in Chester-le-Street. During the course of his career, Captain Marvel broke, fractured or dislocated 24 bones in the United and England cause.

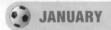

Monday January 12

....

Tuesday January 13

....

Wednesday January 14

1969 Sir Matt Busby retires.

....

Thursday January 15

1977 Steve Coppell begins the longest run of consecutive league appearances by a United player. It ends 206 games later on November 7 1981.

....

Friday January 16

....

Saturday January 17

1948 The biggest ever league crowd of 81,962 is recorded for United's game against Arsenal. It is played at Maine Road, because of bomb damage at Old Trafford.

Wolves v Utd **Premiership**

....

Sunday January 18

1890 Newton Heath's debut in the FA Cup is not auspicious. They lose 6-1 to Preston, double-winners in the previous season.

....

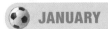

Monday January 19

2003 Wes Brown scores his first goal for United, in a 2-1 home win over Juventus in the European Cup, on his 111th appearance for the club. Of current outfield players John O'Shea has now played most often for United without scoring.

....

Tuesday January 20

1994 Sir Matt Busby dies, aged 84.

Worthington Cup Semi-final 1st leg

....

Wednesday January 21

1975 Nicky Butt born in Manchester.

Worthington Cup Semi-final 1st leg

....

Thursday January 22

1995 Andy Cole makes his debut after his record £7m transfer from Newcastle United.

....

Friday January 23

....

Saturday January 24

FA Cup 4th round

....

Sunday January 25

1995 Eric Cantona takes a detour to the dressing room, via the chest of mouthy Palace fan Matthew Simmons. He is banned for nine months and sentenced to community service.

....

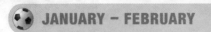
Monday January 26

2003 United defeat West Ham 6-0 in the FA Cup fourth round – The Reds' highest ever cup score against a team from the top flight.

Tuesday January 27
Worthington Cup Semi-final 2nd leg

Wednesday January 28
Worthington Cup Semi-final 2nd leg

Thursday January 29

Friday January 30

Saturday January 31
Utd v Southampton **Premiership**

Sunday February 1

Monday February 2

1999 For the first time, United are officially the world's richest football club. Their turnover in the previous season (£87.94m) is almost £30m more than second-placed Barcelona.

Tuesday February 3

Wednesday February 4

Thursday February 5

Friday February 6

1958 Munich air disaster. Twenty-three people die, including eight United players: Roger Byrne, Duncan Edwards, Tommy Taylor, Eddie Colman, Mark Jones, Liam Whelan, Geoff Bent and David Pegg. Johnny Berry and Jackie Blanchflower survived but never played again.

Saturday February 7

1970 George Best scores six against Northampton Town in the FA Cup, the most by a United player in a single game.

Everton v Utd Premiership (likely Sky kick-off/date change)

Sunday February 8

1984 Fat crook Robert Maxwell makes £10m bid to control United.

Monday February 9

....

Tuesday February 10

....

Wednesday February 11
Utd v Middlesbrough **Premiership**

....

Thursday February 12
1949 Biggest ever FA Cup win: home against Yeovil Town 8-0.

....

Friday February 13
1901 Worst ever FA Cup defeat: away to Burnley 1-7.

....

Saturday February 14
FA Cup 5th round

....

Sunday February 15

....

Monday February 16

....

Tuesday February 17

....

Wednesday February 18

1975 A proud day for Mr and Mrs Neville Neville of Bury: their son Gary is born.

International Friendlies

....

Thursday February 19

1910 First ever game at Old Trafford; Liverpool are the visitors and win 4-3. The crowd is officially 50,000, but many more sneak in without paying.

....

Friday February 20

1945 Matt Busby's first day in charge of United.

....

Saturday February 21

Utd v Leeds Premiership

....

Sunday February 22

....

Monday February 23

....

Tuesday February 24
UEFA Champions League Group Stage First knock-out round, 1st leg

....

Wednesday February 25
UEFA Champions League Group Stage First knock-out round, 1st leg

....

Thursday February 26
2003 United win 3-0 at Juventus, the Italian club's worst-ever home defeat in European competition.

....

Friday February 27
2002 Alex Ferguson signs a new three-year contract, just two months after insisting his decision to retire is final.

....

Saturday February 28
1972 Martin Buchan signed for £135,000 from Aberdeen.
Fulham v Utd Premiership

....

Sunday February 29
Worthington Cup Final (Millennium Stadium, Cardiff)

....

Monday March 1

....

Tuesday March 2

....

Wednesday March 3

....

Thursday March 4

....

Friday March 5
1953 Tommy Taylor signs from Barnsley for £40,000. He goes on to score 128 goals in 189 appearances.

....

Saturday March 6
FA Cup 6th round

....

Sunday March 7

....

Monday March 8

....

Tuesday March 9
UEFA Champions League Group Stage First knock-out round, 2nd leg

....

Wednesday March 10
UEFA Champions League Group Stage First knock-out round, 2nd leg

....

Thursday March 11

....

Friday March 12

....

Saturday March 13
City v Utd **Premiership**

....

Sunday March 14

....

Monday March 15

....

Tuesday March 16

....

Wednesday March 17

....

Thursday March 18
1964 United record their worst ever defeat in Europe, losing 0-5 away at Sporting Lisbon in the European
Cup Winners Cup.

....

Friday March 19

....

Saturday March 20
Utd v Tottenham **Premiership**

....

Sunday March 21

....

Monday March 22
1994 Eric Cantona is sent off in the game at Highbury, for the second time in successive matches. He was sent off five days earlier against Swindon.

Tuesday March 23
UEFA Champions League Group Stage Quarter-finals, 1st leg

Wednesday March 24
UEFA Champions League Group Stage Quarter-finals, 1st leg

Thursday March 25

Friday March 26

Saturday March 27
1994 Andrei Kanchelskis becomes the first ever player to be sent off in a League Cup final as United lose their bid for a domestic treble in a 1-3 defeat by Aston Villa, who are managed by former United boss Big Ron Atkinson.

Arsenal v Utd Premiership (likely Sky kick-off/date change)

Sunday March 28
2001 Seven Manchester United players (Gary Neville, Brown, Butt, Scholes, Cole, Beckham and Sheringham) are on the pitch at the same time for England in the World Cup qualifier against Albania.

Monday March 29

2003 David Beckham scores his tenth goal for England in a 2-0 Euro Championship qualifying win over Liechtenstein. He is the fifth player to score ten goals for England while at United after Tommy Taylor, Bobby Charlton, Bryan Robson and Paul Scholes.

Tuesday March 30

Wednesday March 31

International Friendlies

Thursday April 1

2000 West Ham's goalie Craig Forrest lets in seven at Old Trafford. The last time he had played at the ground, then for Ipswich, he let in nine.

Friday April 2

2002 United beat Deportivo – the Reds' first win in Spain since 1956.

Saturday April 3

Utd v Charlton Premiership

Sunday April 4

1953 Duncan Edwards makes his debut against Cardiff City. He went on to make 175 appearances and score 21 goals.

FA Cup Semi-finals

Monday April 5
1975 United secure promotion from the Second Division with a 1-0 win at Southampton.

....

Tuesday April 6

....

Wednesday April 7
1973 Denis Law makes his last appearance for United.

UEFA Champions League Group Stage Quarter-finals, 2nd leg

....

Thursday April 8
1956 United win their fourth league title, the second under Busby.

UEFA Champions League Group Stage Quarter-finals, 2nd leg

....

Friday April 9
1969 Wilf McGuinness appointed youngest ever United manager at the age of 31.
1999 BSkyB's bid for United is blocked by the Monopolies and Mergers Commission.

....

Saturday April 10
1926 Worst ever league defeat, away at Blackburn in Division One, 0-7.

Birmingham v Utd Premiership

....

Sunday April 11 *Easter Day*
1957 United lose their first European Cup semi-final against Real Madrid, 1-3 in the Bernabau.

....

Monday April 12 *Easter Monday*

1992 United win the League Cup for the first and only time, 1-0 against Nottingham Forest.

2003 United win 6-2 at St James's Park, Newcastle United's worst home defeat since 1961.

Utd v Leicester Premiership

....

Tuesday April 13

....

Wednesday April 14

1999 Ryan Giggs scores the finest ever FA Cup goal to win the semi-final against Arsenal and keep the treble on course. In 2001, Arsenal lose at Middlesbrough, securing United a seventh Premiership.

....

Thursday April 15

....

Friday April 16

....

Saturday April 17

Portsmouth v Utd Premiership

....

Sunday April 18

....

Monday April 19

1930 United's longest sequence without a league win begins. It ends sixteen games and six months later on October 25. The last fourteen matches were all defeats.

2003 Ryan Giggs plays his 540th game for United in the 3-1 home win over Blackburn Rovers, moving to third place in the all-time club appearance table, behind Bill Foulkes (688) and Bobby Charlton (759).

....

Tuesday April 20

1957 With a 4-0 win over Sunderland, United win their fifth Championship.

UEFA Champions League Group Stage Semi-finals, 1st leg

....

Wednesday April 21

1991 United lose 0-1 to Sheffield Wednesday (managed by Big Ron Atkinson) in the League Cup final.

UEFA Champions League Group Stage Semi-finals, 1st leg

....

Thursday April 22

....

Friday April 23

....

Saturday April 24

1909 United win the FA Cup for the first time, beating Bristol City 1-0 at Crystal Palace.

Utd v Liverpool **Premiership (likely Sky kick-off/date change)**

....

Sunday April 25

....

Monday April 26

1908 United secure their first ever Championship, winning the First Division by four points from Aston Villa. On this day in 1965 they win it again.

2003 United win the FA Youth Cup for record ninth time, with a 3-1 aggregate victory over Middlesbrough. Next best are Arsenal who have won the trophy six times. United have appeared in a record twelve finals.

Tuesday April 27

1951 Busby wins his first title as United beat Arsenal 6-1; 1974 Denis Law backheels City's winner in the derby as United are relegated; 2001 Ruud van Nistelrooy signs for record £19m; 2003 Ruud Van Nistelrooy scores his fortieth goal of the season in United's 2-0 win at Spurs, only the second player in United history to score 40 goals in a season.

Wednesday April 28

Thursday April 29

Friday April 30

1910 United win the Championship for the second time.

Saturday May 1

1976 United lose FA Cup final against Second Division Southampton 0-1.

Blackburn v Utd Premiership

Sunday May 2

1993 Oldham beat Aston Villa, clinching United's first title for 26 years and Alex Ferguson's first. On the same day the following year, Coventry beat Blackburn, handing the Premiership to United for the second season running.

Monday May 3

2003 United's final game of the season at Old Trafford (a 4-1 victory against Charlton) is watched by 67,721 – the highest for a competitive game at Old Trafford since 1939, and the second highest-ever for a League game at the ground. (Though the highest post-war crowd officially remains the 67,957 for Ryan Giggs's testimonial against Celtic in 2001.)

Tuesday May 4

1931 United relegated from the First Division with a then-record low number of points: 22. Only 4,000 fans turn up for their last game in the top flight, a 4-4 draw with Middlesbrough. 2003 United are champions as Arsenal lose 3-2 at home to Leeds. It's the club's eighth League title in eleven years.

UEFA Champions League Group Stage Semi-finals, 2nd leg

Wednesday May 5

1971 Pat Crerand makes his last appearance for United.

UEFA Champions League Group Stage Semi-finals, 2nd leg

Thursday May 6

1967 United win the title by winning 6-1 at West Ham. 1997 United win the Premiership for the fourth time in five seasons after Liverpool lose at Wimbledon and Newcastle draw at West Ham.

Friday May 7

1921 Billy Meredith makes his last appearance for United. At 46 years, 281 days, he is also the oldest player ever to wear a United shirt.

Saturday May 8

Utd v Chelsea Premiership (likely Sky kick-off/date change)

Sunday May 9

Monday May 10

Tuesday May 11

2003 In winning the final game 2-1 at Everton, United finish the season with 25 wins and 8 draws, one of the club's best title campaigns. Statistically it is exceeded in points per game (adjusting for different points systems) only by the 1999-2000 and 1993-94 championships. Ruud van Nistelrooy equals his own club record (shared with Billy Whelan in 1956) of scoring in eight consecutive league matches.

Wednesday May 12

1979 United lose the FA Cup final 2-3 to Arsenal, despite scoring twice in the last five minutes.

Thursday May 13

Friday May 14

1994 United win their first double, when they beat Chelsea 4-0 in the FA Cup final.

Saturday May 15

1991 The first European trophy since 1968 is popped in the cabinet when United beat Barcelona 2-1 in the Cup Winners Cup final in Rotterdam: Mark Hughes scores twice.

Aston Villa v Utd Premiership

Sunday May 16

1906 After being banned from football for a year for illegal payments (he was getting £7 a week instead of the maximum wage of £4), Billy Meredith signs for United from City.

1999 United beat Tottenham to win the Championship – the first leg of the treble.

Monday May 17

1990 United beat Palace 1-0 in the FA Cup final replay, securing Alex Ferguson his first trophy for the Reds. The goal was scored by Lee Martin, who never scored again for the club.

Tuesday May 18

1995 United win the FA Cup final 1-0 against Everton, despite Kevin Moran becoming the first ever player to be sent off in an FA Cup final.

Wednesday May 19

Thursday May 20

Friday May 21

1977 United win the FA Cup final 2-1 against Liverpool, thus stopping the Merseysiders becoming the first ever team to win the treble.

Saturday May 22

1999 Goals from Paul Scholes and Teddy Sheringham see United through against Newcastle in the FA Cup final. A third double for Alex Ferguson – and the treble is in sight.

FA Cup Final (Millennium Stadium, Cardiff)

Sunday May 23

Monday May 24

....

Tuesday May 25

1963 United beat Leicester 3-1 in the FA Cup final to secure their first trophy since Munich.

2001 Scholes, Beckham and Sheringham score in England's 4-0 win over Mexico – the first time three players from the same club have scored in a match for England.

....

Wednesday May 26

1999 United achieve the first ever treble of Championship, FA Cup and European Cup by beating Bayern Munich in Barcelona 2-1.

UEFA Champions League Final (Gelsenkirchen, Germany)

....

Thursday May 27

1983 At 18 years, 18 days, Norman Whiteside becomes the youngest ever player to score in the FA Cup final when United beat Brighton 4-0 in a replay.

....

Friday May 28

UEFA Under-21 Championships begin Portugal

....

Saturday May 29

1968 United win the European Cup, beating Benfica 4-1 at Wembley. Each player was on a win bonus of £800 for the game.

....

Sunday May 30

....

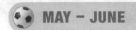

Monday May 31

....

Tuesday June 1

1981 Ron Atkinson becomes United manager, arriving from West Brom.

....

Wednesday June 2

....

Thursday June 3

2003 Phil Neville becomes the sixth United player to captain England (after Charlton, Wilkins, Robson, Ince and Beckham) when he wears the armband for 27 minutes during the friendly against Serbia and Montenegro. United (briefly) have six players on their books who have captained their countries – Keane, Giggs, Veron, Solskjaer, Philip Neville and the soon-to-depart Beckham.

....

Friday June 4

....

Saturday June 5

....

Sunday June 6

UEFA Under-21 Championships Final (Porto, Portugal)

....

Monday June 7

. . . .

Tuesday June 8

1971 Former Leicester boss Frank O'Farrell appointed manager.

. . . .

Wednesday June 9

. . . .

Thursday June 10

. . . .

Friday June 11

. . . .

Saturday June 12

1999 Alex Ferguson is knighted in the Queen's birthday honours list.

Euro 2004 Championships begin Porto (Portugal)

. . . .

Sunday June 13

. . . .

Monday June 14

....

Tuesday June 15

1989 Neil Webb signs from Nottingham Forest for £1.5m.

....

Wednesday June 16

....

Thursday June 17

2003 David Beckham is sold for £25m, on instalments, to Real Madrid. Real hope to sell 40m Beckham
shirts in the Far East alone.

....

Friday June 18

....

Saturday June 19

....

Sunday June 20

....